THE CARLYLES AT HOME AND ABROAD

Essays in Honour of Kenneth J. Fielding

The Carlyles at Home and Abroad

Edited by

DAVID R. SORENSEN
St Joseph's University, USA

RODGER L. TARR
Illinois State University, USA

ASHGATE

Published by
Ashgate Publishing Limited
Gower House
Croft Road
Aldershot
Hampshire GU11 3HR
England

Ashgate Publishing Company
Suite 420
101 Cherry Street
Burlington, VT 05401-4405
USA

Ashgate website: http://www.ashgate.com

British Library Cataloguing in Publication Data
The Carlyles at home and abroad : essays in honour of
Kenneth J. Fielding
1. Carlyle, Thomas, 1795-1881 2. Carlyle, Thomas, 1795-1881 – Criticism and interpretation 3. Carlyle, Jane Welsh, 1801-1866 4. Authors, Scottish – 19th century – Biography 5. Authors' spouses – Scotland – Biography
I. Soresen, David II. Tarr, Rodger L. III. Fielding, Kenneth J. (Kenneth Joshua), 1924-
828.8'09

Library of Congress Cataloging-in-Publication Data
The Carlyles at home and abroad : essays in honour of Kenneth J. Fielding / edited by David R. Sorensen and Rodger L. Tarr.
p. cm.
Includes bibliographical references and index.
ISBN 0-7546-0387-3 (alk. paper)
1. Carlyle, Thomas, 1795-1881—Criticism and interpretation. 2. Carlyle, Jane Welsh, 1801-1866. I. Sorensen, David R., 1953- II. Tarr, Rodger L. III. Fielding, K. J. (Kenneth J.)

PR4434.C285 2004
824'.8—dc22

2004001153

ISBN 0 7546 0387 3

Printed and bound in Great Britain by MPG Books Ltd, Bodmin, Cornwall

Contents

Abbreviations

CL	*The Collected Letters of Thomas and Jane Welsh Carlyle*. Senior Advisory Ed. K. J. Fielding. Eds. Ian Campbell, Aileen Christianson, Sheila McIntosh and David Sorensen. Associate Eds. Brent Kinser and Liz Sutherland. Duke-Edinburgh Edition. 31 vols. Durham, NC: Duke UP, 1970-2004- .
Froude, Life	J. A. Froude, *Thomas Carlyle, A History of the First Forty Years of His Life, 1795-1835* (1 & 2); *A History of His Life in London, 1834-1881* (3 & 4). London: Longman and Green, 1882; 1884.
HE	*Historical Essays*. Ed. Chris R. Vanden Bossche. Strouse Edition. Berkeley, CA: U of California P, 2002.
HHW	*On Heroes, Hero-Worship, & the Heroic in History*. Ed. Michael K. Goldberg. Text established by Michael K. Goldberg, Joel J. Brattin, and Mark Engel. Strouse Edition. Berkeley, CA: U of California P, 1993.
Houghton	Houghton Library, Harvard University.
NLS	National Library of Scotland.
Reminiscences	K. J. Fielding and Ian Campbell, eds. *Reminiscences*. By Thomas Carlyle. London: Oxford UP, 1997.
Strouse	Norman and Charlotte Strouse Carlyle Collection MS, University of California, Santa Cruz.
SR	*Sartor Resartus*. Ed. Rodger L. Tarr. Text prepared by Mark Engel and Rodger L. Tarr. Strouse Edition. Berkeley, CA: U of California P, 2000.
Works	Thomas Carlyle. *Works*. Ed. H. D. Traill. Centenary Edition. 30 vols. London: Chapman and Hall, 1896-99.

Acknowledgements

Many of the essays in this collection were originally delivered as lectures at the Carlyle conferences held in Philadelphia and Edinburgh in 2000–1. At Saint Joseph's University, Philadelphia, we are grateful to Fr. Nicholas Rashford, Judi Chapman, Brice Wachterhauser, and Kevin Robinson for their encouragement and financial support, as well as to the staff of the Honors Program and to Tom Malone of the University Press for his expert preparation of the manuscript in Camera Ready Copy. In Edinburgh, we are particularly grateful to Ian Campbell, Aileen Christianson, Cairns Craig and Anthea Taylor, and to those who helped sponsor the conference, including the National Portrait Gallery of Scotland, which hosted a memorable reading of Carlyle arranged by Kenneth J. Fielding and performed by Tom Fleming. The editors of the *Collected Letters of Thomas and Jane Welsh Carlyle* have provided essential cooperation and assistance. We are also indebted to David Southern, Managing Editor of the Carlyle Letters at Duke University, for responding promptly and tirelessly to our inquiries.

List of Contributors

Ruth apRoberts is Emeritus Professor of English Literature at the University of California, Riverside. Her publications include *Trollope, Artist and Moralist* (Vintage, 1971), *Arnold and God* (California, 1983), *The Ancient Dialect: Thomas Carlyle and Comparative Religion* (California, 1988), and *The Biblical Web* (Michigan, 1994). She is currently editing the Strouse Edition of Carlyle's German Essays.

Rosemary Ashton is Quain Professor of English Language and Literature at University College, London. Her publications include *The German Idea* (Cambridge, 1980) and *Little Germany* (Oxford, 1996), and critical biographies of G. H. Lewes (Oxford, 1991), Coleridge (Blackwell, 1996), George Eliot (Hamish Hamilton, 1996), and Thomas and Jane Welsh Carlyle (Chatto, 2002). She is currently working on a study of Victorian radical publishing, in particular the circle surrounding John Chapman of 142 Strand.

Ian Campbell is Professor of Scottish and Victorian Literature at the University of Edinburgh, and since 1967, one of the editors of *The Collected Letters of Thomas and Jane Welsh Carlyle*. He has written on Scottish, English, Victorian, and modern literature, and edited a number of works by Scottish writers.

Aileen Christianson is Senior Lecturer, Department of English Literature, University of Edinburgh, and since 1967, one of the editors of *The Collected Letters of Thomas and Jane Welsh Carlyle*. She has published essays on Jane Welsh Carlyle, as well as twentieth-century Scottish women writers, including Muriel Spark and Candia McWilliam; she is currently writing a book on Willa Muir.

Kathy Chamberlain, formerly a member of the English Department at the Borough of Manhattan Community College, is Chair of 'Women Writing Women's Lives,' a seminar for biographers and memoirists at the City University of New York. Her essays have been published in the *Virginia Woolf Bulletin*, *Carlyle Studies Annual*, and *Tikkun*. She is currently writing a series of biographical essays about Jane Welsh Carlyle.

Norma Clarke is Senior Lecturer in the Department of English, Kingston University, Surrey. Her publications include *Ambitious Heights, Writing, Friendship, Love: the Jewsbury Sisters, Felicia Hemans and Jane Welsh*

Carlyle (Routledge, 1990), *Dr. Johnson's Women* (Hambledon, 2001), and *The Rise and Fall o the Woman of Letters* (Random House, 2004). She is currently writing a biography of Laetitia Pilkington, to be published by Faber.

Cairns Craig is Professor of Scottish and Modern Literature at the University of Edinburgh, and is Director of the Centre for the History of Ideas in Scotland. His publications include *Out of History: Narrative Paradigms in Scottish and English Culture* (Polygon, 1996), *The Modern Scottish Novel* (Edinburgh, 1999), (with R.D.S. Jack, eds.) *The History of Scottish Literature* (Mercat, 1999), and most recently, *Iain Banks's Complicity: A Reader's Guide* (Continuum, 2002).

David J. DeLaura was Avalon Foundation Professor in the Humanities and Professor of English at the University of Pennsylvania from 1974–1999. His current project is nineteenth-century cults of friendship in school and university settings.

Vanessa Dickerson is Professor of English at DePauw University where she directs the Black Studies Program. Her publications include *Victorian Ghosts in the Noontide: Women Writers and the Supernatural* (Missouri, 1996), and (with Michael Bennett, eds.) *Recovering the Black Female Body: Self-Representations by African American Women* (Rutgers, 2000). She has recently completed a study of black Victorians.

Owen Dudley Edwards is Reader in History at the University of Edinburgh. He has written on Macaulay, Conan Doyle, P. G. Wodehouse, Irish nationalism, and Irish, Scottish, and American cultural and intellectual links.

Mark Engel is a professional editor and independent scholar with interests in philosophy and history. He established, with Michael K. Goldberg and Joel J. Brattin, the text of the Strouse Edition of *On Heroes, Hero-Worship & the Heroic in History* (California, 1993), and with Rodger L. Tarr, he established the text of the Strouse edition of *Sartor Resartus* (California, 2000). He is presently working with David R. Sorensen to establish the text of the Strouse *French Revolution*, which is forthcoming.

Marylu Hill is Assistant Director of the Core Humanities Program at Villanova University. Her publications include *Mothering Modernity: Feminism, Modernism, and the Maternal Muse* (Garland, 1998). She has also published articles on Tennyson and photography, and Carlyle's historicism and religion, Victorian themes in post-modern literature and cinema, and Christina Rossetti's poetry. She is currently working on a study of Victorian literature and the retrieval of the past.

Alain Jumeau, a former editor of *Études Anglaises*, is Professor of English at the University of Paris-Sorbonne and President of the Société Française d'Études Victoriennes et Édouardiennes. He has published widely on Victorian prose-writers and novelists, particularly George Eliot. He has translated Robert Louis Stevenson's *The Master of Ballantrae* (Gallimard, 2000), Walter Scott's *The Black Dwarf* (Gallimard, Pléiade, 2003), and George Eliot's *The Mill on the Floss* (Gallimard, 2003).

Brent E. Kinser is an assistant editor of the print edition of *The Collected Letters of Thomas and Jane Welsh Carlyle* since 2002, and the coordinating editor of the project's electronic edition. He is a senior Teaching Fellow at the University of North Carolina, Chapel Hill, where he is finishing his dissertation on the American Civil War and the rise of British democracy. He has published on the Carlyles, D. H. Lawrence, Emily Dickinson, and Marjorie Kinnan Rawlings.

Sheila McIntosh has been one of the editors of the *The Collected Letters of Thomas and Jane Welsh Carlyle* since 1993. She has published several essays on the Carlyles, including 'Two Victorian Heroes' (Pescara, 1996), 'Carlyle and his Presents to America' (Carlyle Society Papers, 1997-8), and 'Literary Portraits' (Carlyle Studies Annual, 200–2).

David R. Sorensen is Professor of English at Saint Joseph's University, Philadelphia. He has been one of the editors of *The Collected Letters of Thomas and Jane Welsh Carlyle* since 1999. His publications include (with K. J. Fielding, eds.) *The French Revolution*. By Thomas Carlyle (Oxford, 1989) and *Jane Carlyle: Newly Selected Letters* (Ashgate, 2004). He is presently collaborating with Mark Cumming and Mark Engel to establish the text and to annotate the Strouse edition of Carlyle's *The French Revolution*.

Rodger L. Tarr is University Distinguished Professor, Emeritus, Illinois State University. His recent publications include, *Max and Marjorie: The Correspondence of Maxwell E. Perkins and Marjorie Kinnan Rawlings* (Florida, 1999), the Strouse edition of Carlyle's *Sartor Resartus* (California, 2000), and *As Ever Yours: The Letters of Maxwell Perkins and Elizabeth Lemmon* (Pennsylvania UP). His edition of *The Love Letters of Marjorie Kinnan Rawlings*, published by Florida, is forthcoming.

Andrew Taylor is a lecturer in American literature at the University of Edinburgh. He has recently published *Henry James and the Father Question* (Cambridge, 2002).

Chris R. Vanden Bossche is Professor of English at the University of Notre Dame and editor-in-chief of the University of California Strouse edition of the writings of Thomas Carlyle. He is the author of *Carlyle and the Search for Authority* (Ohio State UP, 1991) and editor of the Strouse edition of Carlyle's *Historical Essays* (California, 2002).

Ronald Wendling is Professor of English at Saint Joseph's University, Philadelphia. He has published *Coleridge's Progress to Christianity* (Bucknell, 1995). He is currently writing about Coleridge's presence in the work of Carlyle and other Victorians.

Kenneth J. Fielding: A Dedication

DAVID R. SORENSEN

In *Heroes and Hero-Worship* (1841), Carlyle spoke of the benefit to be derived from the company of a distinguished man: 'He is the living light-fountain, which is good and pleasant to be near' (HHW 3). Kenneth J. Fielding's 'light' is everywhere apparent in this volume, serving both as an inspiration and stimulus to those studying the significance of the Carlyles, both 'at home and abroad'. It is a mark of his intellectual fortitude and curiosity that seventeen years after being honoured in an issue of *Prose Studies* on the occasion of his retirement from the Department of English Literature at the Edinburgh University, K. J. F. continues to pursue fresh inquiries and to initiate new research. From the start of his association in 1966 with the Duke-Edinburgh edition of *The Collected Letters of Thomas and Jane Welsh Carlyle*, Fielding has stressed the importance of understanding the Carlyles in relation to their remarkably broad range of friendships. Patiently and tenaciously, he has mined what he fondly calls 'the rockface' of manuscript evidence, much of it ignored or overlooked by modern scholars and biographers.

Without fuss or fanfare, Fielding has quietly exposed the often threadbare quality of the biographical and critical assumptions that have surrounded the Carlyles since the publication of James Anthony Froude's four-volume life of Thomas in 1882 and 1884. In introductions and notes, and in separate essays, he illuminated previously unknown connections between the Carlyles and a host of major and minor figures. His work has quietly produced a major shift in knowledge about the Carlyles and their world, though many commentators continue to disregard his discoveries. In an age of theory and cultural studies, the close study of the Carlyles' biographical and intellectual environment may seem outdated to those in search of more ambitious and fashionable topics. Yet as Fielding has repeatedly insisted, critical generalizations carry little force unless they are rooted in a sound knowledge of the Carlyles' world. Thomas Carlyle surmised that the 'meaning of life here on earth might be defined as consisting in this: To unfold your self, to work what thing you have the faculty for' (HHW 193). Students of Victorian history should be deeply grateful that Kenneth Fielding continues to 'unfold' himself in his work with such indefatigable energy and insight.

Chapter 1

Justice to Carlyle's Memory: The Later Carlyle

KENNETH J. FIELDING

Readers sometimes have the good or bad habit of making sense of a book by first looking to the end. Hence the subject of 'the later Carlyle'. Can we understand him better by looking at the lengthy latter part of his life, after Jane's death? It raises many questions that arise mainly because the extent of the material to be looked at is so daunting that it has not been properly done - or not done at all. Naturally we know that the *earlier* periods are more interesting. They match the time when Carlyle's powers were strongest, his impact most forcible, and the Carlyles' combined circle of friends gave them the greatest interest and effect. As we know, the story of their marriage in this period has allowed particularly dramatic treatment. Yet the *later* period has great interest, when Carlyle's influence was wider if more diffused, when he was much Boswellised, and certainly had more readers.[1] It was when his outer defences began to give way, and his inner nature showed more openly.

I hope to show part, or a small fraction, of what can be found in the last fifteen years after Jane's death, and even to turn back to disputes which many Carlyleans are reluctant to re-open, though often not to pronounce on. I venture into it now, using some of the unread papers of Alexander Carlyle, and Carlyle's *Journal* or 'Notebook IV' - also making use of the Ashburton Papers recently added to the National Library of Scotland (especially the letters of Louisa Lady Ashburton *to* Carlyle), John Forster's letters *to* Carlyle from the Armstrong-Baylor Library at Waco, Texas (touched on by others, but about which different views are possible), and the extensive and partly unpublished letters at Harvard *to* Carlyle of Charles Eliot Norton.[2] Can we, therefore, glance at this barely known later Carlyle in order to see him more directly, rather than as the *shadow* of a man whom contemporaries accepted as someone who 'essentially modified the mind of his time' (Martineau 4:437).

This inevitably means questioning the view of Carlyle stamped on him by his first or official biographer, James Anthony Froude. For little or none of this material has been used in previous biographies, including Froude's, D.A. Wilson's, Fred Kaplan's, or Simon Heffer's, and it now reveals a different Carlyle. Yet we still have to turn to Froude's biography, again with its apparent finality, to bring the new evidence into focus. But perhaps I can first turn to what we find in some of the letters of Alexander and Mary Aitken Carlyle (niece and nephew), with whom their uncle lived and died at Cheyne Row. He lived with her for up to thirteen years, and with both from their marriage in 1879, when he went with them on their honeymoon. We can especially look at Alexander and Mary's correspondence with Charles Eliot Norton, editor of many volumes of Carlyle's letters and co-editor with Mary of the *Reminiscences*.

It is not necessary to go into their detailed and often captious criticisms of Froude. But we should be aware of their superior knowledge and what they testify. By chance their papers have survived, whereas Froude notably made sure that most of his did not.[3] What do these new papers tell us? They certainly confirm that, in answering Froude, Alexander and Mary made the mistake of concentrating too much on his inaccuracies. Yet what really disturbed them was his whole strategy in the biography, and especially his concentration, in his last volume, in giving long, gloomy, or 'remorseful' extracts from the later *Journal*. They come in the last few chapters, matching Froude's own pessimism, and though we rarely return to those pages now, they deeply colour the conclusion.

Alexander Carlyle wrote to Norton (20 Feb. 1902) about the later *Journal*, which he calls 'Notebook IV', when they were considering what should be done with it:

> My opinion of my Uncle's 'Notebook IV' coincides very closely with yours...But I think it is not so much 'grief overmastering character and serenity of soul' as severe bodily ailments influencing mind and feelings (as is often the case especially in so extraordinarily sensitive a being as Carlyle was) that overclouded his judgment and all but deranged his intellect. Certainly the loss of his wife in such exceptionally painful circumstances was a crown of sorrow; but he bore this greatest of losses in a manful and dignified way *at the time* and for *months after the event*, as his Journal & Letters of the period show. It was not till later when his health of body (what little health he ever had) totally failed that he began to write down the vain lamentations and useless complaints that abound in his Notebook IV.
>
> It would be impossible to give an adequate description of his state of state of mind at that time (1867-1873). My late dear Wife [Mary] who came to live with him in 1868, often told me in what a lamentable condition of health she found him...By abstinence from proper food he was practically starving himself, and the Doctors (there were several in succession) for fear of offending him allowed him to have his own way.

He grew more and more nervous thin and weak, till his mind, especially in the mornings was often 'wandering' through sheer want of bodily nourishment...

This went on for several years, when, a crisis arising, she called in another Doctor Dr. Blakiston, at once ordered nourishing diet in plenty, rich soups and fat in various forms, giving pepsine to digest it.[4] Almost immediately the symptoms improved, he began to grow stronger, slept much better;...his spirits rose, and he became calm, cheerful and comparatively happy and contented. I lived with him for more than *two years* after this (1879-81) and never noticed any trace of querulousness, misanthropy, or morbid despondency such as parts of the Notebook exhibit. He often spoke to me of his Wife, and always calmly and with a dignified sorrow perfectly natural, and without the slightest sign of 'remorse'.

It was during that dreary time of conspicuously bad health and spirits that Notebook IV was written; and its tone is a reflex of what he was feeling, - despairing & morbid. Considering this I am not much surprised at the tone; but it seems marvellous that he should have thought it his *duty* to write at all in such a condition as he was in! And, unfortunately, he nearly always chose a day to write in this Notebook when he was feeling particularly sad and ill. Mary has often remarked to me that, after he passed a sleepless night, or after any untoward event...the Notebook was sure to be brought out and an entry made; whilst for weeks or months, during which he was fairly well and in good spirits the unlucky Note-book was never touched! Froude is about right (for once) when he says that 'his Journal contains chiefly a record of his sorrows'. The pity is that Froude has made public so much of the Note-book. And the portions he has printed have got many a sordid twist in passing through the mill. This makes me feel that it would perhaps be scarcely prudent to destroy the original notebook. Had Froude not printed any of it, or even had his selections from it been accurately printed, the decision to burn the original would have been a much simpler matter. But as the case now stands by destroying the original one would destroy the only certain means of ever effectively & authoritatively correcting Froude's mistakes and misrepresentations.

There is no reason why a new copy of such portions of the Book as you suggest should not be made for ordinary use. After this were done, the typed copy you now have ought to be burnt and the original kept safely under lock and key, to be seen by no one except trusted members of the family. No-one but Froude has seen the Note-book, and no one but you and Professor Masson have seen my copy

Much arises from this, and not simply that in corroborating the independent judgement of one's reading of Froude's confusing later chapters and his use of the *Journal*. It is that Alexander and Mary, who were so close to Carlyle, and Norton who knew him well and was the first to go independently over all the Carlyle papers, agree in their view of a benign and rational later Carlyle. For Froude, who was away in South Africa after his wife's death and at the time of Carlyle's recovery from illness about 1873-74, may have missed the change that Alexander mentions. Certainly in the *Life* he seems to be bewildered by what he saw as a contrast between Carlyle's often extraordinary sympathy and capacity for friendship and the way in which he says they were frequently betrayed by a volcanic bitterness.

He leaves us with an impression of Carlyle as a tormented genius who paid for his achievements by a destructive insanity. He finds it, for example, in *Latter-Day Pamphlets*, in which he says that Carlyle ferociously strikes at 'honoured names' though really the 'most tenderhearted of men', whose savagery was 'affection turned sour' (*Life* 4:30). He tells us that Carlyle's whole soul was loaded with a 'bilious indignation' flung off in 'a torrent of sulphurous denunciation' (*Life* 4:41). Carlyle is quoted on his own 'temper of a rat-trap' (*Life* 4:61). He 'growls' in print, and though his welcoming friends always enjoyed his visits, his imagination wove 'dark webs' when he was with them like Hamlet's 'black stithy' (*Life* 4:85). Carlyle is said to vent his exasperation like Swift, living 'in what he had described as "an element of black streaked with lightning"' (*Life* 4:122). Froude even likens him to Friedrich Wilhelm in *Frederick the Great*, who actually beat his family and courtiers with his stick, following this with bursts of passion and remorse, 'with wild words...and sometimes worse than words', which 'must have sadly reminded Mrs. Carlyle of occasional episodes in Cheyne Row' (*Life* 4:205).

Yet this extraordinary open charge that his friend was physically violent is entirely unsupported, and all the time such remarks are interwoven with recognising that Carlyle's ferocity was combined with gentleness, both in life and writing. After Jane Carlyle's death, we are even told that the much-quoted *Journal* becomes 'soft and melodious', as if the 'sense of duty heroically performed had composed and consoled him'. Froude goes further: 'Time and sorrow had softened the angry tones' of 'earlier days' and 'his talk generally was as calm as the entries in his Journal' (*Life* 4:383, 392). When Carlyle trusted him with his papers in 1873, his 'outward conduct' was that of 'the same noble-minded, simple-hearted man' Froude 'had always known him to be' and his 'heroic decision' to publish Jane's *Letters and Memorials* was 'so beautiful, so unexampled in the whole history of literature' that Froude 'could but admire it with all my heart' (*Life* 4:414, 410). Yet 'the loved disciple' is still ready to say that his friend was 'not what is commonly called an amiable man' (*Life* 4:456).

He was totally bewildered by Carlyle's divided nature, and it is hardly surprising that his personal criticism was deeply resented by Mary, Alexander, and Norton. This was not mainly because of what has been said to be the cause, namely their 'three bones of contention': ownership of Carlyle's papers, his 'bad treatment of Jane' and the later 'imputation of sexual impotence' (Moore 347).[5] They were not always right, but Mary and Alexander's newly-examined letters to and from Norton give their own reasons and demonstrate their real distress. They can be quoted only selectively, mostly passing over Mary Aitken Carlyle's shock at Froude's edition of the *Reminiscences*, when she wrote to Norton (15 Nov. 1881). She reported that 'Mr Froude told me when I saw him a week or so after the 5th of February that her uncle "had once blackened his Wife's wrists when they had quarrelled", as false and vulgar a story as was ever told'. He had 'heard it from a friend of my Aunt's, now dead [Geraldine Jewsbury]. So he said and has often repeated'.

Then, to Norton (9 Aug. 1882), about the first two volumes of the biography, and Froude's 'artful, malicious and sometimes almost imbecile comments on the text. He is a villain & has an utter disregard of the truth...He blames my Uncle for selfishness in making his wife live in solitude at Craigenputtoch never having the candour to say that her Mother was living some fourteen miles away in exactly the same conditions. Nor (as a reason for ill-health more likely than the one he advances) that she lived *much* longer than any one of the numerous Welshes of her own generation'. He 'gives an etching of my Aunt and coolly states it is in his own possession', when in fact it was from a photograph of the original in her 'own keeping' and so on.

It was not a question of factual details or minor mistakes. She was dismayed at the way that someone they admired and loved was unjustly maligned. Mary, Carlyle, and Norton had been affectionately writing to each other for years, exchanging books and presents, including Carlyle's for Norton's little daughter Sally; and Mary had written to Norton in 1875 about her uncle's being in 'better spirits; an American lady reported in a newspaper that he had repeated to her a line from Ossian, "Age is dark and unlovely", but he looks so well; enjoys reading so much, and has such a very loud laugh when he does laugh'. Now they were shattered, quite apart from having the trouble of successfully having to reclaim the fees due to her for the chapter on Jane Carlyle which Froude had misappropriated for his version of the *Reminiscences* without permission.[6]

Norton's exchanges are in the same spirit. Much later, as he was editing his series of Carlyle's letters, he writes to Mary (23 May 1892) that his selection was first governed by the wish to give a clear account of her Uncle's life and work, and then 'to give his descriptions of notable friends and acquaintances' and 'remarks on public events'. His aim was 'to present a true image' of Carlyle's 'constant and tender sympathy with and consideration for those whom he loved, his devoted affection for them, his kindness of heart &c., &c...No one could read this vast mass of letters as I have done, without being deeply impressed by the simplicity, integrity and essential sweetness of character which they reveal'. As he returns the Carlyle papers to Alexander (4 Dec. 1893), he does so 'with regret. I thank Mrs. Carlyle...But my chief regret in sending them back to her is that it seems to put an end to the hope that by their means justice might be done to your Uncle's memory, and the great wrong inflicted upon it in part, at least, be redressed. I trust that at some future time the work may be done by someone who may accomplish what the present indifference of the public has prevented me from doing'.

He kept a copy of the earlier journal, part of which he edited for the Grolier Club as *Two Note Books* (1897). From their correspondence we can see that, far from wanting to dispute the 'three bones of contention', the Carlyles and Norton sought to change the impression left on us by what Norton calls 'the contrast they show between Carlyle's inner and outer life', in which we should have enough insight to see 'the quiet depths of character' (23 May 1892).

*

Norton's remark leads to the second part of this account, in which we can sample how Carlyle's later correspondence illustrates his friendship with John Forster, and with Harriet's successor, Louisa, the third Lady Ashburton. Their love or affection for him is shown in their letters *to* Carlyle, while the letters *from* him can be left for the *Collected Letters*. Those to Forster were perhaps unavailable to Froude, though he calls him Carlyle's 'dearest friend', and he may well have read Louisa's letters since he offered to return them to her a little presumptuously, and he mentions her in connection with her invitation to Carlyle to Mentone after Jane's death. Yet misgivings arise not just because he completely passed over such letters, but because of the entire spirit of what they show. We may appreciate the difficulty of Froude's tremendous task, but he would not have had to give them at length any more than it can now be done here.

Good use has already been made of Forster's letters by James Davies in his *John Forster: A Literary Life* and by Jude Nixon in an article in the *Carlyle Studies Annual* (1988). Virginia Surtees has drawn on Louisa's letters in her biography of Louisa Lady Ashburton, *The Ludovisi Goddess* (1984). By taking these works together we can concentrate on a single aspect: their constant assertion of love for Carlyle, and the obvious affection and tenderness he aroused. It is not possible for me to agree with everything in Davies' and Nixon's accounts, full as they are in comparison with what can be said now. In questioning Forster's motives they are more critical. They see his steady affection for Carlyle as subservient, 'obsessive' and even 'pathological', and Carlyle's as too dominating. Their friendship in old age is said to arise from 'loneliness', though neither was alone. Yet, even if we accept that Forster's deep affection was unusual, it is hard to read all his letters to his friend as showing anything but what Carlyle called 'unwearied kindness and helpfulness' (*New Letters* 2:325), one inspired by generous and open affection, and much more than a friendship based on shared interests.

We already know about their common concerns up to the time of Jane's death: Forster's willingness to be Carlyle's literary agent, his readiness to publish him in his weekly *Examiner*, their intense interest in history and the Cromwellian period, Forster's liking for Jane, their wide circle of friends, and a shared quasi-radical outlook in which Carlyle was dominant but which was always held by Forster. Forster has sometimes been regarded as a lackey, bully, and Podsnap. But what irradiates his letters to Carlyle is his loving generosity, and a humanity to which he knows Carlyle will respond. His later letters are without pretence, full of jokes and gossip, and very different from the lugubrious slabs of *Journal* that Froude confines his attention to.

It may be difficult to convey this aspect of their friendship, because there is something almost ridiculous in love- or loving-letters. Of course Forster wrote to Carlyle with extra warmth on Carlyle's eightieth birthday, 'to say...that all the wishes of my heart are with you today'. Too ill to visit Carlyle, Forster wrote that 'The grief is to be *here*, and to think that you will not read these few words until many days later...But I do not think that you will need any assurances that I am indeed thinking of you...God bless you, dear Carlyle, and preserve you...for the sake of all who love and honour you'. A letter soon followed thanking his eighty-year old friend for calling, and hoping he will 'reward me by coming again...It is the little gleam of coming pleasure on which meanwhile I shall live'. Racked with gasping asthmatic attacks, he writes, 'in pleasure and in pain I think of you' (5 July 1874), 'I am always thinking of you', 'I am quite *weary* to see you again' (14 Nov. 1874); and again, 'I had been wearying to hear from you', while Carlyle had been away in Scotland (14 Nov. 1874), where 'all my heart goes with you, and; and I am as ever yours' (3 Sept. 1874). Still earlier, 'You cannot imagine, dear Carlyle, with what eagerness your letter was received this morning', and a little later when they could not meet, 'you cannot tell with what bitter disappointment'. It was relieved by a New-year note, sent as a 'poor sort of substitute for the *First Foot*...A poor substitute...if it could only make audible in dear old Cheyne Row the wish that will beat [in] our hearts to the exclusion of every other...for more honoured years for a noble life, precious and dear beyond all others to us' (31 Dec. 1873).

These letters seem remarkable, yet this is how Carlyle appeared to many of his friends, and was accompanied by a happy relationship between Forster's wife and Carlyle's niece, with lively interchanges about their activities, reading, and books. It is the brighter aspect of Carlyle, while the later Journal is the shadow. There is nothing 'obsessive' about the details of their shared concerns for Carlyle's sales returns, news of close friends, or mourning for Dickens, Bulwer Lytton, and Bryan Waller Procter. Their correspondence is full and vigorous. They could disagree about such matters as Carlyle's disappointing judgement of Landor, whose *Life* by Forster had appeared in 1869. But the golden letters that Carlyle wrote to him as he received each volume of Forster's life of Dickens, sunk 'deep' into his 'heart'. Of the last of them Forster wrote, 'I shall leave it as an instruction when I die that it be printed on the flyleaf before the book as long as my representatives have power to give such a direction' (18 Feb. 1874; Berg MS, in Davies 205).

Among their shared friends was Louisa Lady Ashburton, Lord Ashburton's second wife (a widow from 1864), to whom Carlyle had introduced Forster once she needed practical help when her home at Melchet was burned down. Forster's letters to Lady Ashburton show Carlyle in a different situation again, necessarily absent from Froude's life, and missing from other biographies. Throughout 1873, in his letters to her soon after the disastrous fire, Forster gives a steady stream of comments about Carlyle, which may have arisen from an extraordinary misunderstanding between Carlyle and Louisa (Surtees 158-60; Ashburton Papers 25:57).

Carlyle had felt compelled to tell her that his niece Mary, who was his housekeeper-companion, suspected Lady Ashburton of wanting to marry her seventy-eight year old uncle. Mary told her mother. The situation somewhat unnerved Louisa, and was the one crisis in which Forster was not willing to help. Forster's frequent references to Carlyle at this time when writing to Louisa may come from a wish to reassure her that all was well in spite of this *contretemps*. In a series of letters he detailed his friend's activities: 'I have been with Carlyle' (2 Aug. 1873); 'I enclose accounts of Carlyle, who…is now at Dumfries (20 Aug. 1873); he is about 'to go on a pilgrimage to Haddington of which I rather dread to hear' (20 Aug.); he is 'not as well as I could wish' (7 Sept. 1873). Forster invites Louisa to dinner with Carlyle and Lord Shaftesbury (April 1874), and he and Carlyle involve themselves in finding a possible teacher for her daughter (April 1874).

1875 brightened for Carlyle, though the 'Eternal Silences' (1 Feb.) were close when Forster was desperately ill. But Disraeli had offered Carlyle the Grand Cross of the Bath or GCB. Forster reported to Louisa: 'Carlyle has been here, but I could not see him', adding, 'I am happy to think…that he is the last man on Earth of whom we need to have fear that he could ever permit himself to be called

(G)reat

(C)onceited

(B)ooby

And again (19 March 1875), perhaps thinking that the anniversary of Lord Ashburton's death was coming round: 'Dear old Carlyle had a baddish cold...and yet he came again yesterday, in the bitter North breeze...Wonderful old man! And yet he has somehow got it into his head that this is to be his last winter - speaking comfortably about it, and a long laugh. He comforted me with old Scottish proverbs'. He is constantly 'Dear Carlyle', 'Dear old Carlyle', the devoted friend who had brought them together.

In under a year Louisa was to write to Carlyle from Egypt, on Forster's death: 'We are brothers in sorrow - having both lost what we can *never never* find again - most tenderly and truly do I mourn with you...where shall I ever find again such a tender heart, with such a strong *wise* head - *nowhere* - this blessed life that God sent me, is taken away...I never forget that to you I owed him...I fear that to *you* also he will leave a blank that will never be filled - & indeed I feel with you in all tenderness' (27 Feb. 1876).

Yet this friendship of Carlyle and Louisa is another story, only some of which may be familiar from the biographies of Jane Carlyle by the Hansons and of Louisa Lady Ashburton by Virginia Surtees. Louisa's marriage to the much older, second Lord Ashburton, just over a year after his wife's death, and Jane Carlyle's at first doubtful response to it, followed by their ecstatic devotion, is a familiar story. Yet Louisa's loving kindness to Carlyle after Jane's death is less well known.

It has to be acknowledged that Louisa and Forster shared a strong tendency for hero-worship and for expressing their affections freely. For though there had been an element of calculation in her marriage to the wealthy Lord Ashburton, she was extraordinarily warm-hearted and impulsive. She inspired the love of Sir Edwin Landseer (to no purpose), had a hopeless love for William Stirling of Keir (who was devoted to Caroline Norton), and won the adoration of numerous women friends, including the American lesbian-inclined sculptor Harriet Hosmer, Jane Stirling (one of Jane Carlyle's circle), Margaret Trotter (a kind of Mrs Sparsit), and the entirely sensible Lady Pauline Trevelyan. The story of these friendships is told in *The Ludovisi Goddess* and the Ashburton Papers. My present concern is to urge that we find a warmer and gentler side of Carlyle reflected in Louisa's letters, though her affections were always so exuberant that some adjustment may need making for exaggeration. In all Carlyle's relationships, in fact, one has to allow for the dominant attraction of his immense reputation. Even so, it is the way this takes of recognising his gentle humanity that is striking.

In 1865 she tells Monckton Milnes how happy she is to have Carlyle stay: 'He is like my beloved one in so many ways - loved him so truly - that I cling to him'. Quite early in the friendship with Jane, she takes Carlyle into her gushing affection. She is glad to hear of his tears when Jane's pet dog Nero died, 'but he is made up of *tenderness*, that is what I felt most in his nature' and she hopes to know him better, 'for I am a good deal in love'. A few months later she wishes Jane lived close by: 'I saw Mr. Carlyle today, a sight which always makes my heart beat' (*CL* 27:29). Jane's death brought them more sharply together. Surtees gives one of the two letters she at once wrote from Switzerland offering to return to her 'nearest and best loved friend' (120). But there are other letters, recording Louisa's last visit from Jane, their shared sadness when Lord Ashburton died, or when her daughter Mary was dangerously ill: 'I feel that so much more is known to me of your Past - than to others living - During that last visit to me she told me all her life with a sort of presentiment that she would never tell again - and I have been brought face to face with you in other ways - so *sacred it all* is...though it is all too sacred, ever again to be alluded to'.

Her answer to Carlyle's reply is new:

> I wish I *cd* tell you how grateful I was for that letter - & how constantly I am with you in the thought - It is a kind of consolation to know how tenderly she was loved wherever she was known & that her memory will always be a precious possession to all there. For myself, I can indeed say - *that* is gone with her which can *never* come back - I never look to have such a friend in my life, & miss the consciousness of the truth & devotion even at this distance...If so with me - what it must be to *you* - whose whole life was encompassed by her love. (25? April 1865)

She sent Thomas a copy of Jane's last letter, and 'to yourself, beloved friend - take whatever you like best to have—of loyal & affectionate... How much these last years have made us to each other!...Oh how one longs to go where they are gone' (*CL* 27:40). We can also turn to *The Ludovisi Goddess*, which gives Louisa's reply when Carlyle told her of his niece's jealousy: 'I feel I have nothing to reproach myself with. How can I fail to revere and love you? - you who were my young enthusiasm, the prophet of my soul...and who have been my unchanging friend all these years' (Surtees 159).

Much of the story is unfamiliar, though we have known a little from the *Reminiscences*, and even from the mainly unpublished letters of

Professor John Tyndall, who escorted the bereaved Carlyle to the south of France, and was another devoted friend who saw him as a gentle and attractive companion. No doubt, though Carlyle liked Louisa's affection, he occasionally found her excessive, impulsive, and changeable, and importunate in demands for help, as over her commissioning works from Thomas Woolner. But there was no difficulty in her commissioning the Woolner bust of Carlyle (one of his best portraits), or the maquette by Jacob Boehme (now in the NLS), the first of a series culminating in the version at the Scottish National Portrait Gallery, and others at Ecclefechan and on the Embankment near Cheyne Row. It is astonishing how Louisa, Froude – who commissioned Millais – and Forster – who chose Watts – competed to memorialise Carlyle. Louisa's daughter Mary was taken to see Boehme's work, and like Sarah Norton exchanged charming letters with her mother's friend. They write as if one family, and prompt the question whether it was really surprising that Forster should have told the inquiring Froude that the first Lady Ashburton was also 'deeply in love with Carlyle'.[7] Biographers have followed Froude in rejecting and mostly concealing this statement. Lady Harriet's and Louisa's were returned to Louisa. Little was to appear in Carlyle's official biography, and an air of embarrassment still hangs over the stories of Carlyle's affections.

Yet after all, what does this tell us? Perhaps a great deal. For example, that earlier accounts of Carlyle are not just incomplete but unreliable, and Froude's whole interpretation and especially the fourth volume may be skewed. Of course, the new papers also enlarge the canvas, fulfil curiosity, and decidedly reveal a different and more attractive Carlyle. The friendships with Lady Ashburton and John Forster are typical of the later Carlyle's other relationships. And they certainly explain the dismay felt by many who knew him when the official biography appeared, which encouraged readers to see Carlyle's life and work coincide.

Tennyson catches the mood in his doggerel 'The Dead Prophet', in which (no doubt after reading Froude's accounts) he sees the prophet's female admirer, at first join in admiring him, 'So great and noble was he!' But then:

> She tumbled his helpless corpse about
>   Small blemish upon the skin!
> But I think we know what is fair about
>   Is often as foul within.[8]

More prosaically, whatever we think, we can understand why so many of those close to Carlyle (not only Norton, Mary and Alexander, but David Masson, the Wedgwoods, Browning, John Tyndall, William Allingham, and many lesser-known), could not recognise the cantankerous and self-absorbed figure of the journals in Froude's final volume. The later Carlyle has still to be revealed.

Notes

1 Non-Carlylean readers should know that there was a strong and bitter controversy about Carlyle's life between Froude, who wrote his sometimes accusatory biography in 4 vols. (1882-84), and his editions of Carlyle's *Reminiscences* (1881) and *My Relations with Carlyle* (1903), and Carlyle's niece and nephew Mary Aitken and Alexander Carlyle. Each side, without being entirely right, has attracted supporters; and though acceptance of Froude's account has been challenged, it has been difficult to dislodge. These new papers should change this; see the Works Cited.

2 Alexander and Mary's mainly unpublished letters to Charles Eliot Norton, are in the Houghton Library, Harvard University, Norton Papers bMS Am 1088 (970). Warm acknowledgements are due for permission to quote, as they are also to the copyright holders and to the Carnegie Foundation of the Universities of Scotland for travel assistance. Thanks are also due to Professor Ian Campbell, and others concerned, for the opportunity to see Norton's unpublished letters in reply. The Ashburton Papers are now in the NLS, Acc. 11388, including the letters of Louisa Lady Ashburton, in using which I was helped by Dr Isla Jack. Grateful thanks are due to the National Library. I am also indebted to Dr Mairi Rennie, librarian of the Armstrong-Browning Library, Baylor University, Waco, Texas, for help and support in using its extensive letters from Forster to Carlyle. Letters are cited by date. Carlyle's *Journal* was largely quoted in the later vols. of Froude's *Life*, and is used in CL. It has been consulted in MS and typed copy, and is otherwise private.

3 With some exceptions he made certain that they were destroyed. In his will he asked his executors to 'destroy all his private papers' and 'all such letters papers and memorials of or relating to the late Jane Welsh Carlyle as came to me for my private property' under Carlyle's will, and 'any unpublished manuscripts' relating to the Carlyles (Dunn 2:633). Not unnaturally Norton wrote to Mary Carlyle that he could not 'interpret this in any sense favorable to Froude. It seems either like a bit of posthumous malice, or as if due to a more or less consciousness on his part that it would be well for him that the papers should be destroyed, in order that they might not give evidence of his misuse & misinterpretation' (4 March 1895). Browning's letters were to be edited by Alexander Carlyle, *Letters of Thomas Carlyle to John Stuart Mill, John Sterling, and Robert Browning*, who quotes Browning to Norton about his own 'enduring gratitude' and Carlyle's 'goodness and sympathy' and 'love' (x). We need not be hostile to Froude, a man of great powers and good intentions, but questionable judgement. Looking at his own life, it is not his unhappy childhood that may strike us, but his deep sorrow for his own two wives from whom he was unhappily bereaved, and a wish to rescue him from his partisan biographer Waldo Dunn, equally a man of good will to all but the Norton party. There was obviously something unhappy about Froude, at odds in his life with the world about Ireland, the empire, South Africa, his adversary Edward Freeman, what he calls 'niggers' in the West Indies, the American-Irish, and about his own religious crises. He was only

too well adapted to be Carlyle's biographer. But out of all this I am struck by the fact that it was not just the magnitude of the task that distracted him from Carlyle's later friendships, but that they did not interest him nearly as much as the way that his own gloom and forebodings had come to match Carlyle's.

The following letter from Alexander Carlyle to Norton (of 20 Feb. 1902) has been published before by John Clubbe, 'Grecian Destiny: Froude's Portraits of Carlyle'. Yet he derives from it a conclusion that it is impossible to accept whatever allowances are made for differences of opinion. For, unlike Norton and A. Carlyle, Clubbe thinks that the 'letter would seem to confirm' that Froude's picture of Carlyle 'in his later years' was 'in essence true to…Carlyle's fourth notebook'. Quite rightly at that time he warned that we did not know what was contained in the notebook. But some of us certainly know *now*, as well as having read further in the later letters. Certainly Norton and A. Carlyle and others believed Froude unjust, and perhaps we need not wait for the complete notebook and last letter to be published.

4 See Fielding and Jackson 51-9.

5 There is no doubt of the bruises but no evidence of their cause; see Fielding and Campbell, *Reminiscences* x-xi, 446.

6 This has raised contention, for which see Fielding and Campbell, *Reminiscences*, xxii-xxv and Fielding, 'Froude and Carlyle: Some New Considerations', based on newly-traced executors' papers, which now happily agree with the Norton/Carlyle letters and refute W. D. Dunn's repeated charges that Mary Aitken Carlyle was a blackmailing mercenary (Dunn 2:486). He relied too much and too closely on Froude's surviving children. It might be possible to see this more closely by examining Dunn's papers, now at Wooster College, Ohio.

7 Froude, *My Relations*, 15 is confusing. Is it even remotely possible that he mistook what Forster said about Louisa Lady Ashburton for Lady Harriet?

8 See Ricks, *Tennyson*, 1322-26, wrongly dated 1822 but in fact 1882-84. Tennyson unconvincingly denied that he meant Froude, and that he had said that Froude 'had sold' his 'master for thirty pieces of silver'. Hallam Tennyson noted his father as saying of the marriage, 'I am sure that Froude is wrong. I saw a great deal of them. They were always "chaffing one another", and they could not have done that if they had got on so "badly together" as Froude thinks'. Tennyson evidently wrote the last stanza of the poem thinking of Froude's introductory note: 'The fire in his soul burnt red to the end, and sparks flew from it which burnt hot on those about him, not always pleasant, not always hitting the right spot or the right person' (*Life* 3:6; Ricks 1323).

Works Cited

Ashburton Papers. NLS, Acc. 11388.

Carlyle, Alexander, ed. *New Letters of Thomas Carlyle*. 2 vols. London: Lane, 1904.

———, ed. *Letters of Thomas Carlyle to John Stuart Mill, John Sterling and Robert Browning*. London: Fisher Unwin, 1923.

Charles Eliot Norton Papers. Houghton Library. Harvard University.

Clubbe, John. 'Grecian Destiny: Froude's Portraits of Carlyle'. *Carlyle and His Contemporaries, Essays in Honor of Charles Richard Sanders.* Ed. John Clubbe. Durham, NC: Duke UP 1976. 316-53.

Davies, James A. *John Forster: a Literary Life*. Leicester UP, Leicester UK, 1976.

Dunn, Waldo Hilary. *James Anthony Froude: A Biography*. 2 vols. Oxford: Clarendon Press, 1961-3.

Fielding, Kenneth J. 'Froude and Carlyle: Some New Considerations'. *Carlyle Past and Present*. Ed. Fielding and Rodger L. Tarr. London: Vision Press, 1976. 239-69.

———, and Peter Jackson. 'Carlyle's Reminiscences: Dr. Peyton Blakiston'. *Carlyle Newsletter* 9 (1988): 51-9.

Forster Collection. Armstrong Browning Library. Waco, Texas.

Froude, James Anthony. *My Relations with Carlyle*. Ed. Ashley A. and Margaret Froude. London: Longmans, 1903.

———, ed. *Reminiscences*. By Thomas Carlyle. 2 vols. London: Longman's, 1881.

Hanson, Lawrence and Elisabeth. *Necessary Evil: The Life of Jane Welsh Carlyle*. London: Constable, 1952.

Martineau, Harriet. *A History of the Thirty Years' Peace*. 4 vols. London: Bohn's, [1877-78].

Moore, Carlisle. 'Thomas Carlyle'. In *The English Romantic Poets & Essayists*. Revised Edition. Ed. Carolyn W. and Lawrence H. Houtchens. New York: Modern Language Association of America, 1966. 336-78.

Nixon, Jude V. 'The Forster/Carlyle Unpublished Letters and Re-Tailoring the Sage'. *Carlyle Studies Annual* 18 (1988): 83-122.

Ricks, Christopher, ed. *The Poems of Tennyson*. London and Harlow, UK, Longmans, 1969.

Surtees, Virginia. *The Ludovisi Goddess*. Salisbury, UK: Michael Russell, 1984.

Chapter 2

The Historian as Shandean Humorist: Carlyle and Frederick the Great

RUTH APROBERTS

Carlyle's *The History of Frederick the Great* (1858-65) is so enormous and various that it has been rather difficult to think of, and it has discouraged or even disgusted many readers. Yet there is a way in which one can come closest to knowing Carlyle through this vast work. It is the most personal of his histories, marked by intimate addresses from writer to reader, informal, colloquial, and frequently witty. We can get closer to knowing the book through remembering Carlyle's debts to Laurence Sterne. His general sympathy with Sterne cannot be underestimated. In his essay 'Jean Paul Friedrich Richter' (1827) Carlyle calls him 'our last specimen of humour, and, with all his faults, our best; our finest if not our strongest' (*Works* 26:17). The 'faults' are Sterne's unVictorian indelicacies. But later in 'Characteristics' (1831), Carlyle echoes Sterne's wish for a reader '"that would give up the reins of his imagination into his author's hands, and be pleased he knew not why, and cared not wherefore"' (*Works* 28:24).

In *The History of Frederick the Great*, Carlyle is continually courting, inviting, communing with, encouraging, and admonishing this wished-for reader. He is related to Sterne also in a larger philosophical sense, insofar as Sterne stands in the light of Locke. All we can know comes out of our sensations, our experience. And it is indeed a Lockean base on which stand Hume and the Scottish tradition that shaped Carlyle. Everywhere in *Frederick* we see the insistence on what is observable, and a general refusal to shape history by theoretical philosophy. Congruent with this is Carlyle's insistence on the limitations of our knowledge, the principle he elaborates as Nescience.[1] Nescience is Sterne's theme, outlined in Sterne's favourite passage from Locke's *Essay Concerning Human Understanding* (1689): 'He that knows anything, knows this in the first place, that he need not seek long for Instances of his Ignorance. The meanest, the most obvious Things that come in our way, have dark sides, that the quickest Sight cannot penetrate into. The clearest, and most enlarged Understandings of Thinking Men find themselves puzzled and at a loss, in every Particle of matter' (*Essay*, ed. Peter H. Nidditch, 4.3.22; quot. in Briggs 94). As Peter Briggs observes, Sterne echoes Locke in this passage in *Tristram Shandy* (1759–67): 'But mark, madam, we live amongst riddles and mysteries – the most obvious things which come in our way, have dark sides, which the quickest sight cannot penetrate into; and even the clearest and most exalted understandings amongst us find ourselves puzzled and at a loss in almost every cranny of nature's works' (*Tristram Shandy*, Florida edn., 4.17.350; quot. in Briggs 94).

In small things and large there are traces of Sterne in Carlyle's *Frederick*, which is his most Shandean work. His sense of the difficulties and yet the importance of history dominates here, and his authorial communion with the reader is elaborate. Throughout *Frederick* Carlyle is supremely conscious of the difficulty of ever knowing anything, and muses often on the problem. He clings to what is definitely *there*, observable. Sterne emerges both in the details and in the broad conception of the work. Carlyle remarks that in 1719, there took place an English '"Descent on Vigo"', with Lord Cobhan leading an attack on this Gallician port. Participating in it was a certain 'Lieutenant of Foot, by name *Sterne*, who had left, with his poor Wife at Plymouth, a very remarkable Boy called Lorry, or *Lawrence*; known since to all mankind. When Lorry in his *Life* writes, "my Father went on the Vigo expedition", readers may understand this was it. Strange enough: that poor Lieutenant of Foot is now pretty much all that is left of this sublime enterprise upon Vigo, in the memory of mankind; hanging there, as if by a single hair, till poor *Tristram Shandy* be forgotten too' (*Works* 13:31).

In an accompanying note Carlyle cites Sterne's *Memoirs*, which he has to hand. The author of *Tristram Shandy* reappears at the Siege of Gibraltar in 1727:

> A siege utterly unmemorable, and without the least interest for existing mankind...if it be not, once more, that the Father of *Tristram Shandy* was in it: still a Lieutenant of foot, poor fellow; brisk, small, hot-tempered, loving, 'liable to be cheated ten times a day if nine will not suffice you'. He was in this Siege...Little Lorry is still living; gone to school in Yorkshire...the poor Lieutenant Father died, soldiering in the West Indies; and we shall not mention him again. But History ought to remember that he is 'Uncle Toby', this poor Lieutenant, and take her measures! – The Siege of Gibraltar, we still see with our eyes, was in itself Nothing. (*Works* 13:99)

Some readers will notice also the reference to the siege of Namur, 1746, in which the fictional Toby took part (*Works* 16:206). As in *Tristram Shandy*, the hero of Carlyle's epic takes a long time getting born; technically he is born in Book I, Ch. II (*Works* 12:20), but his story is not taken up again until his childhood begins in Book IV, Ch. I (*Works* 12:319), and there are 798 more pages before he succeeds to the throne. There is considerable Shandean anticipating and backing and filling: So and so 'will turn up in the next chapter'; another so and so comes back into the story, he 'at whose wedding we assisted...long since...if anyone now remembered' (*Works* 16: 160, 19).

At one stage, three problems confront the king, one and two are described, and then 'Question *Third* is – But Question Third, so extremely important was it in the sequel, will deserve a Chapter to itself' (*Works* 16:390), this being the wars in North America. In the middle of a chapter on newcomers to Berlin, Carlyle describes some but remarks, 'By far the notablest arrival...is M. de Voltaire's...But that arrival will require a Chapter to itself' (*Works* 16:248) and he goes on with those of less account. These 'next chapter' promises are all kept. He prepares us for meeting a Miss Barbara Wyndham long before she appears 448 pages later (*Works* 16:305, 17:343–6). This wealthy English lady in 1758 made a present of £1000 to King Frederick out of sheer admiration. He graciously accepted, and with part of the money he bought himself a new flute. Sterne was a great annotator; Carlyle in his very different project, doing real historical research, annotates most plentifully and meticulously. An annotative touch that may endear Carlyle particularly is a reference to one of his sources, a certain Förster. his note reads, 'Förster (place *lost*)' (*Works* 14:219). On another occasion where he has been telling how the Swedish military lived, oddly, on some sort of dried fish instead of the sensible oatmeal, he gives his source as Montalambert, but the page of 'the demand for Norse *porridge*, which interested me, I cannot find again' (*Works* 17:339). Similarly, Carlyle admits that he once knew what the Opera House in Berlin had cost Frederick, 'but the sibylline leaf is gone again upon the winds!' (*Works* 15:367). In such circumstances, the reader can feel secure in the knowledge of the historian's honesty and integrity.

Throughout the volumes, Carlyle takes on a diverting variety of *dramatis personae*. There is, chiefly, the Editor, who is coping with a vast resource of documents which he studies and combs through in order to save his readers the enormous labour. He selects those passages that illuminate the subject and give his readers contact with it. Specifying the real sources (mostly bad, occasionally good, and very occasionally useful), he complains mightily of the tomes of Dryasdust. Even the great Ranke is remiss in giving *his* sources (Clive 207). To make the history accessible, he abridges and comments in order to clarify, to emphasise or to be humorous. There is the 'tourist' persona, very often representing Carlyle's own researches on his two trips to Germany, and he supplies maps in plenty. There is 'Smelfungus', which was Sterne's name for Smollett, who represents the splenetic view of things, useful enough. And then there is 'Sauerteig', Carlyle's own invention, Professor Gottfried Sauerteig, who figured in 'Biography' as the spokesman for the 'significance that lies in REALITY' (*Works* 28:49) and later as 'an open soul, looking with clear eye and large recognising heart over all accessible quarters of the world' ('Dr. Francia', *Works* 29:304), and sounds like Carlyle's ideal historian self. In all these capacities he very personally relates himself to the reader. Mark Cumming has well said how in the case of *The French Revolution* Carlyle 'enlists its reader as co-worker and co-creator, sharing in the author's imaginative difficulties' (3). This is even more true in the case of *Frederick*. In the language of Reader-Response criticism, the narratee is on loan to the author.

More than once, Carlyle will say a matter is *entre nous*, as though he had just button-holed us, or he will say he owns up to some opinion 'privately' (*Works* 16:198). Typically he explains he will be as brief as he possibly can: 'Courage, reader; by good eyesight, you will still catch some features of Friedrich as we go along' (*Works* 16:199). He admires a certain source book, Walpole's *George The Second*, but complains it has no index, and no dates on the top of the page; soon after, the reader realises that this missing information has been provided by the author (*Works* 17:158). The typographical variety in *Frederick the Great* is both unique and significant. Carlyle frequently resorts to fine print for most quotations of documents or for summaries of situations or events. He is consistently kind to his readers – he invites them to skip passages if they are restless. On the other hand, readers are expected to contribute. On some complicated matter, he will try to give a true outline, and decipher the ambiguous records: 'not impossible, if readers will loyally assist' (*Works* 16:268). He manfully confronts difficult place names: 'Krezeczhorz (let us write it Kreczor for the future)'; he is relieved that 'Radowesnitz' is 'a pronouncable little Village' (*Works* 17:174).

Preparing to describe Frederick's first encounter with Voltaire, Carlyle remarks that 'all readers are on the alert for it, and ready to demand of me impossibilities about it! Patience, readers. You shall see it, without and within, in such light as there was...if you will coöperate' (*Works* 14:348). Sometimes readers are reproved. He does not think much of Frederick's skill in writing verse, but for the sake of his sentimental readers, he allows himself at one point to quote a longish example. His indulgence is brief: 'Sad doggerel...readers see what their foolish craving has brought on them!' (*Works* 14:334). He urges his audience to collaborate with him, as he heroically copes with the sources:

> As the history of Friedrich...is still little other than a whirlpool of simmering confusions, dust mainly, and sibylline paper-shreds in the pages

> of poor Dryasdust, perhaps we cannot do better than snatch a shred or two (of the partly legible kind, or capable of being made legible) out of that hideous cauldron; pin them down at their proper dates; and try if the reader can, by such means, catch a glimpse of the thing with his own eyes. (*Works* 13:374)

In the next volume, he comforts his readers by assuring them that he is through with war for a while, leaving it 'to dance itself out, well in the distance, not encumbering us further, like a circumambiant Bedlam, as it has hitherto done. Courage, reader!' (*Works* 16:2) Still, certain important particulars must be noticed: '[T]he reader is to note well this Treaty of Warsaw, as important to Friedrich and him', 'him' meaning the reader. (*Works* 16:75) Carlyle will save his reader an effort where possible. A certain document is 'not worth following' (*Works* 14:128); another is 'studiable by Editors only' (*Works* 14:225). At one point Smelfungus complains about the unedited state of the Voltaire-Frederick correspondence: 'Will it be possible to pick out the small glimmerings of real light?' Carlyle replies, 'It will be very difficult, my friend; – why did not you yourself do it?...Letters a good few...which all *had* their bit of meaning; and have it still, if well tortured till they give it out...but you have not tortured them; you have left it to me, if I would! As I assuredly will not (never fear, reader!) – except in the thriftiest degree' (*Works* 16:313). In another passage, Carlyle explains a complex military manoeuvre and remarks: 'Meaning what? Be vigilant, my young friend' (Works 16:162).

In his abridgements of narratives or letters, he often adds his own comments. For example, when a letter reads 'I wrote to the Abbé', he interjects, 'never mind what Abbé' (*Works* 16:186). Sometimes he is impatient with his readers. When a Kur-Pfalz reappears in the narrative, Carlyle notes, 'Need we repeat, – lazy readers having so often met him, and forgotten him again, – this is a new younger Kur-Pfalz: Karl Theodor, this one' (*Works* 16:142). Later he reminds his readers of an action of a certain Algarotti 'of which the reader has lost remembrance' (*Works* 16:319). Nearing the end of a series of battles, he acknowledges that 'the wearied Reader's imagination [is] left to conceive for itself...with small help from a wearied Editor!' (*Works* 18:330). In his discussion of Voltaire's allegations against Frederick, he insists that his readers must sift through the false reports to decipher the truth. It is 'laborious, perhaps disgusting; not impossible, if readers will loyally assist' (*Works* 16:268). He also reminds them not to 'be not too severe on poor Voltaire! He is very fidgety, noisy; something of a pickthank, of a wheedler; but, above all, he is scorbutic, dyspeptic; hagridden as soul seldom was; and (in his oblique way) *appeals* to Friedrich and us, – not in vain' (*Works* 16:333). Throughout *Frederick*, the editor is very frank with his audience. Occasionally, he admits his notes are defective. One reference is missing a date but he does not mind – 'sleepy Editor feeling no want of any' (*Works* 16:189). Elsewhere, he concedes that he does not know the provenance of an Irish Jacobite general (*Works* 18:176) and forgets how many times the Austrian General Loudon tried a certain ploy: 'Say six times in all' (*Works* 18:213). One of Frederick's own historical essays 'is not very illuminative...on the first perusal, but I intend to read it again' (*Works* 18:139–40).

Much of *Frederick the Great* consists of long passages quoted from documentary sources, and of course most of these are in French or German. Carlyle's translations are remarkably deft and witty. Typically, he interjects comments of his own and frequently offers the original foreign word by way of explanation. When Frederick and his sister Wilhelmina were young, they used a kind of 'cipher speech' against the tyrant father, 'Ragotin'. Carlyle translates this French word as 'Stumpy', and indeed the French word does mean short and fat and surly, as he says it does (*Works* 12:429). In the case of some thieves put to the torture, Carlyle says 'they blabbed' and then gives the original '*ils ont jasé*' (*Works* 14:287). This catches the low tone of the French word, and is accurate as well as witty. In another case, one must please those in power even though they are stupid, for '*l'amour de ces grands colosses*' is translated as 'all for the sake of those Big Blockheads' (*Works* 13:392). '*Sanssouci*' might be familiar enough to be let go, but we are nevertheless told it means '*No*-Bother', which loses the French elegance, but is very English, and also echoes the Scots 'nae bother' (*Works* 16:203). The '*Count de Boursoufle*' becomes the 'Count de Windbag'. '*Entre deux vins*' becomes 'half-seas over' (*Works* 16:322). '*Si vous nous trompez, vous serez écrasés*' becomes 'if you deceive us, you will be squelched' (16:322).

One could object that he has read too much French: he employs those very French words *hebetude* and *hebetate* as though they were standard English (*Works* 16:143). 'Hebetude' is just allowed in English dictionaries but is hardly idiomatic. He translates the very common denigratory French word '*canaille*' as 'Doggery' (*Works* 13:190 *et passim*), which evidently pleases him. German words too get translated, especially if they are humorous. He enjoys German honorifics, such as *Höchstdieselbe*, 'Highest-the-Same' (*Works* 17:49). A set of 'disagreeing, thin skinned, high-pacing...Generals' is from the German original '*uneinige, piquirte*' as though of ill-trained horses (*Works* 17:215). Proper names are often humorous: Candidate *Linsenbarth* is candidate 'Lentilbeard' (16:248) and Herr Schimmelman is Mr '*Mouldyman*' (*Works* 18:334). Another notable Shandean feature of *Frederick the Great* is Carlyle's eccentric vocabulary, which is both vivid and vigorous. The threatened general Seckendorf is 'puckered into dangerous anxieties' (*Works* 14:71). The ill-trained battalions are in a 'jumbly' condition; hard marching is 'shogging' (*Works* 16:125,127). Complaints arise 'of a very *shrieky* character'. When the Catholic King August is dying, an Archbishop is summoned, 'with his extreme unctions and soul-apparatus' (*Works* 14:368, 90). On the eve of an attack, officers are 'watching, messaging about...assiduously keeping their [generals] in tune' (*Works* 18:42). When a certain source he quotes says something obvious, Carlyle exclaims in a very modern idiom, 'Thank you for reminding us of that' (*Works* 16:347). He refers to the pensioned ex-lovers of Catherine the Great as her '*emeriti*' (*Works* 18:428).

Such language suggests remarkable candour on Carlyle's part. But how frank can he be when his material becomes controversial? The question of Frederick's sexuality is bound to come up in the reader's mind in the early chapters, where Friedrich Wilhelm objects so strenuously to the son's foppishness, and calls him - and Carlyle quotes - an '*effemenierter Kerl*' (*Works* 12:422). When Frederick and his friend Katte attempt to evade the fatherly control by a wild escapade, and are caught and arrested, the audience must follow the horrifying events of their imprisonment and trial, and the execution of Katte before the eyes of Frederick. The horror of the punishment would seem to suggest that the crime was homosexuality. At this point (*Works* 13:332-42), Carlyle does not take up the matter at all, nor does he when the attractive Italian Algarotti becomes part of Frederick's circle. Algarotti had become known for his writings on opera, on science; his *Newtonianisme pour Les Dames* gave him entrée to Voltaire and to Frederick's circle. He was witty, charming and handsome, and associated with various free queer spirits like Lord Hervey. Carlyle lets this suggest what it may but does not address the issue of Algarotti's sexuality. But later in the history, he is obliged to mention an article published in 1752, in what he calls 'The Demon Newspaper', which describes the king's activities at court, including the multifarious business, correspondence, music, learned discussions, and witty dinner-parties. 'Dark' revelations then follow: 'Dinner lasts one hour...upon which the King returns to his Apartment with bows. It pretty often happens that he takes with him one of his young fellows. These are all handsome, like a picture (*faits à peindre*)'. Translating from the French, Carlyle refers to 'poisonous malice mixing itself, this time, with the human darkness...This Demon's Paper abounds with similar allusions; as so the more desperate sort of Voltaire utterances, - *Vie Privée* [Voltaire's work] treating it as known fact' (*Works* 16:343).

The Demon and Voltaire both might have been merely malicious, Carlyle implies, but he admits there are other disinterested individuals who speak of it as 'a thing credible':

> And, beyond the least question, there did a twice-abominable rumour of that kind run, whispering audibly, over all the world; and gain belief

> from those who had appetite...explaining also, to the dark human intellect, why this King had commonly no Women at his Court. A most melancholy portion of my raw-material, this; concerning which, since one must speak of it, here is what little I have to say:...That proof of the *negative*, in this or any such case, is by the nature of it impossible. That it is indisputable Friedrich did not now live with his Wife...That an opposite rumour [gossip about heterosexual liaisons] – which would have been pretty fatal to this one...was equally current...That, for me, proof in the affirmative, or probable indication that way, has not anywhere turned-up. (*Works* 16:343-4)

Carlyle goes on to say that *he* will not 'value the rumour at a pin's fee', and mocks the public's appetite for such things: '[A]re there no obscene details at all, then? grumbles the disappointed idle public to itself, something of reproach in its tone' (*Works* 16:345). Modern scholars tend to grant Frederick's homosexual interests, but question whether he took an active role. Certainly Frederick and his circle joked extravagantly on deviant sex, then highly illegal. All this was no doubt troubling to Carlyle, and probably increased his ambivalence toward his hero.

Yet Carlyle is also surprisingly sympathetic to Frederick's obscene military humour, exhibited in a short poem that he wrote to celebrate the Prussian victory at Rossbach:

> [T]he famed *Congé de l'Armée des Cercles et des Tonneliers*; a short metrical Piece; called by Editors the most profane, most indecent, most etc.; and printed with asterisk veils thrown over the worst passages. Who shall dare, searching and rummaging for insight into Friedrich, and complaining that there is none, to lift any portion of the veil; and say, 'See-Faugh!' [He, Carlyle, will.] The cynicism, truly, but also the irrepressible honest exultation, has a kind of epic completeness, and fulness of sincerity; and, at bottom, the thing is nothing like so wicked as careless commentators have given out. Dare to look a little: '*Adieu, grands ecraseurs de rois*', so it starts: 'Adieu, grand crushers of kings; arrogant windbags...' [and so on]. Enough to say, the Author, with a wild burst of spiritual enthusiasm, sings the charms of the rearward part of certain men; and what a royal ecstatic felicity there sometimes is in indisputable survey of the same. He rises to the heights of Anti-Biblical profanity...quoting King Nicomedes's experiences on Caesar (happily known only to the learned); and, in brief, recognises that there is, on occasion, considerable beauty in that quarter of the human figure, when it turns on you opportunely. A most cynical profane affair: yet, we must say by way of parenthesis, one which gives no countenance to Voltaire's atrocities of rumour about Friedrich himself in this matter; the reverse rather, if well read; being altogether theoretic, scientific; sings with gusto the glow of beauty you find in that unexpected quarter, – while *kicking*

> it deservedly and with enthusiasm. 'To see the' – what shall we call it: seat of honour, in fact, 'of your enemy': has it not an undeniable charm?... 'And oh', next stanza says, 'to think what our glory is founded on', – on view of that unmentionable object, I declare to you! – And through other stanzas, getting smutty enough (though in theory only), which we need not prosecute farther. A certain heartiness and epic greatness of cynicism, life's nakedness grown almost as if innocent again; an immense suppressed insuppressible Haha, on the part of this King. (*Works* 17:281–2)

My authority on the matter of male military humour tells me this is all rather standard and innocent, in the mode of 'We beat hell out of them, or we fucked them to a faretheewell, we really buggered them for good'. Carlyle clearly appreciates the 'smutty' style. He also enjoys another example of Frederick's military idiom, when he congratulates Duke Ferdinand on a victory over the French: 'May you *fleur-de-lys* every French skin of them; cutting out on their' – what shall we say (*leur imprimant sur le cul*) [impressing on their bottoms] 'the Initials of the Peace of Westphalia...' tatooed on that latest extremity of fashion' (*Works* 17:348). Later, Carlyle translates Frederick's suicidal declaration – '*N'ya-t-il donc pas un bougre de boulet que puisse m'atteindre*?' – as 'Is there not one b_____ of a ball that can reach me, then?' The 'b_____' is clearly '*bougre*' or 'bugger' (*Works* 18:80). Carlyle did not have to quote this, yet apparently the statement seems for him to reveal an important aspect of his hero's psyche. He also has no qualms about speaking of Frederick's state of health, and mentions both his haemorrhoids and diarrhoea (*Works* 16:316;18:171).

The Voltaire-Frederick relationship is endlessly interesting, with a wealth of documentation. It originates in Frederick's wonderful zeal for things intellectual and cultural, and his great court Academy. Early in his career, his dream was to invite Voltaire, and in various interesting stages, the dream is gradually realised. Frederick is, of course, ostensibly Protestant, which manifests itself in his mockery of Roman Catholicism. In fact, he objects to all forms of supernaturalism. Carlyle is as circumspect about his hero's unbelief as he is about his own. During the reverses of the Seven-Years War, Carlyle observes of Frederick, 'there is in those grim days, a tone *as of* [my italics] trust in the Eternal, *as of* real religious piety and faith, scarcely noticeable elsewhere in his History' (17:312). The friendship of Voltaire and Frederick develops on a foundation of anti-religious sympathy, with the King delighting in the philosopher's learned and witty epigrams. Frederick looks to Voltaire for literary guidance, and sends him his poems, which Voltaire politely reviews. Carlyle himself has little respect for these writings: 'Ever and anon through his life, on small hint from without or on great, there was found a certain *leakage* [my italics] of verses, which he was prompt to utter' (*Works* 14:239). Of his collected *Poésies*, Carlyle asserts: 'Copies have now fallen extremely rare (and are not in request at all, with my readers or me)' (*Works* 16:241). In Frederick's very worst period when defeat seemed imminent, he produced what Carlyle calls his 'Lamentation Psalms': '[He] took to verses, by way of expectorating himself, and keeping-down his devils. Not a bad plan in the circumstances, - especially if you have so wonderful a turn for expectoration by speech' (*Works* 17:240).

In a retrospective passage, Carlyle uses a sexual metaphor to describe the relationship between Voltaire and Frederick. They are a 'pair of Lovers hopelessly estranged and divorced; and yet, in a sense, unique and priceless to one another'.[2] In their correspondence, Frederick has 'always with something of banter audible in him; as has Voltaire too, but in a finer *treble* tone, being always female in this pretty duet of parted lovers. It rarely comes to any scolding between them; but there is or can be nothing of cordiality. Nothing, except in the mutual admiration, which one perceives to be sincere on both sides; and also, in the mutual practical estrangement' (*Works* 18:188). Carlyle sees the two of them as embodying the historical essence of the century: '"Voltaire was the spiritual complement of Friedrich" says Sauerteig once: 'what little of lasting their poor Century produced lies mainly in these Two...But what little it *did*, we must call Friedrich; what little it *thought*, Voltaire...They are, they for want of better, the two Original Men of their Century' (*Work* 14:177). In his recreation of this famous friendship, Carlyle continues to address the reader as though intimately and informally. He writes colloquially, often with sentence fragments, and interjections, and little glimmers of light about himself break through. At one point when Voltaire's position at Berlin is troubled, he nevertheless works on his history of *Louis Quatorze*. As Carlyle notes, it must have been 'a potent quietus in these Court-whirlwinds inward and outward.... He did *not* go mad in that Berlin element, but had throughout a bower-anchor to ride by' (*Works* 16:314-15). One cannot but think of Carlyle himself, who in spite of his complaints, found a certain peace in the 'bower-anchor' of his own history writing.

In the *History of Frederick the Great*, Carlyle presents a remarkable three-way relationship between himself, Frederick, and the reader, which is both open and perpetually shifting. Modern historians have agreed with Carlyle's verdict that Frederick is a very difficult subject, and that aspects of his personality seem strangely discordant.[3] Yet because he was responsible for shaping so much of modern Europe, we are almost obliged to try to fathom him. This is the challenge Carlyle took on, determined in his Lockean way to stick to what is really there, and as a proper *nescient*, to keep his mind open to what Sterne called 'the riddles and mysteries' of life. He is faithful to the evidence, the written record of a monarch who himself left more written documents than any other. These together with observers' accounts are mediated to the reader by translation, abridgement, and comment. Carlyle's attitudes shift as he progresses, and his readers' attitudes to himself and to Frederick are likewise in motion. The whole enormous work ends with Carlyle saying, 'Adieu, good readers; bad also, adieu' (*Works* 19:300). This has been considered ungracious; on the contrary, it is gracious, charitable, Shandean - and humorous.

Notes

1 See apRoberts. John B. Lamb has perceptively drawn Sterne and Carlyle together, but he does not refer to *Frederick*; Morse Peckham in his notable appreciation of *Frederick* acclaims the book's Shandean quality (45); Georg Tennyson notes Shandean elements in TC's early writings, especially in *Illudo Chartis* (198-215); and John D. Rosenberg observes 'Shandyesque self-mockery' in *Frederick* (160). It is also worth pointing out that there are important echoes of Sterne at various points in Carlyle's works: *The Life and Opinions of Tristram Shandy* stands behind 'The Life and Opinions of Herr Teufelsdröckh'. The central idea of *Heroes*, that 'the true Shekinah is Man', is also from *Tristram Shandy*.

2 Carlyle may be borrowing the metaphor from Varnhagen von Ense, with whom he corresponded. See McDonogh 230.

3 For Carlyle and recent Frederick biography, see Sorensen.

Works Cited

apRoberts, Ruth. 'Carlyle and the History of Ignorance'. *Carlyle Studies Annual* 18 (1999): 73-81.

Briggs, Peter M. 'Locke's Essay and the Tentativeness of *Tristram Shandy*'. Critical Essays on Laurence Sterne. Ed. Melvyn New. New York: Hall, 1998. 88-109.

Carlyle, Thomas. *History of Friedrich II of Prussia called Frederick the Great.* Ed. and abridged with an introduction by John Clive. Chicago and London: U of Chicago, 1969.

Cumming, Mark. *A Disimprisoned Epic*. Philadelphia: U of Pennsylvania, 1988.

Lamb, John B. 'A 'Chaos of Being': Carlyle and the Shandean Web of History'. *Clio* 20 (1990): 23-37.

McDonogh, Giles. *Frederick the Great*. New York: St Martin's Press, 1999.

Peckham, Morse. 'We are Insane'. *Victorian Revolutionaries*. New York: Braziller, 1970. 44-83.

Rosenberg, John D. *Carlyle and the Burden of History*. Cambridge, MA: Harvard UP, 1985.

Sorensen, David. '"Tyrannophilia": Carlyle and the Myth of Frederick the Great'. *The Carlyle Society Papers*. New Series, No. 15 (2002).

Tennyson, G. B. *Sartor Called Resartus*. Princeton, NJ: Princeton UP, 1965.

Chapter 3

Carlyle and the 'Insane' Fine Arts

DAVID DELAURA

The changes and continuities of Carlyle's views about and knowledge of the Fine Arts, in the broadest sense of the term, evolved, culminating in the fierce denunciation of French Art and Literature at mid-century. How did Carlyle respond to the arts *before* his attack against the 'Throne of Hypocrisy' (*Works* 20:321) in *Latter-Day Pamphlets* (1850) and *The Life of John Sterling* (1851)? His first serious engagement with the arts came during the 1820's, when he was devouring large quantities of modern German literature and thought. He sought, famously, to reconstruct his world-view, with the help of German poets and Idealist philosophers; but he was decidedly less than fully 'German', in retaining much of his hereditary Calvinist moralism and biblical rhetoric, while deftly blurring the firm outlines of orthodox supernaturalism.

In contrast, Weimar high aesthetics, and especially the thought of Goethe and Schiller, was soon transformed into an educational ideal associated with a cluster of terms like *Bildung* (self-cultivation), Culture, the Humanities, Hellenism and eventually (especially in American colleges) the modern Liberal Arts curriculum.[1] It is relevant to note that this backward-looking and would-be 'classical' goal of personal development by means of literature - through Matthew Arnold and on to the Great Books movement in the twentieth century - showed little interest until much later in troublesome 'modern' literature and gave next to no attention to the fine arts in our own contemporary use of the term. The Arnoldian ideal of 'the best that is known and thought in the world' ('The Function of Criticism', 1864; 3:268) has of course in recent decades steadily lost ground, particularly in American higher education.

Nonetheless, Carlyle's familiar terms need close examination, in context. His rather nebulous but still impressive statements about Symbols and Emblems in *Sartor Resartus* (finished in 1833) have been traced back, often in loose ways, to Goethe, Novalis, Fichte, and Schelling, with Spinoza on the more distant horizon. But when Carlyle announces that 'Highest of all Symbols are those wherein the Artist or Poet has risen into Prophet, and all men can recognise a present [that is, a still existent and active] God, and worship the same' (SR 165), he makes clear that these high roles, swelling with capitals, belong in his words to 'a stage of culture' long past. It is notable too that even in his last troubled days as a disciple of the Goethe whom he had already tamed and moralised, the terms Art and Artist in no way encompassed the visual arts. In fact, most Britons, even the educated, had scarcely begun to come to terms with the various forms of popular visuality bursting on the European scene - and soon to be disseminated widely by new means of mechanical reproduction. One of the most resistant was this still young Scot, raised in a severe Presbyterian sect with a strong iconoclastic tradition.

In *Sartor*, Carlyle was thinking instead of heroic and prophetic works that defined traditional cultures - and he mentions 'Homer's Epos' and the Norse Eddas (SR 165–6). Not surprisingly, Carlyle was in the same period dismissing the actual world of 'modern' literature, in effect the great age of English and Continental Romanticism, and doing so in revealingly gendered terms. Though he struggled 'manfully' and was 'our English sentimentalist', 'filled with fire', Byron was also 'spasmodic' and finally 'driven mad' (*CL* 26:243, 218, 317; 27:435; 10:290). He was, in effect, unstable and verging on hysteria. The 'wail' of Shelley was, notoriously, like the 'grief and weeping of forsaken infants' (*CL* 28. 331). Only Goethe, after struggle, attained spiritual 'Manhood', 'mild and kindly and calm' (*CL* 27: 440, 435); he was, in short, the sole adult creative figure of the age.

Carlyle's rejection of contemporary literature began in his 'German' phase and persisted into the major works of social denunciation. In his discussion of the Hero as Poet in *On Heroes and Hero-Worship* (1841), only Dante and Shakespeare qualify. The modern Hero as Man of Letters concentrates on Samuel Johnson and Burns, and the dubiously relevant figure of Rousseau. Apart from glancing at Goethe, Carlyle does not include a single nineteenth-century figure. The gender-anxieties underlying this entire network of art-and-poetry passages suffuse a curious and memorable vignette Carlyle offers in *Sartor*. His semi-autobiographical protagonist, Teufelsdröckh, down and out and in urgent need of 'solid pudding', instead receives an invitation from a countess to 'a wash of quite fluid *Aesthetic Tea*!' The Editor (who also is a partial version of Carlyle) speculates that Teufelsdröckh, at that cultivated tea party filled with 'Musical and Literary Dilettanti of both sexes', must have been 'like a hungry lion invited to a feast of chickenweed'. For the titled hosts, he notes, 'Literature and Art, attracted and attached from without, were to serve as the handsomest [mere] fringing' (SR 96).[2]

Even in the early 1830's, while still entangled to some extent in the High Art-talk emanating from Germany, Carlyle subjected the lofty pretensions of contemporary literature and art (and even music) to ironic deflation. For him, the Arts were deeply tainted by artifice and artificiality, and – to use the parlance of our times – inauthenticity. More prophetically, his own vulnerabilities, a prime source of the angers and repulsions that governed so much of his career, are unmistakable here, in the implied ineffectuality of the arts, which are now tamed and domesticated, the province of women and unmanly men. The implied distinction here between Goethe's and Schiller's high-art Weimar doctrines, and the actual art and literature of nineteenth-century Europe, provides semantic signposts through Carlyle's even more vehement engagements with Art on either side of 1850.

A notebook entry in October 1831, soon after he finished *Sartor*, marks his seemingly abrupt decision to reject the allure of Goethe's and Schiller's would-be '*higher*' morality, in which Good and Evil can now co-exist '*without* hostility, with peacefulness' (*Two Note Books* 204). Carlyle's disillusionment, partly rooted in a certain embarrassment about his own credulity, can be measured in Emerson's report in *English Traits* about their famous walk on Salisbury Plain, in July 1847. 'Art' and 'high art' is a favourite target of his wit: '"Yes, *Kunst* is a great delusion, and Goethe and Schiller wasted a great deal of good time on it...As soon as men begin to talk of art, architecture, and antiquities, nothing good comes of it"' (*Works* 276). The broad categories get tangled: transcendental Art doctrines, and actual (if unnamed) 'works of art' (*Works* 276). It was possible perhaps to read the new 'coarse' and 'Brutish' arts as partly the outcome of the elaborate juggling of categories in the *Goethezeit*, but Carlyle, determined not to tarnish Goethe's reputation in public, did not make this connection himself. He may have been thinking of *Faust* II and the hero's failed plan to reclaim the land from the sea, when he told Emerson that Goethe had recognised the 'delusion' of *Kunst* as well, 'and, in his later writings, changed his tone' (*Two Note Books* 204).

For Carlyle, the situation of the arts in France, in the 1840's and beyond, could more plausibly be read as one lurid proof of the accuracy of his earlier denunciations of Wertherism, Romantic Egoism, Byronism, Dandyism, and the Satanic School. His amusing earlier satire about sipping aesthetic tea in German art circles now seemed rather tame, or merely foolish, compared with his vision of an Art-Hell in France, where a significant number of thinkers and painters had laid down the historic Western moral and social burdens and had embraced the ideal of developing 'the senses, the apparent self, all round'. That phrase is Matthew Arnold's, thirty years later, and the new prophets by then were Hugo, Zola, and Renan (*Literature and Dogma*, 1873; 6:390).

It is easy to forget that Carlyle, born in 1795, came to maturity after 1825, as something of a late bloomer, and wrote his most influential essays and books (*Sartor*, *The French Revolution*, *Heroes*, and *Past and Present*) by 1843. These years of his greatest creativity were an unsettled period in English letters and society at large. He was, to put it simply, a post-Romantic and a pre-Victorian who, to be sure, during these same years 'invented' much of the moral rhetoric and social attitudes of some major mid-Victorians. This matter of timing also explains why, despite the Condition of England and the Captains of Industry, Carlyle did not grapple quite directly with the new urbanism, the factory-system, and the suffering and degradation of the 'hands', as Dickens and Gaskell were to do in the 1850's, and Ruskin soon thereafter.[3]

But the question remains: why the violent assault on, precisely, the 'mad' and 'prurient' Fine Arts? His earliest wrestlings with German thought, up to the early 30's, coincided with the struggle to extend the franchise, culminating in the First Reform Bill in 1832. The demand for more thoroughgoing reform fuelled the Chartist Movement from 1837 until its ignominious collapse in 1848. The atmosphere of dangerous social agitation, bolstered by the shock of European revolutions in that latter year, was the continuous context of Carlyle's reactionary social and political commentary up to 1850. The pace of intellectual change was at least as rapid, if less spectacular. Carlyle's writings played a central role in defining a new, and finally even more momentous, battle for the 'mind' of Britain – the same Britain that had by and large resisted the revolutionary and democratising efforts on the Continent earlier in the century. John Henry Newman, who could speak with unusual frankness for an orthodox clergyman, noted in 1865 that the incipient rationalism detectable at Oriel College in the 1820's was scarcely 'liberal' at all, 'in the sense in which the bulk of the educated classes through the country are liberal now' (256).[4]

Carlyle caught some of these European changes, on the wing, in 1850 – changes delayed in Britain for the most part until the 1860's and beyond, and evident then in the bolder free thought in the serious journals, in the loss of the traditional religious character of the universities and perhaps most glaringly in the openly erotic tone of the poetry of Swinburne and Rossetti. But in Britain the growing scepticism and licentiousness were tempered, even subjected to self-censorship, long after the barriers were lowered in France, which was living out the logical consequences of the Enlightenment and the successive revolutions from 1789 onward. Carlyle saw that the French contagion would inevitably spread across the Channel. More pertinently, he saw that literature and the arts had become, by mid-century, a central and contentious arena in which to fight the cultural wars of the newly democratising and fragmenting 'modern' world, as distinguished from older contentions in fields like theology, biblical scholarship, or political economy. They now bore heavy ideological burdens – they were challenging conventional thinking, from both left and right, more than they had in the heyday of the second-generation Romantics, even in Byron's *Cain*.

Carlyle ridiculed John Sterling's 'habit' of eagerly seeking out 'picture-galleries, pictures, statues and objects of Art', during his Continental journeys of 1838–39 and 1843: 'It is expected in this Nineteenth Century that a man of culture shall understand and worship Art: among the windy gospels addressed to our poor Century there are few louder than this of Art' (*Life of Sterling*, *Works* 11:174). But that earlier phase of art-tourism, in the 1830's and 40's, helped by new art-guides and new museums, and later by the railroads, was nevertheless, like the scorned dilettanti sipping aesthetic tea, both slightly comical and still comparatively harmless.[5]

In measuring the rapid cultural changes of that quarter-century, it helps to note just where Carlyle's two major outbursts against France and the Arts occur in *Latter-Day Pamphlets*, the central topic of which is the 'deranged condition of our affairs' (*Works* 20:48). The first comes near the end of No. 2, 'Model Prisons', the theme of which is the demand for Justice and even Revenge in 'the punishment of our criminals', in a world where a soft new 'Prurient influenza of Platform Benevolence' is leading to the 'Dim oblivion of Right and Wrong, among the masses'. The presumptive final loss of clear moral standards (especially the distinction between the authentic hero and the scoundrel) is manifest in the new lascivious and specifically aesthetic French religion of 'Universal Love, with Sacraments mainly of *Divorce*, with Balzac, Sue and Company for Evangelists, and Madame Sand for Virgin' (*Works* 20:80). The second, more explicit eruption dominates No. 8, 'Jesuitism', the finale of the whole book. The 'wretched' Ignatius Loyola, who 'ruined our Fine Arts', is the source and symbol of the cant and lying in these 'Latter Days', and under his guidance 'All arts, industries and pursuits...are tainted to the heart with foul poison; carry not in them the inspiration of God, but...that of the Devil'. In both cases, the nimble Carlylean leap is from a growing moral laxity to a lurid Boschian vision of dilettanti, at once refined and trivial, wallowing in a libidinous trough and 'French cookery' (*Works* 20:319).

No one seems to have looked closely at the actual terms Carlyle uses in his vehement broadside against high/low French lubricity at mid-century. Most importantly, his repeated use of Art, the Arts, and the Fine Arts usually has little to do, as the terms did for later generations, with 'the arts of design': painting, sculpture and architecture (OED). In fact, Carlyle is primarily exercised by contemporary French *fiction*, and to some extent drama: he names Balzac, Eugène Sue, George Sand, and Scribe. And the 'strange new religion' he jeers at is not merely an abstract 'Worship of the Beautiful', but much more pointedly, 'a *new* astonishing Phallus-Worship' (*Works* 20:81,

318).[6] As for Art in the narrower sense, the new galleries only encourage 'pretended raptures' (*Works* 20:321), and apart from his personal interest in the portraits of his heroes (such as John Knox), Carlyle shows little knowledge of art history and he looked closely at few if any paintings of any period.[7] In any case, he ends his discussion with his own rather prurient fantasy: the contemporary Arts serve up 'supple dancing-girls', who will, with 'lascivious fire' and by 'rhythmically chanting and posturing', perform for the modern 'monster of opulence'. He indignantly points the finger at 'The Loves of Vishnu, Loves of Adonis, Death of Psyche, Barber of Seville' (*Works* 20:327–8), the last presumably a reference to the Rossini opera. At one point he winds himself up to a shout: 'May the Devil fly away with the Fine Arts!' Their 'condition' is 'insane' (*Works* 20:320, 321).

Underlying this elaborate entanglement with French (and perhaps Italian) lubricity is Carlyle's obsession, even fiercer than in 1831, with 'manliness', including his own, expressed negatively, and in very 'northern' terms, as sexual self-control and moderation. Carlyle was as enraged by the effeminating sexual indulgence of European heterosexual culture, as Charles Kingsley was by a creeping new homoerotic sensibility he associated with a threatening network of signs of the times, including the Oxford Movement, neo-medievalism and the Christian Art Movement, and monkish celibacy. In short, Carlyle had given up the earlier high-German Art and Culture talk in something like grief and disillusionment; but the actual Arts (meaning mostly Literature) of mid-century Paris he now resists volcanically and with a deeply personal contempt. The rage of the *Latter-Day Pamphlets* is the index of Carlyle's renewed despair, but now with the knowledge that there *will be* no solution to his own spiritual, intellectual, and emotional dilemmas.

Poetry is a revealing test-case of Carlyle's uneasiness with virtually all contemporary creative work. Despite the grandeur of his own prose, and the visionary elements opened up at times to his readers, he was notoriously deaf to the music of poetry and the deep pleasure it affords. William Allingham noted in his *Diary* (1907) in 1872 that, although Carlyle read 'a vast quantity of Poetry', and could even spare praise for some poets, 'his ignorance of the technique of Poetry – *i.e.* the form and body of it, is astonishing' (211). Another acquaintance comes even closer to the truth when he speculates: Carlyle 'seems to have regarded poets as inferior persons, or rather the writing of poetry as an inferior pursuit, not altogether creditable to those engaged in it' (Macdonald 81–2). Similar concerns govern Carlyle's even stronger resistance to the nineteenth-century novel. There was overwhelming hostility to the novel as a genre, with only a few novelists excepted, up until the second decade of the century, when Walter Scott's first novels helped to begin the elevation of the form 'to a position near that poetry and drama'. This is the deep background of Carlyle's own unshakable rejection of fiction. Rodger L. Tarr, in his expert summary, notes that Carlyle's 'concept of the form and content of the novel', formed by 1834, 'never appreciably altered' (27, 39). His standard was didactic and moral, and the familiar terms he invoked are Belief, Reality, and Truth.

Unsurprisingly, Carlyle rejected the Fashionable Novel of the period, and especially the work of Bulwer-Lytton, with scorn. But the disapproval extended even to the Waverley Novels, because in his view Scott sees as the task of Literature, only 'that of harmlessly amusing indolent languid men', a mode fit for precisely 'an age fallen languid, destitute of faith and terrified of skepticism'. A painful paradox is that, although Carlyle was deeply influential on virtually all of the newly 'serious' novelists of the 1840's and 50's - and in some cases even later - he was in conversation and letters 'scathingly critical of almost every major Victorian novelist' (Gallaway 1059). Another is that he 'left little comment on the novel that he was so instrumental in shaping' (Tarr 31, 38–9, 30). A few rays of almost wistful hope for Literature, in a fairly broad sense of the term, do break through the sulphurous gloom of the *Latter-Day Pamphlets*. In 'New Downing Street' (No. 4), Carlyle even attempts, though not very coherently, to connect Literature - 'that strange entity' (and his own calling) - to the needs of the State for 'manly wisdoms and virtues' and for wise men who 'can command and obey'. But there is hope only if Literature continues 'to be the haven of expatriated spiritualisms, and have its Johnsons, Goethes, and *true* Archbishops of the world'. But it is more likely, he admits, to dwindle into 'mere merry-andrewism, windy twaddle, and feats of spiritual legerdemain, analogous to rope-dancing, opera dancing, and street-fiddling' (*Works* 20:167–8).

The paradoxes grow more intense, when Carlyle offers familiar advice to the 'brave young British man', even one with 'a Talent for Literature', that silence is better than speech 'in these tragic days', when 'hearts, in this loud babbling, sit dark and dumb towards one another'. He deplores, especially, the lack of 'a Poet', who would assume the Shakespearean burden of pulling together the 'incondite' materials of history, and write a 'National Bible' for England (*Works* 20:212–13, 282). And yet, a gleam of hope will peep through even during the second of his two major tirades against the contemporary Fine Arts. He acknowledges that, in 'Literature, poetry, and other kindred arts', 'a certain manliness of temper, and liberty to follow truth, prevails or might prevail'. There, 'the world's chosen souls do now chiefly take refuge'. But then, in a characteristic self-referential turn, he nominates 'the Poet in Speech', Fichte's 'Scholar' or 'Literary Man', as in fact the *only* kind of 'Priest' we have now, his task being to see that literature is 'vitally blended' with what remains of religion (*Works* 20:318–19).

It is notable again that, apart from the aging Goethe, not a single nineteenth-century figure, among those chosen souls and manly truth-seekers, is named in these self-defeating prophecies. The strain is particularly evident when Carlyle links an expansive definition of the Fine Arts to one final, and even more unconvincing, prophecy. He invites 'all my artist friends, of the painting, sculpturing, speaking, writing, especially of the singing and rhyming department', to give up 'fiction, idle dross of every kind', and ground their work, as Homer and the Hebrew Bible did, on 'the Interpreting of Fact' (*Works* 20:322–23). In short, they should march straight back to the irrecoverable past. In situating his undoubtedly extreme views, it helps to realise that Carlyle was not entirely alone in resisting the new arts culture. As noted above, only recently had middle-class England entered a vivid new world of illustrated newspapers and novels, new museums, galleries and fine arts reviews in the weeklies and monthlies, as well as the revolution in self-awareness brought about by the rapid spread of photography. Prominent persons - including Carlyle - could now work on their public 'image'.

In the longer perspective, attacks on 'modern' civilisation, and a sharp contrast between the brilliant but artificial and corrupt 'arts and sciences', on the one hand, and 'nature' and fundamental human needs, on the other, begin in the mid-eighteenth century, precisely at the height of the French Enlightenment. Of course Carlyle had trouble coming to terms with Rousseau's call for (in Carlyle's sceptical words) 'either bodily or intellectual Nudity, and a return to a savage state' (SR 153, 368 n.).[8] But even a few of Carlyle's near-contemporaries shared his disquiet with modern secular culture and its chief instruments, the newly unconstrained arts and literature. Intriguingly, the three examples I offer are decidedly not associated with the most conservative political and religious views of the period. Although Dickens was a cautiously liberal reformer, immersed in modern social realities, Michael Goldberg has stressed the similarities of his and Carlyle's aversion to art, past and present.[9] On the other hand, I would argue that Dickens looked at a good many art works, as Carlyle did not; and his hostile reactions - in *Pictures from Italy* (1844) and reviews in *Household Words* - laced as they are with nationalistic and religious prejudice, are less ignorant than deliberately offensive. In his derisive treatment of the arts - for example, Correggio, the Pre-Raphaelites, and St. Peter's - Dickens seemed helplessly drawn into his own worst Cockney performance manner.

But there are at least two truly thought-provoking doubters about 'modern' literature and the arts. Benjamin Jowett, perceived then and now as a very 'broad' Broad Churchman, and a biblical scholar of dubious orthodoxy, is a mixed case. Although he genuinely loved art, music, and literature - his unadventurous tastes ran to Shakespeare, Rembrandt, Haydn, and Corelli - he linked 'Art' to periods of scepticism and cultural 'corruption': 'Art is the bloom of decay' (Tollemache 100). In his letters to Florence Nightingale, he can sound like Carlyle, when he declares that a poet 'ought to be a prophet' (Oct. 1864; Quinn 37). He admits to her that he is 'sometimes inclined to think that Plato is right in banishing [poets]', especially his contemporaries, who are men of 'mere talent or imagination' (1 Aug. 1869; Quinn 175). In another letter, he decries the 'love of art', blaming Goethe and 'a man named Pater, of Brasenose' for 'turning all things, including human characters, into forms of art'. Speaking in virtual Carlylese, though informally, Jowett declares that, apart from 'the Hebrew prophets & some parts of the Greek tragedians', they 'have never understood that their calling was to be the great teachers of mankind' (4 July 1871; Quinn 210). But of course Jowett, from the mid-1860's on, had become the close observer of the new aesthetic atmosphere at Oxford, bringing with it a 'perverse' sexualisation of the literary impulse itself.[10]

And there is William Morris, who near the end of his career revealed the extremity of his alienation not only from capitalism but also from the new 'sickly' arts culture, when he simply banished all modern literature from his ideal pastoral Utopia in *News from Nowhere* (1891). His dismissal of latter-day works, filled with 'a long series of sham troubles' and 'dreary introspective nonsense about [characters'] feelings and aspirations' (16:150-1), seems pretty clearly an extension of Carlyle's attacks on the enfeebling 'self-consciousness' of the Romantic poets and their successors. But when W. B. Yeats asked Morris late in his life 'what led up to his movement', Morris replied, 'Oh, Ruskin and Carlyle, but somebody should have been beside Carlyle and punched his head every five minutes' (98).[11] After 1850, Carlyle spent even less time exploring the rapidly changing world of literature and the arts, than he had in rounding up his rogues' gallery for the *Latter-Day Pamphlets*. And yet his own continuing influence, in a number of important literary and artistic careers in England and France, lasted longer than we have yet fully calculated. He remained conspicuous, first in a literal way through his numerous portraits; and then not only as a social prophet and the assessor of the costs of modernity, but in less familiar roles both as one conduit of the attenuated 'German' Symbolist doctrine later in the century, and as a personal moral anchor in a number of boundary-breaking lives. The intriguing examples include van Gogh, Gauguin, Burne-Jones, Wilde, and Proust.[12] The effort of recovery would reveal often neglected aspects of the 'modern' creative process, especially an understudied but often integral recursive 'turn' towards origins, for some creative figures not fully prepared to discard the personal and cultural past entirely. It would also help students of the 'Sage of Chelsea', still embarrassed by the use and misuse of his political thought in the last century, to explain the enduring qualities in his life and teaching, and to justify Arnold's acknowledgement, in the late conservative phase of his own career, that the 'scope and upshot of [Carlyle's] teachings are true' ('Emerson', 1884; 10:182).

Notes

1 The German history of these themes was explored by Bruford in his two indispensable volumes. While Wilhelm von Humboldt is the key figure in this tradition, other originating names recur: Wieland, Fichte and Herder, whose term *Humanität* may be as central as *Bildung*. The strongest claims for Herder's place in the tradition are made by apRoberts. See my two essays for Goethe's place in English culture; for Carlyle's ambivalence about Goethe's influence, see Sorensen.

2 The source of 'solid pudding' is Pope's *Dunciad*, 1.54, which seems to rule out 'haggis' as the allusion. Tennyson, 240 n., notes the use of 'aesthetischen Tee' in a work by Wilhelm Hauff of 1825-26; but no one seems to have explored the possible relevance to Carlyle's passage. The OED cites Coleridge disparaging 'aesthetic' in 1821 as not 'familiar', as well as Carlyle's own reference in *The Life of Schiller* (1825; *Works* 3:174) to the 'Kantian' term '*Aesthetics*', 'the doctrine of sentiments and emotions' - the italics I think impling novelty. OED: 'But Baumgarten's use of aesthetic found popular acceptance, and began to appear [in English] after 1830, though its adoption was long opposed'. A citation of 1842: it is growing in use, but is 'a silly pedantic term'.

3 In '*Chartism*' (1839; *Works* 29:42-4), Carlyle shows genuine concern over the state of 'poor peasants' and 'the handloom weaver' - and refers, somewhat indistinctly, to 'the class of operatives'. That last word was essentially a new term in the first decades of the century (OED). Although one of the wide range of meanings is someone 'employed in a mill or factory', it is rare, and Carlyle's usage seems closer to 'engaged in production as a workman or artisan', for example, a 'mason'. Later, in *Latter-Day Pamphlets*, he does speak of 'Mill operatives' (possibly a pun on James and John Stuart Mill), but in a context of 'all manner of free operatives' and 'all kinds of Industry' - and offers examples: 'shoe-making, plough-making...house-building' (*Works* 20:166). Interestingly, all later uses seem to move away from 'production' and refer to those who perform assigned tasks (e.g., detectives and spies).

4 The remark appears in a note, 'Liberalism', added to the second edition, entitled *History of My Religious Opinions* (1865).

5 Dorothea Brooke's unhappy honeymoon visit to Rome, in chapters 19 and 20 of *Middlemarch* (1871-72), took place between 1828 and 1830 - the very period of Sterling's first visit. Eliot, who visited Rome in 1860 and again in 1869, goes out of her way to emphasise the great changes of the previous 'forty years': 'Travellers did not often carry full information on Christian art either in their heads or their pockets'. The new enthusiasm was only 'fermenting...in certain long-haired German artists' -

that is, the Nazarenes. Eliot's review of *The Life of John Sterling* (1851), more admiring of the author than of his subject, appeared in the *Westminster Review* for January 1852.

6 'Phallus-worship' appears twice in 'Model Prisons' and once in 'Hudson's Statue' (*Works* 20:81-2, 289). Carlyle's phrase, not listed in OED until 1987, though allusively anthropological in form (worship, etc.), seems to be the first non-scholarly use in English - and thus all the more aggressive an impropriety. He is explicit about 'lascivious' dancing-girls as the focus of attention; and so, his presiding figure of the rampant male generative organ remains somewhat puzzling. Though he is probably not alluding to nudity in contemporary art, even in France, that issue in fact preoccupied art circles in the period, and the male nude steadily 'disappeared'. See the brilliant discussion in Solomon-Godeau, esp. 186-203. Kestner draws on a large body of recent studies of Greek and nineteenth-century male nudity to describe the vexed relationship between the 'vulnerable' (actual) penis and the phallus, which symbolises the mythical code of 'male dominance'. In an ironic twist worth pursuing, Carlyle regularly appears in such works as the embodiment of 'standards of maleness' - such as courage, loyalty, strength, and self-reliance - that maintain the 'phallic order' (273, 35); see also Kaplan.

7 The notable exception is his interest in the 'face and figure' of his own subjects. In an influential letter of 1854, he called for a national portrait gallery, and declared that in all his historical work 'one of the primary wants [has been] to procure a bodily likeness of the personage enquired after' (*Works* 29:404-13). For an extensive and revealing treatment of the subject, concentrating on 'The Portraits of John Knox' (1876; *Works* 30:313-67), see Barlow.

8 Rousseau's call for a return to nature was most fully imagined in Bernardin de St.-Pierre's *Paul et Virginie* (1787), a once-popular fantasy of young love on a tropical isle - Mauritius in fact - long before Gauguin, Robert Louis Stevenson or films like *The Blue Lagoon*. Most intriguingly, Carlyle's brother John was the English translator of the novel in 1824, and as Marrs has argued, Carlyle himself 'played some part, perhaps some considerable part' (43-5) in overseeing the work.

9 For Dickens and the fine arts, see Goldberg.

10 For Jowett's central role in Pater's near 'fall' in 1874, see Inman.

11 For Morris and aesthetics, see Fredeman's important introduction. Carlyle's own influential discussion of modern self-consciousness appeared in 'Characteristics' (1831).

12 The evidence of influence is suggestive: Van Gogh refers to Carlyle's writings in his letters; Carlyle's *Sartor Resartus* appears in Gauguin's painting of his friend Meyer de Haan; Gaunt remains a luminous source for Carlyle and the Pre-Raphaelites; Ellmann points out that Wilde admired 'the Rabelaisian moralist' and 'could quote long passages from *The French Revolution*' (35, 207) - after Carlyle died, Wilde bought his writing table; and Proust hangs a photograph of Whistler's Carlyle in his bedroom (see Fraser).

Works Cited

Allingham, William. *A Diary*, 1824–1889. Ed. H. Allingham and D. Radford. Harmondsworth, MX: Penguin, 1985.

apRoberts, Ruth. *Arnold and God*. Berkeley: U of California P, 1983.

Arnold, Matthew. *The Complete Prose Works*. Ed. R. H. Super. 11 vols. Ann Arbor: U of Michigan P, 1960–77.

Barlow, Paul. 'The Imagined Hero as Incarnate Sign: Thomas Carlyle and the Mythology of the 'National Portrait' in Victorian Britain'. *Art History* 17 (1994): 517–45.

Bruford, W. H. *Culture and Society in Classical Weimar*, 1775–1805. London: Cambridge UP, 1962.

———. *The German Tradition of Self-Cultivation: 'Bildung' from Humboldt to Thomas Mann*. London: Cambridge UP, 1975.

Carlyle, Thomas. *Two Note Books*. Ed. Charles Eliot Norton. New York: Grolier Club, 1898.

DeLaura, David. 'Heroic Egotism: Goethe and the Fortunes of Bildung in Victorian England'. *Johann Wolfgang von Goethe: One Hundred and Fifty Years of Continuing Vitality*. Ed. Ulrich Goebel and Wolodymyr T. Zyla. Lubbock, TX: Texas Tech UP, 1984. 41–68.

———. 'Arnold and Goethe: The One on the Intellectual Throne'. In *Victorian Literature and Society: Essays Presented to Richard D. Altick*. Ed. James R. Kincaid and Albert J. Kuhn. Columbus: Ohio State UP, 1984. 197–224.

[Eliot, George]. 'Life of Sterling'. *Westminster Review* 57 (Jan. 1852): 132–4.

Ellmann, Richard. *Oscar Wilde*. New York: Knopf, 1988.

Emerson, Ralph Waldo. *English Traits*. Vol. 5 of *Complete Works. Centenary* Edition. 12 vols. Boston: Houghton and Mifflin, 1903–4.

Fraser, Robert. *Proust and the Victorians: The Lamp of Memory*. London: St Martin's Press, 1994.

Fredeman, William E. 'William Morris: "What may he not yet do?"' *Victorian Poetry* 13 (1975): xix–xxx.

Gallaway, W. F. 'The Conservative Attitude Toward Fiction'. *PMLA* 55 (1940): 1041–59.

Gaunt, William. *The Pre-Raphaelite Tragedy*. London: Jonathan Cape, 1942.

Goldberg, Michael K. 'Gigantic Philistines: Carlyle, Dickens, and the Visual Arts'. *Lectures on Carlyle & His Era*. Ed. Jerry D. James and Rita B. Bottoms. Santa Cruz, CA: University Library, 1985. 17–43.

Inman, Billie Andrew. 'Estrangement and Connection: Walter Pater, Benjamin Jowett, and William M. Hardinge'. In *Pater in the 1990s*. Ed. Laurel Brake and Ian Small. British Authors Series, No. 6. Greensboro, NC: ELT Press, 1991. 1–20.

Kaplan, Fred. '"Phallus-Worship" (1848): Unpublished Manuscripts III: A Response to the Revolution of 1848'. *Carlyle Newsletter*. No. 2 (1979): 19–23.

Kestner, Joseph A. *Masculinities in Victorian Painting*. Aldershot, UK: Ashgate, 1995.

Macdonald, Frederic W. *Recreations of a Book-Lover*. London: Hodder and Stoughton, 1911.

Marrs, Jr., Edwin W. 'Carlyle, Bernardin de Saint-Pierre, and Madame Cotton'. *Victorian Newsletter* No. 33 (Spring, 1966): 43-5.

Morris, William. *News From Nowhere*. Vol. 16 of *Collected Works... with Introductions by His Daughter May Morris.* 24 vols. London: Longmans, Green, 1910-15.

Newman, John Henry. *Apologia Pro Vita Sua: Being a History of His Religious Opinions*. Ed. Martin J. Svaglic. Oxford: Clarendon Press, 1967.

Quinn, Vincent and John Prest, eds. *Dear Miss Nightingale. A Selection of Benjamin Jowett's Letters to Florence Nightingale 1860-1893*. Oxford: Clarendon Press, 1987.

Solomon-Godeau, Abigail. *Male Trouble: A Crisis in Representation*. London: Thames and Hudson, 1997.

Sorensen, David R. 'Selective Affinities: Carlyle, Goethe, and the French Revolution'. *Carlyle Studies Annual* No. 16 (1996): 61-73.

Tarr, Rodger L. '"Fictional High Seriousness": Carlyle and the Victorian Novel'. *Lectures on Carlyle and His Era*. Ed. Jerry D. James and Charles S. Fineman. Santa Cruz, CA: The University Library, 1982. 27-44.

Tennyson, G. B. *Sartor Called Resartus*. Princeton, NJ: Princeton UP, 1965.

Tollemache, Lionel A. *Benjamin Jowett. Master of Balliol*. Third Edition. London. Edward Arnold, 1896

Yeats, William Butler. *Autobiography*. New York: Collier, 1965.

Chapter 4

'A Scotch Proudhon': Carlyle, Herzen, and the French Revolutions of 1789 and 1848

DAVID R. SORENSEN

Writing of Carlyle in the October 1843 issue of the *British and Foreign Review*, Mazzini remarks that his 'points of view are always elevated; his horizon always extends beyond the limits of country; his criticism is never stamped with that spirit of nationalism...which is only too much at work amongst us, and which retards the progress of our intellectual life by isolating it from the universal life, palpitating among the millions of our brethren abroad' (*Writings* 68). Other European radicals also noticed Carlyle's very unEnglish characteristics. In the same year Frederick Engels reviewed *Past and Present* (1843), and declared that 'Carlyle's book is ten thousand times more worth translating into German than all the legions of English novels which every day are imported into Germany'. In England, Carlyle is a '"phenomenon", and for the practical and sceptical English a pretty incomprehensible one', whereas for Germans, his 'theoretical viewpoint' is familiar (Marx & Engels 3:467, 460).

What Mazzini and Engels observed has largely been ignored by Carlyle's biographers, both Victorian and modern. Their preoccupation with the authoritarian 'Calvinist prophet' has led them to underestimate his appeal among a diverse group of European political activists, journalists, writers, and theorists. No. 5 Cheyne Row was a magnet to exiles throughout the 1840s, 1850s, and 1860s, and not simply because its inhabitants were celebrities. They sought out Carlyle because he addressed issues that were vital to them, and participated in a debate that was largely peripheral to the English political tradition. Living in England, Engels noticed that 'For all questions they have just two answers, a Whig answer and a Tory answer; and these answers were long ago prescribed by the sage supreme masters of ceremony of both parties, you have no need of deliberation and circumstantiality, everything is cut and dried' (Marx & Engels 3:445).

In his attitudes to history, politics, religion, and society, Carlyle stood outside these categories. He opposed the dominant Benthamite liberal version of the individual as monadic entity pursuing happiness, without any connections to society. He was equally contemptuous of the 'old clothes' of organised religion, which he believed was incompatible with either personal or political reform. Following many continental thinkers, he speculated that new myths of identity, which were situated in the character and spirit of a nation – what Europeans called 'ideologies' – would need to be invented. It was no coincidence that in the nineteenth century, some of his most astute critics were foreigners. Though his views often irritated them, they took him seriously, knowing that he shared many of their assumptions about class-conflict, democracy, and individualism. A striking proof of Carlyle's idiosyncratic reputation is the influence that he exercised on Alexander Herzen (1812–70), the great Russian revolutionary exile and founder of the populist movement. When he came to London from Paris in late August 1852, Herzen immediately contacted Carlyle and sent him several books, which included recently published German translations of his first seven *Letters From France and Italy* (1855) and his philosophical dialogue, *From the Other Shore* (1850). Carlyle may have taken the books with him to Germany, where he had gone on August 28 to do research on Frederick the Great. Jane Carlyle wrote back to Herzen, who told his friend Carl Vogt, 'Today I was invited to visit Mrs. Carlyle. She is the wife of the author of the *French Revolution*, a work that you know. He himself was not in, but he liked *From the Other Shore* very much and wanted to meet me' (14 Sept. 1852). To another friend he wrote, 'It appears that Carlyle likes my incidental pieces as much as I admire his history' (16 Sept. 1852; Stelling-Michaud 325).

Their meeting in December was a Carlylean 'conflux of two eternities' (*Works* 2:134). Herzen recalled that he spent a whole evening with Carlyle, and that 'he is everything that we would imagine him to be from reading his *History of the French Revolution* – a talent touched by genius, paradoxical, energetic in his verdicts and endowed with a streak of folly'. He 'argued fiercely with him; against his fantastic notion that despotism would save the world and that obedience would render socialism unnecessary'. In a revealing exchange, Herzen asked his host, 'Have you ever read the *History of the French Revolution*? There is a writer who understands things more clearly and profoundly than you do'. Their debate broke down in mutual laughter (Stelling-Michaud 325–6). Herzen had arrived in London without friends, devastated by personal and political tragedy. The scandal of his broken marriage, his wife's adulterous relationship with a fellow revolutionary and her subsequent death, the drowning of his mother and one of his children, the collapse of the revolutionary movement in France, and its brutal suppression during the June days in Paris - all of these factors contributed to Herzen's despair in 1852. In his *Memoirs* (1852–1868) he remarks, 'It seemed as though I had needed to be brought again and again into physical contact with familiar truths in order that I might renew my belief in what I had long known or ought to have known' (3:1023). The meeting with Carlyle evidently raised Herzen's spirits. He informed Vogt that Carlyle was 'a man with huge talent, but very paradoxical. One might call him the Scotch Proudhon' (5 April 1853; Stelling-Michaud 326). The allusion to the French philosopher and radical Pierre-Joseph Proudhon (1809–65) suggests that Carlyle had brought Herzen back into direct contact with 'familiar truths'.

Herzen's identification of Carlyle with Proudhon indicates an astute awareness of his own intellectual development and the Frenchman's impact on it. As Aileen Kelly has shown, Proudhon was a seminal influence in turning Herzen against utopian schemes of history (100–5). In more practical terms, Proudhon stood out as a beacon of integrity in the aftermath of the June days. In 1849 Herzen financed and contributed to Proudhon's radical journal *Le Peuple*, and encouraged his political attacks against all factions, including the revolutionary Montagnards. Proudhon not only prepared Herzen for the defeat of the revolutionary movement, but he also provided him with a compelling explanation of its failure. Like Carlyle, Proudhon was an unsystematic thinker. His ideas did not conform to the pattern of his country's thought, and they were lampooned and dismissed by critics intolerant of his alien mentality. Marx accuses him in a letter to Pavel Annenkov of being 'nothing but social contradiction in action' and Engels laments to Marx 'that he won't understand German philosophy even should he persist with it until his corpse is in the final stage of decomposition (28 Dec. 1846, Marx & Engels 38:105; 11 Aug. 1851, 38:422).

In a scathing review in 1847, Marx rechristened Proudhon's *Système des contradictions économique, ou Philosophie de la misère* (1846) as *La Misère de la Philosophie* and dismissed the Frenchman's confused historical philosophy: 'M. Proudhon has nothing of Hegel's dialectics but the language. For him the dialectic movement is the dogmatic distinction between good and bad' (Marx & Engels 6:168). Herzen took an opposite view. He regarded the *Philosophie de la misère* and Hegel's *Phenomenology of the Spirit* (1807) as the two most important works of the century, and believed the two books were compatible. According to Herzen, Proudhon 'is as much the poet of dialectics as Hegel is, with the difference that one stands on the tranquil summit of the philosophic movement, and the other thrusts into the hurly-burly of popular commotions and the hand-to-hand fighting of parties' (*Memoirs* 2:807). It was this same quality of 'hurly-burly' that attracted the Russian thinker to Carlyle's *The French Revolution*.

Proudhon agreed with Herzen's interpretation of Hegel. He admired the German philosopher's ambitious objectives, but he was repelled by his philosophy of history. In his critique of Hegel in *De la justice dans la révolution et dans l'Eglise* (1858), he questions the purpose of such thinking: 'What have we become, when the wisest theories are those that suggest historical movement is always regulated by an inflexible reason, which operates unknown to us, despite us, and, if need be, against us?' He seeks to distance himself from revolutionaries who used Hegel's scheme to glorify the principle of collective sacrifice for the sake of distant ends, justifying terror and violence by appealing to the iron laws of historical change: 'Those who will claim that the highest political liberty, for the citizen consists in knowing how to be governed by absolute power, are also the friends of perpetual dictatorship and divine right' (*Oeuvres* 8, Pt. 3:501). Proudhon was no more impressed by the German philosopher Ludwig Feuerbach's effort to humanise Hegelianism in *Introductory Theses to the Reform of Philosophy* (1841). Feuerbach envisaged society being reunited with its ideal self by appropriating the qualities that it had projected onto a divine 'other'. As Proudhon wryly remarks in *Philosophie de la Misère*, 'With such a doctrine, man will inevitably discover that he is neither a god, nor saint, nor sage, and throw himself once again into the arms of religion; in the final analysis, all that the world will gain from the negation of God will be the resurrection of God' (*Oeuvres* 1:395). Feuerbach's thesis - welcomed by Marx in 1845, but revised by him to serve revolutionary ends - promised the end of religion while creating new and more dangerous idols for people to worship. For Proudhon, what distinguished this faith was that it abolished all restraint on the exercise of political power by conflating it with religious revelation.

In his posthumously published *Contradictions politiques* (1870), he describes the inevitable conflict between malleable human nature and inflexible theory:

> A man cannot do what he wants with a system, though he may invent it a thousand times: nothing is more rebellious, more inflexible, and, if I dare say so, more stubbornly complete. As a result of having free will, man has the faculty of avowing and disavowing, of accepting everything; he can infinitely modify his thought, his will, his action, his speech; his life is only a succession of transactions with his fellow men and with nature. An idea, on the contrary, a theory, a system, a

> constitution, a pact, all that which derives from language and logic expression and form, is a thing defined and consequently definitive; an inviolable thing, which does not bend, which does not yield; which cannot be given up for another, but which cannot assume new properties, that is, which does not become another while remaining itself. (*Oeuvres* 13:159)

Proudhon's letter to Marx on 17 May 1848 illustrates the philosophical distance between them. Responding to Marx's invitation to join the new Communist Correspondence Committee, he declares his antipathy to Hegelian patterns of thought:

> I profess with the public an almost absolute anti-dogmatism in economics. Let us work together, as you want, to discover the laws of society, the manner in which these laws are realized and the process by which we are able to discover them. But, for God's sake, when we have demolished all *a priori* dogmas, do not let us think of indoctrinating the people in our turn...I applaud with all my heart your desire to exchange our opinions; let us have a good and honest polemic; let us set the world an example of wise and farsighted tolerance, but because we are leaders of a movement let us not initiate a new intolerance, or establish ourselves as the apostles of a new religion, even if it be a religion of logic or of reason...Perhaps you still hold the opinion that no reform is possible without a sudden *coup de main*, without what used to be called a revolution but which is quite simply a jolt...I do not think that this is what we need in order to succeed; and in consequence we must not suggest *revolutionary* action as the means of social reform because this supposed means would simply be an appeal to force and to arbitrariness, in short a contradiction...I would rather burn property little by little than give it new strength by making a Saint Bartholomew's Day of property owners. (*Correspondence* 2:198–200)

Proudhon was hopeful that an alliance between the petit-bourgeoisie, the urban proletariat, and small landowners might gradually check the power of capitalism, though he had no faith in universal suffrage or political reform (Labry 32). Marx was contemptuous of such compromise, and in the conclusion of *The Poverty of Philosophy* he echoes George Sand: '[T]he last word of social science will always be: "Le combat ou la mort; la lutte sanguinaire ou le néant. C'est ainsi que la question est invinciblement posée"' (Marx & Engels 6:212). Nonetheless, Proudhon had struck a nerve. Marx was uneasily aware that his 'scientific' doctrine, which promised damnation to the bourgeoisie and salvation for the proletariat, contained within itself the elements of a potent religion.

Carlyle's interpretation of history was similarly grounded in a Proudhonesque rejection of 'world-historical' masterplans. In his essay 'On

History'(1830), he represents the past as 'an ever-living, ever-working Chaos of Being, wherein shape after shape bodies itself forth from innumerable elements'. History is a 'Prophetic Manuscript', yet 'the whole meaning lies far beyond our ken' (HE 8, 6-7). Engels regretted that Carlyle had not yet broken free from this 'pantheism', and in his review of *Past and Present*, he urges him to embrace Feuerbach's descendentalism and purge his religious inclinations entirely :'Carlyle has still enough religion to remain in a state of unfreedom; pantheism still recognises something higher than man himself. Hence his longing for a "true aristocracy", for "heroes"; as if these heroes could at best be more than *men*. If he had understood man as man in all his infinite complexity...he would have seen the social function of talent not in ruling by force but in acting as a stimulant and taking the lead'. Still, Engels argues, to 'surmount the contradiction in which he is working, Carlyle has only *one* more step to take' (Marx & Engels 3:466, 467). It was a step that Carlyle could never take after he wrote *The French Revolution*.

He often said that the 'French Explosion' (*Works* 2:61) helped him to appreciate the true meaning of history. In his judgement the tragedy of the Revolution was the failure of its leaders - with the exception of Mirabeau and Danton - to understand the people as human beings rather than equations. Men such as Condorcet, Turgot, Necker, Sieyès, Bailly, Lameth, and later, Roland, Dumont, Barbaroux, Buzot, and Robespierre lived in a fog of philosophical 'cant', cut off from the actual circumstances of ordinary Frenchmen and women. The *philosophes* and their revolutionary admirers forget that 'all theories, were they never so earnest, painfully elaborated, are, and, by the very conditions of them, must be incomplete, questionable, and even false' (*Works* 2:54). Ironically, the French revolutionaries repeated the error of their reactionary enemies when they lumped together 'twenty to twenty-five millions...into a kind of dim compendious unity...[known]...as "the masses"'. By categorising them in these terms, they ignored the basic truth 'that every unit of these masses is a miraculous Man...struggling, with vision or with blindness, for *his* infinite Kingdom (this life which he has got, once only, in the middle of Eternities); with a spark of Divinity, what thou callest an immortal soul, in him!' (*Works* 2:34). In the eyes of the revolutionaries, these 'units' were instruments of justice, through which the prescriptions of 'Jean-Jacques' would be forcibly realised.Though he sympathises with their repudiation of 'Sham' government, Carlyle foresees the consequences of their myopia: 'Thou wouldst not *replace* such extinct Lie by a new Lie, which a new Injustice of they own were; the parent of still other Lies?' (*Works* 2:33-4). The Jacobin's preached emancipation, yet their vision of history promised greater tyranny.

Carlyle regards these system-builders as the precursors of later nineteenth-century 'motive Millwrights' - Saint Simonians, Fourierists, Comtists, Hegelians, Marxists, and Utilitarians (*Works* 1:176) - who went beyond Rousseau in their effort to create precise blueprints for the reconstruction of human nature. What they shared in common was an arrogant indifference towards common humanity and an infinite faith in the power of 'victorious Analysis' (*Works* 2:31). In his review of *The French Revolution* in 1843, Mazzini complains that 'Carlyle does not recognise in a people - nor, *à fortiori*, in Humanity - any collective life or collective aim. He recognises only individuals' (*Writings* 118). Unwittingly, the Italian patriot here explains Carlyle's appeal to the leader of the Russian populists. It is not clear when Herzen first read Carlyle's *The French Revolution*, but he was probably familiar with it prior to visiting France in 1847. In the work he discovered an historical perspective that resembled Proudhon's and strangely anticipated his own. Carlyle had detected a fatal tendency in European radical thought, which would undermine all subsequent attempts in the nineteenth century to change society. Throughout his life Herzen detested what Isaiah Berlin has called 'the despotism of formulas - the submission of human beings to arrangements arrived at by deduction from some kind of *a priori* principles which had no foundation in actual experience'. He was 'among the very few thinkers of his time who in principle rejected all general solutions, and grasped, as very few thinkers have ever done, the crucial distinction between words that are about words, and words that are about persons or things in the real world' (200, 209). Proudhon had stated that theory 'does not bend...does not yield'. In Carlyle, Herzen encountered the first historian of the French Revolution to understand the tragic consequences of the effort to 'bend' human nature to fit with the 'formulas' of philosophy.

Reading *The French Revolution*, Herzen would have quickly understood that he and Carlyle had followed a similar intellectual path. As young men, both had studied science and rejected religion. Conscious of the need for inwardness in a world dominated by 'mechanism', they derived personal strength and hope from the writings of Schiller and Goethe. Politically, both men had been inspired by the example of the Saint-Simonians, and their vision of a society that substituted communal principles of labour for democracy and laissez-faire. They were also attracted to the Saint-Simonian philosophy of history, which regarded the French Revolution as the destructive culmination of a 'critical' epoch and the starting-point of new 'organic' era. Yet significantly, both men rejected the messianic aspect of Saint-Simonianism because it was dependent on the supposedly logical laws of historical change. Carlyle agreed with the Saint-Simonians that society be organised for the sake of work rather than profit, but he suspected they were resurrecting religion in a more 'mechanical' guise. In a letter to one of their leaders Gustav d'Eichthal in 1831, he admits his doubts: 'The more curious am I to understand how, in your minds, Scientific insight has transformed itself into Religion; or in what sense, not of exaggerated metaphor, men of cultivated talent, strong power of thought, and far above all superstition and deception, use these extraordinary words: *Dieu est revenue à France en Saint-Simon, et la France annoncera au monde le Dieu nouveau*' (*CL* 5:137). He rightly surmised that d'Eichthal would not respond directly to his criticism. Goethe had warned him a year earlier about the Saint-Simonians - 'Von der Société St Simonienne Sich fern zu halten' (17 Oct., 1830; *Correspondence* 225) - and he now knew why. Goethe had applied his vision of nature to that of history, at once stressing the transient intricacies of its processes and the indeterminacy of its ends. On the contrary, the Saint-Simonians had unwittingly inherited the Jacobin habit of rewriting the script of history to accord with their prophecies. Carlyle had identified a theme to which he would shortly return.

In *The French Revolution* he deliberately shaped his interpretation of the 'fire-drama' in opposition to the views of Philippe-Joseph-Benjamin Buchez (1796–1865), and Pierre Célestin Roux-Lavergne (1802–74), the Saint-Simonian editors of his major source, the *Histoire parlementaire de la Révolution française* (1834–38). Buchez and Roux wrote philosophical prefaces to many of the volumes in the series, in which they argued that the French Revolution was the culmination of a long historical process to reconcile liberty, equality, and fraternity with Roman Catholicism. In the epoch following this cataclysm, a new religion of humanity would unite the world. Carlyle ridiculed these essays, the content of which 'rattles and rumbles, concerning Progress of the Species, *Doctrine du Progrès*, Exploitations, le Christ, le Verbe, and what not'. Nonetheless, they were valuable historical documents: 'Whoever wants to form for himself an image of the actual state of French Meditation, and under what surprising shackles a French thinking man of these days finds himself gyved, and mechanised, and reduced to the verge of *zero*, may open M. Roux's Prefaces, and see it as an expressive summary' (HE 238). In his interpretation, Carlyle satirised the efforts of 'Quacks' who, like Buchez and Roux, treated the French Revolution as the harbinger of the socialist New Jerusalem. The final prophecy of Cagliostro, the 'Arch-Quack', served as his commentary on philosophers who had privileged access to the script of history.

In the same period Herzen debated the merits of Saint-Simonism with his friend Ogarev. Writing to him in 1833, Herzen tries to separate the social and political elements from the religious aspect of Saint-Simonism:

> We feel...that the world is awaiting a rebirth, that the revolution of 1789 destroyed and did only that, but that it is necessary to create a a new *paligenetic* epoch, it is necessary to give other foundations to the societies of Europe is the actual meaning of our experiences - this is Saint-Simonism. I am not speaking of its recent fall, as I call its religious form (P. Enfantin, etc.). Mysticism always takes hold of a young idea. Let us take the pure foundation of Christianity. How fine and lofty it is; then look at its adherents - a dark and gloomy mysticism. (Malia 121)

Herzen's youthful premonition that 'Mysticism' was inextricable from systems that claimed to read the '*libretto*' (*Other Shore* 39) of history would later be corroborated by the revolutions of 1848. In the interval, he developed his own very idiosyncratic interpretation of Feuerbach and Hegel, which partly reflected Proudhon's influence. For Herzen the Hegelian dialectic was essentially a personal rather than an historical reality, a conflict in the human psyche between the desire for certainty and the impulse of doubt. This struggle - a version of Teufelsdröckh's battle between the 'Everlasting No' and the 'Everlasting Yea' - was never-ending, yet its fruits were the development of an autonomous, spiritually free individual who declined to believe in abstract goals or ideological absolutes that were independent of the individual will. Like Carlyle in *Sartor Resartus* and *The French Revolution*, Herzen insisted that personal emancipation must precede any genuine political change. In *From the Other Shore* he exclaims, 'If only people wanted to save themselves instead of saving the world, to liberate themselves instead of liberating humanity, how much they would do for the salvation of the world and the liberation of humanity!' (128). But whereas Carlyle envisaged the process of liberation culminating in sacrifice to the '*the Duty which lies nearest thee*', Herzen associates freedom with the process of fulfilment and thinks 'of life, and therefore of history, as an end attained than as a means to something else' (SR 145; *Other Shore* 35). This distinction between their outlooks sharpened as political events in Europe soon cut against the possibility of liberation being achieved, either personally or politically.

When Herzen visited Cheyne Row in 1852, he knew that Carlyle had courted controversy as a result of 'The Negro Question' (1849) and *Latter-Day Pamphlets* (1850). Like other European radicals, Herzen was less offended by Carlyle's harsh invective and racist caricatures than English liberals such as Mill. Continental socialists were accustomed to comparing the condition of industrial workers to that of slaves. In the *The Condition of the English Working Classes* (1845), Engels observed that Manchester factory operatives 'are worse slaves than the Negroes in America, for they are more sharply watched, and yet it is demanded of them that they shall live like human beings, shall think and feel like men' (Marx & Engels

4:468). In his letter to Pavel Annenkov attacking Proudhon's *Philosophie de la misère* in 1846, Marx chastised the Frenchman for his naive proposals to end slavery, reminding his correspondent that 'slavery has existed in all nations since the beginning of the world. All that modern nations have achieved is to disguise slavery at home and import it openly into the New World' (Marx & Engels 38:101).

In this context, Carlyle's ridicule of 'Quashee' and the abolitionists possessed a certain perverse and brutal logic. Moreover, Carlyle's hostility to 'Exeter Hall' in *Latter-Day Pamphlets* was consistent with his earlier hostility to political 'formulas'. As the French critic Joseph Antoine Milsand pointed out in a review of the pamphlets in *Revue des Deux Mondes* in 1850, Carlyle's satirical target remained fixed: 'Under different faces, it is always the same fatal spirit of theory that blindly marches towards the ideal, that always begins by demanding how it might realize its highest dream, and uses its power to choose the most suitable way to its goal, ignoring the issue of impossibility' (Milsand 1084). Where Herzen broke from Carlyle was over the question of freedom in history. Carlyle had successfully recreated the revolutionary mentality because he sympathised with the Jacobin urge to apply violent methods in the battle against 'lies' and 'shams'. He was a baffling mixture of the liberal and the illiberal. Though he rejected historical blueprints, he was intrigued with those who attempted to impose them by force, and who sacrificed themselves and others for the sake of a political abstraction. The Russian rightly found him 'paradoxical' because his authoritarian views conflicted with his profound understanding of history, and the importance he attributed to contingency, uncertainty, and unpredictability.

In their review of *Latter-Day Pamphlets* in 1850, Marx and Engels accused Carlyle of capitulating to the bourgeoisie, ignoring class conflict...substituting the 'eternal laws of nature...[and]...bowing to nature's noble and wise: the cult of genius'. In Carlyle's ideal world, they remark, 'the whip imagines it possesses genius' (Marx & Engels 10:309). Herzen was equally critical of Carlyle's preoccupation with authority, and he especially resented his praise of Czar Nicolas I in *Past and Present*. He was perplexed that Goethe's disciple should substitute a static and hierarchical model of nature in place of the German poet's vision of dynamic flux. As Herzen points out, 'In nature everything is independent and everything is in correlation, everything is on its own and everything is united. Nature in no way seeks to fulfill laws; on the contrary, wherever possible, it evades them' (*Letters* 166). Carlyle had misread Goethe's 'open secret', confusing arbitrary hierarchy with natural law. But despite Carlyle's extremism, Herzen did not dismiss him as another radical who had succumbed to 'petit-bourgeois' prejudice, as Marx and Engels did. He was moved by Carlyle's vehement satire against philanthropic liberalism, parliamentary democracy, universal suffrage, 'stump-oratory', 'the cash nexus', Jesuitism, and the spiritually bankrupt middle-classes. Herzen shares his pessimism, and is convinced that '[e]verything in Europe is rushing with extraordinary speed toward either radical transformation or radical destruction; there is no final point where one can support oneself. Everything is burning, as in a fire – traditions and theories, religion and science, new and old' (*Letters* 162). Moreover, Carlyle's conception of history helped him clarify the meaning of 1848 and repudiate Marxist 'final destinations'. As Carlyle must have realised from a reading of *Letters From France and Italy* and *From the Other Shore*, considerable common ground lay between them.

Herzen's description of the revolutionary situation in France in 1848 revealed the impact of Carlyle's history on his intellect and imagination. The Russian judged the upheaval in relation to the dominant Carlylean 'Facts', hunger and oppression. In *The French Revolution* Carlyle had stressed the divorce between revolutionary rhetoric and these fundamental forces: '*Liberty, Equality, Fraternity*, these are words; enunciative and prophetic. Republic for the respectable washed Middle Classes, how can that be the fulfilment thereof? Hunger and nakedness, and nightmare oppression lying heavy on Twenty-five million hearts; this, not the wounded vanities or contradicted philosophies of philosophical Advocates, rich Shopkeepers, rural Noblesse, was the prime mover in the French Revolution; as the like will be in all such Revolutions, in all countries' (*Works* 4:115). For Herzen too, poverty and oppression took precedence over political slogans and theories. Much of the political discussion was ignored by the masses, who 'are too much poets and children to be attracted by abstract thoughts and purely economic theories. They live incomparably more by their heart and custom than by their mind; moreover, destitution and heavy labor make it just as difficult to see things clearly as do wealth and lazy surfeit' (*Letters* 56).

Following Carlyle, Herzen faults the main actors in 1789 because of their reliance on 'formula', yet like the author of *The French Revolution*, he also reveres their fanatical fervour and heroic intensity, and sympathises with their violent desire to extinguish 'lies'. In contrast to the 'worn, pale, half-hearted, cautious personalities of Lamartine and company', Mirabeau, Danton and Robespierre were 'giants of war and…civic life'. The original Jacobins 'believed that they were saving the world, that their salvation was the only possible one, and hence they really saved it'. But the leaders of 1848 – Ledru-Rollin, Louis Blanc, and Blanqui – lack the 'restless spirit that tore apart the old, that broke it up without turning back, that was impudent and angry in relation to the past, and found satisfaction in destruction'

(*Letters* 170, 146). In 1848 'genius' and 'greatness' were lacking because the leaders were now too far removed from the emotional and spiritual origins of 1789.

What separated them was the July Monarchy, which Carlyle had characterised as the 'Evangel of Mammon' and 'Aristocracy of the Moneybag' (*Works* 4:314). Herzen uses similar language to describe the reign of the 'Citizen-King' Louis Philippe. The July Revolution initiated a period in which 'political economy' became the sole contract of society. Comments Herzen, 'Instead of "noble" ideals and "elevated" goals, the lever that sets everything in motion is money. Where there used to be discussions of the inalienable rights of man, state policy, and patriotism, people are now occupied with political economy'. The passion for wealth has transformed the institutions of society: 'Life was reduced to the means of coining money; the state, the court, and the army to means of protecting property' (*Letters* 52, 57). The triumph of bourgeois values subtly shaped future events. Inspired by liberals and moderates, radical leaders consumed their energies fighting for principles such as universal suffrage, republican government, and constitutional reform, which served the interests of the middle-classes rather than the masses

Herzen's analyis of the failure of 1848 strongly suggests Carlyle's influence. Avoiding 'dialectical' explanations, he endorsed Carlyle's conception of the French Revolution as an epic act of vengeance, an exhibition of 'the destructive wrath of Sansculottism'. As Arno Mayer has argued recently in his aptly titled *The Furies*, to study revolution in relation to the neglected theme of vengeance is also to avoid 'exaggerating the role of ideology and of the great leader, or of the two combined' (171). Herzen appreciated Carlyle's evenhanded approach. His sympathies were also carefully balanced between his respect for the dispossessed, and his recognition that their aims were incoherent. Their demands were rooted in material circumstances, yet their needs were also 'transcendent': 'The people demand a prepared doctrine, a belief; they need a dogma, a definite goal. Individuals who were strong at criticism were weak at creation; the people listened to them but shook their heads and still sought something'. Herzen attacked liberals who offered them '*the same* civil rights as Rothschild' while ignoring their physical 'well-being' (*Letters* 55).

Though he sided with those behind the barricades, Herzen did not sentimentalise their plight. Their actions were futile because their goals were solely destructive. His assessment is as sober as Carlyle's in *The French Revolution*: 'Perhaps the masses will not understand for a long time what will relieve their misfortune, but they will understand how to tear rights from the hands of the unjust, not to make use of them, but to destroy them, not to enrich themselves, but to ruin others' (*Letters* 58). Unlike Marx and Engels, he could take no satisfaction in witnessing the great machinery of history repeating the tragedy of 1789 in the form of a 'farce', with Louis Napoleon taking on the role of emperor. After the June massacres in Paris, he despaired of political solutions, and speculated that France might 'regress to a stage not merely prior to 1830, but prior even to 1789' (*Letters* 143). His faith in European radicalism now shattered, Herzen re-assessed his political philosophy in *From the Other Shore*, the title of which may owe something to Carlyle, who often uses the metaphor in *The French Revolution* to describe his vantage point as an historian: 'Standing wistfully on the safe shore, we will look, and see, what is of interest to us, what is adopted to us' (*Works* 4:120)

In his fictional dialogue Herzen pondered the fate of European revolutionary movements since 1789. At various stages he seems to echo passages from 'On History', *Sartor Resartus*, *The French Revolution*, *Heroes and Hero-Worship,* and *Past and Present*. Elsewhere he challenges assumptions that are more pertinent to *Latter-Day Pamphlets*. Throughout he attempts to redeem history from the efforts to define its plot, and to free individuals from the logical 'mechanisms' of ideology. Herzen's notion of history, similar to Carlyle's 'chaos of Being', emphasises the fluidity of experience: 'In this ceaseless movement of all living things, in this universal change, nature renews herself and lives on; in them she is eternally young. That is why each historical moment is complete and self-contained, like each year with its spring and summer, its winter and autumn, its storms and fine weather. Addressing the accusation that he was robbing history of meaning, Herzen's narrator replies, 'I prefer to think of life, and therefore of history, as an end attained than as a means to something else' (*Other Shore* 35). In *The French Revolution* Carlyle had identified 'prophecy' as the chief political tendency of the times, and linked it to the dominant personality of Rousseau. 'That a new young generation has exchanged the Sceptic Creed, *What shall I believe*? for passionate Faith in this Gospel according to Jean Jacques...betokens much' (*Works* 2:54), he asserts. The Swiss outcast invented a revolutionary sensibility, and transformed himself into a symbol of purity and martyrdom. For the French Revolutionaries, the attainment of Rousseauistic 'vertu' was both a personal and a civic goal, and they made no distinction between the private and public spheres of behaviour. Carlyle represents Robespierre's Festival of the Supreme Being as a doomed effort to establish a 'New Religion' based on Rousseau's character. In Carlyle's estimate the distinctive feature of the revolutionary gospel is its 'mechanical' aspect: '[T]his new Deity of Robespierre...is a *conscious* Mumbo-Jumbo, and *knows* that he is machinery' (*Works* 4:267). Robespierre's 'formula' was fatal, since it had to be imposed by force. The 'machinery' necessary to realise 'vertu' was terror.

Herzen's arguments against such 'Gospels' were close to Carlyle's own. He links the phenomenon of revolutionary violence in Europe to the confusion of prophecy and politics: 'The submission of the individual to society, to the people, to humanity, to the Idea, is merely a continuation of human sacrifice, of the immolation of the lamb to pacify God, of the crucifixion of the innocent for the sake of the guilty. All religions have based morality on obedience, that is to say, on voluntary slavery. That is why they have always been more pernicious than any political organization. For the latter makes use of violence, the former – of the corruption of the will'. This was the 'liberation' proposed by the disciples of Rousseau in 1789. Buoyed by the certainties of Hegelian philosophy, their descendants continued to affirm it in 1848. As Herzen bitterly notes, 'We know your kind of liberation. You open the prison doors and want to drive the convict out into the open, assuring him that he is free. You demolish the Bastille, but build nothing in its place, leaving only an empty site' (*Other Shore* 135–6, 27). The possessors of this freedom had no sense of how to use it.

Surveying the carnage of 1848, Herzen cautions against further prophecy: '[W]e have seen all the hopes of the theorists derided, and the demonic pattern of history makes a mockery of their learning, their thought, their theories, turns the republic into a Napoleon, the revolution of 1830 into a deal on the Bourse'. Like the *philosophes* in 1789, the liberals of 1848 constructed a bookish version of 'the people', and 'dressed it up in a Roman toga or a shepherd's cloak. No one thought about the real people. It lived, laboured, suffered nearby, round the corner, and there was anyone who knew it, it was its enemies – the priests and the legitimists. Its lot remained unchanged, but the fictitious people became the idol of the new political religion' (*Other Shore* 93–4). When this 'idol' revealed its true nature, the liberals abandoned their worship: 'They came to their senses when, from behind the half-demolished walls, there emerged the proletarian, the worker with his axe and his blackened hands, hungry and half-naked in rags – not as he appears in books or in parliamentary chatter or in philanthropic verbiage, but in reality' (*Other Shore* 60). The hungry and the oppressed were once again betrayed by the propagators of 'formula'. Herzen pleaded for free will and individualism in history against those who condemned the 'sacrifice of thousands to the role of wretched galley slaves, up to their knees in mud, dragging a barge filled with some mysterious treasure and with the humble words "progress in the future" inscribed on its bows' (*Other Shore* 30, 34, 37–8). History was an open door, and opportunities for change existed without having to insist that the present be sacrificed for the sake of an intellectual delusion.

Herzen believed that the forms and traditions of European civilisation were incompatible with liberty, equality, and fraternity, and that the attempt to impose these by force would only cause more bloodshed. 'Democracy' was an intoxicating dream, but its origins lay in the confusion of the past. Drawing on Carlyle's metaphors of the clothes-philosophy and the Phoenix-rebirth, Herzen envisages the creation of a new 'Mythus' woven in different circumstances:

> Democracy, anyway, does not go so far – it is still on the Christian shore. It has a vast fund of ascetic romanticism, of liberal idealism. It has a terrifying power of destruction, but as soon as it starts to create, it gets lost in school-boy experiments, in political exercises. Of course, destruction creates: it clears the ground, and that is already creation; it removes many falsehoods, and that already is truth. But there is no real creation in democracy, and that is why it is not the future. The future is outside politics, the future soars above the chaos of all political and social aspirations and picks out from them threads to weave into a new cloth which will provide the winding-sheet for the past and the swaddling clothes for the new-born. (*Other Shore* 89)

Whereas Europe's future remained open and mysterious, its present offered little scope for individual initiative. Herzen used Proudhon's example to recommend a socialism grounded in reality and directed towards tangible ends. The Frenchman's resistance to the political orthodoxies of 1848 was a solitary illustration of Herzen's own principles at work: 'The year which has passed...offered us a terrible spectacle: the fight of *a free man against the liberators of humanity*. The bold words, the mordant scepticism, the fierce denial, the merciless irony of Proudhon angered the official revolutionaries no less than the conservatives...they were terrified of his atheism and his anarchism, they could not understand how one could be free without a state, without a democratic government (*Other Shore* 37, 132). It was perhaps not surprising that when Herzen arrived in England after the debacle of 1848 and Louis Napoleon's ascent to power, he sought the company of a 'Scotch Proudhon', who had similarly alienated all political factions with his fierce invective.

What is surprising is that Carlyle and Herzen continued to maintain contact, even after their first stormy meeting in December 1852. In London Herzen had turned away from European politics and instead concentrated on Russia, where he thought he saw political salvation. He had lost patience with French radicalism, which promulgated 'rhetorical morality unconnected to practical life' (*Letters* 160). In the communal organisation of the Russian peasants, he discerned socialist principles that had grown up spontaneously in the midst of despotism and deprivation. In the village *obshchina* (Venturi 8) personal freedom and dignity were compatible with a collective enterprise. Herzen speculated in *On the Development of*

Revolutionary Ideas in Russia (1853) that his country, uncontaminated by the political traditions of Western Europe, might provide solutions to the intractable social and economic problems of the continent. In the preface he declares, 'We do not prophesize, but we are not convinced that the destinies of humanity are tied to occidental Europe. If Europe cannot transform itself, other countries may assist; there are several that are ready to initiate this movement, while others are still preparing. One is already known – the States of North America; the other is full of youthful vigour as well as savagery, yet it is hardly known or not known at all' (vii). In the rural communes of Russia, European democratic socialists would discover a society worthy of close study.

Herzen voiced this argument at a rally organised by the English socialist Ernest Jones at St. Martin's Hall on February 27, 1855 to commemorate the revolutions of 1848 and protest the Anglo-French alliance. The *Leader* reported that Herzen seconded Jones's declaration that 'there was an oppressed nationality in every country where labour was not the master of capital', condemned the despotism of Louis Napoleon, and argued 'that the natural tendency of the Russian people was towards democracy' (3 March 1855; no. 258, 200). Perhaps familiar with Carlyle's proposals for 'Industrial Regiments' in *Latter-Day Pamphlets* and his contempt for Palmerston's Crimean policies, Herzen sent him a copy of his speech

The Crimean crisis had revived interest in Carlyle's pamphlets, and as Thomas Ballantyne pointed out in a selection of passages from them published by Chapman and Hall in June 1855, 'no small amount of "Stump Oratory" is likely to be expended in proving that Mr. Carlyle was a true prophet in 1850, when he denounced the whole system of procedure by which Governments are appointed and broken up in this country' (4). Carlyle gratefully received Herzen's 'eloquent Discourse on Russian revolutionary matters, which manifests a potent spirit, and high talent, in various respects; and in which, especially, there is a tone of tragic earnestness not to be mistaken by the reader, nor to be judged lightly by him, whatever he may think of your programme and prophecy as to Russia and the world'. But Carlyle saw no future in socialism, or in Herzen's idea that the *obshchina* would provide Europe with a new model of democracy in action.

Carlyle proclaims that he would prefer 'Tsarism itself, or Grand-Turkism...to the sheer Anarchy...which is got by "Parliamentary Eloquence", Free Press and counting of heads'. What distinguished Russia from Europe was not its fledgling socialist democracy, but its '*talent of obeying* – which is much out of vogue in other quarters just now!' He adds that 'the want of *it* will be amerced to the last due farthing, sooner or later;

and bring about huge bankruptcies, wherever persevered in. Such is my sad creed in these revolutionary times' (quot. in Herzen, *Memoirs* 4:1796–7). Fearful in this period that his work on Frederick the Great had cut him off contemporary politics, Carlyle relished debate. He asked Herzen to return to Cheyne Row, and held out the hope they might also meet at the Russian's home in Fulham.

Herzen replied in a long and thoughtful letter, employing arguments from *Letters From France and Italy* and *From the Other Shore* that partly reflected his reading of Carlyle's *The French Revolution*. He was still insisting that had Carlyle known of this book, he would have encountered a writer whose ideas were more profound than his own. He agreed with Carlyle's criticism of 'universal suffrage', admitting 'I have never been an ardent admirer of [it]'. But he was sceptical of his terms 'Anarchy' and 'talent of submission', and argued that they required greater clarity: 'If anarchy means disorder, arbitrariness, the rupture of mutual responsibility, a break with reason, then socialism opposes it more than it does monarchy'. Shrewdly echoing Carlyle's criteria for true heroes, Herzen reminded him that the 'ability to submit in agreement with our conscience is a virtue; but the ability to resist, which demands that we shall not submit against our conscience, is also a *virtue*!' (*Memoirs* 4:1798). Few of Carlyle's heroes, including Frederick the Great, would have dissented.

Herzen again rejected Carlyle's assumption that the order of society should mirror that of nature. Writing to Proudhon from London in 1851 he had asked, 'Is there an idea in existence today that is more impoverished than that of "order" - abstract order - it is mechanical, the negation of change and metamorphosis' (Mervaud 153). Goethe had repudiated this idea, and in *The French Revolution* Carlyle had described him at the Battle of the Argonne, performing experiments on 'cannon-fever', while simultaneously pronouncing the 'Death-Birth of the World' (*Works* 4:55). Goethe had discovered in his scientific studies what Carlyle had confirmed in history, that the old monarchical and aristocratic plan of the world was based, like the new Rousseauistic mythus, on the fallacy of order in nature. Anarchy, Herzen insisted, did not mean 'a tangle of whims and freaks'. On the contrary, 'Nature presents itself to us as the hugest harmonious anarchy, and for that reason in nature everything is in order that proceeds on its own course' (*Memoirs* 4:1798).

Carlyle must have realised that he was engaged in debate with a man who knew his writings thoroughly and understood the contradictions in his outlook. His praise of 'obedience' clashed oddly with his religious scepticism, which had sharpened his antagonism to the same revolutionary 'librettos' that Herzen himself despised. His biography of Frederick the Great was less a paean to despotism and 'drill' than a description of an iconoclast who challenged the corrupt monarchies of Europe an prepared the way for the Revolutionary outbreak that would rid Europe of monarchy, aristocracy, and 'Respectability'. Indicating his indebtedness to Carlyle, Herzen reminded him that '[w]ithout the talent for struggle and opposition the world would still be standing where Japan stands: there would be neither history nor development'. He cited the case of the apostle Paul, a rebellious Roman citizen, communist, and blasphemer who declared 'There is no power but of God' and was later 'executed by Caesar for the very reason that he did not find in him the talent for submission sufficiently developed' (*Memoirs* 4:1798). Appropriately, Herzen left the 'paradoxical philosopher' with a riddle that he could not solve.

Herzen's assessment of Carlyle was astute. He understood that the author of *The French Revolution* was a 'prophet' in one vital respect - he had anticipated the consequences of revolutionary utopianism, which Andrzej Walicki has linked to the attitude of 'treating individuals, as well as entire classes and nations, as mere instruments of history and...justifying this instrumental attitude by the greatness of the final result of historical development: the universal collective liberation of mankind' (16). In the early twentieth century, the reputation of both Carlyle and Herzen declined. Carlyle was condemned as an authoritarian reactionary, while Herzen was categorised as a 'romantic exile' (Carr). Ironically in Russia, Lenin resurrected Herzen as a disciple who grasped the 'algebra of revolution', and taught the valuable lesson that 'selfless devotion to the revolution and revolutionary propaganda among the people are not wasted even if long decades divide the sowing from the harvest' (Lenin, *Works* 19:26, 31). Yet in the wake of the totalitarian catastrophes of the twentieth century - engineered by revolutionaries who justified a bloody 'harvest' by appealing to the immutable laws of nature and history - it is instructive to look again at Herzen's debate with Carlyle. Orlando Figes has recently described the Russian Revolution as a 'people's tragedy' in an effort to show 'that what began as a people's revolution contained the seeds of its own degeneration into violence and dictatorship' (xvi). This is a perspective that would have appealed to both Carlyle and Herzen - two strong-minded eccentric, and curiously solitary figures, who contemplated the social and political life of their time from another 'shore', where few of their contemporaries were prepared to wander.

All translations are my own, unless otherwise indicated.

Works Cited

Ballantyne, Thomas. *Passages Selected from the Writings of Thomas Carlyle.* London: Chapman and Hall, 1856.

Berlin, Isaiah. *Russian Thinkers.* Ed. Henry Hardy and Aileen Kelly. Harmondsworth, UK: Penguin Books, 1978.

Carr, E. H. *The Romantic Exiles*. London: Gollancz, 1933.

Figes, Orlando. *A People's Tragedy: The Russian Revolution, 1891-1924.* London: Cape, 1996.

Herzen, Alexander. *Mémoires de L'impératrice Catherine II, écrits par elle-même, et précédés d'une préface par A. Herzen.* Londres: Trübner, 1859.

———. *From the Other Shore and The Russian People and Socialism. An Open Letter to Jules Michelet.* Trans. Moura Budberg and Richard Wollheim. Intro. Isaiah Berlin. London: Weidenfeld and Nicolson, 1956.

———. *Memoirs.* Trans. Constance Garnett. Intro. Isaiah Berlin. 4 vols. London: Chatto and Windus, 1968.

———. *Letters from France and Italy, 1847-1851.* Ed. and Trans. Judith E. Zimmerman. Pittsburgh and London: U of Pittsburgh, 1995.

———. *Du développement des idées révolutionnaires en Russie*. Séconde édition revue par l'auteur. Londres: Jeffs, 1853.

Kelly, Aileen. *Views From the Other Shore. Essays on Herzen, Chekhov, and Bakhtin.* New Haven and London: Yale UP, 1999.

Labry, Raoul. *Herzen et Proudhon.* Paris: Bossard, 1928.

The Leader. No. 1-510. London: 30 March 1850 - 31 December 1859.

Lenin, V. I. 'In Memory of Herzen' (1912). Vol. 19 of *Collected Works.* 45 vols. Moscow: Progress Publishers, 1968. 25-31.

Malia, Martin. *Alexander Herzen and the Birth of Russian Socialism.* New York: Grosset and Dunlap, 1965.

Marx, Karl and Frederick Engels. *Collected Works*. 47 vols. New York: International Publishers, 1975-95- .

Mayer, Arno J. *The Furies. Violence and Terror in the French and Russian Revolutions.* Princeton, NJ: Princeton UP, 2000.

Mazzini, Joseph. 'On the Genius and Tendency of the Writings of Thomas Carlyle' and 'On the History of the French Revolution by Thomas Carlyle'. Vol. 4 of *Life and Writings of Joseph Mazzini.* London: Smith, Elder, 1867. 56-109, 110-44.

Mervaud, Michel. 'Herzen et Proudhon'. *Cahiers du Monde Russe et Sovietique* 12 (1971): 110-88.

Milsand, J.A. 'Les Pamphlets de Thomas Carlyle'. *Revue des Deux Mondes* No. 2 (1850): 1083-1111.

Norton, C.E. *Correspondence Between Goethe and Carlyle.* London: Macmillan, 1889.

Proudhon, Pierre-Joseph. *Correspondance.* 14 Tom. Paris: Lacroix, 1874-5.

———. *Oeuvres complètes.* Nouvelle éditon. Ed. C. Bouglé and H. Moysset. 19 Tom. Paris: Rivière, 1923-59.

Stelling-Michaud, Sven. 'Herzen et Thomas Carlyle'. *Autour d'Alexandre Herzen.* Documents Inédits publiés par Marc Vuilleumier, Michel Aucouturier, Sven Stelling Michaud et Michel Cadot. Genève: Libraire Droz, 1973. 325-9.

Walicki, Andrzej. *Marxism and the Leap to Freedom. The Rise and Fall of the Communist Utopia.* Stanford, CA: Stanford UP, 1995.

Chapter 5

'True Thomas': Carlyle, Young Ireland, and the Legacy of Millenialism

OWEN DUDLEY EDWARDS

It is not every day that the Supreme Powers send any *Missionary*, clad in light or clad in lightning, into a Country, to act and speak a True Thing there.

(TC to Charles Gavan Duffy, 12 March 1846; *CL* 20:141)

'"O no, O no, True Thomas", she says
"That fruit maun not be touched by thee,
For a' the plagues that are in hell
Light on the fruit of this countrie"'.

Thomas the Rhymer[1]

Andrea. *Unglücklich das Land, das keine Helden hat!...*
Galileo. *Nein. Unglücklich das Land, das Helden nötig hat.*

—Bertolt Brecht, *Leben des Galilei* (1938–9), Sc.13.

Carlyle's relations with Ireland, and in particular with the Irish nationalist intellect and culture, are predictably forceful but paradoxically startling. The editor-biographer of Cromwell might seem an appropriate hero for Irish Unionists, but their hero-king was William III, whose grandfather's head was cut off by Cromwell's necessities. Nor did Ulster Presbyterians share kind ancestral memories from Scotland concerning the victor of Dunbar. Presbyterian or episcopalian, the Ulster Protestant Unionists gave pride of place to Carlyle's rival Thomas Babington Macaulay, notwithstanding his zealous support for Catholic emancipation and his electoral defeat for speaking and voting for the increased grant to the Catholic seminary in Maynooth.

Ulster provided Carlyle with two of his most conspicuous Irish nationalist followers, Charles Gavan Duffy (1816–1903), Roman Catholic, and John Mitchel (1815–75), Unitarian. The chemistry that induced their devotion was initially literary. The two future Young Irelanders warmed to Carlyle (as would many of their colleagues) long before meeting him. Their enthusiasm might seem odd, racially and spiritually. Carlyle went to great lengths to extol the Teuton at the expense of the Celt (and everyone else). Religion also divided him from Young Ireland, whose many liberal Protestants demanded more political and cultural power for Catholics. Carlyle had never cared for the Catholic cause beyond a sardonic leer at the revolutionary acquisition of Catholic Emancipation in 'Signs of the Times' (1829)

Carlyle's conquest of Young Ireland was nonetheless carried out with Irish troops. *Sartor Resartus* was brought into being by Irish voices. Jonathan Swift and Laurence Sterne are its most obvious literary godparents, and *Fraser's*, for which its first (1830) version was intended, and where its full text in 1833–34 was to appear, became for Carlyle that '"drunk man's vomit" of an (Irish) Magazine' in which the editor himself was 'like to get *drowned* one day' (*CL* 8:13).[2] Carlyle had been familiar with Irish migrants to the southwest of Scotland from his early youth, and had been philosophical about his consequent adventures. He had shared a bed with two Irish doctors, one of whom seems to have become ardent in his affections towards his theologically terrified colleague. Carlyle recounted the episode with realism rather than reproach, a tone he sought to maintain with Ireland (*CL* 1:70). It at least prepared him for the inspiring lunacies of *Fraser's Magazine* and its first editor Dr William Maginn (1794–1842), who was a Corkman, Protestant, child prodigy (matriculated in Trinity College, Dublin aged 12, in 1805), polymath, early contributor to *Blackwood's*, explosive wit, embattled High Tory, spendthrift, and alcoholic. Maginn is a prime example of what Roy Foster has called 'marginal men', squandering the capital of Irish origins on British conquests, fragmenting his genius in journalism, staging his Irishness, and infecting with his lifestyle, prejudice, anger, and folly a generation of figures more staid than himself (Foster 290).

Carlyle was at first dismissive of the *Fraser's* entourage. Ian Campbell shows him as early as 1824 summing up Maginn, his fellow-Irishman George Darley, and the English wit Theodore Hook as 'spotted fry that "report" and "get up" for the "Public Press"; that earn money by writing calumnies, and spend it in punch and other viler objects of debauchery. Filthiest and basest of the children of men!' (Campbell 10; *CL* 3:234). But the publication of 'On History' – one of the greatest essays on History ever written – softened the attitudes of both men. Maginn understood Carlyle's genius and its frustrations. He continually denounced the Whig literary darling as 'Thomas Babbletongue Macaulay' just when Macaulay was plainly overshadowing Carlyle in the rival *Edinburgh Review*. Carlyle might loftily disdain the Maginn's malice in enhancing *Fraser's* by lampooning the *Edinburgh* in so personal an assault, but Maginn was wise in his generation and beyond it. In 1842, the year of his death, the *Edinburgh* published Macaulay's essay 'Frederick the Great', which inspired the most disproportionate literary response ever accorded to a magazine essay - Carlyle's six-volume *History of Friedrich II of Prussia* (1858-65).

From Maginn, Carlyle derived a rich sense of the Irish political Saturnalia, and a sharp antipathy to the two major political parties in Britain. The admission of Daniel O'Connell (1775-1847), and with him all electable Roman Catholics, to the House of Commons in 1829 meant the end of the Protestant state of the United Kingdom of Great Britain and Ireland. O'Connell's triumph presaged the ultimate fall of Protestant Ireland. Maginn's consequent hatred of O'Connell saturated Carlyle. That the architect of that United Kingdom, William Pitt the Younger (1759-1806), had intended admission to Roman Catholics to its Parliament as part of the package of 1800 was irrelevant. Pitt had been foiled, and by 1829 a large Protestant evangelist faction - led by journalists such as the Reverends Samuel (1790-1851), and Mortimer (1791-1859) O'Sullivan, Caesar Otway (1780-1842), and James Wills (1790-1868) - had recruited widespread polemical support in Ireland. Converts increased, activists proliferated, writers multiplied, and even the traffickers with Catholic emancipation such as George Canning (1770-1827) and his successor Lord Goderich (1782-1859) had held Prime Ministerial office without the insidious Papist foot entering Westminster.

And then in 1829 the Protestant cabinet headed by Ireland's most illustrious Protestant, the Duke of Wellington (1769-1852), had capitulated to O'Connell, his middle-classes, and his mobs. The less than reverend Dr. William Maginn might seem disreputable company for the embattled clerics, but he was a doctor of their university and scholar of their college. What was done could not be undone. Maginn declaimed in 'Our Confession of Faith', with which he inaugurated *Fraser's* in February 1830, that 'Whig' and 'Tory' had lost any doctrinal meaning, and that *Fraser's* regarded political life, as it had been known, as dead:

> [W]e have seen, within a couple of years, the Roman Catholic question carried by a ministry which got into power on the avowed grounds of opposing it. We have seen the freedom-loving patriots of Covent Garden and elsewhere, supple servants of the ministry, and rebuking the people for daring to express their opinion against any measure coming from authority...And how can we pretend to say what is party at present? (*Fraser's* 1:4).

Maginn helped shape Carlyle's hatred of politics and politicians, nourishing his interest in people beyond power and alerting him to the revolutionary potential of the Irish in Britain. Happy in his cups among Irish ragged vagrants, Maginn can be heard in *Sartor Resartus*, into whose apocalyptic close Carlyle introduces the Drudge. He belongs to 'another British Sect, originally, as I understand, of Ireland, where its chief seat still is; but known also in the main Island, and indeed every where rapidly spreading'. These sects 'go by a perplexing multiplicity of designations, such as *Bogtrotters, Redshanks, Ribbonmen, Cottiers, Peep-of-day Boys, Babes of the Wood, Rockite, Poor-Slaves*...Enough for us to understand, what seems indubitable, that the original Sect is that of the *Poor-Slaves*; whose doctrines, practices, and fundamental characteristics, pervade and animate the whole Body, howsoever denominated or outwardly diversified' (SR 205). This passage declares that all Irish tenant-farmers, landless labourers, agrarian criminals whether Protestant or Catholic, are victims of the same process. The anti-Catholic vigilante Peep-o'-Day Boys are diagnosed as fundamentally indistinguishable from the sectarian Catholic assassins of landlords or secret intimidators of blackleg tenants; hopeless poverty is the root-cause of the activities of all.

Carlyle's ecumenical diagnosis and sureness of touch show the hand of Maginn, as does his final to his editor: 'Thou too, miraculous Entity, that namest thyself YORKE and OLIVER, and with thy vivacities and genialities, with thy all-too Irish mirth and madness, and odour of palled punch...have we not lived together, though in a state of quarrel!' (SR 218). *Sartor Resartus* established Carlyle as a sound and original authority on Ireland, two qualities essential to win over Young Ireland: true Thomas had also to be new Thomas. For Maginn was no crude Protestant partisan. Like the finest of his fellow evangelicals, he was ready to love the Catholics if it would help make them Protestants. He saw religion, not ethnicity, as their blemish. But Carlyle, while appropriately anti-Catholic, could not very well urge conversion to a Protestantism he no longer professed save in outline.

He did not follow Maginn in wanting Irish Catholics to adopt habits of thrift, foresight, industry, and self-reliance, which the Dublin evangelicals took to be side-effects of conversion to Protestantism (and he would have added temperance). But Maginn's political disillusion gave Carlyle space to be vehement and sardonic - and whimsical - without any specific political agenda that might win respect in Ireland, which was over-run with political agenda. And whether alone or with Maginn, Carlyle produced a revolutionary prophecy of Ireland's place, which he would return to in *The French Revolution* and *Chartism*, impressively anticipating the analysis of Marx and Engels.[3] Maginn fathered Carlyle's revolution, much as Hegel inspired Marx, and Carlyle, like Marx unmasking Hegel, had to turn Maginn from past to future and stand him on his head.

The idea of British revolution fuelled, if not ignited, by Irish labourers seems to have lain at the back of Maginn's mind in his 'The Burnings in Kent, and the State of the Labouring Classes':

> It is in evidence...that they assemble in large numbers more openly than has yet occurred in any of the Rockite counties of Ireland. That they warn the farmer to employ at his peril threshing machines. They intimidate, in no equivocal terms, their resolution to destroy these machines in case he should contravene their inhibition. They require clergymen, overseers, and others, to subscribe to their injunctions, and engage to pay such a rate of wages as they decree. (*Fraser's* 2:577)

Maginn may have drunk with some of the Irish agrarian activists in Kent. The non-existent head of the movement soon became known as 'Captain Swing', exactly as in Ireland agrarian outrages were credited to 'Captain Rock'. 'Swing', like 'Rock', was a signature on threatening notices. The names may originate in the idea of an officer, originally Jacobite, turning highwayman (or, in the Irish word, a tory). 'Rock' may have been connected with the 'Mass-rock', on which the outlawed Catholic Mass was celebrated with sentinels posted during the early eighteenth century; 'Swing' may allude to the fate of highwaymen and other felons. There is a hint of ghostly status inviting the filio-pietism required by Hamlet's father for revenge duties: the guardian of the rock, the victim of the gallows. In *Sartor* Carlyle too sees the likelihood of rebel unity, in language Manichaean and millennarian:

> If indeed, there were to arise a *Communion of Drudges*, as there is already a Communion of Saints, what strangest effects would follow therefrom!...To me it seems probable that the two Sects will one day part England between them; each recruiting itself from the immediate ranks, till there be none left to enlist on either side...I might call them two boundless, and indeed unexampled Electric Machines...with batteries of opposite quality; Drudgism the Negative, Dandyism the Positive...till your whole vital Electricity, no longer healthily Neutral, is cut into two isolated portions of Positive and Negative (of Money and of Hunger); and stands there bottled up in two World-Batteries! (SR 210)

Not surprisingly, within months of its appearance in *Fraser's*, Carlyle had started work on *The French Revolution*. Once again, Ireland haunted his closing lines. His meditations on garments had naturally concluded on those who lacked them, and now his obituary for the Sansculottes in his French epic recalled their local equivalent:

> History ventures to assert that the French Sansculotte of [Seventeen] Ninety-three, who, roused from long death-sleep, could rush at once to the frontiers, and die fighting for an immortal Hope and Faith of

> Deliverance for him and his, was but the *second*-miserablest of men! The Irish Sans-Potato, had he not senses then, nay a soul! (*Works* 4:312)

This may not have been a call for revolution, but to Carlyle's mind, it was a call to truth. If others read revolutionary agenda from his observation, was that his fault? Maginn, who wanted an Irish revolution in the theological beliefs of Catholics, had given him data, description, atmosphere, and polemic. Carlyle diagnosed an Irish potential for revolution with a consistent, Maginn-like disillusioning of his audience. He may have done no more than visibly see through human self-delusion, forcing his readers to look through as well, beneath and beyond. But Romanticism was in the making, and Carlyle's own denunciation of political pragmatics in the name of the human spirit undermined the rationality of his own argument, while simultaneously investing it with a Yeatsian 'terrible beauty'.

Young Ireland quickly responded to the force of Carlyle's vision. Reading the history in 1838, the 23-year-old John Mitchel told his bosom fellow-Ulsterman John Martin (1812–75) that it was 'the profoundest book, and the most eloquent and fascinating history, that English literature ever produced...Such men as Carlyle are the salt of the earth' (Dillon 1:37; quot. in Fielding 135). The Roman Catholic Gavan Duffy, from central Ulster like Mitchel, remembered how Carlyle's 'daring theories moved me like electric shocks' (Duffy 1898, 1:52). Quoting Herman Merivale's *Edinburgh Review* notice, Kenneth J. Fielding has pointed out the probable impact of *The French Revolution* as a whole with its echo of the 'inarticulate and confused cry of...millions struggling – not for the paper "rights of men", but for their "rank as fellow men"' (135; Seigel 79–80). As Hillaire Belloc pertinently remarked, 'The Revolution filled [Carlyle] as he proceeded and was, in a sense, co-author with him of the shock, the flames, and the roar, the innumerable feet, and the songs which together build up what we read achieved in these volumes' (1:xviii). The Irish finale of the *The French Revolution* would have completed the conquest of Mitchel and Martin, but Belloc's idea of the upheaval as co-author was most immediately sensed by Mitchel alone. He intended to enter on that partnership, with or without Carlyle, alternating pen with sword when desirable.

The Young Irelanders active in Dublin (not yet including Mitchel) broke all records with their weekly journal the *Nation*, which sold 10,000 copies within weeks of its foundation in 1842. They refuelled themselves intellectually and emotionally over frugal supper-parties, where 'intoxicating effects of Thomas Carlyle's literary style and searching denunciation of humbug later led to the suppers being dubbed "tea and Thomas"' (Duffy 1898, 1). 'Thomas' was short for 'true Thomas', another testament to their view of Carlyle as millenarian prophet: they knew the verses commemorating Thomas the Rhymer (1220? - ?), and to the Ulsterman among them, the poem's Scottish origins may have better affirmed their cultural identities than, say, pocalyptic noises of the Rockites in the southern counties foretelling destruction of the Protestants in 1825, or the more learned if no less impassioned prayers of southern Protestant evangelicals of the same decade. Yet Rockites and proselytisers prepared much more sophisticated Irish Catholic and Protestant minds for the music of Carlylean prophecy, all the more comforting because it announced no dates that subsequent history might refute. Thomas the Rhymer derived his prophecies from his visits to a conspicuously nonsectarian elfland, and while among mortals was, like Carlyle, a Borderer, ranging from Dunbar to Ayr.

Carlyle had given Young Ireland suppers more strong meat (or as he would have put it, potatoes) with the publication of *Chartism* (1839) and *Past and Present* (1843). *Chartism* returned to the theme of the 'Sanspotato' latter-day Sansculotte: 'A government and guidance of white European men which has issued in perennial hunger of potatoes to the third man extant, - ought to drop a veil over its face and walk out of court...expecting now of a surety sentence either to change or die' (*Works* 29:136). Read before the famine, this is chilling enough. Read after it, it is a vindication of Carlyle's status as millenial prophet. He had told the truth, and Mitchel learnt from him that the truth would prevail, even if it took famine to reveal it. Echoing his master in his *Jail Journal* (1854), Mitchel exalted, '[A] lie, be it never so current, accepted, endorsed, and renewed many times, is quite sure (thank God!) to get protestated at last...Is it not so written in the great book of *noster* Thomas?' (86) More dangerously, Carlyle celebrated the triumph of blood-sacrifice, which he advocated in *Past and Present*:

> Await the issue. In all battles, if you await the issue, each fighter has prospered according to his right. His right and his might, at the close of the account, were one and the same. He has fought with all his might, and in exact proportion to all his right he has prevailed. His very death is no victory over him. He dies indeed; but his work lives, very truly lives. A heroic Wallace, quartered on the scaffold, cannot hinder that his Scotland become, one day, a part of England: but he does hinder that it become, on tyrannous unfair terms, a part of it...Scotland is not Ireland: no, because brave men rose there, and said, 'Behold, ye must not tread us down like slaves; and ye shall not - and cannot!' Fight on, thou brave true heart, and falter not, through dark fortune and through bright. (*Works* 10:12)

This line of reasoning is especially crucial to Mitchel. Duffy's antecedents may have given him some Scots tradition, as may his youthful schooling from a Monaghan Presbyterian minister. But Mitchel came to intellectual maturity with no sense of any native Irish derivation to point his nationalism. *Past and Present* gave him cultural roots from an ancestral Scotland as well as an Irish agenda. Its argument of the triumph of failure, the necessity for blood-sacrifice, and the indispensability of the god-hero, wrote a vital - and pernicious - doctrine into the heart of Irish revolutionary nationalism, one which seems to have had no place in the thought of the United Irishmen, however illustrious their martyrs. From Wolfe Tone to Robert Emmet, they wanted to win and intended to do so. The Easter Rising of 1916 was the classic exposition of blood-sacrifice - with Pearse well-schooled and well ready to school anyone else in the gospel of John Mitchel. It also accounts for the hari-kiri element in Irish republican violence since then, whether in hunger-strike or in self-destruction in violent action. Carlyle may have opposed violence in the *French Revolution*, but as Kenneth J. Fielding has observed, the work was 'a handbook for revolutionaries' (136). And in *Past and Present* Carlyle abdicated responsibility as to the truth or falsehood of a cause: the choice lay with the dealer. At best, Carlyle had given children the right to strike matches and to decide when they should be struck.

The Young Irelander most noticeably resistant to Carlyle's influence was Thomas Davis (1814–45), who pointedly paralleled Carlyle in finding a quasi-religious voice to reject the materialism and worldliness of the ruling Whigs and (for Davis implicitly, for Carlyle explicitly) of their ally Daniel O'Connell. He sharply reminded the Trinity College Historical Society in 1840 - the same year that Carlyle delivered his lectures on heroes - that 'the chatter of contemporary fame may have concealed the good by the celebrity of the great, yet Washington is more dear to history than Frederick, Brutus than Caesar'. Davis prophesied Carlyle's own future cults and their limits. He saw him as 'a more honest, but less learned thinker than Coleridge. Their opinions are unsafe but their works are of the greatest use, in tempting men by their enthusiasm, or forcing them by their paradoxes, to think' (*Prose Writings* 26). But Carlyle's Irish 'solution' - to drop O'Connell, and forge a revolutionary alliance with the British workers - remained a prescription for endless violence, which Davis rejected.

The appearance of *Oliver Cromwell's Letters and Speeches* on 27 November 1845 severely tested the loyalty of the Young Irelanders to Carlyle. Yet his conception of the Protector as a hero for all seasons and eras was appealing to them. For Mitchel and many of his followers, Cromwell was proof that what England had been to Ireland, it could be again. While it might seem that Cromwell's Irish campaign of 1649–50 might alienate them from 'true Thomas', they simply adopted his version and painted it green. If Carlyle verged on making Cromwell divine, Young

Ireland reciprocated by making him diabolic. Mitchel fully embraced Carlyle's gospel of curing Ireland's ills by force. Ironically, the Irish theme was incidental to Carlyle's story of Cromwell, since Michael Jones's victory in the last pitched battle of the Irish War at Rathmine had secured victory two weeks before the Protector's arrival in 1649. Having happened, the Irish campaign had to be there, and Carlyle had to make the most of it. According to Carlyle, Cromwell brought order from chaos, and Ireland, on the arguments of *Sartor*, the *French Revolution*, and *Chartism* was a moving chaos, bringing its anarchy to the destruction of England. That Carlyle had been led to this view above all by an Irish lord of misrule in the shape of the late William Maginn, the doctor in drink, deepened the belief: *res ipsa loquitur*.

Cromwell had gone to Ireland and imposed order where chaos had reigned (and reigned once again in the 1830s and 1840s, with its O'Connells on high and its Rockites below). What Ireland needed now was what Cromwell had given it then. In a thinly veiled allusion in *Cromwell* to the Ireland of the 1830s and 1840s, and the duplicity of O'Connell, Carlyle acknowledges that 'Every idle lie and piece of bluster this Editor hears, he too, like Oliver, has to shudder at it; has to think: "Thou, idle bluster, not true, thou also art shutting men's minds against the God's Fact; thou wilt issue as a cleft crown to some poor man some day; thou also wilt have to take shelter in bogs whither cavalry cannot follow"' (*Works* 7:51).

O'Connell had recently been released on a technicality when the House of Lords upheld his appeal against imprisonment by Sir Robert Peel's government prosecution in 1844. He was aware of Carlyle's hostility to him and his association with the Young Irelanders, and replied to his attacks at a meeting of the Repeal Association in Dublin on 21 December 1845, a summary of which was published in the *Nation*. In a deft demolition of Carlyle's version of the slaughter at Drogheda, O'Connell questioned the author's loyalties: 'Dr Carlyle...speaking of Cromwell, says – They rejected his summons and terms at [Drogheda]; he stormed the place, and, according to his promise, put every man of the garrison to death...To our Irish friends we ought to say, likewise, that this garrison...consisted mostly of Englishmen. Perfectly certain this; and, therefore, let 'the bloody hoof of the Saxon', &c., forbear to continue itself on the matter'. O'Connell went on to quote from a contemporary Royalist historian writing in 1683, remarking that 'no manner of compassion or discrimination was showed either to age or sex; but that little children were promiscuously sufferers with the guilty' (*Nation*, 27 Dec. 1845; see *CL* 20:95–6n.). Duffy and Mitchel must have writhed, as O'Connell probably intended them to writhe at his virtuosic appeal to Irish glee in the face of pomposity.

O'Connell was facing an imminent break with Young Ireland on the issue of the right to use violence in Irish nationalist causes. He cunningly ridiculed their Scots guru's half-evasive, half-frank justification of violence, and hinted that Young Ireland would make a genocidal Cromwell their exemplar. Carlyle might pass it off as 'balderdash', (*CL* 20:95), but Gavan Duffy knew it for hard politics. Thomas Davis had prevented previous breach by bursting into tears, but he had died four months earlier, and the Carlylean Young Irelanders now served a more dry-eyed oracle. In April three of them had visited the Carlyles in Chelsea, and Duffy had made a life-long friendship with him.

The *Nation* reviewed Carlyle's *Cromwell* on 10 January 1846, anonymously. Mitchel, its author, was hagiographic. That he was a Carlylean and a physical force man before reading *Cromwell* is obvious. What the book provided was the means and the exemplar around which to crystallise his thought. It supplied Mitchel with a Scottish Calvinist identity for Irish nationalism. As Kenneth J. Fielding has noted, his review was a homage not only to Carlyle, but also to Cromwell: 'A book to be opened with reverence...The greatest writer, and profoundest philosopher, now living upon English soil, with eloquence, the like of which has not uttered itself in English speech since John Milton's time deals in this book with the most glorious and terrible epoch of his country's history, and the divine (or diabolic) man, who is at last recognised'. Mitchel went further. Though he was critical of Carlyle's treatment of Cromwell and Ireland, he admitted that 'he never would have been, as he is, a determined Repealer and Irish Nationalist, but for his reverent study of the same great writer' (10 Jan. 1846; quot. in Fielding 104–5n.).

From O'Connell's perspective, Mitchel's analysis amounted to a declaration of war. Through his *Cromwell*, Carlyle had become the rock upon which the Repeal Association would be wrecked. O'Connell was not only prejudiced against such hagiography for its implicit worship of violence, but he also realised he could no longer sponsor a newspaper principally read by Catholics making a cult of an infidel defender of anti-Catholic mass-murder. Carlyle himself read the review as a repudiation of O'Connell, and though he thought Duffy had written it, he 'could not but pronounce it heroic'. From the author of *Heroes*, this was the highest of praise. He recognised that an Irish nationalist taking his part against O'Connell was risking his future in Irish public and literary life: 'That you across such a mahlstrom of Irish indignation, have nevertheless discerned that the man *was* a Hero, full of Manhood, Earnestness and Valour, – this I think, is the creditablest thing I have yet known of you, and to me also is a very great satisfaction' (*CL* 20:104–6).

Carlyle may have eased Duffy's own departure from the Young Ireland movement. When Mitchel saw this letter, he was delighted. Carlyle's conclusion seemed directly relevant to his own position as Young Ireland's new messiah: 'Ireland, which means many millions of my own brethren, has again a blessed chance in having made a man like you speak for her' (*CL* 20:104–6). Mitchel would have recognised that Duffy was a stopgap editor, and that he – an Irishman of Scots Presbyterian ancestry – was the real leader of the movement. Carlyle's letter foreshadowed the breach between Mitchel and Duffy, which resulted in Mitchel's foundation of his own newspaper, the *United Irishman*, two years later. It also foreshadowed a life for Duffy in British constitutional service that culminated in a knighthood, and a life for Mitchel in permanent rebellion against the British Empire, and later, the United States of America.

Carlyle's *Cromwell* may never have convinced Mitchel as to Cromwell's restraint in Drogheda and elsewhere, but it made a 'Cromwell' of him. Carlyle's hero began as a constitutional rebel, swept the constitutional leaders out of the way of revolt, and then swept away constitutionalism altogether and rebuilt it around himself. In Young Ireland's eyes, Mitchel swept away O'Connell, whom he might identify with Pym, Fairfax, or Charles I, according to taste. Mitchel saw himself abolishing democracy, asserting the pre-eminence of violence, and establishing the authority of the racially pure idea of nationhood. That all of this coincided with the Great Famine, now about to enter its full force in 1846, supplied Mitchel with the means to transform himself into a literary Cromwell. His articulation of the cry of murder against the British government transferred the Cromwell debate from the 1640s to the present. Cromwell and Carlyle charged the native Irish with massacres in 1641, which the modern Irish nationalists denied. Cromwell was charged by modern Irish nationalists with massacres in 1649, which Carlyle denied. Mitchel charged the British government with the greatest massacre of all. While denying that the Irish Catholics massacred in 1641, he adopted Cromwell's use of the charge as justification for his own conduct, and made his conviction of British genocide in the Great Famine the justification for a lifetime of hatred.

Kenneth J. Fielding speaks of Carlyle's *The French Revolution* 'presenting various revolutionary directions' (136) to Duffy and Mitchel. Certainly both men were at logger-heads as soon as the break with O'Connell had been completed. Duffy fought off attempts at prosecution and never sought to take apostleship of violence beyond the rhetorical need to merit O'Connell's denunciation. But the longterm effect was to leave Irish nationalism with a straightforward ethos of violence, and an alternative use of constitutionalism with a violent option. Irish nationalism was destined to oscillate between imitation of the spirit of Cromwell at

Drogheda and that of Cromwell at Westminster, just as it oscillated between Mitchel's ideas and Gavan Duffy's.[4] It also lost O'Connell's universalist vision of non-violence, and his identification with the sufferings of black slaves as well as his championship of Jews, both causes anathema to Carlyle and Mitchel. Even Duffy, admirably humble and noble as he was, could not resist endorsing the Irish nationalist tradition of explaining violence by appealing sympathetically to its context. Carlyle had given Duffy's Catholic enemies weapons against him, yet Duffy's break with O'Connell simply impaired his otherwise good credentials to lead Irish constitutional nationalism after O'Connell's death on 15 May 1847. Essentially he sought to play that role in 1850–55, cruelly impaired by his inability to plead O'Connell's memory against clerical pressure, although by now bitterly at enmity with Mitchel and his violent solutions.[5]

When Carlyle saw and heard O'Connell speak in Dublin at the Repeal headquarters ('Conciliation Hall') on 7 September 1846, he sensed that his nemesis would not live much longer: 'Poor Daniel, Conciliation Hall and he seemed verging to their consummation, and not long for this world without a change!' Carlyle described him as 'the Prince of Humbugs', and in a memorial worthy of William Maginn, referred to him as the 'chief quack of the then world': 'Conciliation Hall something like a decent Methodist chapel; but its audience very sparse, very bad, and blackguard-looking; brazen faces like tapsters, tavern keepers, miscellaneous hucksters and quarrelsome male or female nondescripts, the prevailing type; not one that you would have called a gentleman, much less a man of culture; and discontent visible among them. The speech – on potato rot (most serious of topics) – had not one word of sincerity, not to speak of wisdom in it. Every sentence seemed to you a lie, and even to know that it was a detected lie' (*CL* 21:25).

Naturally, Carlyle's recollections of Mitchel and Duffy were far more generous. Ireland always remained somewhat unreal to Carlyle (as it did to Maginn), and his account of his relations with the two Young Irelanders betrays this sense of incredulity:

> Mitchell's wife, especially his mother (Presbyterian parson's widow of the best Scottish type), his frugally elegant small house and table, pleased me much, as did the man himself, a fine elastic-spirited young fellow with superior natural talent, whom I grieved to see rushing to destruction, palpable by 'attack of windmills' but on whom all my dissuasions were thrown away. Both Duffy and him I have always regarded as specimens of the best kind of Irish youth, seduced (like thousands of others in their early days) into courses that were at once mad and ridiculous and which nearly ruined the life of both, by the Big Beggarman, who had 15,000 a year (and proh pudor! the favour of English

> ministers instead of the pillory from them) for professing blarney, with such and still worse results. (*CL* 21:25)

Returning to England in 1849, Carlyle left behind Mitchel and Duffy to pursue their incendiary careers, the authorities to pursue them both in due course, and the country to lose a million and a half people by death. 'Poor Mitchel! I told him he would most likely be hanged, but I told him too they could not hang the immortal part of him', Carlyle said to Froude. Carlyle's biographer, in his own eyes the master-historian of Ireland, rather sanctimoniously dismissed the 1848 Irish rebellion as 'a blaze of straw' that 'had ended in a cabbage garden' (Froude, *Life* 3:429). Yet Froude's analysis of Young Ireland's role in the forging of an Irish revolutionary identity was shrewd: 'Mitchel has lately died in America [he died in Newry, co. Down, Ireland, 1875]. The 'immortal part' of him still works in the Phoenix Park and in dynamite conspiracies; what will come of it has yet to be seen' (Froude, *Life* 3:430).

Froude's chain of ideology from Mitchel to the Phoenix Park murders of the Irish Chief Secretary and Under-Secretary on 6 May 1882 and to the dynamiters (who included Thomas J. Clarke, future leader of the 1916 insurrection) was sound, yet it strangely excluded Carlyle's name. The railway sabotage proposed in November 1845 for which Duffy was indicted, is perfectly consistent with urban guerrilla warfare of later times. Irish nationalist terrorists would return to the name of Mitchel, generation after generation.[6] But Froude was as anxious to absolve Carlyle from blame as Carlyle was to absolve Cromwell: 'He could not see even the surface of Ireland without recognising that there was a curse upon it of some kind, and these young enthusiasts were at least conscious of the fact and were not crying "Peace" when there was none' (Froude, *Life* 3:428). The 'Facts' contradict such complacency. After Carlyle had made the cult of Cromwell and the inevitable suppression of his Irish enemies a matter of transcendental inevitability, Mitchel could neither compromise his principles nor conceal them.[7] Carlyle assured him of his immortality as gallows-fodder. He had no alternative left to him but to follow the path to glory, gallows, and grave.

Carlyle's invective against O'Connell fatally undermined the movement for non-violence, encouraged Young Ireland in its defiance, and helped produce the mentalité immortalised by John Mitchel in his *Jail Journal*. His diatribe against O'Connell, prompted by Mitchel's thought of the Africa he was now approaching as the 'fruitful mother of monsters', neatly illustrates the Carlylean influence:

> Poor old Dan! – wonderful, mighty, jovial, and mean old man! with silver tongue and smile of witchery, and heart of melting truth! – lying tongue!

> smile of treachery, heart of unfathomable fraud! What a royal, yet vulgar soul with the keen eye and potent swoop of a generous eagle of Cairn Tual – with the base servility of a hound, and the cold cruelty of a spider! Think of…the 'gorgeous and gossamer' theory of moral and peaceful agitation, the most astounding *organon* of public swindling since first man bethought him of obtaining money under false pretences. (*Jail Journal* 141)

The ghost of William Maginn lurks in every line of Mitchel's invective. Inspired himself by the hurly-burly rhetoric of *Fraser's*, Carlyle taught Young Ireland how to demolish O'Connell, but left them nothing to fight with except vague appeals to 'Veracity'. If they were not crying 'Peace', and this exceptional silence was meritorious, they had but one alternative, summarised in Yeats' 'Under Ben Bulben' (1938): 'We who Mitchel's prayer have heard / Send war in our time, O Lord!

Much has been written on the millennial phenomena of Ireland in the early nineteenth century. It was by no means limited to uneducated peasants. The aspirations of evangelical Protestants had their own millennialism, and the transfer of that evangelicalism to politics carried its spirit. Carlyle as a historian had breathed millennial air from the period bringing Cromwell to power, although never fully vindicated by Cromwell himself. It was an obscure English writer in Ireland who most perfectly caught the character of Carlyle as a millennialist thwarting his followers. In *The Warden* (1855) Anthony Trollope caricatured the 'Prophet' as Dr. Pessimist Anticant: 'His theories were all beautiful, and the code of morals that he taught us certainly an improvement on the practices of the age. We all of us could, and many of us did, learn much from the doctor while he chose to remain vague, mysterious, and cloudy; but when he became practical, the charm was gone' (128). But the charm was not quite gone, and after Mitchel had been transported and Duffy had risen from the stepping-stones of his prosecutors' dead cases to higher things, he would travel around Ireland with Carlyle, who produced a sour record of the visit in *Reminiscences of My Irish Journey* (1849). Duffy himself wrote a more charming memoir of their friendship in *Conversations with Carlyle* (1892). Neither book made an impact on any save the antiquary and the anthologist. If they served any purpose, they were symbolic grains of sand in the desert that twentieth-century Irish nationalism made of Anglo-Irish relations. Maginn had fired Carlyle's soul with hostility to politics and politicians. In turn, 'True Thomas' had handed on this millennial habit of mind to those who were incapable of acknowledging its limitations, and who were contemptuous of compromise.

Carlyle's *Cromwell*, so far from converting the Irish to the cause of his canonisation, hardened Irish Catholic hatred of his memory where previously he had been but one of a large number of hostile English generals and administrators, and far from the worst, in many views. Carlyle had in fact written so well, and placed his zeal for Cromwell's heroic stature in such challenging form, that the very male chauvinist spirits he sought to arouse necessarily felt called on to give him battle and hence to give Cromwell the pre-eminent diabolic status. Mitchel in the *Nation* had summed up the alternatives: 'divine' or 'diabolic'. Catholic Ireland would not concede divine honours to the grand opponent of its priesthood, and hence Cromwell in even scholarly accounts no less than in popular culture became a devil of the proportions his servant John Milton would give to Satan in *Paradise Lost*.[8] Before Carlyle, the Irish had little cause to demonise a man so abhorred by the English; after him, they had little alternative.

Yet Carlyle had done great service in his collection of texts, showing the beauty and kindness, piety and generosity, vigour and courage that mixed with the brutality and inflexibility in Cromwell's character. Equally, we cannot understand the measure of Carlyle's influence on Young Ireland if we fail to see the sweetness, kindness, good nature, wit, humour, charm, strength, and charisma that obviously made him the most extraordinary of phenomena - a Briton to whom Irishmen listened, without attempt to subvert, and frequently even without right of reply. We might give the final word to the love that kept his memory so green to Gavan Duffy:

> It has been a personal pain to me in recent times to find among honourable and cultivated people a conviction that Carlyle was hard, selfish, and arrogant. I knew him intimately for more than an entire generation - as intimately as one who was twenty years his junior, and who regarded him with unaffected reverence as the man of most undoubted genius of his age, probably ever did...a man of generous nature, sometimes disturbed on the surface by trifling troubles, but never diverted at heart from what he believed to be right and true. (Duffy 1892, 6-7).

Notes

1 For 'Thomas the Rhymer', see Watson 194.

2 For the political repercussions of Carlyle's debt to Swift, see Sorensen; for *Fraser's*, see Thrall.

3 For Marx and Engels on Ireland, see Fox; for a broader discussion of Carlyle's influence on them, see Sorensen.

4 At Westminster Duffy developed the strategy, later brought to a fine art by Parnell, of

an independent Irish party whose members were pledged not to accept office until their demands were met. This tendency is chronicled by Duffy in *The League of North and South* and subjected to reliable historical scrutiny in Whyte.

5 For the consequences of this division, see Nolan, 1963 and 1965.

6 Griffith's edition of *Jail Journal* in 1913 canonised that text, letting it for the use of Pearse in 1915–16, which virtually made it a holy relic of Pearse's martyrdom, established in his last essays as it was. After the Treaty split IRA supporters were somewhat embarrassed at the dependence of their ideologue Mitchel on editing by the (by now) pro-Treaty Griffith. But Mitchel remains in the vestibule of their Valhalla to the present day.

7 Carlyle had taught Mitchel the meaning of 'terrible beauty'. As Worden points out in his graceful and illuminating essay on Carlyle and Cromwell, 'At Drogheda and at Wexford, Cromwell used the brute force that is hideous when practised by the wicked but has a dreadful beauty in the hands of the righteous' (145).

8 For the Cromwell and Ireland debate, see Barnard in Richardson, and Canny 574–8.

Works Cited

Belloc, Hilaire, intro. *The French Revolution*. By Thomas Carlyle. 2 vols. London: Dent, 1929.

Barnard, Toby. 'Irish Images of Cromwell'. *Images of Oliver Cromwell*. Ed. R. C. Richardson. Manchester UK: Manchester UP, 1993. 180–206.

Campbell, Ian. *Thomas Carlyle*. London: Hamish Hamilton, 1974.

Canny, Nicholas. *Making Ireland British 1580–1650*. Oxford: Oxford UP, 2001.

Carlyle, Thomas. *Reminiscences of My Irish Journey in 1849*. London: Sampson & Low, 1882.

Davis, Thomas W. Prose Writings. Ed. T.W. Rolleston. London: Walter Scott, [1890].

Dillon, William. Life of John Mitchel. 2 vols. London: Kegan Paul, Trench, 1888.

Duffy, Charles Gavan. *The League of North and South*. London: Chapman and Hall, 1886.

———. *Conversations with Carlyle*. London: Sampson & Low, 1892.

———. *My Life in Two Hemispheres*. 2 vols. London: Unwin, 1898.

Fielding, Kenneth J. 'Ireland, John Mitchel and his "sarcastic friend" Thomas Carlyle'. In *Literatur im Kontext / Literature in Context. Festschrift für Horst Drescher*. Ed. J. Schwend, S. Hagemann, and H. Volkel. Frankfurt and New York: P. Lang, 1992. 131–43.

Foster, R. F. *Paddy and Mr. Punch*. London: Penguin, 1993.

Fox, Ralph W. *Marx, Engels and Lenin on the Irish Revolution*. London: Modern Books, [1933].

Maginn, William. 'Our Confession of Faith'. *Fraser's Magazine* 1 (1830): 1–7.

———. 'The Burnings in Kent, and the State of the Labouring Classes'. *Fraser's Magazine* 2 (1830): 572–81.

Mitchel, John. *Jail Journal.* Pref. by Arthur Griffith. Dublin: Gill, 1913.

Nolan, Kevin B. *Charles Gavan Duffy and the Repeal Movement.* Dublin: University College, 1963.

———. *The Politics of Repeal.* London: Routledge and Kegan Paul, 1965.

Seigel, Jules P. *Thomas Carlyle: The Critical Heritage.* London: Routledge, 1971.

Sorensen, David R. '"Guts in the Brain": Carlyle, Swift and the French Revolution'. *The Carlyle Society Papers.* New Series, No. 8 (1995): 9–28.

———. 'One More Step to Take: Marx & Engels, Carlyle, and the French Revolutions of 1789 & 1848'. *The Carlyle Society Papers.* New Series, No. 12 (1998–9): 30–40.

Thrall, Miriam H. *Rebellious Fraser's*. New York: Columbia UP, 1934.

Trollope, Anthony. *The Warden*. Ed. Robin Gilmour. Harmondsworth UK: Penguin, 1982.

Watson, Robert, ed. *The Poetry of Scotland: Gaelic, Scots and English 1380–1980.* Edinburgh: Edinburgh UP, 1995.

Whyte, John H. *The Independent Irish Party 1850–59*. Oxford: Oxford UP, 1958.

Worden, Blair. 'Thomas Carlyle and Oliver Cromwell'. *Proceedings of the British Academy: 1999 Lectures and Memoirs.* Vol. 105. Oxford: Oxford UP, 2000. 131–70.

Chapter 6

Translating Carlyle's French Revolution: A French Perspective

ALAIN JUMEAU

French academics have come to respect the work of Thomas Carlyle, even though he is largely unknown among them. His *The French Revolution, A History* is no exception. Those who are interested in literature tend to discard it because it is a history book, and French historians are ready to discard it because it is a purely literary work that does not meet the high scientific standards of modern historiography. It is indeed a very special book, paradoxical in that it is both a history and more than a history. It is highly personal, yet it is also a prophetic parable for Victorian England. The first thing that strikes a French reader is the subject itself. Why did Carlyle choose to write about French history in the first place? And in what way was his subject relevant to the situation of England in 1837? Carlyle was born weeks after the Insurrection of Vendémiaire, which according to him marked the conclusion of the French Revolution. In certain respects he was a child of the event. It belonged to the past and to history, but it was close enough to him that he knew many people of his parents' generation who had experienced it or heard about it when Britain was at war with France. He found himself in the same situation as young European historians writing about World War II at the end of the twentieth century.

Yet researching the book in the mid-1830s, Carlyle also realised that he lived at a reasonable distance from the event, so that he could grasp it fully and understand its significance for himself and for his readers. When the book was published in June 1837, just before the coronation of Queen Victoria, England was in a state of unrest. The passage of the Reform Bill in 1832 had not satisfied the demands of the people for a greater political representation. Their frustration would soon manifest itself with the birth of the Chartist movement. The Industrial Revolution caused a huge migration of workers from country to town; the new proletariat worked long hours for low wages and endured terrible conditions. As Engels remarked in his *The Condition of the English Working Classes* (1845) – a work itself influenced by Carlyle's analysis - 'Everywhere barbarous indifference, hard egotism on one hand, and nameless misery on the other' (69). Unemployment was a permanent threat and the workers knew that in case of absolute destitution, their fate would be harrowing in the workhouses established by the New Poor Law of 1834. Popular discontent was reaching a climax. Carlyle was aware that he was writing in what seemed to be a pre-revolutionary context.

He chose to treat his subject as a professional historian. David Sorensen has recently offered convincing proof of the extent of his commitment, and it will be valuable to have a definitive account of the sources Carlyle used when the forthcoming Strouse edition f *The French Revolution* is published. To write his history, Carlyle consulted a wide range of very different sources - many of them became 'standard' works in the nineteenth century - including histories, memoirs, dictionaries, biographies, newspapers, periodicals, pamphlets, and other publications (Sorensen 1-3). These materials make an impressive whole, but did they provide him with a secure foundation on which he might write a fully documented history? His secondary sources were not always supported by his primary ones, and some of his primary sources wanted checking. Carlyle could not afford to do the sort of field-work in France that he did later in Germany for *Frederick the Great.* In 1837 his knowledge of France was limited. He spent a fortnight there in 1824, but he did not enjoy the experience. He chastised the French for their religion, superficiality, lack of discipline, and impetuosity.

Though he did little field work, Carlyle still managed to produce a remarkable study of the French Revolution, demonstrating that vision is perhaps more important to the historian than meticulous source-checking. Inevitably, he commits errors. At times his geography of France is confusing. For instance, he sees Avignon in the South-West instead of the South, la Vendée in the South-West instead of the West, and Thionville in the North instead of the East. He seriously miscalculated the distance between Paris and Varennes, thereby giving the impression that the coach carrying the Royal Family was traveling at an extraordinarily slow pace (when it was travelling at a modestly slow pace). More idiosyncratic is his chronology. The work is divided into three volumes - 'The Bastille', 'The Constitution', and 'The Guillotine', which correspond with the three well-known phases of the Revolution - the fall of the Bastille, the transfer of power from King to Parliament, and the Terror. But the time-limits of Carlyle's history are unusual. The first volume does not begin in 1789 as one might expect, but many years earlier, in May 1774, when King Louis XV lies on his death-bed. The King's long agony appears as a metaphor illustrating the decay of the Ancien Régime and the concomitant decline of authority in France. Carlyle suggests that the Revolution is simply the end of a lengthy process that started much earlier.

The other time-limit is equally puzzling. After the Terror and the reaction brought about by Thermidor, Carlyle ends his history with the episode of the Insurrection of Vendémiaire 13th (October 1795) quelled by young Bonaparte. He acknowledges that significant events occur between this date and Brumaire 18th (November 1799), when Bonaparte seizes power, but in his view the principle of permanent insurrection is no longer alive. As he later remarked in the chronological summary included in the 1903 Centenary edition, '"The Revolution", as defined here, ends, – Anarchic Government, if still anarchic, proceeding by softer methods than that of continued insurrection' (*Works* 4:338). The Revolution has lasted for six years. Not all historians would agree with this judgment, and many would argue that important links are missing in the chain of events. But Carlyle does not want to cover everything, and he makes clear throughout that his aim is not to write a chronicle of the Revolution in the manner of Alison or Thiers. It is 'A History', rather than 'The History', as he states in the subtitle. Moreover, he was sceptical of 'scientific' approaches to history, which became fashionable as a result of the work of Leopold von Ranke (1795-1886) and his followers. In *The French Revolution* he offers a personal reading, in which his message to his contemporaries is as important as the documented facts.

Carlyle was extraordinarily sensitive to the paradoxical aspects of historical inquiry. He realised that the word 'history' sprung from two sources: Latin *historia*, suggesting 'a narrative of past events', and Greek, denoting 'an inquiry, an investigation'. His contemporaries liked to dwell on the 'dignity of history', which gave pride of place to a restrained, gentlemanly recital of the facts, and not to the figure of the historian, whose presence is bound to obscure clear vision and rational explanation. Carlyle's version of the role of the historian was quite different. In *The French Revolution* he does not refrain from asserting his presence, yet this does not jeopardise the objectivity and impartiality of his study. In the English debate about the French Revolution, he sides neither with Edmund Burke, the arch-enemy of the Revolution, nor with Thomas Paine, the chief advocate of the 'Rights of Man'. At various points in the narrative, he understands both perspectives. With Burke, he accepts that the Revolution marks the end of an era and possibly the end of civilisation; with Paine, he sympathises with the ordinary citizen's desire for recognition and respect. But his vision of the Revolution is global and dialectical, eclipsing the vantage points of both Burke and Paine and anticipating the conclusions of Marx and Engels.

For Carlyle, it is necessary that the Ancien Régime should be destroyed, to allow the birth of a new system. Though he has no sympathy with anarchy of 'Sansculottism', he realises that it has a part to play: 'Sansculottism will burn much; but what is incombustible it will not burn. Fear not Sansculottism; recognise it for what it is, the portentous inevitable end of much, the miraculous beginning of much' (*Works* 2:213). He sees that even the terrible events of that history are of vital importance, for they pave the way for the outcome, when the Revolution, true to its etymological meaning, comes full circle. Thesis and antithesis are transcended in the final synthesis:

> For ourselves, we answer that French Revolution means here the open violent Rebellion, and Victory, of disimprisoned Anarchy against corrupt worn-out Authority: how Anarchy breaks prison; bursts-up from the infinite Deep, and rages uncontrollable, immeasurable, enveloping a world; in phasis after phasis of fever-frenzy; – till the frenzy burning itself out, and what elements of new Order it held... developing themselves, the Uncontrollable be got, if not reimprisoned, yet harnessed, and its mad forces made to work towards their great object as sane regulated ones. (*Works* 2:211-12)

While French historians of the present day continue to accept the Marxist version of the Revolution as a victory of the people and minimise the Terror as an inevitable evil, Carlyle is always ready both to denounce the Terror and to understand it; he sees the event as a huge apocalypse in which violence plays a vital part in the revelation of divine justice.

He is not simply an historian, but an Old Testament prophet addressing his Victorian audience. Unlike French historians, either past or present, he never sees the Revolution in mere political or economic terms – it also has religious significance. Following the religious crisis that he described metaphorically in *Sartor Resartus*, Carlyle focused on the incarnation of the Transcendent in this world – 'Natural Supernaturalism' – and urged his audience to heed the 'Signs of the Times', which had to do with basic questions about justice. In the French Ancien Régime, the King and the aristocrats forgot their mission, which was to guide and protect the people; the Church neglected her duty, which was to educate the people. As a consequence, the condition of the French masses became unbearable: 'For there are from twenty to twenty-five millions of them... Untaught, uncomforted, unfed! A dumb generation' (*Works* 2:33-4). This unjust situation calls for retribution and divine justice, though this justice is implicit in the order of nature rather than the work of a specific 'God'. For Carlyle, the French Revolution is a well-deserved punishment: 'All this... has been storing itself for thousands of years; and now the account-day has come. And rude will the settlement be: of wrath laid up against the day of wrath' (*Works* 2:58). For many centuries, the rulers of the country have ignored their duties to the people. Echoing passages from Proverbs (3:113), Hosea (8:7), and

Romans (6:23), he insists on the moral necessity of retribution: 'Dance on, ye foolish ones; ye sought not wisdom, neither have ye found it. Ye and your fathers have sown the wind, yet shall reap the whirlwind. Was it not, from of old, written: *The wages of sin is death*?' (*Works* 2:48). The French Revolution is a warning to England not to follow the example of France. If the same kind of injustice prevails at home, the same consequences will have to be faced: 'That there be no second Sansculottism in our Earth for a thousand years, let us understand well what the first was: and let Rich and Poor of us go and do *otherwise*' (*Works* 4:313).

It is a regrettable 'sign of the times' that Carlyle's history, with its dialectical structure and its unique political and prophetic perspective, remains unread by the vast majority of French people. A new translation would almost certainly awaken them to the profound originality of Carlyle's contribution to the historiography on the subject. The nineteenth-century translation by Regnault and Barot (1865-7) has long been out of print and cannot be found easily. Moreover, it is not reliable. A close examination reveals a number of errors, misreadings, and misinterpretations. Some difficulties in the original text have been overlooked, and the originality of Carlyle's style is poorly rendered. A modern translator would be wise to heed Carlyle's own estimation of the book: 'a wild savage Book, itself a kind of French Revolution...born in blackness whirlwind and sorrow' (TC to John Sterling, 17 Jan. 1837, *CL* 9:116). Conveying a sense of this 'wild' and 'savage' quality is the chief challenge facing any translator. The problem is compounded by the poetic nature of the Carlyle's work, which constitutes a vital part of its verisimilitude. As John Stuart Mill perceptively remarked in his review of *The French Revolution* in 1837, 'This is not so much a history, as an epic poem; and notwithstanding, or even in consequence of this, the truest of histories. It is the history of the French Revolution, and the poetry of it, both in one' (*CW* 20:133).

This epic quality is perceptible everywhere in the general inspiration of the work, as well as in the minor details, such as the epic similes. How does a translator cope with such phrases as 'sea-green man'? (*Works* 4:8) There is no direct equivalent of this description in French, for the sea is not linguistically associated with the colour green. We say 'vert d'eau' but not 'vert de mer' or 'vert comme la mer'. If the reference to the sea has to be dropped, then what needs to be preserved is Carlyle's emphasis on the unusually green colour of Robespierre's face, which betrays stiffness and dyspepsia. A pejorative suffix might serve this purpose, such as 'Robespierre au teint verdâtre'. The epic dimension accounts for many other stylistic idiosyncrasies. Carlyle frequently abolishes the distance between past and present, uses metonymy and apostrophe, and litters his texts with exclamation marks and hyperbolic language. In short his epic style amounts to what he calls an 'Imbroglio', which would pose difficulties for even the most determined translator. But the task is worth taking up for several reasons. Not only will Carlyle's history help the French to understand the history of their own country in a fresh light, but it will also give them new insight into Victorian culture and society. In his time Carlyle's contribution to history and literature was decisive, and his stature was comparable to, if not higher than, Michelet's.

In a curious way, his closing words in *The French Revolution* stand as an invitation to a French translator to render his history 'an incarnated Word' for a new audience:

> Et voici venu, ô lecteur, le temps pour nous deux de nous séparer. Elle a été pénible la route que nous avons suivie ensemble; elle n'a pas été sans heurts; mais nous sommes parvenus à son terme. Pour moi, tu as été comme une ombre chérie, l'esprit désincarné, ou pas encore incarné, d'un frère. Pour toi, je n'ai été qu'une voix. Mais notre relation a été quasiment sacrée; n'en doute pas! Car, même si des choses jadis sacrées se transforment en jargons creux, quand la voix de l'homme parle à l'homme, n'as-tu pas là cette source vive d'où tout ce qui est sacré a jailli et jaillira encore? L'homme, par sa nature, se définit comme 'un verbe incarné'. Malheur à moi si j'ai parlé faussement; il t'appartenait aussi d'écouter sincèrement. Adieu.

Works Cited

Engels, Friedrich. *The Condition of the Working Class in England*. Ed. Victor Kiernan. Harmondsworth, UK: Penguin, 1987.

Kaplan, Fred. *Thomas Carlyle: A Biography*. Cambridge: Cambridge UP, 1983.

Mill, John Stuart. 'Carlyle's French Revolution'. *Essays on French History and Historians. Vol. 20 of Collected Works*. Ed. John M. Robson. London and Toronto: Routledge & Kegan Paul; Toronto UP, 1985. 133-66.

Sorensen, David. 'In Pursuit of Fact: Carlyle's Use of Sources in *The French Revolution*'. Carlyle 2000 Conference, Philadelphia. 6-8 April 2000.

Chapter 7

The 'Magical Speculum': Vision and Truth in Carlyle's Early Histories

MARYLU HILL

The action of looking backwards marks a distinctly nineteenth-century approach to the intersection of past and present in historical writing. In contrast to earlier ages when ardent history enthusiasts were isolated as a dusty class of antiquarians and pedagogues, the Victorians as a society desired desperately to see and feel the past as it was, through artefact, photograph, and visual experience. At the same time, there is a poignant awareness in Victorian literature that the act of looking backwards is a fleeting one at best, involving 'magical speculums' (*Past and Present*, *Works* 10:43) which all too soon reduce both view and viewer to ghosts in the landscape of memory.

Carlyle was particularly interested in the '*eye*' ('On History', HE 13) of historical perception, and in the use of vision and incantation for resurrecting the past. He borrows this concept of vision from the romantic writers of the early nineteenth century, who were adept at using the visionary as a frame for a poetic sense of the past, but he applies it instead to a new way of writing history. Through the vision of a 'magical speculum', Carlyle hoped to integrate 'Dryasdust' historical facts with the experiential quality of romance, encouraging the reader to 'feel' the past even while preserving a necessary awareness of 'strange dualistic life of ours' caught between 'Memory and Oblivion' ('On History Again', HE 20). In his historical writings, Carlyle strives to overcome, or at least lessen, the 'fatal discrepancy' ('On History', HE 7) between the past as it was and the past as it is perceived in the present.

Carlyle was not alone in his concern to connect historical fact with experiential feeling. In his essay 'History' (1828), Macaulay describes historical writing as 'under the jurisdiction of two hostile powers...instead of being equally shared between its two rules, the Reason and the Imagination, it falls alternately under the sole and absolute dominion of each. It is sometimes fiction. It is sometimes theory' ('History' 51).[1] Pressing his case further in his review of Hallam's *Constitutional History* (1828), he insists that the novelist has usurped the role of the historian: 'To make the past present, to bring the distant near, to place us in the society of a great man, or on the eminence which overlooks the field of a mighty battle, to invest with the reality of human flesh and blood beings whom we are too much inclined to consider as personified qualities in an allegory...these parts of the duty which properly belongs to the historian have been appropriated by the historical novelist' (67).

Like Macaulay, Carlyle lamented the inability of historians to offer a flesh-and-blood recreation of the past. He agrees with him that the old description of historical writing as 'Philosophy, teaching by Experience' is at best inadequate and, at worst, nothing more than an 'owl on housetop, *seeing* nothing, *understanding* nothing, uttering only, with such solemnity, her perpetual most wearisome *hoo-hoo*'. The consequence for Carlyle is the promise of a 'feast of widest Biographic insight' reduced to a 'mere Ossian's "feast of *shells*", – the food and liquor being all emptied out and clean gone, and only the vacant dishes and deceitful emblems thereof left!' ('Biography', *Works* 28:47). The shells lack the nourishment of the historical imagination – the challenge to the historian, according to both Macaulay and Carlyle, is to find a method for revitalising these dead objects.

Always striving to outdistance his rival, Carlyle proposes a more radical solution to bridge the chasm between historical romance and the writing of history. With the essays 'On History' (1830) and 'On History Again' (1833), he began to explore a methodology that later bore fruit in *The French Revolution* (1837) and *Past and Present* (1843). In these works, Carlyle developed a clear vocabulary of optical allusions to draw the reader into an experience of the past that is at once familiar and strange. He borrows from romance not only the language of dreams, but also the theatrical effects that seem better suited to conjuring up myths and legends rather than to writing history. Taking a radically original approach, he introduces a variety of visually-oriented time machines in his books, the two most memorable of which are the 'camera lucida' (as opposed to the better known camera obscura) and the 'magical speculum'. These 'inventions' clearly deserve a place next to other, real-life Victorian optical wonders such as the stereoscope, the magic lantern, and, of course, the camera. Their purpose is similar. Using these techniques deftly, Carlyle conveys the magical quality of 'Facts'.

He moves history far beyond 'Philosophy, teaching from Experience' into a new realm of expression. The vehicle for his magic is the prosaic and unromantic bedrock of all human historical writing – the primary source, whether it be chronicle, first-person narrative, or personal correspondence. For Carlyle, the beginning of all history truly is the word, for, as in John's Gospel, the word can become flesh through the historian's efforts. *Past and Present* offers the most vivid account of this transformation. In it, Carlyle describes the path of Jocelin's chronicle as it emerges from its Pompeii-like existence as a Camden Society manuscript, covered 'with the lava-ashes and inarticulate wreck of seven hundred years' (*Works* 10:40). The new edition, courtesy of Jocelin's editor, Mr Rokewood, makes the 'crabbed manuscript' newly audible. It also makes it truly visible as the now 'clear print' restores Jocelin's likewise 'clear eyes', permitting him to once again look 'on us so clear and cheery' which in turn allows his readers to see themselves reflected in the newly restored mirror of his 'neighborly soft-smiling eyes' (*Works* 10:42, 44). Venerating this sacred source, Carlyle applauds Mr Rokewood for 'standing faithfully by his text' (*Works* 10:42) and allowing it to speak for itself with the help of judiciously-placed explanatory notes.

In *The French Revolution*, Carlyle exhibits the same fidelity to his own sources. As David Sorensen has recently argued, 'Carlyle's narrative power springs not merely from his skill as a word-painter, but from his deep intellectual engagement with the content and spirit of his sources' (3). For example, in a lengthy and incisive footnote on Madame Campan's description of the moments following Louis XV's death, Carlyle demonstrates a delicate balance between source and commentary, allowing for the emotion of the moment even while he interprets the description in hindsight: 'One grudges to interfere with the beautiful theatrical "candle", which Madame Campan has lit on this occasion, and blown out at the moment of death. What candles might be lit or blown out, in so large an Establishment as that of Versailles, no man at such distance would like to affirm: at the same time, as it was two o'clock in a May afternoon, and these royal stables must have been some five or six hundred yards from the royal sickroom, the "candle" does threaten to go out in spite of us. It remains burning indeed – in her fantasy' (*Works* 2:24-5). The candle is at once palpably real yet improbable. Carlyle strikes a balance here between truth and imagination, and combines vision and judgement in a way that demonstrates both his empathy and his understanding.

For Carlyle the historian vision is an ocular manifestation – an act of seeing as a vehicle for transportation to the past. The primary challenge for the historian is to persuade his reader to 'see' the past in its true guise, whatever that may be. The intersection of the artefact – be it book, object, or building – with the viewer constitutes the terrain of real history, where past and present meet and interact in the mind of the viewer. Carlyle describes the process in 'Biography':

> Half the effect, we already perceive, depends on the object; on its being *real*, on its being really *seen*. The other half will depend on the observer; and the question now is: How are real objects to be *so* seen; on what quality of observing, or of style in describing, does this so intense pictorial power depend? Often a slight circumstance contributes curiously to the result: some little, and perhaps to appearance accidental, feature is presented; a light-gleam, which instantaneously *excites* the mind, and urges it to complete the picture, and evolve the meaning thereof for itself. (*Works* 28:57)

The image of the 'light-gleam' is crucial to Carlyle. The glimmer of light is thrown, not on myths or grand events, but on small details that are pregnant with imaginative meaning. In 'Biography', Carlyle casts the 'gleam' on shoes lent to Charles I by a poor cottager when the king was fleeing Cromwell's army:

> [How comes it] that this poor pair of clouted Shoes, out of the million hides that have been tanned and cut, and worn, should still subsist, and hang visibly together? We see him [the cottager] but for a moment; for one moment, the blanket of the Night is rent asunder, so that we behold and see, and then closes over him - forever. (*Works* 28:55)

The shoes 'hang visibly' in the mind's eye, as Carlyle's shutter opens momentarily, revealing the objects in motion.

Carlyle also throws a glimmer of light on individuals by using incantatory phrases such as 'here he is' or 'there they are', which function as a magical formula to awaken the dead. Jocelin of Brakelond is introduced to us in this theatrical way as the curtains of time are whisked away: 'Here he is; and in his hand a magical speculum, much gone to rust indeed, yet in fragments still clear; wherein the marvellous image of his existence does still shadow itself though fitfully and as with an intermittent light. Will not the reader peep with us into this singular *camera lucida*, where an extinct species, though fitfully, can still be seen alive?' (*Works* 10:43). As John Rosenberg notes, Carlyle accomplishes this feat of revelation in distinct stages: 'The paragraph opens with the double-frame of Carlyle's observing the clear-eyed Jocelin as Jocelin observes King John. It ends with the reader drawn through the frame and into the picture' (22). Carlyle's aim is to use the tools of fiction and romance in order to move the reader beyond dream into an encounter with the past as a *real entity* - not just one that once lived, but one that 'lives, moves and has its being' in the present.

In *The French Revolution* he achieves a similar result in his description of the 'Merovingian Kings slowly wending on their bullock-carts through the streets of Paris, with their long hair flowing...into Eternity' (*Works* 2:7). With this image, he creates a visual effect that anticipates the cinematic technique of instant replay, as the kings seem captured in a ghostly time loop that keeps them wending through the streets of Paris forever. With typical concision, he describes the experience of inner vision in 'Biography':

> [L]et any one bethink him how impressive the smallest historical *fact* may become, as contrasted with the grandest fictitious event; what an incalculable force lies for us in this consideration: The Thing which I here hold imaged in my mind did actually occur; was, in very truth, an element in the system of the All, whereof I too form part; had therefore, and has, through all time, an authentic being; is not a dream, but a reality! (*Works* 28:54)

As the 'reality' unfolds, Carlyle juxtaposes these glimpses of the past with reminders of the strangeness of our existence in history. As quickly as the light beam comes, just as quickly it disappears, abruptly reminding readers of the elusiveness of historical knowledge. In the conclusion of 'The Ancient Monk' section of *Past and Present* Carlyle remarks that 'the miraculous hand, that held all this theatric-machinery, suddenly quits hold; impenetrable Time-Curtains rush down; in the mind's eye all is again dark, void; with loud dinning in the mind's ear, our real-phantasmagory of St. Edmundsbury plunges into the bosom of the Twelfth Century again, and all is over' (*Works* 10:125). The reader is jolted back, as it were, into the language of dreams, with its dark void and loud dinning; the transition itself suggests the 'strange dualistic life' that envelops both past and present.

But the point of vision for Carlyle is not simply seeing; it is the inner vision – the vision linked to prophecy – that matters most. In 'On History', Carlyle identifies History as the 'true fountain of knowledge', yet he acknowledges that it is 'covered over with formless inextricably-entangled unknown characters – nay, which is a *Palimpsest*, and had once prophetic writing, still dimly legible there'. It demands a special reader, who reads by both sight and insight, with an eye for 'an Idea of the Whole'. If 'History is a real Prophetic Manuscript', then the historian must be both prophet and artist to be able to decipher truly even a little portion of it (HE 8). While Carlyle's use of the word 'prophet' retains its Old Testament undertones, he does not mean it precisely as one who predicts the future, but rather as one who tells the *truth* – who reads the past both accurately and sensitively. The art of history does not consist of making up fictitious details to force a false sense of empathy on the reader. On the contrary, for Carlyle it resides in the 'seeing' and loving heart that 'opens the whole mind, quickens every faculty of the intellect to do its fit work, that of *knowing*; and therefrom, by sure consequence, of *vividly uttering-forth*' ('Biography', *Works* 28:57).

Early in *The French Revolution,* Carlyle uses the vivid image of Newton and his Dog Diamond to illustrate the complexity of the historian's vision:

> For indeed it is well said,'in every object there is inexhaustible meaning; the eye sees in it what the eye brings means of seeing'.To Newton and to Newton's Dog Diamond, what a different pair of Universes; while the painting on the optical retina of both was, most likely, the same! Let the Reader here, in this sick-room of Louis, endeavour to look with the mind too. (*Works* 2:5)

The historian must simultaneously be a truth-teller, master-conjurer, and translator to truly recreate the past. This inner vision is the real inspiration for historical truth:'By critics, such light-gleams and their almost magical influence have frequently been noted: but the power to produce such, to select such features as will produce them, is generally treated as a knack, or trick of the trade, a secret for being 'graphic'; whereas these magical feats are, in truth, rather inspirations' ('Biography', *Works* 28:57). Inspiration for Carlyle is thus based in a sense of wonder - the amazing realisation that 'the thing which I here hold imaged in my mind did actually occur' ('Biography', *Works* 28:54) and the surprise that Jocelin, like a 'deep-buried Mastodon' can still speak to us from 'amid [his] rock-swathings' (*Past and Present*, *Works* 10:43).

Carlyle's emphasis on the practicality of the historian as visionary and his own well-publicised lapses in accuracy made him suspect to historians of the late nineteenth and early twentieth centuries, who adopted the constrictive analytical prescriptions of Ranke's 'science of history'. Ironically, when R. G. Collingwood memorably attacked this school in *The Idea of History* (1933), he did so using Carlylean arguments. In this study, Collingwood speaks of history as 'the re-enactment of past thought in the historian's own mind' (215) as well as a discipline that requires the exercise of what he calls the 'historical imagination', namely,'the activity of the imagination by which we endeavour to provide this innate idea with detailed content' (247).

Collingwood's description of historical re-enactment and historical imagination entails taking the 'dry bones' of facts and re-animating them, not with fictionalised details, but with 'the flesh and blood of a thought which is both his [the historian's] own and theirs [the past]' (305).The process of re-animation begins when the historian sympathetically enters the mind of his subjects and attempts to think and feel as they do.Whereas Carlyle called this process 'mystical', Collingwood is content to define it merely as being 'pre-adapted' to the historical period or historical figure in question:

> The gulf of time between the historian and his object must be bridged, as I have said, from both ends. The object must be of such a kind that it can revive itself in the historian's mind; the historian's mind must be such as to offer a home for that revival…It means that he must be the right man to study that object. What he is studying is a certain thought: to study it involves re-enacting it in himself; and in order that it may take its place in the immediacy of his own thought, his thought must be, as it were, pre-adapted to become its host. (304)

This re-enactment entails a connection with history that goes beyond the visual to one that is directly experiential: 'To the historian, the activities whose history he is studying are not spectacles to be watched, but experiences to be lived through in his own mind; they are objective, or known to him, only because they are also subjective, or activities of his own' (218). The result, for Collingwood as for Carlyle, is that 'the gap between present and past [is] bridged not only by the power of the present thought to think of the past, but also by the power of past thought to reawaken itself in the present' (294). For both writers, there is a primary assumption that the past is not dead and gone, but can be awakened through the transformative power of the sympathetic eye and the active imagination. Collingwood describes the process of thinking historically as possessing the same sort of mysterious relationship with time – that is, both of and beyond the time continuum – that Carlyle attempts to create in his historical writing: 'In a sense, these thoughts [of historical re-enactment] are no doubt themselves events happening in time; but since the only way in which the historian can discern them is by re-thinking them for himself, there is another sense, and one very important to the historian, in which they are not in time at all' (217).

Carlyle and Collingwood both demonstrate the process whereby history becomes visionary in its ability to re-animate the past, not like taxidermic forms aping (and distorting) life, but as a living entity bodied forth in the present.[2] In Carlyle's hands, this process is both 'rich and strange' in a Shakespearian manner. For as much as Carlyle champions the vision of historical truth, he consistently makes the strangeness of that vision an integral part of his approach to writing the past. Indeed, his striking awareness of the tension between vision and dream marks Carlyle's method as distinctly modern and even post-modern. Carlyle's magical speculums, magic mirrors, and camera lucidas are the vehicles for both the insight of his vision and the strangeness inherent in that gaze. Though it allows the past to breathe again, the magical speculum also prevents the possibility of true dialogue. As Carlyle says of Jocelin, 'we have a longing always to cross-examine him…but no; Jocelin, though he talks with such clear familiarity…will not answer any question: that is the peculiarity of him, dead these six hundred and fifty years, and quite deaf to us, though still so audible!' (*Works* 10:44).

Brought face to face with Jocelin, the reader is reduced to the condition of an eavesdropping ghost, mirrored in Jocelin's eyes but still 'invisible' (*Works* 10:50). The magic mirror itself is fragile, making our 'understanding of [past events] altogether incomplete' ('On History', HE 6). And there can be no guarantee that the magical speculum is necessarily accurate, since eyewitness accounts will vary according to bias and perspective. The visual power is inevitably interwoven with the visionary faculty. The 'real cardinal points' of an event may be completely overlooked, 'because no Seer, but only mere Onlookers, chanced to be there' ('On History', HE 7). As a consequence, the published historical record needs to be treated sceptically. The supposedly authoritative 'Letter of Instructions' is often 'falsified, blotted out, torn, lost, and but a shred of it in existence; this too so difficult to read, or spell' ('On History Again', HE 16). The frustration and challenge of history is to fathom the meaning of this 'Letter' - read without inward vision, it will remain 'lost'.

Notes

1 The interest of both Macaulay and Carlyle in bridging disciplines and genres in their quest for an appropriate style may be due to the fact that neither belonged to the community of professional historians writing at this time. As Levine points out, they were 'more accurately part of an older tradition of essayists and reviewers' rather than part of the 'wider historical community' (3).

2 See Bann's discussion of taxidermic practices of the nineteenth century, 16-17.

Works Cited

Bann, Stephen. *The Clothing of Clio: A Study of the Representation of History in Nineteenth Century Britain and France*. Cambridge: Cambridge UP, 1984.

Collingwood, R. G. *The Idea of History*. Oxford: Oxford UP, 1993.

Levine, Philippa. *The Amateur and the Professional: Antiquarians, Historians, and Archaeologists in Victorian England, 1838-1886*. Cambridge: Cambridge UP, 1986.

Macaulay, Thomas Babington. 'History'. *Critical, Historical and Miscellaneous Essays*. NY: Sheldon, 1860. 51-67.

Rosenberg, John. *Carlyle and the Burden of History*. Cambridge, MA: Harvard UP, 1985.

Sorensen, David. 'In Pursuit of Fact: Carlyle's Use of Sources in *The French Revolution*'. Carlyle 2000 Conference, Philadelphia, 6–8 April 2000.

Chapter 8

Prophet and Friend: The Reflective Politics of Carlyle and Coleridge

RONALD C. WENDLING

David R. Sorensen has recently argued that Professor Teufelsdröckh's career in *Sartor Resartus* is a progress from aloof reflection to social engagement (2001:212–13).[1] A similar development in Carlyle himself would help explain his early images of Coleridge atop Highgate hill as a man of disabled force – 'a steam-engine of a hundred horses power – with the boiler burst', 'a seventy-four-gun- ship, but water-logged, dismasted', metaphors famously elaborated over twenty-five years later in the *Life of John Sterling* (*CL* 3:139, 351–2). And yet Carlyle was unsure of his claim that an excessive inwardness had robbed Coleridge's work of decisive impact on a changed world. He disdained, for example, the reviewers' triumphant condemnations of *The Friend* and the *Biographia Literaria* as obscure, calling them instead 'living brooks' that, though momentarily hidden under mountains of difficulty, may one day 'roll forth in their true limpid shape' to a more appreciative reception (*Works* 27:3).[2] This suspicion of a latent energy and transparency in the seemingly unproductive haze of Coleridgean theorising significantly qualifies Carlyle's abhorrence of the sage of Highgate's fussy self-involvement (Sanders 148). Carlyle believed, as Coleridge did, in a form of self-consciousness that could renovate personal and social life. They both distinguished such engaged subjectivity from the detached introspection characteristic of a self-indulgent mysticism (STC *Works* 9:388–94). In fact, Carlyle trusted the productivity of political reflection even more than Coleridge, who deplored its tendency to absolutes when uncorrected by the receptive faculty he called 'Understanding'. Understanding, which can only mimic engaged reflection in Carlyle, keeps it responsive in Coleridge to the practical demands of action and work.[3]

Carlyle's dislike of the kind of subjectivity that is merely mystifying should not blind us to the patience he showed in the late 1820's and early 30's with the reflective cast of mind generally, especially as manifested in the inward-looking tendency of German philosophy. English readers call the Germans mystical, he argues in the 'The State of German Literature'

(1827), because they mistakenly expect spiritual realities, like God and the soul, to be treated with the same clarity and definiteness as material, visible objects (*Works* 26:71–3).[4] They label emotional intensity in argument 'Kantism', conveniently ignoring the distinct conceptions and iron logic of Kant's own writing. Kant, Fichte, and Schelling are not mad, says Carlyle, merely because the English refuse their works the same steady application they willingly give to physics and mathematics.[5] When read with some care, these philosophers are in fact the very opposite of mystics. Coolly rational and purposeful men, they ground their admitted inwardness in the partly spiritual nature of reality. 'Nowhere does the world, in all its bearings, spiritual or material, theoretic or practical, lie pictured in clearer or truer colours', according to Carlyle, 'than in such heads as these' (*Works* 26:76).

This recognition that the priority of reflection in German philosophy involved no necessary neglect of the material and the practical does not make the early Carlyle himself a disciple of Kant. Unwilling to pronounce 'Kantism' either true or false, he asserts merely that there is some truth in it, along with hope for the future of society. The Germans correctly insist, against the empiricists, that the bedrock of certainty is neither the world received through the senses nor the common sense of human kind, but rather certain 'obscured but ineffaceable characters, within our inmost being' (*Works* 26:81). A consciousness of these internal imprints at least indicates the existence of God, the soul, and the responsible will, truths in which the reflective spirit may find not refuge from observation and action, but the source of their meaning. In Kant, as in Plato, not only does the truest knowledge originate in self-knowledge, but the internal realities at first obscured by the material world become the very basis for engagement in that world.[6] These realities are known, moreover, not by mystical intuition, but by a reflective power belonging to the ordinary constitution of the human mind: Kant's reason, or *Vernunft*, as distinguished from the understanding, *Verstand* (*Works* 26:81–2).

Carlyle does not formally accept this distinction in 'The State of German Literature', nor does he pretend to do justice to the subtleties in Kant's presentation of it (*Works* 26:83). His sympathetic sketch of the distinction indicates the strength, however, of his attraction to it. 'Understanding' in Kant, as Carlyle explains it, organises the information we gather from our senses, constitutes the world as it materially appears to us, and constructs practical sciences like political economy. Focusing on the relation of means to ends, Understanding also drives our conduct of the ordinary business of life. But because it cannot grasp the immaterial, Understanding can function successfully only so long as it confines itself to this work of managing surfaces. The realities of the soul, God, and moral duty are so far beyond it that any effort the Understanding may make to establish their existence ends up distorting them. Understanding can see no more in virtue, for example, than utility, in prudence than self-interest, in art than formal expertise.[7] But the world is not so hollowed out, according to Carlyle: altruism and inspiration do exist, and matter has the vital interior the Germans see in it (*Works* 26:85–6). 'That religion is not hope and fear, or duty and prudence, or art a skill to please, that behind the sensible there lies a spiritual, and beneath all relative phenomena an absolute reality was', wrote James Martineau, Carlyle's 'first inspiration' (267). Nothing exists more certainly than God and the soul, he thought, and with anyone who would deny these immaterial realities he must, as he says, 'agree to differ' (*Works* 26:70–1).[8]

Carlyle's belief in a non-phenomenal order of existence does not mean that he accepts Kant's Reason, however, as the power of apprehending it. Without the reflective introspection Reason makes possible, religion and poetry remain for him the faint caricatures of themselves available to Understanding, and duty itself a mechanical round of actions without meaning. So reductive of the significance of life does Carlyle find Understanding, in fact, that he thinks philosophically establishing Reason as a value-giving power distinct from Understanding is vital to anyone concerned about nineteenth-century Europe's fading sense of the spiritual. Personally, Carlyle has no doubt that the mind has valid knowledge of invisible objects. The Kantian's Reason is no mere philosophical contrivance, in his view, to make the old religious prejudices look objective. He even admires the Kantians for holding the middle ground between the empiricists, who equate affirmation of the existence of Reason with enthusiasm or mysticism, and the religious, who suspect it of infidelity. But he cannot make that affirmation himself because the Kantians have not yet proven it, as he says, 'scientifically'. Carlyle regrets the spread of scepticism about the possibility of knowing immaterial realities because it has created a culture of mere Understanding that leaves 'no home for the soul' (*Works* 26:83, 85). And while the Germans have still not created a spiritual culture to contest the new supremacy of Understanding, the hope they offer for such a future, however slight, is to be acknowledged and encouraged.

In 'Novalis's, first published in the *Foreign Review* (1829), Carlyle tests out the possibility of such a future. Novalis was no 'mystic', he says, in the sense that he is impossible to understand (*Works* 27:22). He lived and wrote in the spirit of Fichte and of 'Kantism, or German metaphysics generally' (*Works* 27:23), which sought to overthrow the empiricists' naïve faith in the self-subsistence of matter. German metaphysics is no 'mere intellectual card-castle, or logical hocus-pocus', Carlyle insists, 'with no bearing on the practical interests of men' (*Works* 27:26). Carefully understood, it does not deny the existence of the material world, but only their independence of our categories for perceiving them. Nor is this internal character of matter absolute because it may likewise be, as in Fichte, an impression, or 'Manifestation of Power', from something outside, or beyond, the human self (*Works* 27:25).[9] Here again Carlyle, without himself adopting the German view of material objects as phenomena of mind, understands its 'boundless importance', especially to morals and religion, if it were to become widespread (*Works* 27:26). If time and space are simply human categories for organising the world, for example, an eterna , omnipresent God transcending those categories would appear much easier to argue, as would the origin and subsistence of the world in such a transcendent mind.[10] But Carlyle clearly foresees that such an idealising tendency will not necessarily usher in some unambiguous culture of the spirit.A philosophy in which knowledge is governed not by the external world, but by an apparatus of mind that could just as well have been constructed differently, may indeed open the way to a new theology, but it may just as easily encourage doubt about the objectivity of any knowledge whatsoever. In such a philosophy, as Carlyle says, 'all inductive conclusions, all conclusions of the Understanding, have only a relative truth;' they 'are true only for *us*, and *if* some other thing be true' (*Works* 27:27).

Carlyle distances himself from these mixed consequences of German metaphysics under the figure of Novalis, who in this respect anticipates the fictional Teufelsdröckh of *Sartor Resartus*. Novalis represents the German effort to head off the relativism of the Understanding by positioning Reason's confident knowledge of the immaterial over against it. Carlyle doubts neither the realities of spirit Reason seeks to guarantee nor their availability to an ordinary, non-mystical power of the mind. He too wishes to ground poetry, religion, and ethics in some such capacity for reflecting on the imprints of the soul, God, and the responsible will within the self, and he sees clearly that Kant's Understanding can offer no such ground 'except a false one' (*Works* 27:27). Carlyle is wary of that self-reflective power, however, because of the ease with which it effectively annihilates the material world.[11]

For Carlyle's Novalis, matter is not only an appearance but a transparent manifestation of the divine without any solidity of its own. Spirit is so near and objective to Novalis that it is, according to Carlyle, his 'only reality' (*Works* 27:28). Not that he avoids observation and detail: Novalis reveres nature as the voice of God, and his writings make remarkable order and sense out of the complex history of thought (*Works* 27:29, 36). Carlyle appreciates the synthetic power of Novalis's mind and sympathises with his Pauline feeling that in God we 'live, move and have our being' (*Acts* 17.28). But he infers that the preference of Novalis for synthesising the facts of nature and history, rather than breaking them down into their separate parts, overlooks the intractability of those facts. Novalis's desire to make the world a 'universally connected Whole' neglects it as a 'divisible Aggregate' (*Works* 27:28).

Carlyle in no way denies that the material world is an aggregate, or that we have a reflective power to know it as such. He insists merely that nature and fact have a weight of their own at enmity with the tendency to order and unify them. History, the body, objects of sensation – these are the realities closest and most objective to Carlyle. Novalis's proximity to a spiritual order prevailing within them, as reluctant as Carlyle is to doubt it, is foreign to him. Nor does he think that such an order, real as it may be, is supported by Kant's Understanding, to which nature and history appear hostile to spirit. Carlyle's Novalis avoids this 'hostility of matter' (*Works* 27:26) by converting facts into types of God's presence before he confronts their disordered particularity. In short, he lived too exclusively in the 'Light of Reason'. Carlyle agrees with Novalis that the temporal world only distantly parodies the 'Eternal City' and offers no 'home for the soul' (*Works* 27:29; 26:85). The utility that unreflective minds mistake for virtue, for example, merely mimics it. But utility has a reality for Carlyle that Novalis is too ready to turn into a mere 'vassal' before the 'Majesty of Reason' (*Works* 27:28). Novalis needs an Editor, as will Teufelsdröckh, to speak up for the degree of reality the earthly city does have, shadow though it is of a world beyond it.

Carlyle simultaneously respects the visible world and finds it soulless. He wants the relative permeable to be spiritual, but he dislikes Kant's Reason for being too spiritual. Every effort of the Understanding to rise above the relative, he believes, merely caricatures the absolute. Reason alone provides certainty, yet it is at the expense of the ephemeral, as in Novalis's mysticism. Carlyle moves beyond these dilemmas in 'Characteristics' (1831) by distinguishing between a healthy and a diseased form of self-consciousness. The healthy kind, as self-reflectively spiritual as Reason, nevertheless remains immersed in nature and history. It is exemplified in the old dogmatic metaphysics, which explained phenomena in such a way as to provide a basis for confident action. Diseased self-consciousness occurs when new phenomena, unexplainable by past certainties, prompt a necessary scepticism, like Hume's, that can seek certainty only by denying its possibility. This negative form of reflection effectively discourages action by forever questioning the grounds of it (*Works* 28:26–8). It is reflection for its own sake, not for the world's, and it transcends the needs of society and the demands of politics as falsely as any sublimely self-involved mysticism ever did.

Carlyle endorses the energising reflection that gives meaning to action.[12] He believes it necessary, in fact, if the supremacy of the relativistic and sceptical Understanding is to be overthrown and a more affirmative phase of culture is to be ushered in ('Characteristics', *Works* 28:42–3). The only self-consciousness Carlyle deplores is the kind that can 'listen only to itself', whether it is sceptical like Hume's or semi-mystical, as he thought Coleridge's was (*Works* 28:25). Even so acute a reader as Martineau erroneously believed that in 'Characteristics' Carlyle rejects self-consciousness altogether, when in fact he there advocates an engaged form of it. Effective activism requires a self aware of its own depths – 'a region of meditation', as Carlyle calls it, 'underneath [that] of argument and conscious discourse'. All goodness, religion, and poetry (as opposed to mere precept, observance, and artfulness) comes from that region. Martineau mistook this reflective descent into the self for a plunge into 'currents of indistinctive nature' devoid of conscious rationality (270). Carlyle did not recommend unreason, however, but Kantian Reason as he interpreted it – a power in the self to access the 'vital force' at the source of its creative, not 'merely manufactured', work (*Works* 28:4–5).

As heedless as Coleridge could be of the listeners to his talk, or of the daily business of living and writing, he taught a form of reflection even closer to empirical fact than that espoused by Carlyle. 'Of all systems that have ever been presented', he said of his own philosophy, 'this has the least of Mysticism' (*Coleridge Letters* 4:706). Carlyle regarded matter as antagonistic to spirit, and Kant's Understanding as instinctively at odds with Reason.[13] The more we know nature and history, he thought, the more we find our vision of the realities of spirit impaired. Understanding, in Carlyle's secularised version of Christianity, is the prideful milieu of our fallen condition. It keeps doubting the 'mysterious Self-impulse of the whole man, heaven-inspired and in all senses partaking of the Infinite' until nothing remains of that inspired centre but its 'outward Mechanism' (*Works* 28:9). It is not a healthy awareness of our centre that makes us egotistical, in Carlyle's view, but this sceptical reduction of it to its material shell – the absence, in other words, of a complete self-consciousness. Here is the source of the diseased introspection that turns intuition into logic-chopping, affection into benevolence, moral action into moral theories, and religion into metaphysics. We can never entirely escape this disease since it is the 'material', says Carlyle, 'which Action has to fashion into Certainty and Reality' (*Works* 26:26). But we must defy it anyway with a confident subjectivity – Teufelsdröckh's 'Everlasting Yea' – that becomes psychologically possible at a time of personal crisis, and anyone incapable of so becoming 'a new creature' will 'necessarily founder' (*Works* 28:6).

Paradoxically, Carlyle's dislike of mysticism ends up depending on the illuminated subjectivity of some select, 'saved' individuals.

The kind of reflection that informs action in Coleridge's thought is not as antagonistic to Understanding as that recommended by Carlyle, but instead continuously open to self-correction by external circumstances. This strikingly empirical element in his thinking is evident as early as 1809 when, attacking the political philosophy of Hobbes on the one hand and Rousseau on the other, Coleridge warns readers of *The Friend* not to misinterpret his admiration of Reason as slighting Understanding (STC *Works* 4:104).[14] Hobbes, he there argues, thinks that governments originate from human minds subject to the senses, whereas Rousseau maintains that they are formed from 'Principles contained in the REASON of Man' (STC *Works* 4:101, 105). Coleridge rejects both theories, but especially Rousseau's, which he finds far too dependent on absolute views of what the principles of Reason require, and hence 'undisciplined, and unhumbled, by practical Experience' – in short, 'the essence of JACOBISNIM' (STC *Works* 4:105). He therefore adopts a theory that, while recognising the union of sense, Understanding, and Reason in every act of the human mind, does not hesitate to take Understanding, 'the faculty of suiting Measures to circumstances', as the principal guide to political conduct. Coleridge believes that government is derived 'from human *Prudence*', and the need to adjust the universals of Reason to what Experience has proved to be expedient (STC *Works* 4:103–4). Like Carlyle, he is aware of the tendency of Reason, when forgetful of Understanding, to degenerate into solipsistic disregard of the world as it is. More acutely than Carlyle, he recognises its potential for a dangerous political absolutism.

However carefully they qualified their discussions of philosophical Reason, Coleridge and Carlyle both thought some form of it was necessary to effect significant political change. They agreed that the immaterial is real, and that the only way to know it is through the reflection on the spiritual self that gives meaning and value to action. They also agreed that Europe's increasingly mechanised present threatened the capacity for reflection that had driven its religious, ethical and aesthetic past. Each denied that this capacity is confined to an initiated few. Introspection might seduce some into spiritualising nature and history out of existence on the one hand or, on the other, emptying them of spirit altogether. But Coleridge and Carlyle both pinned their hopes for a humane future on a form of reflection that engaged with the external world through the empirical Understanding. They realised that the Understanding, competent though it is to constitute knowledge, advance science, and increase efficiency, cannot deal with the inner activities of religious contemplation, moral decision-making, and aesthetic appreciation without turning them into parodies of themselves.

Each asked how, in an age that overvalued Understanding, the works of Reason were to go on? Had not Kant's destruction of metaphysics - his denial that Reason could achieve any theoretical certainty that God, the soul, and moral freedom even existed - robbed the culture of spirit of the solid foundation it was once thought to have?

Carlyle and Coleridge answered these questions in substantially different ways. Carlyle doubted the power even of substantial numbers of reflective individuals to contest the post-Enlightenment supremacy of Understanding, which had moved the intangibles of Reason to the edges of cultural concern.[15] A dominant analytical cast of mind had not merely distorted the realities of spirit (as in supposed 'proofs' of God's existence or 'explanations' of aesthetic response), but it had also eroded the reflective habits that nourished awareness of these realities. Carlyle chose to attack the cult of Understanding not on its own grounds, but by insisting on the prerogatives of spiritual intuition. He had no doubt that experience posed formidable obstacles to distinguishing justice from self-interest, and that the two were generally confused. But he thought reflection could afford a sense of the 'the just' that, combined with a will to act, could become the basis for productive social change (*Works* 28:41). Carlyle believed that the patient study of particulars was as necessary a spur to effective political action as prophetic certainty. But the indignant vehemence of his style suggests that he considered the latter by far the more important of the two.

Coleridge had responded to the prevailingly material and practical concerns of his age far differently. He had subdued the Miltonic voice of such early reflective poems as 'Religious Musings' and 'The Destiny of Nations' and adopted a more accessible, conversational form of address. The poet-prophet of 'France: an Ode' and 'Fears in Solitude' became the poet-sufferer of 'Dejection: an Ode' and 'Work without Hope' - one who himself struggled with the impoverishment of spirit he protested in society at large. For his first periodical venture in 1796 Coleridge named himself a *Watchman* after Ezekiel and Isaiah; in the second (1809-10) he became simply *The Friend* (STC *Works* 2: xxix).[16] A 1796 letter to his radical friend, John Thelwall, anticipated this shift of self-image from aloof decrier of social ills to sympathetic sufferer of their consequences. Coleridge there insisted that his preference for metaphysics, psychology, and religion by no means excluded historical and scientific inquiry and that his impassioned opposition to the error of irreligion implied no 'personal asperity' toward the irreligious. Reflection on the realities of spirit did not neglect mundane facts any more in Coleridge than in Carlyle. Coleridge's opposition to materialism and historicism does not reject matter and history, and if he appears to reject materialists and historicists, it is only because he is 'ever so swallowed up' in their theories as to 'perfectly forget' the individuals who held them

(*Coleridge Letters* 1:260). Carlyle believed Coleridge took refuge from history in arcane philosophical speculations. On the contrary, Coleridge thought that history originated in just such speculations: '[T]he mighty epochs of commerce, that have changed the face of empires', along with the most important 'discoveries and improvements in the mechanic arts', were due primarily not to statesmen and businessmen, but to philosophers. Their 'visions' do not escape history, but reshape it (STC *Works* 6:14).[17]

The error at the root of his times, in Coleridge's analysis, was applying the empirical Understanding to truths of spirit that only Reason can conceive, let alone subject to coherent discourse. Coleridge had learnt from Kant that the Understanding found such truths ('Before Abraham *was*, I *am*', for example) contradictory and inexpressible (STC *Works* 9:233). Accepting the inadequacy of the Understanding outside its own province, Carlyle substituted for it the prophet-hero's firm grasp of the principles of Reason and his willingness to act on them decisively. When Coleridge called Reason an inner eye that beheld the spiritual, just as the outer eye beholds the sensible, it may seem that he leaves himself as liable as Carlyle to imposing some supposedly objective absolutes on a society whose moral vision he regards as comparatively dim (STC *Works* 9:223–4). But Coleridge's renovated society was not as centred as Carlyle's on the reflective capacity of certain 'seers'. It depended rather, to Carlyle's dismay, on 'the idea of a National Church' – that '*idea*' being the aim, only progressively realisable, of measuring the existing institutions of society against the universal truths of Reason (STC *Works* 10:56–7).

While Coleridge had opinions about the principal social issues of his time, he did not generally appeal to his own vision of those universal truths to support specific political changes or to suggest how they should be implemented. In his view reform should not depend on prophets alone. He was equally sceptical of relying on Reason to propose political solutions without consulting the Understanding. Coleridge's expectations of reform were less urgent and apocalyptic than Carlyle's. He based them on the national church not because he thought the current forms of that church approximated the 'idea' of it, but because it diffused reflective communities throughout society and so increased the chances of getting Reason's work done.[18]

Notes

1 See also 'Instinctive Kantian' 60.

2 On this division in Carlyle's response to Coleridge see Harrold 52–3 and Ashton, 73–4.

3 Harrold (51, 124, 131–4), Sanders (48, 165–6) and Ashton (47, 74) all emphasise the similarity in Coleridge's and Carlyle's version of the Reason/Understanding distinction and sharply differentiate both their versions from Kant's. But Coleridge, despite his frequent slighting of the understanding, almost as frequently praises it and shows himself, in this respect, much more aware than Carlyle of the high regard in which Kant held it.

4 See Ashton (1–2, 18–19, 67–9) on the impetus and influence of this essay, originally published in the *Edinburgh Review*, and on the English resistance to German thought that Carlyle, like Coleridge before him, had to contest.

5 According to Ashton (94), however, Carlyle himself lacked the 'stamina' to understand Kant carefully. See also Harrold (10, 11–12). For a different view, see Sorensen (1998:56,59), who emphasises Carlyle's responsiveness to Kant as a practical moralist while acknowledging Carlyle's tendency to assimilate Kant's views into those of Fichte, Schelling, Novalis, and Hegel.

6 Significantly, however, the ideas of Reason merely regulate action in Kant; they yield no certainty of corresponding metaphysical realities.

7 Harrold's important differentiation of Kant's doctrine of the understanding from Carlyle's version of it (127–34) does not directly concern us here.

8 See Sanders (168) on Carlyle's fundamental agreement with Coleridge on this issue.

9 On Carlyle's tendency to conflate Fichte with Kant, see Harrold 102–3.

10 This is an argument Kant himself would have rejected, as Harrold (95) and Ashton (97) correctly point out.

11 Harrold (92, 103) overemphasises both the unreality of the empirical world to Carlyle and his early attraction to the Germans' spiritualising of it. Matter had value to Carlyle beyond its usefulness as an instrument for the realisation of spirit.

12 He also knew 'that thought itself was a form of action, and might be for individuals or epochs the duty that lay nearest to them' – a duty especially for his own epoch 'when the skeptical philosophy of Hume had to be met with a new constructive or dogmatic metaphysic' (Muirhead 135).

13 See 'Novalis', *Works* 27:27, where Carlyle seems to approve of, without entirely endorsing, Friedrich Heinrich Jacobi's untraced statement that 'it is the instinct of Understanding to *contradict* Reason'. Carlyle here appears also to confuse Jacobi (1743–1819) with his elder brother Johann Georg (1740–1814), who was a poet (see Harrold 17, 125, 254).

14 Coleridge did not increasingly debase the Kantian understanding 'as he pressed metaphysics into the service of religion' (Ashton 47), nor did Reason ever lose 'all its Kantian meaning' for him and become exclusively 'an organ of faith' (Harrold 124).

15 See Sanders 165–6, 174.

16 The prophetic stance lingers on in Coleridge, as in the 1817 collection of his poems he called *Sibylline* Leaves, but much less insistently.

17 See Sanders 65–6.

18 On the ideas of community and the national church in Coleridge, see Wendling, 88–9, 173.

Works Cited

Ashton, Rosemary. *The German Idea: Four English Writers and the Reception of German Thought 1800–1860*. Cambridge: Cambridge UP, 1980.

Coleridge, Samuel Taylor. *Collected Letters of Samuel Taylor Coleridge*. Ed. E. L. Griggs. 6 vols. Oxford: Oxford UP, 1956–71.

———. *Collected Works of Samuel Taylor Coleridge*. Ed. Kathleen Coburn, Bart Winer, et al. 16 vols. Princeton NJ: Princeton UP, 1969–2002.

Harrold, Charles Frederick. *Carlyle and German Thought: 1819–1834*. 1934; rpt. London: Archon, 1963.

Martineau, James. 'Personal Influences on Present Theology'. *National Review* (Oct. 1856); rpt. *Essays, Reviews, and Addresses*. 4 vols. London: Longmans, Green, 1890–91. 219–81.

Muirhead, John Henry. *Coleridge as Philosopher*. London and New York: Allen and Unwin; Macmillan, 1930.

Sanders, Charles Richard. *Coleridge and the Broad Church Movement: Studies in S. T. Coleridge, Dr. Arnold of Rugby, J. C. Hare, Thomas Carlyle and F. D. Maurice*. 1932; rpt. New York: Octagon, 1972.

Sorensen, David R. 'An Instinctive Kantian: Carlyle, Kant and the Vital Interests of Men'. *Carlyle Studies Annual* 18 (1998): 53–63.

———. '"The Invention of Reality": Carlyle's Allegorical Autobiography in *Sartor Resartus*'. In *La Littérature autobiographique en Grand-Bretagne et en Irlande*. Ed. Robert Ferrieux. Paris: Ellipses, 2001. 206–16.

Wendling, Ronald C. *Coleridge's Progress to Christianity: Experience and Authority in Religious Faith*. Lewisburg, PA: Bucknell UP, 1995.

Chapter 9

Carlyle and Symbolism

CAIRNS CRAIG

In 1899, Arthur Symons published his influential study of *The Symbolist Movement in Literature*, which provided the first account in English of the radical changes that had been taking place in French literature since mid-century. The book's relevance was noted by T. S. Eliot in 1930: 'I myself owe Mr Symons a great debt: but for having read his book I should not, in the year 1908, have heard of Laforgue or Rimbaud; I should probably not have begun to read Verlaine; and but for reading Verlaine, I should not have heard of Corbière' (Symons xv). As Eliot recognised, Symons established the foundations of modern poetic theory in the Anglophone world. His influence is apparent not only in Yeats's theory of symbols and *A Vision* (1927), but also in Eliot's notion of 'the objective correlative' and Pound's 'imagism', in which the image is little more than the secularisation of the hieratic 'symbol' of Symons's book.

Rodger L. Tarr has remarked in his introduction to *Sartor Resartus* that Carlyle 'anticipated by fifty years the Symbolist Movement' and that his conception of the 'symbol' can be found in many places in late nineteenth- and early twentieth-century literature (SR xxvii). Such appearances, however, are not necessarily the result of a direct indebtedness to Carlyle. Yet in the single most influential critical book of the 1890s, Symons opens with an epigraph from *Sartor Resartus* – 'It is in and through Symbols that man, consciously or unconsciously, lives, works, and has his being: those ages, moreover, are accounted the noblest, which can the best recognise symbolical worth, and prize it at the highest' (1). Later, he cites another passage from *Sartor Resartus* that had been frequently used by French symbolists:

> In a symbol there is concealment and yet revelation: hence therefore, by Silence and by Speech acting together, comes a double significance... In the Symbol proper, what we can call a Symbol, there is ever, more or less distinctly and directly, some embodiment and revelation of the Infinite; the Infinite is made to blend itself with the Finite, to stand visible, and as it were, attainable there. (2)

Using Carlyle's definition of the symbol, Symons identifies the key developments of modern French poetry, extending from Baudelaire to Mallarmé. In turn, Anglophone writers of the first four decades of the twentieth century absorbed Carlyle's influence through their reading of *The Symbolist Movement in Literature.*

The context of Carlyle's assertion of the significance of the 'symbol' is his development of the idealism of German post-Kantian philosophy, and particularly the work of Schelling. He regarded Germanic idealism as an antidote to the constrictive and 'mechanical' conceptions of the working of the mind in the Scottish tradition. But as Ralph Jessop has persuasively demonstrated, 'Carlyle's writings can be valuably related to Scottish philosophical discourse' (10). Ostensibly, Carlyle's argument represented a counterblast to the thinking of Thomas Brown, his professor of philosophy at Edinburgh University. Brown had developed the associationism of Hume into a thoroughgoing 'mental chemistry' that could account for even the most complex states of mind on the basis of simple constituents:

> In this spontaneous chemistry of mind, the compound sentiment that results from the association of former feelings has in many cases, on first consideration, so little resemblance to these constituents of it, as formerly [existed] in their elementary state, that it requires the most attentive reflection to separate...the assemblages which even a few years have produced. (Warren 79)

Just as Coleridge developed his idealist philosophy by rejecting the associationism of Hartley's *Observations on Man* (1749), so too did Carlyle embrace 'natural supernaturalism' by repudiating the Brown-Hume tradition. For both men, the crucial failure of associationism lies in its inability to account for the workings of the creative imagination. As Carlyle observes in 'Signs of the Times' (1829), associationism represents art in a brutally reductive manner:

> We have our little *theory* on all human and divine things. Poetry, the workings of genius itself, which in all times, with one or another meaning, has been called Inspiration, and held to be mysterious and inscrutable, is no longer without its scientific exposition. The building of the lofty rhyme is like any other masonry or bricklaying: we have theories of its rise, height, decline and fall, – which latter, it would seem, is now near, among all people. Of our 'Theories of Taste', as they are called, wherein the deep, infinite, unspeakable Love of Wisdom and Beauty, which dwells in all men, is 'explained', made mechanically visible, from 'Association' and the like, why should we say anything. Hume has written us a 'Natural History of Religion'; in which one Natural History and all the rest are included. (*Works* 27:76)

The connections he establishes here summarise his relationship with the traditions of Scottish philosophy in the half century before he went to Edinburgh University. His allusion to 'taste' embraces a broad philosophical tradition, which originated with David Hume and received its most complete expression in Archibald Alison's *Essays on the Nature and Principles of Taste* (1790). For both Hume and Alison, poetry and art could be explained by the principle of associationism. Carlyle would have known Alison's work through Francis Jeffrey, who reviewed the second edition of the book in *The Edinburgh Review* in 1811.

Jeffrey's article exerted a considerable influence because it later formed the basis of the entry on 'Taste' in the *Encyclopedia Britannica*. He agreed with Alison that the principle of association accurately defines the experience of art. The value of the work of art is not *in* the work of art itself, but in the mind of the person who experiences it. Suspended from ordinary utilitarian occupations, the mind is allowed to revive and explore its own associations and to follow them wherever they might lead. In effect, the work of art says nothing by itself: it is simply the occasion for an exploration of the associative patterns of memory. As Jeffrey argues in his review of Alison's work:

> The grand mistake, indeed, which seems to have misled almost all the inquirers into this curious subject, consists in their taking it for granted, that beauty, in whatever variety of objects it might be found, was always in itself one and the same; and that, in order to explain the beauty of any one particular thing, it was necessary to show that that it had some quality in common with all other things that were beautiful...But if it be true, that the emotions which we receive from beauty are thus various in themselves, and that they partake thus largely of the character of other emotions, why should we not conclude, that they are but modifications of these more familiar affections, - and that the beauty which we impute to external objects, is nothing more than their power of reflecting these several inward affections? (7)

Art's fundamental significance is in reactivating emotions that are significant in the personal life of the aesthetic 'observer'. The most effective art is that which encourages the reader to 'forget' it as an object in itself, and to discover it as reflection of his or her own past emotional experiences. Jeffrey argues 'that these emotions are not original emotions, nor produced directly by any qualities in the objects which excite them; but are reflections, or images, of the more radical and familiar emotions to which we have already alluded; and are occasioned, not by any inherent virtue in the objects before us, but by the accidents, if we may so express ourselves, by which these may have been enabled to suggest or recall to us our own past sensations or sympathies' (8). As his reference to Hume suggests, Carlyle rejects this theory because it reduces art to a merely psychological phenomenon that has no grounding in reality. In an associationist context, all art is simply the stimulus to associations which its audience happen to bring to it. Art has no significance beyond its appeal to those associative clusters that the artist knows in advance will be effective for that particular audience, or which accidentally happen to be produced by that audience. In short, art points to nothing but the workings of the human mind.

Contrary to the claims of many literary historians, the associationist theory did not die as a consequence of its refutation by Coleridge. It was sufficiently alive in 1829 to require Carlyle's dismissal in *Sartor Resartus* and it continued to attract Symon's attention in the 1890s. Describing the work of Mallarmé, a 'symbolist' for whom each word is only the 'notation of the free breath of spirit' (70), Symons reverts to an associationist account of how the poet composes:

> Remember his principle: that to name, is to destroy, to suggest is to create. Note, further, that he condemns the inclusion in verse of anything but, 'for example, the horror of the forest, or the silent thunder afloat in the leaves, not the intrinsic, dense wood of the trees'. He had received, then, a mental sensation: let it be the horror of the forest. This sensation begins to form in his brain, at first probably no more than a rhythm...Imagine the poem written down, at least composed. In its very imperfection, it is clear, it shows the links by which it had been riveted together: the whole process of construction can be studied. Now most writers would be content: but with Mallarmé the work has only begun...By the time the poem has reached, as it seems to him, a flawless unity, the steps of the progress have been only too effectually effaced: and while the poet, who has seen the thing from the beginning, still sees the relation of point to point, the reader, who comes at it only in the final stage, finds himself in a not unnatural bewilderment. (71–2)

Symons redefines the transcendental force of the 'symbol', which is an 'embodiment and revelation of the Infinite'. In his version, Mallarmé's style of writing is designed to destroy our ability to follow the poet's associational process, thus leaving us entirely in the grip of our own associations. This was to be the pattern of much of nineteenth-century British aesthetics: the transcendentalist argument was frequently challenged by a vigorous empiricist tradition that sought to explain higher spiritual or aesthetic realities in empirical terms.

Carlyle was familiar with this tactic, since the most dedicated extrapolator of empirical explanations of 'transcendental' truths was his early follower (and later, his implacable opponent) John Stuart Mill. Against both the romantic notion of art and the renewed 'common sense' tradition of Dugald Stewart and Sir William Hamilton, Mill defended the associationist principles put forward by his father James Mill in *Analysis of the Phenomena of the Human Mind* (1829). Mill Sr. sought to prove that complex experiences that *appear* to be of an entirely different order can be derived from the simple actions of associative connection. In other words, so-called 'mechanical' processes in the mind can give rise to those forms of consciousness that are defined as 'organic'. James Mill uses the metaphor of a spinning prism to describe this process:

> [W]hen a wheel, on the seven parts of which the seven prismatic colours are respectively painted, is made to revolve rapidly, it appears not of seven colours, but of one uniform colour, white. By the rapidity of succession, the several sensations cease to be distinguishable: they run, as it were, together, and a new sensation, compounded of all the seven, but apparently a simple one is the result. Ideas, also, which have been so often conjoined that whenever one exists in the mind, the others immediately exist along with it, seem to run into one another, to coalesce as it were, and out of many to form one idea; which idea, however in reality complex, appears to be no less simple, than any one of those of which it is compounded. (1:68–9)

The 'white light' demonstrates how association can generate higher forms of consciousness entirely out of simple and apparently mechanical operations, which require no postulation of a transcendental consciousness to justify it. In 'Characteristics' (1831) Carlyle employs a similar metaphor to describe the purity of childhood, when 'the body had not yet become the prison-house of the soul'. He regrets the loss of this unconscious spirituality, which renders life 'a pure, perpetual, unregarded music; a beam of perfect white light, rendering all things visible, but itself unseen, even because it was of that perfect whiteness, and no irregular obstruction had yet broken it into colours'. Here the 'perfect white light' is a symbol of spiritual wholeness that will later be shattered and fragmented by 'mechanical' definitions of epistemology. Carlyle insists that 'what [man] can altogether know and comprehend, is essentially the mechanical, small; the great is ever, in one sense or other, the vital; it is essentially the mysterious, and only the surface of it can be understood' (*Works* 28:2–3).

For John Stuart Mill and the empirical psychologists with whom he worked – particularly Alexander Bain of the University of Aberdeen – every 'mysterious' higher unity could be explained by the 'mechanical' associationist principles dismissed by transcendentalists such as Carlyle. For example, in *An Examination of Sir William Hamilton's Philosophy* (1865), Mill shows how, in the act of reading, we construct higher orders of meaning from lower-order processes:

> After reading a chapter of a book, when we lay down the volume do we remember to have been individually conscious of the printed letters and syllables which have passed before us? Could we recall, by any effort of mind, the visible aspect presented by them, unless some unusual circumstances has fixed our attention upon it during the perusal? Yet each of these letters and syllables must have been present to us as a sensation for at least a passing moment, or the sense could not have been conveyed to us. But the sense being the only thing in which we are interested...we retain no impression of the separate letters and syllables. This instance is the more instructive, inasmuch as, the whole process taking place within our means of observation, we know that out knowledge began with the parts and not with the whole. (Mill, *CW* 9:257–8)

Far from having to construct the world from atomistic fragments which could never be combined except by conjunction, association theory worked with 'wholes' that consisted of lesser and often unobserved units. The structure of the 'whole' may be retained by the mind even when its parts have decayed from recollection. From this position, Mill develops his theory of 'signs' as unacknowledged associations that are transmuted almost instantaneously into higher-order wholes of which we alone are conscious. Rather than the universe being a 'language' of symbols, as Carlyle claims in *Sartor Resartus*, language is revealed by Mill as the very demonstration of a material and mechanical process of the human mind, which is association. At every turn, the factors that transcendentalists appealed to as the revelation of a higher form of knowledge were converted by the empiricists into a mental experience explicable through a process of association. Carlyle might declare that 'no meanest object is insignificant; all objects are as windows, through which the philosophic eye looks into Infinitude itself' (SR 55), but the associationist would resolve that experience into a purely psychological phenomena, which says nothing about the external world and reveals only the associative processes of the thinker himself.

The debate between Teufeldröckh's transcendentalism and the Editor's scepticism in *Sartor Resartus* dramatises the conflict analysed by Mill. Carlyle begins with the power of 'SILENCE', which, unlike white light, cannot be broken down into its component parts: 'In a symbol there is concealment and yet revelation: here therefore, by Silence and by Speech acting together, comes a doubled significance' (SR 162). Because 'Speech is of Time, Silence of Eternity', the silence of the symbol makes it gateway to the Infinite:

> In the Symbol proper, what we can call a Symbol, there is ever, more or less distinctly and directly, some embodiment and revelation of the Infinite;

> the Infinite is made to blend itself with the Finite, to stand visible, and as it were, attainable, there. By Symbols, accordingly, is man guided and commanded, made happy, made wretched. He everywhere finds himself encompassed with Symbols, recognised as such or not recognised: the Universe is but one vast Symbol of God. (SR 162–3)

Carlyle defines 'the Symbol proper' – the Symbol as revelation of the Infinite – but he soon distinguishes two different types, which possess either 'extrinsic' or 'intrinsic' (SR 164) value. Symbols which have 'extrinsic' value are those which are simply the products of contingent mental connections – associations – and their significance is simply as testimony to human activity, not as gatekeepers of the infinite. Interpreting Teufesldröckh's philosophy of symbols, the Editor points to the 'clouted Shoe, which the Peasants bore aloft with them as ensign in their *Bauernkriek* (Peasants' War)'. Of such symbols, he remarks that 'Intrinsic significance these had none: only extrinsic; as the accidental Standards of multitudes more or less sacredly uniting together' (SR 164). In this sense, even the Cross of Christianity is nothing but an 'extrinsic' symbol, the effect of the accumulation of associations with which the 'symbol' is imbued in the mind of the perceiver.

However, 'intrinsic' symbols present the interpreter with unique difficulties. As Carlyle explains, 'Another matter it is…when your Symbol has intrinsic meaning, and is of itself *fit* that men should unite round it'. When he attempts to define these symbols, he finds himself trapped in a vicious circle: 'Of this latter sort are all true Works of Art: in them (if thou know a Work of Art from a Daub of Artifice) wilt thou discern Eternity looking through Time; the Godlike rendered visible' (SR 165). What ought to be an aspect of the very form of the work of art becomes an element of its content discernible only to the truly seeing eye of the observer. How can the observer know whether he has engaged with a true 'Work of Art' or with impressions too multiplied, too minute, at once limitless and chaotic?

This problem compounds itself because 'intrinsic' symbols eventually begin to inherit 'extrinsic' qualities: 'Here too may an extrinsic value gradually superadd itself: thus certain *Iliads*, and the like, have, in three-thousand years, attained quite new significance'. Faced with the prospect of boundless interpretation, Carlyle appeals to stabler kinds of symbolism: 'But nobler than all in this kind are the Lives of heroic god-inspired Men; for what other Work of Art is so divine?' (SR 165). He started by trying to establish that the world had a divine symbolic meaning: here he concludes with a rhetorical question that leaves his audience poised over an abyss, since the answer to the question of 'what other work of art is so divine' may be, 'none – and not this one either'. Teufelsdröckh's text asserts the possibility of an 'intrinsic' symbol only to have it decay at each instance into an extrinsic symbol, so that the supposedly transcendental significance decays rapidly into a merely temporal significance.

The symbol as the gateway to eternity turns back into a series of merely associative connections, contingently linked in the memory of the perceiver: 'But, on the whole, as Time adds much to the sacredness of Symbols, so likewise in his progress he at length defaces, or even desecrates them; and Symbols, like all terrestrial Garments, wax old' (SR 165). In this moment of disintegration, a Prophet arrives 'who Prometheus-like, can shape few Symbols, and bring new Fire from Heaven to fix it there' (SR 166), but these too will eventually dissolve. It is the decay of the white light into its component colours, of the pure silence into speech, that haunts Carlyle's texts. The central justification of Teufelsdröckh's connection with the Infinite and justification of transcendentalism proves to be nothing more than the 'extrinsic' symbol already rendered inadequate to fulfil its role. If all symbols decay into the condition of being 'extrinsic' rather than 'instrinsic', then the notion of symbolism itself cannot support the weight of significance Carlyle attaches to it.

The angst of this process of symbol creation as the failed revelation of the divine inspires Carlyle's best historical writings, which convey the frustration of a world busily creating symbols of Infinity that prove to be nothing but the projection of accidental psychological processes. As Carlyle remarks in *The French Revolution*, 'Observe, however, that of man's whole terrestrial possessions and attainments, unspeakably the noblest are his Symbols, divine or divine-seeming; under which he marches and fights, with victorious assurance, in this life-battle' (*Works* 2:8). How do we tell the difference between the 'divine or divine-seeming'? Carlyle concedes that the central affirmation of the 'intrinsic' is always threatened by the 'extrinsic', the transcendental by the merely associative: 'Man, "Symbol of Eternity imprisoned into Time!" it is not thy works, which are all mortal, infinitely little, and the greatest no greater than the least, but only the Spirit though workest in, that can have worth or continuance' (*Works* 2:20–1). He reinforces his sense of uncertainty by appealing to his own definition of symbolism in *Sartor Resartus*. The ground of this symbol is not a defiance of time and history – as would be required by a transcendental notion of the symbol – but only an assertion of Carlyle's own will-to-transcendence, his personal identification with the source of all symbolic truth.

In *Sartor Resartus*, Carlyle unwittingly reinforced Mill's later defence of associationism. In his essay 'Bain's Psychology' (1859), Mill supported the arguments of Bain, who had repudiated John Ruskin's attempt to demolish associationism in *Modern Painters*, and demonstrated that his account of art was entirely compatible with associationist principles:

> Mr Ruskin would probably be much astonished were he to find himself held up as one of the principal apostles of the Association Philosophy in Art. Yet, in one of the most remarkable of his writings, the second volume of *Modern Painters*, he aims at establishing, by a large induction and searching analysis, that all things are beautiful (or sublime) which powerfully recall, and none but those which recall, one or more of a certain series of elevating and delightful thoughts. (*CW* 11:363–4)

Earlier, in *A System of Logic Ratiocinative and Inductive* (1843), Mill had declared that in Bain's work 'the laws of association have been more comprehensively stated and more largely exemplified than by any previous writer', and that author had provided 'incomparably the most complete analytical exposition of the mental phenomena, on the basis of a legitimate Induction, which has yet been produced' (*CW* 8:853n). Mill's belief in the associationist argument against transcendentalism never wavered. With Bain's assistance, he reissued his father's *Analysis of the Phenomena of the Human Mind* in 1869, certain of its continuing significance because its theories had been justified by the work of empirical psychologists such as Bain.

Mill's associationist account of the symbol was to be carried forward into the twentieth century by Yeats. In 'The Symbolism of Poetry' (1900), he echoes Symons in treating the symbol as the realisation of associationist principles: 'All sounds, all colours, all forms, either because of their preordained energies or because of long association, evoke indefinable and yet precise emotions, or, as I prefer to think, call down among us certain disembodied powers, whose footsteps over our hearts we call emotions' (156–7). Eliot too acknowledged the importance of the associationist argument, though more reluctantly. In *The Use of Poetry and the Use of Criticsm* (1933), he found himself unable to evade the language of association in trying to define the power of certain kinds of imagery whose 'intensity' resulted from 'its saturation – I will not say with "associations", for I do not want to revert to Hartley – but with feelings too obscure for the authors even to know what they are' (147–8).

But later in his essay 'The Music of Poetry' (1942), Eliot rehabilitated the language of association. He referred to this 'music' as 'a point of intersection: it arises from its relation first to the words immediately preceding and following it, and indefinitely to the rest of its context; and from another relation, that of its immediate meaning in that context to all the other meanings which it has had in other contexts, to its greater or less wealth of association'. For Eliot, 'Not all words, obviously, are equally rich and well-connected; it is part of the business of the poet to dispose the richer among the poorer, at the right points, and we cannot afford to load a poem too heavily with the former – for it is only at certain moments that a word can be made to insinuate the whole history of a language and of a culture' (32–3). The 'music of poetry' is not in the general process of association but in the poet's control of a particular moment, when the accumulated power of association is able to release into the reader's mind the whole history of a culture, through a memory which is neither personal nor 'mechanical'.

In Eliot's criticism, associationism has to be mitigated so that a symbol can be produced that will be significant to writer and reader, and not serve merely as a function of the reader's recollections. In his effort to restrict the effects of associationist theories, Eliot is the modern mirror image of Carlyle, who denied the associationist theory of symbols but in his own conception submitted to the very empiricist arguments he wished to overthrow. In *Sartor Resartus*, Carlyle dramatised the conflict that lies at the core of almost all modern and post-modern aesthetics. His symbol, which claims transcendental justification, may only be the psychological concomitant of certain associationist effects in the mind of the reader. Equally, the psychological processes of association may never be able to release the reader from anything but a personal response to works of literature. In his essay from 'Work to Text' (1971), Roland Barthes explains the paradoxical consequence of this confinement:

> The logic that governs the Text is not comprehensive (seeking to define 'what the work means') but metonymic: and the activity of associations, contiguities, and cross-references coincides with a liberation of symbolic energy… The Text is plural. This does not mean just that it has several meanings, but rather that it achieves plurality of meaning, an *irreducible* plurality. The Text is not coexistence of meanings but passage, transversal: thus it answers not to an interpretation, liberal though it may be, but to an explosion, a dissemination. (76).

Barthes' 'dissemination' overlaps with the deconstructive theories of Jacques Derrida, to whom Carlyle is also relevant. Derrida's undoing of the logic of a 'presence', with its desire to discover a transcendental signifier and its replacement with the dissemination of *différance,* repeats in a post-modern idiom the crisis of *Sartor Resartus*. In his description of the debate between Teufelsdröckh, who champions 'Symbolism' as a representation of the infinite, and the Editor, who sees in such symbols the play of multiple possible associations, Carlyle anticipates a philosophical 'conflux of two eternities' (*Works* 2:134).

Works Cited

Alison, Archibald. *Essays on the Nature and Principles of Taste*. Edinburgh: Bell & Bradfute, 1811.

Barthes, Roland, 'From Work to Text'. In *Textual Strategies: Perspectives in Post-Structuralist Criticism.* Ed. Josué V. Harari. London: Methuen, 1980. 73–81.

Eliot, T. S. *The Use of Poetry and the Use of Criticsm*, London, Faber, 1933.

———. Eliot, T. S. 'The Music of Poetry'. In *On Poetry and Poets.* London: Faber, 1957. 26–38.

Jeffrey, Francis. 'Alison on Taste'. *The Edinburgh Review* 18 (1811): 1–46.

Jessop, Ralph. *Carlyle and Scottish Thought.* London: Macmillan, 1997.

Mill, James. *Analysis of the Phenomena of the Human Mind*. 2 vols. London: Baldwin and Craddock, 1829.

Mill, John Stuart. *A System of Logic Ratiocinative and Inductive: Being a Connected View of the Principles of Evidence and the Methods of Scientific Investigation.* Vol. 8 of *Collected Works.* Ed. John M. Robson. London and Toronto: Routledge & Kegan Paul; U of Toronto P, 1974.

———. 'Bain's Psychology'. In *Essays on Philosophy and the Classics*. Vol. 11 of *Collected Works* (1978). Ed. John M. Robson. 339–74.

———. *An Examination of Sir William Hamilton's Philosophy*. Vol. 9 of *Collected Works* (1979). Ed. John M. Robson. 1979.

Symons, Arthur. *The Symbolist Movement in Literature.* Intro. Richard Ellmann. New York: E. P. Dutton, 1958.

Warren, Howard C. *A History of the Association Psychology*. London: Constable 1921.

Yeats, W. B. 'The Symbolism of Poetry'. *Essays and Introductions.* London: Macmillan, 1961. 153–64.

Chapter 10

Mark Twain, Thomas Carlyle, and Shooting Niagara

BRENT KINSER

Mark Twain called Thomas Carlyle's *The French Revolution* (1837) 'one of the greatest creations that ever flowed from a pen' (*Fairbanks* 207), and in 1896 made a pilgrimage to Carlyle's home in Cheyne Row, where he saw the only surviving manuscript fragment of the otherwise burnt first volume. Twain read other works by Carlyle as well. In 1883 he tried to convince his friend William Dean Howells to co-write a tragedy based upon *Oliver Cromwell's Letters and Speeches* (1845). Although the play was never written, Twain eventually developed the idea into 'The Death Disk' (1901), a short story which includes an introductory note identifying *Cromwell's Letters* as its source (Twain-Howells 1:455-9). Twain also once insisted to an editor that he had never read *Sartor Resartus* (1833-34); however, shortly after, he admitted to a friend that the clothes-philosophy in his story 'The Czar's Soliloquy' (1901) was inspired by Teufelsdröckh (Gribben 130). In 'My First Lie and How I got Out of It' (1899), he declared. 'I have a reverent affection for Carlyle's books and I have read his *Revolution* eight times' (167). He read it at least once more. Seeking solace on his deathbed, Twain recited passages from his worn copy of Carlyle's epic (Baetzhold 87).[1]

Carlyle's importance to Twain is not merely a question of influence. As Thomas C. Richardson has argued, 'The most significant levels of influence of Carlyle on Twain - or rather the most important responses of Twain to Carlyle for literary purposes - are in Twain's subtle (usually) but powerful adaptations of certain of Carlyle's metaphors to examine the human condition in nineteenth-century America' (6). These Carlylean metaphors occur at an early stage in Twain's career. Two years before Twain first read *The French Revolution* in 1871, the imprint of Carlyle is apparent in his minor sketch called 'A Day at Niagara'. At the end of July 1869, Samuel Clemens, his fiancée Olivia Langdon, and a few friends made a three-day visit to Niagara Falls to see the sights and to investigate the area as a suitable place for the Clemenses to settle. In order to bring stability to a wandering habit of life, Clemens thought of buying a stake in the *Buffalo Express*, a daily newspaper operating in the nearby Lake Erie community of Buffalo, New York. Apparently the visit was a success, for soon after it, he borrowed $12,500 from his future father-in-law, Jervis Langdon, and bought a one-third stake in the *Express*, where, for the next eighteen months, he served as both editor and contributor.

Mark Twain began as the managing editor of the *Express* on 15 August 1869. His custom was to write a signed piece for the Saturday paper. During the remainder of the week, especially on the editorial page and in the column entitled 'People and Things', several short, unsigned pieces appear, many of which bear the recognisable marks of Twain's wit and sarcasm. In one of these Twain addresses Carlyle directly:

> The soul of old Tom Carlyle is still troubled with dire forebodings concerning the future of the awful Democracy of the United States, which has the insufferable assurance to fancy that it can take care of itself and does not need a master. An American letter writer, who must be tolerably callous and indifferent to rough treatment, ventured to make the ancient oracle a visit the other day, and this is the woful [sic] prophecy that he brought away: 'As sure as the Lord reigns', said he, 'you are rushing down to hell with desperate velocity. The scum of the world has got possession of your country, and nothing can save you from the devil's clutches. Not perhaps', cried he, raising his voice to its shrillest notes, 'a hell burning with material fire and brimstone, but the wide, weltering chaos of corruption in high places, and the misrule of the people. A fine republic that! England follows in the train, and is even now on the brink of the infernal precipice – and hell below'. (2)[2]

Sounding like Carlyle, Twain warns 'old Tom' to mind his own business, especially when it comes to the question of the progress of democracy in North America. Ironically, Twain would soon grow to see America in terms of its 'weltering chaos of corruption in high places, and the misrule of the people'. His representation of the Scotsman as an 'ancient oracle' who pronounces 'woful prophecy' brings their future agreement into sharper relief and suggests Carlyle's later impact on his darkening view of humanity (*Express* 2).

The immediate context of Twain's attack is almost certainly Carlyle's pamphlet *Shooting Niagara: And After*? (1867), in which he attacks egalitarianism. Carlyle describes North America as a continent that has been suffering from a demonic flood: 'A continent of the earth has been submerged, for certain years, by deluges as from the Pit of Hell' (*Works* 30:7). Britain's reforming parliament has freed Satan, and 'now hardly any limb of the Devil has a thrum or tatter of rope or leather left upon it. [...] And in fact THE DEVIL (he, verily, if you will consider the sense of words) is likewise become an Emancipated Gentleman' (*Works* 30:8-9). Twain too equates the devil and hell with political corruption, and the 'rushing down' of his parody echoes Carlyle's view that the reform measure of 1867 'pushes us at once into the Niagara Rapids: irresistibly propelled, with ever-increasing velocity, we shall now arrive; who knows how *soon*!' (*Works* 30:10). Carlyle believes that the country will arrive at the Falls, go over, and most likely hit the bottom, disastrously; he metaphorically equates Britain's move towards democracy with '*shooting* Niagara to the bottom' (*Works* 30:14).

Twain was undoubtedly familiar with the intense reaction against *Shooting Niagara* in the American press.[3] Whitman had published an elegant and emphatic response to Carlyle in the December 1867 issue of *The Galaxy*, a magazine to which Twain regularly contributed.[4] Many of the American reviews comment on the Niagara metaphor. As the critic in the *St. Paul's Monthly Magazine* asserts, '[W]e will not allow ourselves to be frightened by this prospect of a Niagara Falls' (305). Twain himself seems sensitive to the charge that the United States is drifting towards disaster. In his first signed piece for the *Express*, 'A Day at Niagara' (21 Aug. 1869), he responded more directly to Carlyle's pamphlet. Six days before commenting obliquely on *Shooting Niagara*, he signed his name to a sketch in which describes himself figuratively plunging into and shooting the rapids of Niagara.

Twain divides 'A Day at Niagara' into three sections. In the first, 'The Tamed Hackman', he reports the fate of Niagara's cab drivers, who were notorious for gouging tourists. An unidentified yet powerful force operates to restrain the cabbies: 'The hackmen have been tamed, and numbered, and placarded, and blackguarded, and brought into subjection to the law, and dosed with Moral Principle till they are meek as missionaries'. Though well controlled by the institutional forces of Niagara, a circumstance that Twain represents in distinctly Carlylean language, the cabbies divide themselves into two clans and begin an internecine war over the tourist trade. According to Twain, they go too far when their squabble becomes public: 'It made the Falls unpopular by getting into the newspapers, and whenever a public evil achieves that sort of success for itself, its days are numbered'. The first section closes in classic Twain style: 'It became apparent that either the Falls had to be discontinued or the hackmen had to subside. They could not dam the Falls, and so they damned the hackmen. One can be comfortable and happy there now' (300). The regulatory forces in Niagara are invisible but pervasive, and though Twain's persona thinks them a positive force in curbing the hackmen, his opinion will change when the rules of Niagara begin to exert their regulatory force on him.

The title of the next section, 'Signs and Symbols', recalls 'Signs of the Times' and the chapter entitled 'Symbols' in *Sartor Resartus*. In *Shooting Niagara* Carlyle continues to describe his theory of symbols in terms of aesthetics: '[G]enuine 'Art' in all times is a higher synonym for God Almighty's Facts, – which come to us direct from Heaven, but in so abstruse a condition, and cannot be read at all till the better intellect interpret them' (*Works* 30:25). Twain sardonically provides a sharply different interpretation of the signs in and around Niagara:

> I drank up most of the American Fall before I learned that the waters were not considered medicinal. Why are people left in ignorance in that way? I might have gone on and ruined a fine property merely for the want of a little trifling information. And yet the sources of information at Niagara Falls are not meager. You are sometimes in doubt there about what you ought to do, but you are seldom in doubt about what you must not do. (300)

Twain implies that Carlyle is incapable of proposing positive solutions to Britain's social problems. In *Shooting Niagara* Carlyle vaguely demands that the 'better kind of our Nobility' and the 'silent Industrial Hero' do something (*Works* 30:18, 30). The pamphlet is more of a compendium of social ills than a list of particular solutions: 'In God's name, let us find out what of noble and profitable we can *do*; if it be nothing, let us at least keep silence, and bear gracefully our strange lot!' (*Works* 30:18-19). Twain subtly ridicules the prophet who disdains the role of legislator. In his emphasis on the 'thou shalt not', he implicitly condemns the negative vagueness and acerbity of Carlyle's social vision in *Shooting Niagara*.

Twain proceeds to give the reader a long list of rules associated with the hotel he is staying at in Niagara: '"Pull the bell-rope gently, but don't jerk". "Bolt your door". "Don't scrape matches on the wall". "Turn off your gas when you retire". "Tie up your dog". "If you place your boots outside the door they will be blacked – but the house will not be responsible for their return"' (301). Parenthetically, he complains about this last rule: '(This is a confusing and tanglesome proposition – because it moves you to deliberate long and painfully as to whether it will really be any object to you to have your boots blackened unless they *are* returned)' (301). The tone and structure of Twain's list of rules seem similar to those of Carlyle, who had a propensity for lists. For example, the 'ARTICLES OF FAITH' in *Sartor Resartus* is a numbered list of fashion regulations, including, 'Coats should have nothing of the triangle about them...No license of fashion can allow a man of delicate taste to adopt the posterial luxuriance of a Hottentot...There is safety in a swallow-tail...It is permitted to mankind, under certain restrictions, to wear white waistcoats'. Teufelsdröckh ends this list of rules with an unequivocal denial of them: 'All which Propositions, I, for the present, content myself with modestly but peremptorily and irrevocably denying' (SR 204-5). Carlyle's list is part of his effort to create and establish a symbolic world of clothes as a metaphor for the body's vestment of the spirit - the symbolic meaning of his list transcends its literal function as a set of fashion laws. In a similarly figurative way, Twain does more than create a list of the literal regulations of Niagara. His aim is to develop an important argument about democracy. Although he is a member of a free and democratic society, he finds the veritable avalanche of rules and regulations in Niagara suffocating.

Twain then moves his story outside of the hotel: '[W]herever you wander, you are intelligently assisted by the signs'. He offers another long list of (fictitious) regulations: '"Keep off the grass". "Don't climb the trees". "Hands off the vegetables". "Do not hitch your horse to the shrubbery"... "Visitors will please notify the Superintendent of any neglect on the part of employees to charge for commodities or services"'. In a sarcastic aside he adds, '(No inattention of this kind observed)' (301). He finishes his catalogue of Niagara's ever-present regulatory signs with a particularly interesting example: 'The proprietors will not be responsible for parties who jump over the Falls'. To which he comments, again parenthetically: '(More shirking of responsibility - it appears to be the prevailing thing here)' (301). Again, Twain alludes to Carlyle's *Shooting Niagara*, the controlling metaphor of which identifies the progress of democracy with a plunge over the Falls. In Twain's Niagara, however, mob rule poses no threat, for as the numerous signs indicate, there are already plenty of rules to keep everyone in line.

For Twain as for Carlyle, going over the Falls is synonymous with expanding the democratic experiment. But as Twain remarks, 'I have always had a high regard for the signers of the Declaration of Independence, but now they do not really seem to amount to much alongside the signers of the Niagara Falls. To tell the plain truth, the multitude of signs annoyed me' (302). They symbolically suggest that democracy itself has been diminished by the rules and regulations of government, the makers of the signs. The danger of democracy is not misrule resulting from too much freedom, which is Carlyle's reading of the signs, but restriction resulting from too many rules. The fact that Twain is in Niagara, the leisure world of nineteenth-century American tourism, adds weight to his ironic commentary on democracy - everyone is free to go to Niagara or to go over Niagara. In the context of Carlyle's *Shooting Niagara*, the Falls had also become an emblem of the dangers associated with the move towards democracy in Britain and the ongoing struggle of the democratic experiment in America.

Twain continues his catalogue of Niagara's signs with a growing sense of perturbation: 'I desired to roll on the grass: the sign prohibited it. I wished to climb a tree: the sign prohibited it. I longed to smoke: a sign forbade it'. Finally, for Twain, enough is enough:

> There was no recourse, now, but to seek consolation in the flowing bowl. I drew my flask from my pocket, but it was all in vain. A sign confronted me which said: 'No drinking allowed on these premises'. On that spot I might have perished from thirst, but for the saving words of an honored maxim that flitted through my memory at the critical moment. – 'All signs fail in a dry time'. Common law takes precedence of the statutes. I was saved. (302)

Twain's attitude to democracy becomes increasingly irreverent. He valorises the law of precedence (the law of the people) over the law of the legislator (the law of the politician). In doing so, he implies that true freedom transcends the restrictions put upon individuals by public institutions; true freedom requires freedom from political and legislative intrusion. For Twain, real democracy demands an individual insistence on individual rights, at least if a fellow needs a drink while standing in front of a no drinking sign. The mob-run-amuck democracy that Carlyle fears in *Shooting Niagara* simply does not exist in Twain's view of democracy, as he expresses it in 'A Day at Niagara'.

In the final section of the sketch, 'The Noble Red Man', Twain confronts the 'natives' of Niagara. Learning from a local clerk that local Native Americans make the souvenirs for the tourist shops and that they are harmless, Twain seeks them out. He notices an 'Indian' sitting under a tree wearing 'a slouch hat and brogans', and he observes that 'baneful contact with our effeminate civilization dilute[s] the picturesque pomp which is so natural to the Indian' (303). He then asks the 'native', in a formal, puffed-up manner, 'Is the Wawhoo-Wang-Wang of the Whack-a-Whack happy? Does the great Speckled Thunder sigh for the war-path, or is his heart contented with dreaming of his dusky maiden?' Unfortunately, he does not get the answer he anticipates. The 'Wawhoo-Wang-Wang' is in fact an Irish worker, one of many hired to make the Indian trinkets for sale in the tourist shops of Niagara.

After his confrontation with 'Wawhoo-Wang-Wang', otherwise known as Dinnis Hooligan, who has threatened to eat him, Twain comes upon a female carving a piece of wood. After commenting on her work, he asks, 'Is the heart of the forest maiden heavy? Is the Laughing-Tadpole lonely? Does she mourn over the extinguished council-fires of her race and the vanished glory of her ancestors?' The name of the 'Indian maiden' is Biddy Malone, and her response to 'the pale-face stranger' closely resembles that of Hooligan. She calls Twain a 'sniveling blagyard' and threatens to throw him over the Falls (303). Again, through his own ignorance, Twain's persona has failed to see the true identity of a person; he is grossly misreading the signs. Thoroughly frustrated with the violent responses that he receives from Hooligan and Malone, Twain then comes upon a camp of 'natives' who sit 'in the shade of a great tree, making wampum and moccasins'. Immediately, he sets out to teach them about their degraded state:

> Noble Red Men, Braves, Grand Sachems, War-Chiefs, Squaws and High-you-Muck-a-Mucks, the pale face from the land of the setting sun greets you!...Trading for forty-rod whiskey to enable you to get drunk and happy and tomahawk your families has played the everlasting mischief with the picturesque pomp of your dress, and here you are, in the broad light of the nineteenth century, gotten up like the ragtag and bobtail of the purlieus of New York! (304)

The figurative core of his speech to the Irish natives is very Carlylean, and their response to it is immediate and violent. The Irish 'natives' attack Twain and tear off his clothes. Twain's persona wants them to reclaim their nobility by throwing off the false garments of the present in exchange for the true vestments of their ancestors. But he has misidentified his savages. Stripped naked in a Carlylean sense, Twain the fictional persona remains what he appears to be, the ignorant brunt of the author's sarcasm. By appearing to ridicule himself, however, Twain produces a complex symbolic and comic effect. It is the misreading of signs that causes trouble. Twain's own nakedness suggests the futility of Carlyle's sign-reading.

Other aspects of 'A Day at Niagara' serve to undercut Carlyle. The Irish workers, who produce shoddy Indian trinkets for Niagara's tourist traps, resemble the blighted inhabitants of his '*Cheap and Nasty*':

> Do you know the shop, saleshop, workshop, industrial establishment temporal or spiritual, in broad England, where genuine work is to be had? I confess I hardly do; the more is my sorrow! For a whole Pandora's Box of evils lies in that one fact, my friend; that one is enough for us, and may be taken as the sad summary of all. Universal *shoddy* and Devil's-dust cunningly varnished over; that is what you will find presented you in all places, as ware invitingly cheap, if your experience is like mine. (*Works* 30:32-3)

Twain's exposure to them emphasises the production of their wares. When he first speaks to the clerk about the natives of Niagara he notices their work: 'I found the shops at Niagara Falls full of dainty Indian bead-work, and stunning moccasins, and equally stunning toy figures representing human beings who carried their weapons in holes bored through their arms and bodies, and had feet shaped like a pie. I was filled with emotion'. When he first sees Hooligan, he is working on a 'bead reticule'. When he first sees

Malone, she has just finished carving 'a wooden chief that had a strong family resemblance to a clothes pin' (303). When he comes upon the group of 'natives', they are 'making wampum and moccasins' (304). The trinkets made by the Irish are quite the opposite of 'stunning' – they are Native American artifacts being made by Irish people merely for the money.

Their falseness and wage mongering make them perfect candidates for the charge of '*Cheap and Nasty*'. The fact that the fictive Twain has misidentified them as Native Americans adds to the complexity of his representation, for they violate their own Irish heritage as much as they pervert Native American culture. They remain dangerous and violent – quite like a mob, and it is Twain's ignorance of the situation that has provoked them. He is attacked and stripped because of his obliviousness, not because the Irish workers are inherently violent or dangerous. They required no assistance from the 'pale face from the land of the setting sun' (304) whose misreading of signs is at the root of the trouble.

By not attacking him individually but as a group, the Irish 'savages' exhibit 'mob' behaviour, which Carlyle defines in *Shooting Niagara* as '*Swarmery*', a phenomenon he detested (30:3). Hooligan and Malone threaten Twain, but do not act. It is only *en masse* (to borrow Whitman's loaded phrase), in an act of '*Swarmery*', that they physically attack Twain. His call on them to proclaim him as their leader drives them to it: 'For shame! Remember your ancestors!... Unfurl yourselves under my banner, noble savages, illustrious guttersnipes – ' (304). It is this cutting swipe at the 'savages' which causes the violence on Twain to commence:

> In the next instant the entire tribe was upon me. They tore all the clothes off me, they broke my arms and legs, they gave me a thump that dented the top of my head till it would hold coffee like a saucer; and to crown their disgraceful proceedings and add insult to injury, they threw me over the Horseshoe Fall and I got wet. (305)

Once the swarm of angry Irish workers has Twain's persona beaten and naked, they pitch him into the nearby river, where he is saved from drowning by getting stuck on a rock. Freeing himself from it, he plunges over Niagara Falls. In *Shooting Niagara* Carlyle uses intense sarcasm to describe England's move towards democracy: 'Bring in more voting; that will clear away the universal rottenness, and quagmire of mendacities, in which poor England is drowning; let England only vote sufficiently, and all is clean and sweet again' (*Works* 30:9). Similar to Twain's persona, who is stuck above the Falls, Carlyle's England sits poised above the precipice of democracy. He sarcastically proclaims that the expanded suffrage created by the reform of 1867 will save England from drowning. However, as Carlyle warns repeatedly in *Shooting Niagara*, the probable result of

England's rescue by 'more voting' is a metaphorical trip over the Niagara Falls. Twain's persona also saves himself from drowning, but in doing so, he goes over the Falls, taking a trip that figuratively echoes Carlyle's vision of 'the Niagara leap of completed Democracy' (*Works* 30:9,3).

The great lesson of Twain's plunge is that he survives. Floating up to the surface at the bottom of the Falls, he is promptly caught in a whirlpool-like eddy. As he circles the vortex, he tries to get closer to a bush to pull himself out, and on the forty-fourth time around, he is confronted by a curious person:

> At last a man walked down and sat down close to that bush, and put a pipe in his mouth, and lit a match, and followed me with one eye and kept the other on the match while he sheltered it in his hands from the wind. Presently a puff of wind blew it out. The next time I swept around he said: 'Got a match?' 'Yes – in my other vest. Help me out, please'. 'Not for Joe'. When I came around again I said: 'Excuse the seemingly impertinent curiosity of a drowning man, but will you explain this singular conduct of yours?' 'With pleasure. I am the Coroner. Don't hurry on my account. I can wait for you. But I wish I had a match'. (305)

Twain is saved not by the coroner – himself oddly resembling the dour Carlyle, surveying civilisation through pipe-smoke – but by a passing policeman, who arrests him for disturbing the peace. He is brought before a Judge, who fines him, unsuccessfully. As Twain explains, 'My money was with my pantaloons, and my pantaloons were with the Indians'. Twain moves his sketch quickly to its conclusion: 'Thus I escaped. I am now lying in a very critical condition. At least I am lying, anyway – critical or not critical' (305). As he undergoes treatment for the wounds suffered on his visit to Niagara, his doctor tells him that only six of his wounds are fatal, a diagnosis to which he responds, 'I don't mind the others'. Twain then asks the doctor, 'It is an awfully savage tribe of Indians that do the beadwork and moccasins for Niagara Falls, doctor. Where are they from?' 'Limerick, my son', the doctor replies. Ignorant to the last, Twain closes: 'I shall not be able to finish my remarks about Niagara Falls until I get better' (306). Though he has misread the signs and continues to misread the signs, Twain survives the Niagara leap and his arrest for disturbing the peace. He will soon be well enough to tell his tale.

Unlike the stern prophet in Carlyle's essay, Twain's narrator is a bumbling fool who gets it all wrong. He staggers through this self-deprecating sketch, in which he cannot tell the difference between an Indian and an Irishman. As a result, the Irish are represented as perfectly sensible participants in the democratic process, who reject the demagoguery of Twain's fictional persona. The contrast in voice reflects a broader disagreement between Carlyle and Twain. Carlyle is correct in viewing the trip over the Falls as unavoidable, but he is wrong to view it as irrevocably disastrous, for Twain demonstrates that it is possible to survive the plunge. Furthermore, his arrest for disturbing the peace shows that democracy is equally restrictive above and below the Falls. The signs of Niagara make it clear that although democracy has its faults, there is no reason to fear it as Carlyle does in *Shooting Niagara*.

In a letter to William Dean Howells in 1877, Twain explains how his different interpretations of *The French Revolution* reflects changes not in Carlyle but in himself:

> When I finished Carlyle's French Revolution in 1871, I was a Girondin; every time I have read it since, I have read it differently - being influenced and changed, little by little, by life and environment [...]: and now I lay the book down once more, and recognize that I am a Sansculotte! - And not a pale, characterless Sansculotte, but a Marat. Carlyle teaches no such gospel: so the change is in me - in my vision of the evidences. (Twain-Howells 2:595)

The letter gives insight into how Carlyle and his apocalyptic social vision and his anxiety about democracy played a role in the darkening of Twain's vision of humanity. Both writers spent their careers struggling with the relationship of the individual to society. Neither could reconcile freedom with mob-rule, which from their point of view was the offspring of too much liberty. As they grew older and as their outlooks descended further into the darkness of misanthropy, neither Twain nor Carlyle trusted the lower classes with democracy. In 'A Day at Niagara', Twain had not yet adopted the hostile attitude to democracy that he later exhibited in *Huckleberry Finn* and *Connecticut Yankee*, and his 'Sansculottism' here is in the spirit of Teufelsdröckh rather than Marat. The story provides one of the last visions of Twain as the liberal defender of the institutional democratic faith, a Girondin who had not yet become an extreme Jacobin.

Notes

1 Recent commentary has done much to confirm Carlyle's influence on Twain. Britton explores the role of Carlyle in Twain's movement towards a more deterministic worldview and philosophy. Through a close study of the marginalia in one of Twain's copies of *The French Revolution,* Fulton adds to earlier work by Baetzhold and Richardson, and establishes that Carlyle's history was a major source for and influence on Twain's *A Connecticut Yankee in King Arthur's Court* (1889). Fulton also mentions *The Adventures of Tom Sawyer* (1876), *The Prince and the Pauper* (1882), and *Adventures of Huckleberry Finn* (1885) as earlier works 'enlivened by references to Carlyle's history and inspired by its philosophy' (82). In his 1990

Carlyle Society lecture, Richardson makes further connections between Carlyle and Twain, particularly in *Sartor Resartus* and *Pudd'nhead Wilson* (1894).

2 McCullough and McIntire-Strasburg warn that it 'is impossible to know ultimately how much Samuel Clemens contributed to the *Express* during his association with the paper' (xxii), and do not include this unsigned reference to Carlyle in their book. However, Baetzhold, Gribben and Britton do attribute the piece to Twain (327 n33; 128; 199). While it is impossible to prove definitively that Twain and not his co-editor Josephus Larned wrote this parody, it seems highly likely that Twain would have seen and approved of the piece before it was sent to press. It is, after all, set as a separate article on the editorial page.

3 As Trela remarks, '[M]ost commentators were appalled by the work and felt it showed nothing more than the diminished rhetorical ability, creative power and political shortsightedness of its author' (30).

4 Whitman entitled his response to Carlyle 'Democracy'. In it he defends Carlyle at the same time as he insists that the prophet's vision is faulty: 'The only course eligible, it is plain, is to plumply confront, embrace, absorb, swallow (O, big and bitter pill!) the entire British 'swarmery', demon, 'loud roughs' and all [...] By all odds, my friend, the thing to do is to make a flank movement, surround them, disarm them, give them their first degree, incorporate them in the State as voters, and then - wait for the next emergency' (749). He eventually expanded this piece in *Democratic Vistas* (1871).

Works Cited

'An Essay on Carlylism: Containing the Very Melancholy Story of a Shoddy Maker and His Mutinous Maid-Servant'. *St. Paul's Monthly Magazine* 1 (1867): 292-305.

Baetzhold, Howard G. *Mark Twain and John Bull: The British Connection*. Bloomington, IN: Indiana UP, 1970.

Berton, Pierre. Niagara: *A History of the Falls*. New York: Kodansha, 1997.

Britton, Wesley. 'Carlyle, Clemens, and Dickens: Mark Twain's Francophobia, the French Revolution, and Determinism'. *Studies in American Fiction* 20 (1992): 197-204.

DeVoto, Bernard. *Mark Twain in Eruption*. NY: Harper, 1940.

Fulton, Joe B. *Mark Twain in the Margins: The Quarry Farm Marginalia and A Connecticut Yankee in King Arthur's Court*. Tuscaloosa, AL: U of Alabama P, 2000.

Goldberg, Michael. 'Carlyle and Ireland'. *Canadian Journal of Irish Studies* 5 (1979): 4-25.

Gribben, Alan. *Mark Twain's Library: A Reconstruction*. Boston, MA: Hall, 1980.

Hollander, Joel A. 'Ford Madox Brown's Work (1865): The Irish Question, Carlyle, and the Great Famine'. *New Hibernia Review* 1 (1997): 100-19.

Richardson, Thomas C. 'Thomas Carlyle and Mark Twain: A Vision of the Evidences'. Edinburgh: *Carlyle Society, Occasional Papers*, 1990. 1-16.

Seigel, Jules. 'Carlyle's Ireland and Ireland's Carlyle'. *Selected Essays on Scottish Language and Literature*. Ed. Steven R. McKenna. Lewiston: Edwin Mellen Press, 1992. 195-209.

Trela, D. J. 'Carlyle's *Shooting Niagara*: The Writing and Revising of an Article and Pamphlet'. *Victorian Periodicals Review* 25 (1992): 30-4.

Twain, Mark. 'A Day at Niagara'. *Collected Tales, Sketches, Speeches, and Essays: 1852-1890*. New York: Library of America, 1992. 300-6.

———. Editorial. *Buffalo Express* 27 Aug. 1869: 2.

———. 'English Festivities: And Minor Matters'. *Buffalo Express* 28 Aug. 1869: 1.

———. *Mark Twain at the Buffalo Express: Articles and Sketches by America's Favorite Humorist*. Ed. Joseph B. McCullough and Janice McIntire-Strasburg. DeKalb, IL: Northern Illinois UP, 1999.

———. *Mark Twain to Mrs. Fairbanks*. Ed. Dixon Wecter. San Marino, CA: Huntington Library, 1949.

———. *'My First Lie and How I Got Out of It'. 'The Man That Corrupted Hadleyburg' and Other Essays and Stories*. New York: Wells, 1923. 167-9.

Twain, Mark, and William D. Howells. *Mark Twain - Howells Letters: The Correspondence of Samuel L. Clemens and William D. Howells*. Ed. Henry Nash Smith and William M. Gibson. 2 vols. Cambridge, MA: Harvard UP, 1960.

Whitman, Walt. 'Democracy'. *Prose Works* 1892. Ed. Floyd Stovall. Vol. 2. New York: New York UP, 1963. 748-51.

Chapter 11

'The same old sausage': Thomas Carlyle and the James Family

ANDREW TAYLOR

In June 1883, Henry James wrote a letter from Boston to Lady Hannah de Rothschild Rosebery, a society hostess and wife of Archibald, a future British Prime Minister. Introduced to the Roseberys three years earlier, James found their friendship a useful means of entry into the aristocratic circles within which he felt so at ease. He had been in America since late 1882, preoccupied with his role as executor of his father's will, and the pull of England, now James's home, was increasingly strong. His analysis of his New England scene demonstrates a wry detachment in its mock anthropological language. 'Newport indeed is given up to billionaires and "dudes" (I will explain the dude when I see you next)', he assures the no doubt bemused Lady Hannah (*Letters* 2:420).

Amid the enervating torpor of Newport's summer heat, literary culture too seems to be underdeveloped:

> Of topics I am afraid that we have none to speak of here just now – now that we have all read Mrs. Carlyle, and 'Mr. Issacs', and even Ernest Renan's *Souvenirs de Jeunesse*. We find Mrs. Carlyle rather squalid, but a great one for saying things well, and we thirst, generally, for the blood of J.A. Froude. (*Letters* 2:420-1)

James's list refers to several literary successes of the day: *Mr. Issacs* (1882), an eroticised Indian adventure novel by the popular F. Marion Crawford, and Renan's *Souvenirs d'Enfance et de Jeunesse* (1883), an autobiographical account of religious crisis, read avidly by those who remembered the controversy surrounding his *Vie de Jésus* twenty years before, with its application of a scientific historical method to the origins of Christianity. The oddly disparaging and complimentary reference to Mrs. Carlyle – somehow she is both 'squalid' and articulate – was prompted by James's reading of Froude's monumental three-volume edition of Carlyle's *Letters and Memorials to Jane Welsh Carlyle* (1883).

As has been thoroughly documented, Froude's editorial labours had caused something of a literary scandal. The revelations of an unhappy marriage and Carlyle's keen sense of guilt at his wife's death were aired for a reading public on both sides of the Atlantic accustomed to propriety and the illusion of domestic harmony.[1] Throughout his career, Henry James was preoccupied with issues of publicity, and with the intrusion of the public world into the private literary realm. As Richard Salmon has recently noted, 'From his earliest writings onwards, James revealed an acute concern with the cultural space of authorship, and its movement across a shifting boundary between private and public spheres' (7).

For James, this was a new and very pressing social problem, indicative of the degree to which hierarchies of taste and decorum had been erased by the general levelling impetus of democracy. Writers and texts were now thrust involuntarily into the public sphere to be avidly consumed by an insatiable and all too 'familiar' readership. In an 1872 review of Nathaniel Hawthorne's *French and Italian Note-Books*, he had raised the 'general question of the proper limits of curiosity', which ought to be focused on those writers whose 'elements are scattered in portfolios and table-drawers'. Noting with alarm the increasing publication of authors' 'literary remains', he predicted a time when 'Artists, of course, will be likely to take the alarm, empty their table-drawers, and level the approaches to their privacy. The critics, psychologists, and gossip-mongers may then glean amid the stubble' (*Essays* 307).

The publication in 1875 of the correspondence by the great Unitarian divine William Ellery Channing prompted a similar anxiety. The letters may possess an 'agreeable suggestiveness', but James is concerned enough to wonder to 'what degree of merit it is that would make it right we should read them at all'. The 'pestilent modern fashion of publicity' undermines the degree to which a man has 'a right to determine, in so far as he can, what the world shall know of him and what it shall not' (*Essays* 212). In a very tangible sense James considered the publication of private texts to be a defilement of the author. The language he employs in his notebook entry – 'invasion', 'devouring', 'extinction' – suggests the degree of metaphoric violence that accompanied such publication. James's comment in the letter to Lady Rosebery about thirsting for the blood of Carlyle's dutiful literary executor neatly turns Froude's vampiric intrusion, as James saw it, back on Froude himself.[2]

This image of corporeal invasion had been employed by James's father, the social and religious philosopher Henry James Sr, in a sketch of Carlyle first published in the *Atlantic Monthly* in 1881. Writing of his subject's acute disdain for reform movements, James Sr declared: 'He did, indeed, dally with the divine ideas long enough to suck them dry of their rhetorical juices, but then dropped them, to lavish contempt on them ever after' (*Literary Remains* 445).[3] But the metaphor of ingestion can also be explored from a reverse perspective. Although both Henry Jameses are quick to assign the language of invasion to others, they tended to perpetuate the same process in their representation of Carlyle. They too had territorial designs on the figure whom James Sr later dismissed as 'the same old sausage, fizzing and sputtering in his own grease' (Perry 1:83).[4]

On 11 May 1843 James Sr wrote to Ralph Waldo Emerson, whom he had met the previous year. He was immediately attracted to the spiritual bravery so evident in the Concord philosopher's religious sensibility, writing at the time of beholding one 'who in very truth was seeking the realities of things' (Perry 1:39). Attaining intellectual maturity just as New England transcendentalism was becoming influential nationally, James Sr was at the centre of what F. O. Matthiessen, borrowing the title of William Ellery Channing's influential 1820 essay, termed 'the moral argument against Calvinism' (6).[5] Yet what distinguishes James Sr from Emerson is his reluctance to dispense altogether with the substance of the old faith. Like Emerson, James Sr could regret the emergence of 'a feeble Unitarian sentimentality', as he put it, yet he prefaces this phrase with a more telling lament: '[R]eligion in the old virile sense has disappeared' (Dupee 11).

Unlike the transcendentalists, the elder James was not interested in founding an alternative religious telos to compete with the one that had dominated spiritual life in America since its colonisation. Instead, he sought to preserve what was still usable, both religiously and culturally, in Calvinism's formulations. Reared as a Presbyterian, James Sr's strong attachment to the stern and austere faith is apparent in the complaint he makes in his letter to Emerson: 'You don't look upon Calvinism as a fact at all, wherein you are to my mind philosophically infirm, and impaired as to your universality. I can see in Carlyle's writing the advantage his familiarity with this fact gives him over you with a general audience. What is highest in Carlyle is built upon that lowest. At least so I read' (Perry 1:47).

James Sr had been an enthusiastic advocate of Carlyle's *Sartor Resartus* (1834) and *Past and Present* (1843), describing their author as 'the very best interpreter of spiritual philosophy... *for this age*, the age of transition and conflict. And what renders him so is his natural birth- and education-place. Just to think of a *Scotchman* with a heart widened to German spiritualities!' Carlyle, a fellow reconstructed Puritan, seemed to offer James Sr precisely what Emerson could not - a philosophical and spiritual assertiveness which called into question the sublime indifference that Emerson seemed to display towards anything which might complicate the serene optimism of his refined perception. The man of the hour, James Sr assured Emerson, would have to be a 'Jonathan Edwards *redivivus*' (Perry 1:47).

The intellectual currents of antebellum New England were particularly hospitable to Carlyle's robust philosophy. As Andrew Hook has explained, the muscularity of Carlyle's prose seemed to resonate for an America striving to define itself as unconventional and defiant. His expansive style seemed to match the nation's spatial extremes, cherished exceptionalism, and anti-dogmatic spirituality. Carlyle's praise of Cromwell, that 'last glimpse of the Godlike vanishing from this England' where 'conviction and veracity [were] giving place to hollow cant and formulism', suited a young nation identifying with Christian dissent (*Works* 6:1). For James Sr in 1843, Carlyle fitted just this mould, and was useful as an antidote to what he felt to be Emerson's more ethereal meanderings.

That James Sr chose to frame his comments on Carlyle in the context of a discussion of Emerson is characteristic. In the writings of both Henry Jameses, Carlyle rarely exists independently. When a whole chapter, entitled 'Some Personal Recollections of Carlyle', is devoted to him in James Sr's posthumously published *Literary Remains* (1884), that chapter sits alongside and is in dialogue with a lengthy account of Emerson elsewhere in the volume. Henry James's most extensive discussion of Carlyle occurs in a review of the Emerson–Carlyle correspondence, and even his 1886 novel *The Bostonians*, he pits Basil Ransom, a character modelled on elements of Carlylean thought, against the faded remnants of Emersonian reformism.[6] Carlyle is brought into focus by both writers for the religious and cultural use which can be made of him, a use that makes no claims for consistency and may be prompted by altogether different motives than a desire to understand him.

James Sr's lecture on Emerson delivered in 1872 (unpublished until 1904) illustrates this tendency. James Sr's personal and intellectual relationship with Emerson had been on the wane for several years. Their temperamental and philosophical differences had widened, to the extent that James Sr could write to his son William on 18 March 1868:

> Emerson's unreality to me grows evermore. You have got to deal with him as with a child, making all manner of allowances for his ignorance of everything above the senses, and putting such a restraint upon your intellect as tires you to death...I love the man very much, he is such a born natural; but his books are to me wholly destitute of spiritual flavour, being at most carbonic acid gas and *water*. (Perry 1:96-7)

Of course what was admitted in private correspondence was very different from the language being used in public. The lecture of 1872 was an attempt by James Sr to recall his earliest feelings of admiration and discipleship in an act of self-rehabilitation.[7] Emerson, he writes, 'at once captured my imagination, and I have ever since been his loving bondman...I have often found myself, in fact, thinking: if this man were only a woman, I should be sure to fall in love with him' ('Emerson' 740). The feminisation of Emerson becomes a useful means for James Sr of assessing him; his feminine qualities come to represent a form of purity and an energising spiritual force. James Sr describes the manner in which Emerson acts as an influence in terms of female infiltration and cleansing, 'as if the spotless feminine heart of the race had suddenly shot its ruby tide into your veins, and made you feel as never before the dignity of clean living' ('Emerson' 741). For him, Emerson's masculinity has become 'so sublimated into feminine or aesthetic force, force of spontaneity, that men instinctively do him homage, as a manifest token of divine power in our nature' ('Emerson' 745).

But what is striking about this lecture is the way in which James Sr is unable to forget his intellectual objections. He does not get drawn into overtly judging his subject, but his prose struggles to maintain that external veneer of esteem against the impulse to criticise. This tension is palpable in his assessment of Emerson's morality: 'He has not the least vital apprehension of that fierce warfare of good and evil which has desolated so many profounder bosoms, which has maddened so many stouter brains' ('Emerson' 743). Emerson's obliviousness has saved him from destruction. Neither desolated nor maddened, he continues to live in perfect serenity. By remaining untouched by fundamental warring impulses he has survived to represent the 'bud of a redeemed life of God in our nature' ('Emerson' 744). Yet by characterising Emerson as a 'bud', James Sr implies that Emerson is both a precursor to a full-flowering of spiritual unity – elsewhere in the lecture he is 'an American John the Baptist' ('Emerson' 742) – and an unformed mystic cocooned in inchoateness.

James Sr redeems Emerson by comparing him to Carlyle, a convenient antagonist whom he employs to bring out Emerson's saintly qualities in stronger relief. After mid-century the appeal of Carlyle to the New England intelligentsia had suffered serious decline following his inflammatory remarks on slavery both before and after the Civil War. David Wasson's 'A Letter to Thomas Carlyle' in the October 1863 *Atlantic Monthly* encapsulated the shift from admiration to opprobrium felt by many of Carlyle's abolitionist readers. Wasson had been an early disciple, reading *Sartor Resartus* 'aloof and on horseback, sleeping with it under my pillow and wearing it in my pocket till pocket and it were worn out'. Yet narrating in highly emotional terms the story of a young slave who had been whipped for disobedience because she had refused the sexual demands of her master, Wasson finds Carlyle complicit:

> Yes, Thomas Carlyle, I hold you a party to these crimes. You, YOU are the brutal old man who would flog virgins into prostitution. You approve the sy tem; you volunteer your best varnish in its commendation; and this is an inseparable and legal part of it. (501)

James Sr's manœuvring of blame and praise in his lecture reflects this change, as he strives to mould Emerson (himself an ambiguous convert to the cause of abolition) into a champion of American democratic promise. In effect Carlyle is used as a prop to help James Sr bolster Emerson's reputation. The project of public endorsement is all too gratefully assisted by a pattern of Manichean simplicity. Compared to Emerson's almost preternatural goodness, Carlyle, 'does not hesitate to regard the good and evil, the true and the false, the strong and the feeble that he discerns in men's persons, as finalities, clothing the universe of the divine administration in impenetrable gloom' ('Emerson' 743). Though Emerson may remain unconscious of the divine drama of good and evil, Carlyle's crime is worse because he accepts the polarities as absolute. For the purposes of his lecture, James Sr accords Emerson the superior position: obliviousness to evil is preferable to a resigned acceptance of its immutable existence.

Two other essays – James Sr's 'Some Personal Recollections of Carlyle' and Henry James's review of Charles Eliot Norton's edition of the Emerson-Carlyle letters – demonstrate further Jamesian efforts to retailor Carlyle for the age. The first was a sketch delivered as a lecture in New York in 1864, at the height of the Civil War. James Sr was concerned about its reception. Writing to Parke Godwin, the organiser of the event, he joked: 'Would it be necessary to take on my own bowie-knife or do [sic] the Association guarantee life to their speakers?' (Habegger, *The Father* 463). It proved to be popular and Charles Eliot Norton expressed an interest in publishing it in the *North American Review*. But James Sr was reluctant for it to appear in print while its subject was still living. He wrote to Norton: 'It is not a literary criticism of the writer but a sketch of the man himself illustrated by facts of observation, and though these are all creditable to Carlyle in the way he seeks to be accredited, they are still not exactly what one would care to publish so long as he survived' (19 July [1865?], Norton Papers, bMS Am 1088 [3834], by permission of the Houghton Library, Harvard University).

Despite these reservations, the lecture became a staple in James Sr's repertoire, with William informing his brother Henry in 1872, eight years after its first delivery, that 'Father read his paper on Carlyle yesterday at the Radical Club very successfully' (*Correspondence* 184). That Henry read the lecture himself is fairly certain: it eventually surfaced as the lead article in the May 1881 *Atlantic Monthly*, separated by a matter of pages from the latest instalment of James's own *The Portrait of a Lady*. What James read was not uniformly critical of its subject, for his father was prepared to acknowledge those qualities which had so attracted him to Carlyle back in the 1840s. James Sr was especially impressed by Carlyle's aesthetic power, which could inhabit the least promising subject and revivify it: '[H]aving an immense eye for color, an immense genius for scenic effect, he seized with avidity upon every crazy, time-stained, dishonoured rag of personality that still fluttered in the breeze of history, and lent itself to his magic tissues' (*Literary Remains* 440-1).

Yet such stylistic alchemy had its dangers if it was separated from issues of morality. This was the trap into which Carlyle had fallen: 'It always appeared to me', James Sr writes, 'that Carlyle valued truth and good as a painter does his pigments, - not for what they are in themselves, but for the effects they lend themselves to in the sphere of production' (*Literary Remains* 451). For all his skill at unmasking human folly, Carlyle's cynicism was felt to be so pervasive and relentless that it hardly left room for anything else - to the extent that there was, finally, something false about his writing, a simulation of rhetorical effect which hid an essential emptiness of thought. Genuine scepticism and critique had become aestheticised into a literary form which had been bled of all moral and spiritual impact.

Repeatedly James Sr uses the word 'picturesque' to characterise his subject's qualities; a 'picturesque palaver' was what Carlyle deployed to engage with 'social problems'; 'picturesqueness...was the one key to his intellectual favor'; and 'he precipitated himself upon the picturesque in character and manners wherever he found it' (*Literary Remains* 425, 429, 433). Whatever Carlyle's substantive opinions might be, they are overpowered by style, 'swallowed up in talk or writing'. He 'obviously meant nothing beyond the production of a certain literary surprise, or the enjoyment of his own aesthetic power'. The deliberate cultivation of style - what James Sr calls Carlyle's 'rococo airs and affectations; his antiquated strut and heroics' - fed a reading audience happy to enjoy the rhetorical flourishes without having to test the validity of the assertions that the rhetoric clothed. And the greatest beneficiary of this, James Sr decided, was Carlyle himself. 'The habit was tyrannous' because of the 'heartless people who hang, for their own private ends, upon the skirts of every pronounced genius, and do their best, by stimulating his vanity, to make himself feel a god' (*Literary Remains* 444, 451, 465, 441).

What may at first seem like a parasitic relationship between Carlyle and his readers (they 'hang' upon him for 'private ends') turns out to be symbiotic. The vampirism here is mutual: the readers feed on the writer's style, the writer feeds on their feeding. Both sides benefit from operating in a moral vacuum. In an ingenious and disarming manœuvre (one worthy of Carlyle himself), James Sr reveals that this characterisation is intended to suggest how America, in her Emersonian innocence, had succeeded in calling Carlyle's bluff. The misguided admiration of antebellum New

England was nevertheless fundamental, he argues, in undermining Carlyle's sense of himself. American readers were different from their amoral and 'heartless' European counterparts:

> This is what made him hate Americans, and call us a nation of bores, – that we took him at his word, and reckoned upon him as a sincere well-wisher to the species. He hated us, because a secret instinct told him that our exuberant faith in him would never be justified by closer knowledge; for no one loves the man who forces him upon a premature recognition of himself. (451)

By a circuitous route, James Sr ends up using Carlyle as evidence of a superior American sensibility, a sensibility all too willing to believe in the sincerity of others. Even before that sincerity is shown to be a sham, America's steadfast belief in itself – its 'exuberant faith' – has the effect of disarming and troubling the deceiver. James Sr's example is Margaret Fuller, who 'no sooner crossed Carlyle's threshold…than her heart offered its fragrance to him as liberally as the flower opens up the sun'. Unused to devotion from 'this clear-eyed barbarian', Fuller 'made him feel himself for the moment the transparent mask or unconscious actor he was'. Having little sympathy with Carlyle's visitor – a 'breathless, silly little maid' (*Literary Remains* 452) – James nonetheless admires her New World freshness and touching faith in her host.

The elder James was wary of what he considered to be transcendentalism's otherworldly qualities. Yet he manages to curb his criticism to the extent that Fuller can be marshalled as a warning of the threat posed by Carlyle, a warning delivered to a lecture audience presumably aware of its earlier and highly vocal praise of the Scot. New England intellectuals, including James Sr, were now having to define a position in relation to Carlyle's anti-abolitionist sentiments. They would have to accommodate criticism of their fallen hero while justifying their antebellum enthusiasm for him.

These were matters of pressing concern for a writer whose generation was still guided by religious authority and divided by sectional conflict. For Henry James, a generation later, the issues were not as personal. The choice between Emerson and Carlyle as spiritual seer had become less relevant to one whose focus was more literary and whose sensibility more cosmopolitan. Like his father, James regards Emerson and Carlyle as operating at opposing ends of sensibility, but unlike James Sr, he has no philosophical agenda which requires him to arbitrate between them. The great novelist admits being unable to describe Carlyle's arrival in New England. It would have been a 'dramatic' situation, James writes, but 'the catastrophe never came off…it is impossible to imagine what the historian of the French Revolution, of the iron-fisted Cromwell, and the Voltairean

Frederick, would have made of that sensitive spot or what Concord would have made of Carlyle' (*Essays* 239).

James's estimation of Carlyle is a familiar and familial one: he was a 'pessimist of pessimists' who had 'a vivid conception of evil without a corresponding conception of good' (*Essays* 242, 243). Carlyle's style similarly comes in for close scrutiny, perhaps not surprising given the preoccupations of one for whom the adjective 'Jamesian' would be coined both as a mark of celebration and as one of belittlement and pastiche. What was already termed 'Carlylelese' (a word used by the *Saturday Review* in 1858) disturbed James as it had his father. Carlyle had 'invented a manner, and that his manner had swallowed him up'. Like his father, James uses the vocabulary of ingestion: Carlyle's literary style has taken him over, to the extent that he has ceased to exist independently of it: 'To look at realities and not at imitations is what he constantly and sternly enjoins; but all the while he gives us the sense that it is not at things themselves, but straight into this abysmal manner of his own that he is looking' (*Essays* 249).

From the outset of the review James tries to establish distance between himself and the world he describes. Echoing his review of Hawthorne's notebooks, James remarks that Froude's biographical revelations had revealed Carlyle with an 'unlooked-for vividness' after the dutiful executor had 'unlocked the cabinets'. Carlyle's 'mysteriousness' has been transformed by his forced appearance in the public sphere, so that he is now 'definite and measurable', reduced and contained in a manner which renders him wholly predictable, 'every feature marked and every peculiarity demonstrated'. Carlyle has become public property, a figure from history no longer possessing the power to startle or to amaze. With Emerson, Carlyle has 'already receded…into a kind of historical perspective', and 'their allusions belong to a past which is already remote'; 'the questions of those years are not the questions of these' (*Essays* 234).

James's distancing of Emerson and Carlyle does more than just introduce a generational perspective of gentle irony – he also uses them to highlight the dangers of literary excess. Carlyle's style has an energy and solidity which, though undeniably attractive, is ultimately nothing more than 'magnificent vocalization' (*Essays* 248). His example shows that style can quickly become frozen into affectation and caricature when it is devoid of discrimination and indeterminacy. Carlyle's polemicism stands opposed to the strategies of ambiguity and tentative exploration, which James's attempts to embody in his own developing style. By burying Carlyle in the past, James protects himself from a sensibility that remains a danger to him in the present.

Neither of the Jameses were particularly sophisticated readers of either Carlyle's or Emerson's work.[8] Both were eager to slip into the comfortable polarities of destructive pessimism and other-worldly perfectionism, and to ignore his love of paradox. Yet curiously, these two members of America's most famous intellectual family were troubled by his legacy. In discussing him, they employed the same hyperbole that they condemned in him. Whether in terms of spiritual or literary identity, Carlyle served as a cipher through which they dramatised their personal and professional anxieties. James Sr might announce that 'Thomas Carlyle is incontestably dead at last, by the acknowledgement of all newspapers' (*Literary Remains* 421), but for both father and son, the 'old sausage' continued to fizz and sputter.

Notes

1 For two useful accounts of the controversy surrounding Froude's biographical enterprise, see Broughton and Gilbert; see also Kenneth J. Fielding's intro. to Carlyle's *Reminiscences*.

2 In an 1886 letter to Charles Eliot Norton, whose own edition of Carlyle's correspondence he had just read, James denounced Froude as 'unspeakable' (*Letters* 3:145).

3 *The Atlantic Monthly* sketch was reprinted unchanged as a chapter of *The Literary Remains of the Late Henry James*. All references are from this printing.

4 The phrase is from a letter which James Sr wrote to Ralph Waldo Emerson from London in 1856, after renewing his acquaintance with Carlyle the year before. He had first met Carlyle in 1843, and the two men seemed to have established a warm relationship. Carlyle, notoriously particular about his friends, wrote to Emerson in November of that year that 'James is a very good fellow, better and better as we see him more - something shy and skittish in the man; but a brave heart intrinsically, with sound earnest sense, with plenty of insight and even humour' (Slater 352).

5 Channing's essay was one of the inaugural texts of American Unitarianism, in which he hoped that the historical force of Calvinism was 'giving place to better views...Society is going forward in intelligence and charity, and of course is leaving the theology of the sixteenth century behind it' (343). For James Sr's intellectual career, see Habegger, *The Father*, and the introductions of Gunn and Perry.

6 Both Bell and Habegger, *Henry James,* draw connections between James's novel and Thomas Carlyle. Habegger's is the less successful of the two, merging the figures of Basil Ransom, James Sr and Thomas Carlyle into a whole so as to argue that James, through Basil, approvingly echoes James Sr's Carlylean conservatism.

7 The lecture was delivered on February 6 at the home of the publisher James T. Fields to a coterie of New England writers. James Sr read it again a fortnight later

at the Emerson home, although significantly he requested that Emerson himself not be present.

8 William James offers a sharp difference in viewpoint from the two Henrys. In an address to Harvard Divinity students in 1884, 'The Dilemma of Determinism', his comments clearly reflect an impatience with the kind of sensitive circumlocutions which his brother's prose exhibited: 'No matter for Carlyle's life, no matter for a great deal of his writing. What was the most important thing he said to us? He said: "Hang your sensibilities! Stop your snivelling complaints, and your equally snivelling raptures! Leave off your general emotional tomfoolery, and get to WORK like men!'"(*Writings* 587).

Works Cited

Bell, Ian F.A. *Henry James and the Past*. London: Macmillan, 1991.

Broughton, Trev. 'The Froude-Carlyle Embroilment: Married Life as a Literary Problem'. *Victorian Studies* 38 (1995): 551-85.

Channing, William Ellery. *The Complete Works of William Ellery Channing*. D.D. London: Routledge, 1884.

Dupee, F. W. *Henry James: His Life and Writings*. New York: Doubleday, 1956.

Gilbert, Elliot L. 'Rescuing Reality: Carlyle, Froude, and Biographical Truth-Telling'. *Victorian Studies* 34 (1991): 295-314.

Gunn, Giles, ed. *Henry James Senior: A Selection of His Writings*. Chicago: American Library Association, 1974.

Habegger, Alfred. *Henry James and the 'Woman Business'*. Cambridge: Cambridge UP, 1989.

———. *The Father: A Life of Henry James, Sr*. New York: Farrar, Straus, and Giroux, 1994.

Hook, Andrew. 'Carlyle and America'. *From Goosecreek to Gandercleugh: Studies in Scottish-American Literary and Cultural History*. East Linton, PA: Tuckwell Press, 1999. 135-59.

James, Henry. *Letters*. Ed. Leon Edel. 4 vols. Cambridge, MA.: Belknap Press of Harvard UP, 1974-84.

———. *Literary Criticism: Essays on Literature, American Writers, English Writers*. New York: Library of America, 1984.

James, Henry, Sr. *The Literary Remains of the Late Henry James* (1884). Ed. William James. Boston: Osgood, 1885.

———. 'Emerson'. *Atlantic Monthly* 94 (1904). 740-5.

James, William. *The Correspondence of William James. Volume 1 William and Henry 1861-1884*. Ed. Ignas K. Skrupskelis and Elizabeth M. Berkeley. Charlottesville: Virginia UP, 1992.

———. *Writings* 1878-1899. New York: Library of America, 1992.

Matthiessen, F. O. *The James Family*. New York: Knopf, 1947.

Norton, Charles Eliot. Charles Eliot Norton Papers. Houghton Lib., Harvard University.

Perry, Ralph Barton, ed. *The Thought and Character of William James*. 2 vols. Boston: Little, Brown, 1935.

Salmon, Richard. *Henry James and the Culture of Publicity*. Cambridge: Cambridge UP, 1997.

Slater, Joseph, ed. *The Correspondence of Emerson and Carlyle*. New York: Columbia UP, 1964.

Wasson, David A. 'A Letter to Thomas Carlyle'. *Atlantic Monthly* 12 (1863). 497-504.

Chapter 12

Cedric the Saxon and the Haiti Duke of Marmalade: Race in *Past and Present*

CHRIS R. VANDEN BOSSCHE

The central concerns of *Past and Present* are announced in its opening sentence deploring the 'condition of England' (*PP* 7). Although the book focuses on England, its range of reference moves far beyond English shores to the Americas, Africa, Asia, and Australia. In addition to its well-known references to contemporary English culture – the seven-foot hat, the white surplice controversy, the corn laws, and so on – there are allusions to Chactaws and the American Commonwealth, the Chinese emperor and the opium war, the Dalai Lama and Buddhist Calmucks, Brahmins and Spinning Dervishes, and 'Indian Empires, Americas, New-Hollands'. Especially resonant are the references to the West Indies and Africa: freed slaves in Haiti, slave-trading Dahomey, the pirate Howel Davies (who operated in the West Indies and on the West African coast), the explorer Mungo Park, the Mandingo people, the Niger expedition (which aimed at reducing the slave trade), and African religious and social practices, including the palaver, mumbo-jumbo, and fetishism. Why, it might be asked, does a book on the condition of England require a global perspective?

Carlyle's views on race, which was at this time the subject of a growing body of scientific, social, and popular investigation, were neither unusual nor systematic. As Douglas Lorimer has suggested in relation to Thomas Arnold's understanding of race, 'we need to be wary of a temptation to tease out a more precise meaning, when its ambiguous, and even contradictory, character was the source of its utility' (14). During this period, race was being transformed from a collection of longstanding prejudices and stereotypes into the concept of biologically-determined race difference. Carlyle's use of race in *Past and Present* might be explained by pointing to his insistence that social order requires hierarchy, an explanation that would agree with assumptions on the part of his contemporaries that there is a hierarchy of races.[1] But this explanation is insufficient because Carlyle does not confine hierarchy to race; he regards all society, including white English society, as hierarchical or requiring hierarchical structures. Furthermore, while he does seem to view races as forming a hierarchy, he does not attempt to legitimate hierarchy on the basis of race, or claim, like some contemporaries, that racial distinctions in English culture provide the basis for hierarchy. While his belief in the importance of social hierarchy certainly plays its part, the role that race plays in his works cannot be explained solely in terms of hierarchy.

Rather than produce an opposition between black and white, empire and metropole, Carlyle uses the racial 'other' as a mirror in which England can see itself and begin to comprehend its 'condition'.[2] In this respect, the relationship between here and there, England and empire, is similar to the relationship Carlyle establishes between past and present. The past as represented by Abbot Samson and Bury St. Edmunds is not an ideal to which the present should aspire, but rather a moment of crisis similar to that faced by the present, a 'magic-mirror' in which the present can see itself (*PP* 51). Similarly, the 'out there', the colonies, serves as a mirror in which his contemporaries 'here' in England can catch a glimpse of themselves.

Given this racial and colonial background, where do the Celts fit? *Past and Present* certainly does not focus exclusively on black and white. While the black/white racial dichotomy is central to the development in Carlyle's writings of a racially-inflected conception of English society, the references to various other groups – Chactaws as vicious killers, Chinese as recalcitrant traders – also rely on racial stereotypes. For example, Carlyle's anti-Semitism is evident in his comment on the fate of a Jewish money-lender in Book II: '[O]ne almost hopes he was one of those beleaguered Jews who hanged themselves in York Castle shortly afterwards, and had his usances and quittances and horseleech papers summarily set fire to!' (*PP* 65). Chapter four of *Chartism* – ironically titled 'The Finest Peasantry in the World' – describes the Irish as '[i]mmethodic, headlong, violent, mendacious' (*Works* 4:137; see also *CL* 13:192). Apart from a passing reference to Christopher Wren's 'mutinous masons and Irish hodmen' (*PP* 198), however, there are only two references to the Irish in *Past and Present*, both sympathetic and both, tellingly, references to real individuals. The Irish widow who is refused help and infects her neighbourhood with typhus is clearly a victim of *laissez-faire* indifference, and, while the Sandys, who killed their children in order to obtain their burial insurance payment, exemplify the brutality to which the working poor have been reduced, Carlyle does not blame the individuals but the system that crushes them (*PP* 9–10). But his sympathetic discussion of these individuals does not mean that he has changed his views about the Irish. Rather, he develops the strategy here that he would bring to fruition in his essay 'The Negro Question' (1849; retitled 'The Nigger Question' in 1853), in which he uses West-Indian blacks as a stand-in for the Irish. During a tour of Ireland in the later 1840s, he would compare Kildare to 'a village in Dahomey', where the Mungo Park incident recounted in *Past and Presen* took place (*Irish Journey* 64; *PP* 211). The Irish are not absent but are rather subsumed into the problem of British labour and mirrored in the West Indian slave.

This contrast between empire and metropole, together with its racial context, is at play in the chapter 'Permanencc', in which Carlyle opposes the Haiti Duke of Marmalade and the freed slave Quashee to Cedric the Saxon and the swineherd Gurth. While the Duke of Marmalade and Quashee belong to the set of references that includes Africa, the West Indies, and slavery, Cedric and Gurth belong to another set of references – early English history and the 'Anglo-Saxon race' – that includes Hengist, Horsa, and the Anglo-Saxon invasions of Britain, the Anglo-Norman Britain of Abbot Samson and Walter Scott's *Ivanhoe*. This passage draws on a rangc of references to race and empire, but it does so in the course of defining the conditions of English society and advancing Carlyle's argument about the modern English worker:

> Gurth was hired for life to Cedric, and Cedric to Gurth. O Anti-Slavery Convention, loud-sounding long-eared Exeter-Hall – But in thee too is a kind of instinct towards justice, and I will complain of nothing. Only, black Quashee over the seas being once sufficiently attended to, wilt thou not perhaps open thy dull sodden eyes to the 'sixty-thousand valets in London itself who are yearly dismissed to the streets, to be what they can, when the season ends;' – or to the hunger stricken, pallid, *yellow*-coloured 'Free Labourers' in Lancashire, Yorkshire, Buckinghamshire and all other shires! These Yellow-coloured, for the present, absorb all my sympathies: if I had a Twenty Millions, with Model-Farms and Niger Expeditions, it is to these that I would give it! Quashee has already victuals, clothing; Quashee is not dying of such despair as the yellow-coloured pale man's. Quashee, it must be owned, is hitherto a kind of blockhead. The Haiti Duke of Marmalade, educated now for almost half a century, seems to have next to no sense in him. Why, in one of those Lancashire Weavers, dying of hunger, there is more thought and heart, a greater arithmetical amount of misery and desperation, than in whole gangs of Quashees. It must be owned thy eyes are of the sodden sort; and with thy emancipations, and thy twenty-millionings and long-eared clamourings, thou, like Robespierre with his pasteboard *Etre Suprême*, threatenest to become a bore to us, *Avec ton Etre Suprême tu commences m'embêter!* – (*PP* 275)

Why does Carlyle allude to Haiti? This passage employs a form of the argument that he returns to in 'The Negro Question': free industrial labourers are worse off than black slaves because industrial labourers have to fend for themselves in the marketplace whereas slaves are protected by a serflike and 'permanent' relationship with their masters.[3] Given that Britain had abolished slavery in the West Indies in 1833 and that many of his countrymen continued to seek an end to the slave trade (hence the references to Exeter Hall and the Niger expedition), it might be expected that Carlyle would use Jamaica as his example, as he does in 'The Negro Question'. However, Haiti, which he had written about in *The French Revolution*, serves his purpose here in a number of ways. It combines abolition and revolution, provides the inspiration for the figure of an ersatz duke to contrast with Cedric the Saxon, and connects revolution to failed democratic institutions in order to argue that the masses are incapable of self-government.

As Carlyle knew from his research for *The French Revolution*, the events of 1789 in France had inspired a revolution in Haiti (then Saint-Domingue). Although he regarded the French Revolution as a historical necessity, he was unequivocal about his feeling that revolution is 'anarchy' (*Works* 1:211–12). In *Past and Present* he links Revolutionary Haiti to the anarchy of revolution, because its hierarchy fails to govern. The successor of the leader of the revolution, Toussaint L'Ouverture, was Henry Christophe (1767–1820), who ruled a portion of Haiti from 1806 to 1820, crowned himself King Henry I, and installed a nobility comprised of four princes, eight dukes, twenty-two counts, thirty-seven barons, and fourteen chevaliers. Among his nobility was the governor of Cape Henry, Jean Pierre Richard (d. 1821), who received the title Duke of Marmalade (taken from the town of that name in northern Haiti). Many contemporaries regarded Christophe as a civilising force, praising in particular his efforts to provide modern education and his success in bringing economic prosperity to Haiti.[4] But Christophe's success was achieved through increasingly draconian rule. In 1820 a group of officers led by Richard deposed him, and in the ensuing years the prosperity of Christophe's reign came to an end. The change in Haiti's fortunes was reflected in an 1830 essay in *Fraser's Magazine* that repeatedly evoked the stereotype of the lazy, ineffectual black man who spends his life 'eating, drinking, and sleeping' ('Mackenzie's Haiti' 62).[5] Accordingly, alongside the duke, Carlyle sets the figure of Quashee – which he here employs for the first time – a widely-used stereotype of the deceitful, lazy, and childlike slave of West African origin (Patterson 174–8).[6] He hints that revolutionary Haiti does not have a genuine hierarchy, and that there is no one to govern the untrustworthy 'Quashee'. The duke is contrasted with Cedric, who embodies Carlyle's paternalist ideal, an ideal summed up in his assertion that 'Cedric *deserved* to be [Gurth's] Master' (3.13.211). However, Carlyle's comparison of the

Duke and Cedric is not intended to make a case for slavery. Rather it contrasts the good government of Cedric and the anarchy of Haiti in order to make the case for turning mill-owners into captains of industry capable of establishing order among the labouring classes.

Carlyle connects the origin of the nation to the need for good government. A lord, he claims, is a '*Law-ward*', whose responsibility is to create social order (*PP* 193). It is the paternalist relationship between Cedric and Gurth, rather than the contemporary Benedictine monastery, that provides him with an alternative to the cash nexus and '*Laissez-faire*': in Cedric's era, he claims, 'no human creature...went about connected with nobody' (*PP* 244). Although Carlyle recognises that serfdom and slavery are no longer viable, he still insists that the hierarchical relationship between master and worker must endure: the solution to the problem of the cash nexus, he concludes, is to turn mill-owners into captains of industry who can '[s]ubdue Mutiny, Discord, wide-spread Despair, by manfulness, justice, mercy and wisdom' and transform it into 'a green flowery World' (*PP* 293–4). While the working class performs the physical labour of making the land productive, captains of industry must do the labour of creating social order by regimenting these workers.

In addition to linking blacks with anarchy, Carlyle associates Africa with the creation of language divorced from practical action The reference to Robespierre echoes a chapter of *The French Revolution*, entitled 'Mumbo-Jumbo', in which Carlyle compares Robespierre's festival of the Etre Suprême to the 'Mumbo-Jumbo of the African woods' (*Works* 3:267). Mumbo-jumbo – a fetish worshipped by West Africans – had come to designate *gibberish* because European travellers could only see mystification in the rituals associated with it.[7] This relationship between revolution, gibberish, and mumbo-jumbo in turn evokes another African allusion, Carlyle's designation of the British parliament as a 'National Palaver' that produces only 'eloquence' and '[v]ain jargon': (*PP* 218, 19, 29). In *The French Revolution*, he alludes to the African origin of the term:

> Yes truly, my Patriot Friends, if Liberty, the passion and prayer of all men's souls, means Liberty to send your fifty-thousandth part of a new Tongue-fencer into National Debating-club, then, be the gods witness, ye are hardly entreated. Oh, if in National *Palaver* (as the Africans name it), such blessedness is verily found, what tyrant would deny it to Son of Adam. (*Works* 2:26).

Carlyle echoes this passage in *Past and Present*: 'The notion that a man's liberty consists in giving his vote at election-hustings, and saying, "Behold now I too have my twenty-thousandth part of a Talker in our National Palaver; will not all the gods be good to me?"' (*PP* 218) According to the OED, *palaver* – a parley or conference, 'with much talk', conducted by African and European traders – was often used contemptuously, as was mumbo jumbo, to describe 'unnecessary, profuse, or idle talk'.[8] The context of Carlyle's statements make it clear, however, that Africa, like Haiti, serves merely as a metaphor for Europe and England. Like Africans speaking gibberish, the Lancashire working class is fundamentally 'inarticulate', incapable of meaningful speech: 'Thus these poor Manchester manual workers mean only, by day's-wages for day's-work, certain coins of money adequate to keep them living…They as yet clamour for no more; the rest, still inarticulate, cannot yet shape itself into a demand at all, and only lies in them as a dumb wish; perhaps only, still more inarticulate, as a dumb, altogether unconscious want' (*PP* 26). Unable to articulate their needs, they are also incapable of making decisions for themselves, and the demand for just wages becomes, for Carlyle, a demand to be governed.

Carlyle advocates universal access to education, but he does not believe that education alone will turn the poor into civilised, productive workers. When he remarks that after being educated 'for almost half a century' the Duke of Marmalade 'seems to have next to no sense in him' he leans to some extent towards the opinions of those contemporary writers on race who insisted that Africans were ineducable and would never achieve civilisation (Young 106). Such views were common among polygenists, who regarded Africans as a distinct species and perpetuated a long-standing association between them and African apes (Stepan 15–19).[9] Carlyle makes a similar association in the paragraph preceding this one, where he claims that permanence of contract separates 'the civilized burgher from the nomadic savage, – the Species Man from the Genus Ape' (*PP* 274). Cedric and Gurth represent the permanent contract of civilised 'Man', while the Duke of Marmalade and Quashee are given the status of 'nomadic savage' and 'ape'. This association between black men and apes in turn echoes the Koranic tale, used elsewhere in *Past and Present*, of the 'tribe of men' who refused to give up 'falsities and outer semblances' and were 'changed into Apes…gibbering and chattering very genuine nonsense' (*PP* 153–4). Nonsense, linked to revolution and Africa, becomes a fact of 'nature', and a sign that the under classes will always require government.

In using Cedric and Gurth throughout *Past and Present* to represent his paternalist ideal (see also *PP* 27, 70–1, 211, 244), Carlyle draws on a longstanding tradition that treats 'Teutonic' peoples as a superior race (see MacDougall chap. 2). It is not immediately apparent that Cedric and Gurth, like the Duke of Marmalade and Quashee, invoke assumptions about race; however, in addition to being contrasted with black men, Cedric and Gurth (as well as Carlyle's source, Scott's *Ivanhoe*) belong to a long-standing racial interpretation of the history of England. During the Reformation, claims that the English church had always been independent from Rome were supported by appeals to an ancient Saxon church and the myth that the Anglo-Saxons were the founding people of England (see MacDougall chap. 2). In the seventeenth century, this myth was revised to argue for a tradition of English liberty and opposition to the 'Norman yoke' (MacDougall chap. 3, Simmons 6–7). Although Scott's use of this mythology is complicated by his conflicting allegiances, *Ivanhoe*, on the whole, continues the tradition of privileging Saxon over Norman character, economy and culture. As Clare Simmons has shown, Scott's novel was an important influence on Augustin Thierry, who, together with his brother Amédée, was among the first historians to use race and class as categories of historical analysis (Young 75–6). In turn, Carlyle cited Thierry's *Histoire de la conquête de l'Angleterre par les Normandes* (1825) in his fictitious 'History of the Teuton Kindred' in *Chartism* (*Works* 4:170; see Simmons 91–2). Consequently, when he took up the story of Abbot Samson, Carlyle represented Samson and his era in the context of a long-standing mythology of a superior Teutonic or Saxon race.

What distinguishes Carlyle's use of the myth from that of many of his predecessors is that he is not concerned to argue that the Saxons were the source of English liberty or parliamentary democracy (which protected liberty by serving as a check on monarchy).[10] On the contrary, *Past and Present* questions the value of liberty, institutional reform, and parliament. While Carlyle does find antecedents of contemporary debates in the history of the Saxons, his version of the founding myth, which focuses on Hengist and Horsa (the English Romulus and Remus), he is not concerned with the Saxon love of liberty. He emphasises instead productive labour and emigration, which he associates with the etymological derivation of the name *Saxon* from the root *sahso*, meaning *knife*.

For Carlyle the Saxons are not creators of an ancient parliament but men of silent action who forcefully break up legislative gridlock. He identifies the key event in their history as the moment when Hengist spurs his men to assassinate Vortigern, leader of the Britons, with the words: '"*Eu Sachsen nimith euer Sachses*, You Saxons, out with your Gully-Knives then!" You Saxons, some "arrestment", partial "arrestment of the Knaves and Dastards" has become indispensable!' (*PP* 210).[11] The reference to knaves and dastards in turn recalls an episode of *The French Revolution* in which the threat of 'Insurrection' leads a man to cry out '"*Je demande l'arrestation des coquins et des lâches*...I also *demand arrestment of the Knaves and Dastards*, and nothing more whatever"' (*Works* 3:308). Through this juxtaposition, Carlyle makes Hengist an opponent of revolution and democratic anarchy. He is a Napoleon bringing an end to 'Palaver', or, as a parallel passage in the Forster manuscripts suggests, a Cromwell dismissing parliament.[12]

In the chapter entitled 'The English' (which must be regarded as alluding to this history of a race), Carlyle contrasts the productive 'done work' of the silent English with the 'spoken Word', implicitly the African 'Palaver' (*PP* 160). While praising the end of palaver, he applauds the productive labour that has created '[t]his English Land…whose real conquerors, creators, and eternal proprietors are…all the men that ever cut a thistle, drained a puddle out of England, contrived a wise scheme in England, did or said a true and valiant thing in England' (*PP* 134–5). Action means work, and work means transforming chaos into order. For Carlyle nothing better exemplifies the power of labour to turn chaos into order than the transformation of 'waste' into 'arable' land (*PP* 201). By making land productive, work produces social order and the nation, which is why the work of captains of industry is to make labour orderly. As Carlyle observes, 'The English are a dumb people. They can do great acts, but not describe them. Like the old Romans, and some few others, *their* Epic Poem is written on the Earth's surface' (*PP* 159).

Carlyle's interest in race and imperialism is therefore linked to the way in which he imagines a national epic and national culture. In his lectures on the history of literature delivered in 1838, he compared English colonisation with the founding of the Roman empire, claiming that the descendants of the Saxons not only conquered more territory than the Romans but also reclaimed 'wild and boundless wastes' and converted them into 'arable land and scenes of civilization':

> If any seer among them in the year 449, when they landed here in the Isle of Thanet, could have looked forward to the year 1838 as we can look back to 449, he would have said, as we may say, that great and remarkable as the foundation of Rome certainly was, it was not a greater fact, nor so great even, as that humble settlement of the Saxons on these shores. He would have seen our present dominion extending from the Gulf of California, from the mouth of the Gulf of Mexico, away up to the Ganges and Burrampootra, descending even to our antipodes. He would have seen these descendants of Saxons conquering more than the Romans did, who subdued men, but these subdued the incoherences and difficulties of Nature, reclaiming wild and boundless wastes and converting them into arable land and scenes of civilization. (149)

The Saxon sword is also a tool – 'Our Epic [has] now become Tools and the Man' (*PP* 247) – that brings forth the land, both the material land, which provides food, and the conceptual fatherland, the nation that demands allegiance.

Carlyle's nationalism and imperialism enable him to envisage emigration as a solution to the plight of the surplus population of workers, for even if every mill-owner became a Cedric, England would still be faced with the fact that there are too many Gurths. In *Sartor Resartus*, he proposed colonial expansion as the solution to feeding Britain's surplus population:

> How thick stands your population in the Pampas and Savannas of America; round ancient Carthage, and in the interior of Africa; on both slopes of the Altaic chain, in the central Platform of Asia; in Spain, Greece, Turkey, Crim Tartary, the Curragh of Kildare? One man, in one year, as I have understood it, if you lend him Earth, will feed himself and nine others. Alas, where now are the Hengsts and Alarics of our still glowing, still expanding Europe; who, when their home is grown too narrow, will enlist and, like Fire-pillars, guide onwards those superfluous masses of indomitable living Valour; equipped, not now with the battle-axe and war-chariot, but with the steam-engine and ploughshare? Where are they? – Preserving their Game!' (SR 170)

In *Past and Present*, Carlyle again draws on the myth of Hengist and Horsa, depicting them as colonists responding to the Malthusian dilemma of over-population: 'Fourteen hundred years ago it was by a considerable "Emigration Service", never doubt it, by much enlistment, discussion and apparatus, that we ourselves arrived in this remarkable Island' *(PP* 265). What he has in mind is stated more explicitly in 'On History Again' (1833), where he claims that Hengist and Horsa had 'determined on a man-hunt in Britain' because 'the boar-hunt at home [had] got over-crowded' (HE 22). As references elsewhere in the passage make clear, he was drawing on Milton's *History of Britain* (1670), which records that 'it was the custom in old *Saxony*, when their numerous off-spring overflow'd the narrowness of thir bounds, to send them out by lot into new dwellings, wherever they found room, either vacant or to be forc't' (*PP* 116). Carlyle uses this ancient precedent to justify new migrations:

> Our little Isle is grown too narrow for us; but the world is wide enough yet for another Six Thousand Years. England's sure markets will be among new Colonies of Englishmen in all quarters of the Globe. All men trade with all men, when mutually convenient; and are even bound to do it by the Maker of Men. Our friends of China who guiltily refused to trade, in these circumstances, – had we not to argue with them, in cannon-shot at last, and convince them that they ought to trade! (*PP* 264).

Emigration would enable colonists to transform '[w]aste desart-shrubs of the tropical swamps...[into] Cotton-trees', which in turn would supply raw materials for English industry (*PP* 169–70). Two basic assumptions underlie these proposals: that there is abundant work available in the colonies for the unemployed and that because the colonies are less populated than England, there is less competition for work. In *Past and*

Present these two notions are intertwined: the idea of waste land suggests that colonial territory is unpopulated and the idea of chaos suggests metonymically that its inhabitants are anarchic, and so must be ordered and regimented by labour.[13] A further benefit of emigration is that in addition to assisting the poor by sending them abroad where they can find work, it would aid those who remained behind by removing surplus labour from the marketplace and reducing competition for work in England.

These views inform Carlyle's juxtaposition of the images of sewers that drain off disease: 'Through the swamps we will shape causeways, force purifying drains' (*PP* 277). Once again the image has both a literal and a figurative register. Carlyle endorses 'Sanitary Regulations' as a means of alleviating material conditions, the 'foul cellar[s]' and 'poison-lanes' of London's slums (*PP* 261–2), but he also imagines symbolic sanitation, slum clearance, and emigration as draining sewage from England.[14]

As Patrick Brantlinger has pointed out, 'Many Victorian social reformers viewed a 'redundant population'...as nonproductive waste, the unfortunate byproduct of the social organism' (117). The metonymy by which the qualities of chaotic, vacant wasteland are transferred to its inhabitants can be seen in Carlyle's discussion of work. In 'Labour', draining swamps is not only a kind of work, it is also a simile for labour itself, which is 'a free-flowing channel, dug and torn by noble force through the sour mud-swamp of one's existence, like an ever-deepening river there, it runs and flows; – draining off the sour festering water gradually from the root of the remotest grass-blade; making instead of pestilential swamp a green fruitful meadow with its clear-flowing stream' (*PP* 197). Like the anarchic inhabitants of Haiti and Jamaica, the English poor are the subjects of labour that transforms them from a chaotic, pestiferous mass into orderly and productive workers. By draining off surplus labour and sending it abroad, emigration reduces domestic competition for labour and reduces the likelihood of anarchic epidemics such as the Manchester Insurrection, a series of violent protests against the reduction of wages that broke out in the industrial midlands in August of 1842 and prompted Carlyle to write *Past and Present*. While he seems to attack telescopic philanthropy, arguing that the needs of the English poor are superior to the needs of 'Quashee', Carlyle collapses the distinction between 'here' and 'there', and between industrial worker and freed slave. The purpose of producing order 'there' is to create order 'here' in Britain. Implicitly, English workers are not orderly Saxons, but anarchic pirates, Mandingos, Chinese or Chactaws, and so must be regimented by Captains of Industry. While Carlyle might place English workers higher than Africans on the chain of being, it is perhaps not insignificant that he describes them as 'yellow' rather than white. As he wrote in a letter to American delegates to the World Antislavery

Convention in 1840, 'the *green* and *yellow* slaves, grown green with sheer hunger in my own neighbourhood, were far more interesting to me!' (*CL* 12:254). For Carlyle, race overlaps with class, the condition of mill workers with that of slaves (see Anderson 149).

Carlyle uses conceptions of the other as a means of understanding what troubles him about his own culture. Not surprisingly, his use of race and advocacy of emigration are often at odds with his critique of the cash nexus. Perhaps because he sees the problem of the cash nexus as a problem of governance – *laissez-faire* as the failure to govern – he does not consider the fact that international commerce and trade depend on cash. This paradox would become apparent in 'The Negro Question', where he insists that 'the gods' prefer that the freed slaves cultivate 'commercial' and 'valuable products' rather than 'pumpkins' (*Works* 29:375, 373). The commercial product Carlyle refers to is sugar, the chief export of Haiti and main ingredient in marmalade. In favouring sugar over pumpkins, he privileges commodity production that involves trade and requires a medium of exchange (*cash*), over domestic, subsistence production. For Carlyle, the difference between commodity and subsistence production seems to be that large-scale commodity production requires hierarchical organisation – overseers or captains who make workers orderly – while small-scale subsistence production can be engaged in by individuals acting for themselves. As John Stuart Mill remarked in his reply to 'The Negro Question', this argument rests on the assumption that spices and sugar are more valuable because they are 'commercial' and that their value is defined by exchange, a startling contradiction of Carlyle's belief that value cannot be defined in purely economic terms (*Essays on Equality* 90, 92).

In *Past and Present,* Carlyle momentarily imagines eliminating the cash nexus by giving workers an 'interest' in production, but he quickly backs away from this possibility with the remark: 'Despotism is essential in most enterprises; I am told, they do not tolerate 'freedom of debate' on board a Seventy-four!' (*PP* 278). His coupling of social order with hierarchy, mediated by the image of colonial swamp-draining, means that race hierarchies underwrite his solution to the cash-nexus. His argument that the captain of industry must do right by his workers means also that the captain must put a stop to 'Palaver', by force if necessary. While he insists that social justice can be achieved only by establishing social order, his use of race demonstrates the contradictions in how he conceives the relationship between 'Cedric' and 'Gurth'.

Notes

1. On hierarchy in Carlyle, see my *Carlyle and the Search for Authority*, 136; on race hierarchy see Stepan 12–14.
2. See Young's discussion of Said 159–61.
3. As Gallagher has shown, this argument was widely circulated before Carlyle took it up, and there were many variants, both pro- and anti-slavery (chap. 1).
4. A *Quarterly Review* article of 1819 (coincidentally titled 'The Past and Present State of Hayti') depicted the revolution as evidence of the equality of blacks to whites, and praised Christophe's administration (a similar view was expressed in an 1825 *Edinburgh Review* article). Similarly, a letter printed in *Blackwood's* in 1821 remarks on Haiti's civilised society and the warm reception provided by the Duke of Marmalade ('Christophe' 546).
5. Carlyle would almost certainly have known this article, which appeared in the August *Fraser's* as he and his brother published several pieces in it that year (Carlyle in February, May, September, and November, and his brother John in May and July of 1830).
6. In the 'The Negro Question', Carlyle presents the full-blown stereotype of Quashee '[s]unk to the ears in pumpkin, imbibing saccharine juices, and much at his ease in the Creation…a merry-hearted, grinning, dancing, singing, affectionate kind of creature' (*Works* 29:352, 357–8).
7. See Gates 220–1. The OED gives the following definitions: '1. A grotesque idol said to have been worshipped by certain tribes or associations of Negroes. 2. *transf.* a. An object of unintelligent veneration. b. Obscure or meaningless talk or writing; nonsense'.
8. Carlyle refers elsewhere in *Past and Present* to Mungo Park's *Travels*, which describe the use of mumbo jumbo and the palaver to solve marital disputes (*PP* 29, 268). On the relationship between meaningless speech and revolutionary anarchy, see Vanden Bossche 84.
9. It should be noted that about this time Carlyle met Richard Owen, who had recently completed research refuting these claims (Stepan 16; see *CL* 15:51).
10. Carlyle would have come across the use of the Saxon myth to argue for the independence of parliament while researching Cromwell (see MacDougall 55–9). Although he had little faith in parliament, he was certainly sympathetic with the parliamentarians' desire to seek independence from Charles I.
11. The source is Nennius, *Historia Britonum*, sec. 46. Other ancient sources report the speech, but omit the first two words (e. g. Geoffrey of Monmouth), which has led some editors to assume that they were added by Carlyle (Hughes 340).
12. Forster Manuscript, National Art Library, Victoria and Albert Museum, London, fol. 38v.
13. In *The History of Jamaica* (1774), Edward Long argued that 'British freedoms' should not be extended to slaves in the colonies because blacks were 'almost incapable of making any progress in civility or science' (quot. in MacDougall 85).
14. Chadwick had sent Carlyle a copy of his 1842 *Report on the Sanitary Condition of the Labouring Population*, and Carlyle was quite familiar with Chadwick's proposals for sanitary reform.

Works Cited

Anderson, Benedict. *Imagined Communities: Reflections on the Origin and Spread of Nationalism*. London: Verso, 1991.

Brantlinger, Patrick. *Rule of Darkness: British Literature and Imperialism, 1830–1914*. Ithaca and New York: Cornell UP, 1988.

[Brougham, Henry.] 'State of Haiti'. *Edinburgh Review* 41 (1825): 497–507.

Carlyle, Thomas. *Lectures on the History of Literature Delivered by Thomas Carlyle April to July 1838*. Ed. Greene, J. Reay. New York: Scribners, 1892.

———. *Past and Present*. Ed. Richard D. Altick. Boston: Houghton and Mifflin, 1965. Quotations from Carlyle's works have been collated against the first edition and corrected when necessary. Altick's edition of *Past and Present* is based on the first London edition of the work, and I have used it throughout in preference to the less accurate Centenary version.

———. *Reminiscences of My Irish Journey in 1849*. New York: Harper, 1882.

'Christophe, late Emperor of Hayti'. *Blackwood's Magazine* 10 (1821): 545–52.

Eldridge, C. C. *The Imperial Experience: From Carlyle to Forster*. New York: St. Martin's Press, 1996.

Gallagher, Catherine. *The Industrial Reformation of English Fiction: Social Discourse and Narrative Form, 1832–1867*. Chicago: U of Chicago P, 1985.

Gates, Henry Louis. *The Signifying Monkey: A Theory of Afro-American Literary Criticism*. New York: Oxford UP, 1988.

Hughes, A. D. M., ed. *Past and Present*. Oxford: Clarendon Press, 1918.

Lamb, John B. 'Carlyle's *Chartism*, the Rhetoric of Revolution, and the Dream of Empire'. *Victorians Institute Journal* 23 (1995): 129–50.

Lorimer, Douglas A. 'Race, Science, and Culture: Historical Continuities, and Discontinuities, 1850–1914'. In *The Victorians and Race*. Ed. Shearer West. Aldershot, England: Scolar Press; Brookfield, Vermont: Ashgate, 1996.

MacDougall, Hugh A. *Racial Myth in English History: Trojans, Teutons, and Anglo-Saxons*. Hanover, NH: University Press of New England, 1982.

'Mackenzie's Haiti, and Bayley's Four Years in the West Indies'. *Fraser's Magazine* 2 (1830): 61–6.

Mill, John Stuart. 'The Negro Question'. *Essays on Equality, Law, and Education*. Ed. John M. Robson. Toronto: U of Toronto P, 1984. 87–95.

Milton, John. *History of Britain*. New York: Columbia UP, 1932.

Park, Mungo. *Travels of Mungo Park*. Ed. Ronald Miller. Rev. ed. London: Dent, 1954.

Simmons, Clare A. *Reversing the Conquest: History and Myth in Nineteenth-Century British Literature*. New Brunswick, NJ: Rutgers UP, 1990.

Stepan, Nancy. *The Idea of Race in Science: Great Britain, 1800–1960*. Hamden, CT: Archon Books, 1982.

Vanden Bossche, Chris. *Carlyle and the Search for Authority*. Columbus: Ohio State UP, 1991.

Young, Robert. *Colonial Desire: Hybridity in Theory, Culture, and Race*. London and New York: Routledge, 1995.

Chapter 13

Performing Blackness: Carlyle and 'The Nigger Question'

VANESSA D. DICKERSON

In 'An Occasional Discourse on the Negro Question' (1849; retitled 'The Nigger Question', 1853), Carlyle was provocatively ungracious and rigid in his stereotyping of West Indian blacks as lazy pumpkin-eating Quashees.[1] As the New England Quaker poet and abolitionist John Greenleaf Whittier declared in 1854 after he read the 'Occasional Discourse', Carlyle 'vituperates the poor black man with a coarse brutality which would do credit to a Mississippi slave driver, or a renegade Yankee dealer in human cattle on the banks of the Potomac. His rhetoric has a flavor of the slave pen and auction-block - vulgar, unmanly, indecent, a scandalous outrage upon good taste and refined feeling - which at once degrades the author and insults his readers' (34, 35–6). Outrageous, scandalous, and insulting as it was, Carlyle's slave pen and auction-block rhetoric did not prompt black nineteenth-and twentieth-century American writers and thinkers to dismiss him completely. They realised that his discourse was so undeniably and powerfully constitutive, that it could not easily be ignored.

The example of the black American writer and fugitive slave William Wells Brown (1814–84) illustrates the complexity of their response. During a visit to England in the 1850s, he found himself riding an omnibus which Carlyle boarded, and recalls how he had read Carlyle's '"Hero-worship", and "Past and Present", and formed a high opinion of his literary abilities'. But Brown's opinion of Carlyle's is adversely affected by the 'Occasional Discourse on the Nigger Question'. Admitting that Carlyle's 'recent attack upon the emancipated people of the West Indies, and his laborious article in favor of the reëstablishment of the lash and slavery, had created in my mind a dislike for the man', he 'regretted that we were in the same omnibus'. Brown revises his high opinion of Carlyle's literary abilities, finding them 'often monotonous and extravagant'. In his view, Carlyle 'generally takes commonplace thoughts and events, and tries to express them in stronger and statelier language than others'. Carlyle 'cares little what he says, so as he can say it differently from others'. Brown came to see Carlyle as a fallen writer who 'holds no communion with his kind, but stands alone, without mate or fellow. He is like a solitary peak, all access to which is cut off. He exists not by sympathy, but by antipathy'.

Brown is simultaneously dismayed and intrigued by the contradictions in Carlyle's outlook:

> He writes one page in favor of reform, and ten against it. He would hang all prisoners to get rid of them; yet the inmates of the prisons and 'workhouses are better off than the poor'. His heart is with the poor; yet the blacks of the West Indies should be taught that if they will not raise sugar and cotton by their own free will, 'Quashy should have the whip applied to him'. He frowns upon the reformatory speakers upon the boards of Exeter Hall; yet he is the prince of reformers. He hates heroes and assassins; yet Cromwell was an angel, and Charlotte Corday a saint. He scorns everything, and seems to be tired of what he is by nature, and tries to be what he is not.

Brown recognises in Carlyle a notable literary ability, whose sympathy is mixed with antipathy, and concludes that in 'somethings Mr. Carlyle is right: but in many he is entirely wrong' (167).

At the turn of the twentieth century, W. E. B. Du Bois (1868–1963) read Carlyle's *Sartor Resartus* and *Heroes and Hero-Worship* and was immediately impressed. As Du Bois' biographer David Levering Lewis has pointed out: 'His immersion in the works of Carlyle had yielded a rhythm and prose ideal for expressing insights and outrage. *The French Revolution*, Carlyle's dazzling, Calvinist history of divine chastisement and human agency, would remain near at hand' (115–16). Du Bois had earlier referred to Carlyle in an editorial at Fisk University, declaring that if Carlyle were to visit the campus, he would find ample opportunity to admonish students who were not working and planning for the future (Lewis 74–5). Du Bois found Carlyle's rugged style and individualistic transcendentalism inspirational, but as Lewis surmises, he was probably unfamiliar with 'The Nigger Question' (Lewis 75). Nonetheless, he discovered in Carlyle's major writings what Brown had noted earlier: a rhetorical strategy and literary demeanour that aligned him with an oral vernacular tradition associated with blacks in the United States.

There is no evidence that Carlyle himself read anything by nineteenth-century black Americans. While critical and rhetorical studies have identified his writings with a 'heterogeneity of materials' (Tennyson 30), these are largely confined to classical, English, German, Scottish, and Irish models of inspiration. But Carlyle is never quite at ease in the Western stylistic tradition. Twentieth-century critics have struggled to describe his disturbing and unclassifiable prose, which has attracted a diversity of labels: 'esoteric', 'crude', 'violent', 'febrile' (Holloway 37, 7); 'violently mannered and extravagant', 'strangely ordered', 'clogged' (Levine, 'Use and Abuse' 107, 110); 'lavish', 'gospelizing' (Tennyson 195, 67); 'barbarous' (Heffer 19), and perhaps inevitably, 'frequently unreadable' (Klingopulos 13).

In certain vital respects, however, the flamboyance of Carlyle's prose, together with its dramatic and demoniacal energy, links it with black American idioms. Some black critics have denied this affiliation. In an essay characterising black expression, the twentieth-century African American novelist and folklorist Zora Neale Hurston has argued that Carlyle's prose bore little relation to 'the characteristics of negro expression'. Describing black expression as 'highly dramatized' and 'impromptu', she found the style of writers such as Carlyle and Milton evasive and abstract. In her view, their language is divorced from action, 'written' rather than 'hierogliphic', which is characteristic of Negroes (50). She reinforces this distinction by comparing it to the evolution of money as a means of exchange: 'In primitive communities actual goods, however bulky, are bartered for what one wants. This finally evolves into coin, the coin being not real wealth but a symbol of wealth. Still later, even coin is abandoned for legal tender, and still later cheques for certain usages' (49). The real thing, bulky as it is, is replaced by a simulacrum. Repeated substitution transforms actualities into symbols, tangibles into intangibles. Rhetorically speaking, language loses its visceral quality. 'Perhaps we might say', writes Hurston, 'that *Paradise Lost* and *Sartor Resartus* are written in cheque words, those furtherest removed from 'real wealth' and detached from action and thus furtherest from the highly descriptive and dramatic verbal exchanges of the 'Negro [who] even with detached words in his vocabulary – not evolved in him but transplanted on his tongue by contact – must add action to it to make it do' (49). Yet as distant as Carlyle's expression appears from that of blacks, Carlylean and black expression are not as 'detached' as Hurston suggests. Carlyle reinvests 'cheque words' with value in the 'Nigger Question' by using dramatic, hyperbolic, and metaphorical devices that resemble black performance style.

In curious ways, Carlyle tried to assume the role of the black poet, which Henry Louis Gates has defined as 'the point of consciousness, a superconsciousness of his or her people' (176). In the black community of the nineteenth century, this role was frequently realised in the preacher, who was so respected for his ability to teach, lead and sometimes sing, that he was called 'professor'. Victorians recognised Carlyle as a sage and a Jeremiah who had gauged the conditions of the age – not unlike a voodooist – by reading the signs of the times. In interpreting these signs, Carlyle drew upon a religious tradition that he shared with African American preachers, for whom the pulpit proved a site of spiritual, cultural, and political renewal. Like them, Carlyle understood the power of the pulpit. As John Holloway has pertinently remarked, Carlyle 'envies the preacher his pulpit...because he feels that his own message has an almost sacred quality' (21).

While there is no denying the differences between the social preaching of Carlyle in 'The Nigger Question' and those of the nineteenth-century black evangelists hostile to slavery, there is equally no denying that Carlyle's prose resonates with the same dramatic expressiveness characteristic of black preaching, poetry, and talk. Contrary to what Hurston argues, Carlyle does not write rhetorical blank cheques. Like the American black writers whom she describes, Carlyle recasts language through 'the use of metaphor and simile...double descriptives...[and] verbal nouns' and makes 'new force words out of old feeble elements' (Hurston 51). Explaining the peculiarly theatrical aspect of Carlyle's style, George Levine asserts that 'the drama is only possible because Carlyle sees what he is discussing not in logical but in metaphorical terms' ('Use and Abuse' 107).

A good example of this method is Carlyle's use of the metaphor of stampede in the 'Occasional Discourse' to describe a society possessed by notions of democracy, majority and equality. In a world in which the principle of hierarchy is absent, no leader will embody 'the extreme *maximum* of wisdom'(*Works* 29:361). The foolishness of 'million-fold majority', Carlyle admonishes, will bring down upon society the advance of 'buffalo-phalanx[es]' or other smaller porcine 'bristly creatures':'Rushing, namely, in wild *stampede* (the Devil being in them, some small fly having stung them), boundless, - one wing on that edge of your horizon, the other wing on that, and rearward whole tides and oceans of them: - so could Folly rush; the enlightened public one huge Gadarenes-swinery, tail cocked, snout in air, with joyful animating short squeaks; fast and ever faster; down steep places, - to the sea of Tiberias, and the bottomless cloacas [sewer, drain, privy] of Nature'(*Works* 29:362). In Carlyle's view, the biblical and metaphorical stampede dramatises a chaos that is sure to befall Victorian society if 'no man in particular be put at the top' and the idea that 'supply-and-demand' is 'the sufficient substitute for command and obedience among two-legged animals of the unfeathered class'(*Works* 29:361). It may be said of Carlyle's stampede, as Henry Mitchell says of black preaching, that the picturesque language and animated delivery - 'rearward whole tides and oceans of them', 'tail cocked, snout in air', 'joyful animating short squeaks; faster and ever faster' - are part of a larger pattern of concreteness and liveliness. Carlyle's prose would satisfy 'African insistence on images and action, tales and pictures with meaning' (31).

Often Carlyle's metaphors speak at the level of a folk language. For example, in his commentary on the value of permanence in relations between master and servant, he refers to 'Marriage by the month' which 'has been tried and is still extensively practised in spite of Law and Gospel; but is not found to do!' (*Works* 29:368). Carlyle establishes the wedding metaphor in the opening pages of the 'Occasional Discourse', where he warns readers about the dangers that are likely to come out of any organised efforts by do-good philanthropists and social scientists. Like a black 'doer of the word', he prefers 'useful concrete visions to learned abstractions' and in his use of the wedding metaphor, he imitates the preacher who lights an 'emotional fire' in the hearts of his listeners (Mitchell 21, 33). The 'Marriage' between 'Exeter-Hall Philanthropy and the Dismal Science, led by any sacred cause of Black Emancipation, or the like, to fall in love and make a wedding of it, – will give birth to progenies and prodigies; dark extensive moon-calves [daydreamers, imbeciles], unnameable abortions, wide-coiled monstrosities, such as the world has not seen hitherto!' (*Works* 29:354). The 'unholy' wedding produces a grotesque word painting that would be familiar to any black congregation.

Carlyle also constructs metaphors using double descriptives, which Hurston has referred to as 'one of the Negro's greatest contributions to the language'(51). In certain respects Carlyle's 'froth-oceans', 'flunky-world', 'sham-kings', 'sham-subjects', and 'life-theories' (*Works* 29:351, 260, 363, 366) resemble and even match such black American expressions as 'low-down', 'top-superior', 'Lady people', 'Kill-dead', 'Hot-boiling', 'Chop-axe', and 'Sitting-chairs'(Hurston 52). While the Carlylean and African-American double descriptives come out of the same need for expressiveness, Carlyle's examples tend to be less informal than black ones. Levine finds that Carlyle's 'coinage' of these 'compound words, suggest[s] the need to break through conventional means of expression'(110), whereas Hurston recognises that the black double descriptives are both adaptive and expressive, since the black speaker takes the 'word evolved in him but transplanted on his tongue by contact' and 'add[s] action to it to make it do' (49).

Black performance art informs the structure as well as the style of Carlyle's 'Occasional Discourse'. In the essay he creates a framework that is designed to contain the outrageousness of his racist propositions. To a notable extent, this strategy imitates the pattern of the African-American trickster tale. Instead of presenting the essay as his own work, Carlyle opens with a prefatory paragraph in which an Editor identifies the essay on the nigger question as the production of an unknown 'Speaker'. Carlyle further distances himself from the essay by introducing yet another player in the ruse he stages – a 'so-called "Doctor" and "Absconded Reporter", Phelim M'Quirk', into whose hands this essay has mysteriously fallen. Readers learn that it is not the 'absconded' M'Quirk who has delivered this essay for which there is 'no speaker named, no time or place assigned, no commentary of any sort given', but his landlady, who has turned the document over to the journal's editor in hopes of recouping some of her financial loss. Meanwhile, M'Quirk has fled, leaving 'debts, extravagancies and sorrowful insidious finance-operations, now winded-up...to the grief of many poor tradespeople...making too much noise in the police-offices at present!' (*Works* 29:348). In setting up this elaborate introduction, Carlyle performs in a way suggestive of the African trickster figures whose business, among other things, it is to outsmart and entertain.

Critics have noticed Carlyle's penchant for trickery, though Levine and Carlisle Moore have remarked that it was 'one of the few traits which Carlyle did not seem to recognize in himself – the love of hoaxing' (*Boundaries* 52). Holloway also observes how Carlyle's use of rhetorical devices 'may unconsciously trick the reader' (55). Yet the black trickster dimension of the essay is significant, though Carlyle's conception of trickery differs in its intent from African notions. As John Roberts has argued, their tales were a means of negotiating black survival in a world in which 'enslaved Africans...were forced to work endlessly to make...[the system] productive while the masters went to great length to limit their autonomy and access to its material rewards' (31–2). The black trickster often engaged in 'the most outrageous behavior', charming and cajoling in order to subvert 'the master's authority and control in ways that did not disrupt the system' (Roberts 30, 32). The trickster tradition is a subtle form of vernacular protest and resistance to what Roberts argues is the slave masters' repeated effort 'to foist on enslaved Africans an illusion of the system as a cooperative enterprise in whose success both master and slave had a significant stake' (31).

While the ruses of the African American trickster are ultimately liberating, Carlyle's tricks in 'The Nigger Question' are derogatory and reactionary. He encourages his audience to be less hostile to his ideas about the necessity for white masters to maintain mastery of their black servants for life. As part of this effort, Carlyle employs the same oratory that has such an important place in the African American community, scripting the 'Occasional Discourse' as an oral performance. The 'Speaker', should he 'be of any eminence or substantiality, and feel himself aggrieved' (*Works* 29:348) is invited in the framing paragraph to make allowances for the way in which his composition has fallen into the hands of the journal's editor. That the composition is meant to be spoken before an audience is apparent in the opening lines where Carlyle uses the Speaker as a device to deflect any objections the audience may have about his proposals for disciplining black Quashee. The Speaker begins, 'My Philanthropic Friends – It is my painful duty to address some words to you, this evening, on the Rights of Negroes'. Ironically, he allows room for resistance among his white audience, even though he will be advancing an argument for the complete submission of Negroes to their white owners: 'Well, you shall hear what I have to say on the matter; and probably you will not in the least like it' (*Works* 29:349).

To moderate the expected hostile response of his reading audience, Carlyle uses another trick by creating an imagined audience in the essay. He sets up a call-and-response structure that is reminiscent of patterns that Fahamisha Brown has detected in black poetry: 'Writing in the presences of an implicit community/congregation, the poet writes responses to both oral and written cultural calls; the call-and-response structures are written into the poems themselves' (26). Carlyle not only creates his congregation, but he also anticipates their emotional and political responses to his controversial opinions, using the imaginary audience indirectly as a safety valve. After the Speaker insults blacks by describing them as pumpkin-eating horses and refers to their philanthropic friends as asses singing 'loud and long-eared hallelujahs of laudatory psalmody', the reading audience learns about the imaginary audience's response in a bracketed stage direction: '[*Some emotion in the audience; which the Chairman suppressed*]' (*Works* 29:351). The congregation has spoken, but Carlyle has the final word. Though his essay shares features of deception, outrageousness, and humour characteristic of the African American tale, his conclusions are hardly consoling to blacks. But in his ambition to echo Jeremiah or Moses, to break through conventional means of expression, to locate an audience and community and to enact his aims dramatically and metaphorically, Carlyle has unwittingly struck a note of rhetorical solidarity with 'Quashee'.

Note

1 The original essay was reissued in pamphlet form by Thomas Bosworth. As Tarr points out, 'There seems no doubt that the reissue would have come and gone with little fanfare had not the blatant alteration been made in the title from "Negro" to "Nigger"' (343).

Works Cited

Brown, Fahamisha Patricia. *Performing the Word: African American Poetry as Vernacular Culture*. New Brunswick NJ: Rutgers, UP, 1999.

Brown, William Wells. *The American Fugitive in Europe. Sketches of Places and People Abroad.* Ed. Paul Jefferson. New York: Wiener, 1991. 71–235.

Gates, Jr., Henry Louis. *Figures in Black: Words, Signs, and the 'Racial' Self.* New York: Oxford UP, 1987.

Harrold, C.F. *Carlyle and German Thought: 1819-1836.* Hamden CT: Archon, 1963.

Holloway, John. *The Victorian Sage: Studies in Argument.* New York: Norton, 1965.

Hurston, Zora Neale. *The Sanctified Church.* Berkeley CA: Turtle Island, 1981.

Klingopulos, G. D. 'Notes on he Victorian Scene'. *From Dickens to Hardy: Volume 6 of the Pelican Guide to English Literature.* Ed. Boris Ford. Baltimore MD: Penguin, 1963. 11-56.

Levine, George. *The Boundaries of Fiction: Carlyle, Macaulay, Newman.* Princeton: Princeton UP, 1968.

———. 'The Use and Abuse of Carlylese'. *The Art of Victorian Prose.* Ed. George Levine and William Madden. New York: Oxford UP, 1968. 101-126.

Lewis, David Levering. *W. E. B. DuBois: Biography of a Race.* New York: Holt, 1993.

Mitchell, Henry H. *Black Preaching: The Recovery of a Powerful Art.* Nashville TN: Abingdon, 1990.

Roberts, John W. *From Trickster to Badman: The Black Folk Hero in Slavery and Freedom.* Philadelphia PA: U of Pennsylvania P, 1989.

Tarr, Rodger L. 'Emendation as Challenge: Carlyle's 'Negro Question' from Journal to Pamphlet'. *The Papers of the Bibliographical Society of America* 75 (1981): 341-5.

Tennyson, G.B. *'Sartor Called 'Resartus': The Genesis Structure, and Style of Thomas Carlyle's First Major work.* Princeton NJ: Princeton UP, 1965.

Whittier, John G. *Literary Recreations and Miscellanies.* Boston MA: Ticknor and Fields, 1854.

Chapter 14

The Carlyles and 'Phantasm Aristocracy'

SHEILA McINTOSH

The story of Thomas Carlyle's friendship with Lady Ashburton and Jane Welsh Carlyle's jealousy of her is well known. A less familiar aspect of the story is the role the Carlyles played in the Ashburton circle. A useful vantage point from which to explore this relationship is the Ashburtons' Christmas house party of 1855, the last given by Lord Ashburton and Lady Harriet Ashburton. Numerous observers wrote about the event, either in letters or in memoirs, and these give a particularly vivid cameo of a Victorian country house party, the Ashburtons' hospitality, and the Carlyles' position in this society.

The Carlyles' membership of the Ashburton circle seems anomalous. In 1843 Thomas wrote in *Past and Present* that the aristocracy had become 'Phantasm-Aristocracy', 'totally careless to *do* its work; careful only to clamour for the wages of doing its work, - nay for higher and palpably undue *wages*, and Corn-Laws and *increase* of rents; the old rate of wages not being adequate now!' (*Works* 10:40). In 1848, in conversation with his friend, the writer Richard Monckton Milnes, he refers to the English aristocracy as 'a tragic spectacle' and wondered how they endured their 'vacant existence':'I always think of the sublime ennui of the Halls of Eblis - of men with burning fire for hearts in their bosoms, who will stand no pity or advice in any way, but suffer on' (Pope Hennessy 274). In 1853 he described life at the Grange as a 'continued series of elegant *idlenesses* thro the waking hours of the 24, this does not tend much to edify me at all' (*CL* 28:103). Jane Welsh Carlyle was no less scathing in her denunciations of aristocratic idleness. Meeting Lady Harriet in 1846, she was baffled by her character: '[She] especially who is the woman of the largest intellect I have ever seen - how can *she* reconcile herself to a life which after all is a mere dramatic representation, however successful, fills me with astonishment and *a certain* sorrow' (*CL* 20:179).

How then had Thomas and Jane become part of the inner core of the Ashburton circle, and what were they doing at the house party of

Christmas 1855? In 1850, Amalie Bölte said that Carlyle had been 'courting intimacy with the aristocracy for years' and that now he was 'the defender of this world of appearances', 'a betrayal of his true self' (*CL* 25:288). But the Ashburtons courted the Carlyles too, particularly Thomas, and as with all complicated people, inconsistency is not always betrayal of the 'true self'. In certain respects the Ashburtons are the protagonists. They determined the 'rules' of their circle and established its ambience and yet there is no full biography of either of them, and only a fraction of their correspondence is accessible. Less is known about them than many other members of their circle, and what is known is fragmentary.

We know that their interests were literary and intellectual but that they were also traditionalists. The author and journalist George Venables said of Lady Ashburton that in spite of her friendships with liberals and radicals, 'her own predilections...were always in favour of ancient beliefs and established institutions' (628-9). This was also true of her husband. As a young man Lord Ashburton played a central role in putting down the 1830 Hampshire Swing riots. The riots, caused by rural poverty and increasingly repressive Poor Laws, were rooted in the aristocratic 'Do-Nothing' attitudes that Carlyle excoriated in *Past and Present.* Lord Ashburton's role is revealed in his letters to Lady Harriet, several of which are in the Hampshire Record Office, and many more in the National Library of Scotland. He entered into the protection of his own and other aristocrats' property with gusto, and on his own admission acted with such rashness while protecting his cousin, Thomas Baring of Stratton Park, that one of the rioters, Henry Cook, knocked him down and was later hanged for the assault (MS:NLS Acc. 11388). Thomas Baring had previously torn down empty houses to stop paupers from acquiring a settlement and he had reduced poor relief in two parishes (Kent 6). The papers in NLS give a more complicated picture of Ashburton. In a letter to Lady Harriet, dated 26 November 1830, he recalled his shame at descending on houses at night to make arrests: 'I swore I never would engage in the like again. But oaths are frail when the excitement returns. My midnight excursion proved to have no danger in it, to relieve the infamy of the occupation' (MS: NLS Acc. 11388).

But the incident did nothing to convert Ashburton to more liberal views. In a letter to the Duke of Wellington in April 1838, he opposed his father, who had argued against the enforced recruitment of the yeomanry into the militia (HRO). He remained suspicious of levelling tendencies. Though his proposal for educational reform in 1851 – the 'Ashburton Movement for the Teaching of Common Things' – was relatively enlightened, it differed sharply from the work of the Rev. Richard Dawes, on which it was based. At King's Somborne School in Hampshire, Dawes introduced means-tested fees so that even the poorest farm workers could afford the fees and pupils were not segregated according to social class. Algebra, geometry, and natural science were taught to all pupils as well as basic reading and arithmetic. Dawes based his practice on the belief that education was 'not as a privilege to be graduated according to men's social condition, but the right of all' (Council of Education 27).

Ashburton agreed that everyone should have the means to develop their skills and ingenuity but insisted that working men should not think of 'quitting their sphere, they should not be learning what those above them learn;...that which really elevates a man is the cultivation of mind, which follows upon its enlightened application to his work' and that work is determined by his station.[1] Writing at the time of the Preston cotton industry strikes of 1853, he said working men should wait until the laws of nature secured them justice. In Carlylean language, he compared the strikers to Israelites who 'passed their children through the fire to win the favour of Moloch and Ashtaroth...they are passing their children through the furnace of affliction and disease and want to win the interposition of a principle just as false, just as delusive' (Ashburton 1854:13-16). In April 1855 in an address to Winchester and Hampshire schoolmasters, he said that the troops' suffering in the Crimea was the consequence of their faulty education. The four-fifths of the troops not educated at all were 'the pariahs of civilization', while the rest were 'spoiled, misdirected children'. He accused the troops of lacking the 'ingenuity and contrivance' needed to provide themselves with food, shelter and clothing in their 'encounter with material difficulties' (*Times* 14 April 1855). Yet Lord Ashburton had not been to the Crimea and was oblivious to the widespread outrage against the conduct of the war and the aristocratic monopoly of the high command.

Lord Ashburton was clearly more progressive and enlightened than those members of his class, who feared that the education of the working man would produce insurrection. In a speech in November 1855 to celebrate the founding of the Birmingham Literary Institution, Ashburton declared that an educated work force was essential if Britain was to compete effectively in world markets (*Hampshire Chronicle* 25 Nov. 1855). Carlyle praised the speech, but questioned Ashburton's methods of getting things done: 'Nothing can be better in the way of a speech, if you will speak to such a pack. My chief dissent, I find always, lies in this, that you *hope* some advance will be made by these methods of institutioning, dinnering &c &c; and that I, unfortunate, see no shadow of salvation on that side'. He reiterates that action is better than words, even, in his inimitable way suggesting that Lord and Lady Ashburton should themselves teach in 'solidly practical' ways the 'common things to the young populations that depend on you...But I know it is supremely difficult, ugly in the doing as any real labour is, only thrice beautiful when *done*' (*CL* 30:126-7).

Carlyle's feelings about the aristocracy were undoubtedly ambivalent. In spite of their failings they were the only ones who could 'save us from the bottomless pit' (Pope- Hennessy 274), representing as they did an older and more stable social hierarchy, infinitely preferable to democracy and laissez-faire. Even though Ashburton lacked Carlyle's intellect they were natural allies. They felt comfortable together and respected each other. Memoirs of Ashburton's friends and his letters indicate that he was an affectionate friend and husband, with a shy and puritanical side to his nature. In an early comment on Thackeray, who later became his close friend, he said that he had little to recommend him and that in his company he felt 'as a modest woman does in loose society even when it puts on its best behaviour...I have lived too little in low society to be able to dispense with refinement unless the want of it be redeemed by undoubted talent, and even then!!' (11 March 1844; MS:NLS Acc.11388). But Carlyle valued this 'refinement', determined to see it even in quite minor acts. Writing to his mother in 1853, Carlyle reports Ashburton's quick response to the news of a fire at a neighbouring farm: 'I admired much the silent promptitude with which Lord A*n*, telling nobody, went out, leaving his dinner in the middle...and galloped off with a groom in the wild squally night...This is what an English country gentlemen is always good for...if he is of the right quality' (*CL* 28:95).

It is perhaps more difficult to explain Lady Ashburton's widely acknowledged reputation for wit. Her appeal must have been the result of her physical presence, which is difficult for even the most skilled memoirist to convey a century and a half later. In a perceptive analysis, Lord Charles Fulke Greville, the politician and diarist described her as 'the most conspicuous woman in society, intelligent, quick and vivacious in conversation' with 'a spirit of genuine benevolence as well as hospitality'. She was kind to children but avoided family talk in case it suggested useless regrets, her own child having died in infancy. In Greville's view it was not difficult for a woman in her position to attract people: 'Lady Ashburton laid herself out for this, while she exercised hospitality on a great scale, she was more of a *précieuse* than any woman I have known'. He said her chief faults were 'caprice and a disposition to quarrels...about nothing' (2:107-9).

Others noticed her despotic tendencies. Richard Monckton Milnes remembers one of her victims saying, 'I do not mind being knocked down but I can't stand being danced upon after' (231). But he also recalled her 'intellectual gaiety' and 'joyous sincerity that no conventionalities high or low could restrain' (231-2). The civil servant Henry Taylor said she was 'the most brilliant phenomenon of London society drawing round her all of it that was much distinguished in social, political and literary life'. Her wit was 'too subtle, swift, born of the moment...to be capable of lending itself to a record' and she was 'a person of continually deepening nature and of great truth, strength and constancy in friendship' (*Autobiography* 309-11). For Goldwin Smith, the liberal thinker and activist, she was the nearest thing in England 'to the queen of the French salon before the Revolution'. He doubted that Lady Ashburton ever gave Welsh Carlyle 'serious cause for unhappiness', though he admitted she was 'a queen, and may like other Royalties, have been sometimes a little high; but she was incapable of doing anything unfeeling' (140). Like many other men, he admired her character as well as her wit.

Lady Ashburton's obituary in the *Annual Register* echoed many of these opinions, and linked her character to a quiet yet significant change in the tenor of English society. It observed that 'her position was one of public utility', and that the Ashburton hospitality, because it was 'open to all excellence and liberal to all opinions', was 'honourable to English manners'. It showed 'the luxury of wealth compatible with simplicity of life, and mental superiority without taint of pride or affectation'. The obituary praised her wit and her humour which 'sometimes astonished a society accustomed to a vapid and colourless conversation', but attracted those who knew 'that her singular good sense, her penetration of character, her solid information, and above all her deep love of truth, were fully to be traced and understood'. The writer regretted that the same apprehension of 'moral and intellectual greatness' which prevented her from patronage in her friendships with writers and scientists also prevented her leaving any evidence of her powers.

Notwithstanding the praise heaped on both the Ashburtons, their influence was ephemeral. Neither lived very differently from other members of the 'idle rich', nor did they seek to disturb the political, social, or intellectual status quo. What distinguished them was their ability to maintain a lively social, intellectual circle, to which the Carlyles, even Jane, willingly belonged. The Christmas party at the Grange in 1855 provides some insight into the appeal that the Ashburtons had for Thomas and Jane. They arrived at the Grange on 17 December 1855 in a sour mood. Jane felt depressed and jealous of Lady Ashburton's hold over her husband, while Thomas, tormented by the burden of *Frederick the Great*, was grimly determined to be amiable for his hosts' sake. Their letters reflected their mutual irritation. Jane wrote to Margaret Welsh on 10 January that with all the talent, wit and champagne around her, she should have been happier: 'God help me! what a number of "distinguished" men have passed through this house since I came into it'. She complained bitterly about Tennyson constantly reading and talking about 'Maud', and regretted the arrival of a steady stream of guests, 'each one of them pretending to be "one and somewhat"' (Huxley, *Cornhill Magazine* 633-5). Thomas appeared only slightly less uncomfortable. He complained to John Forster, his brother, his sister and his assistant Joseph Neuberg about his lack of sleep and the uncongenial company, and bitterly commented that there was neither pleasure nor profit in the visit, except in the medical sense, that he felt older and in 'a sour humour...not...*enjoying* the kind of things and persons that are chiefly here at this season' (*CL* 30:144).

Other guests' comments give a much more dramatic and complex view of the Ashburtons and activities at the Grange, and offer a different perspective from that of the Carlyles. Arriving at the Grange on 14 December, the young American Elisabeth Dwight, Ellen Twisleton's sister, wrote to her older sister Mary Parkman about the size of the grounds, the rooms (the drawing room as big as Boston Common) and their quarters which contained 'everything the human mind could desire'. Surveying the grounds, she comments, 'The place is a superb one, rather for the shape of the ground and from the stately old trees than from any case of money expended on it' (Houghton). She is as amused as well as impressed by the opulence: 'A heavenly servant met us at the door, who carried us through the Door to the Drawing-room, which is about the size of the Common'. Of the paintings she comments, 'We have only a Vandyck in one room and a Paul Veronese in the other...which isn't what we're accustomed to, but we manage to get on, & overlook the omissions of the other great masters' (Houghton; *CL* 30:xix). It may have been in Jane's words 'a country house with a vengeance' (*CL* 21:83) but the grandeur and the graciousness, clearly gave pleasure to most of the guests, including Thomas, whom Henry Taylor remembers telling funny stories and laughing wildly at them (*Correspondence* 214).

Monckton Milnes believed that the presence of Carlyle gave to it and to Bath House a 'reality' that made it 'more human than elsewhere' (236), and Henry Taylor wrote that at the Christmas party, 'there was a 'cloud of savans, physiologists, chemists, mechanists, historians, poets, artists, Doctor this and Professor that; but the Carlyles flashed through the cloud and the Brookfields gleamed through it'. Taylor added, 'there was a great deal that was agreeable and interesting in the party; and had there been three more elements in it, - youth, folly and music, - there would have been nothing wanting to its charm' (*Autobiography* 2:141-2). Tennyson enjoyed himself far more than he expected. Lady Ashburton had corresponded with him since the 1840s and invited him to parties on several occasions, but he had always refused (Moore 80-1). Writing to his wife on 5 January, he said that he could not detect 'the least touch of the haughtiness which fame attributes to [Lady Ashburton]...though like enough she sometimes snubs her own grade now and then when she sees presumption as folly'. It was 'a house not uneasy to live in – only I regret my little fumatory at Farringford. Here they smoke among the oranges, lemons and camellias. That sounds pleasant but isn't' (*Letters* 2:140).

Amongst many others who came and went were Dicky Doyle the illustrator and caricaturist; Henry Drummond, the previous owner of the Grange; Edward Ellice, a politician and close colleague of Lord Ashburton's, whom Carlyle called 'the *oiliest* and best-natured of old men' (30 Dec; CL 30:151); the 'pleasant but sanguinary' Lord Gifford, who had killed fifty six tigers, eleven elephants and a multitude of bears (Taylor, *Autobiography* 129); Lord Lansdowne, patron of the arts and literature, and one of the founders of the London Library; Robert Lowe, the free-trade advocate, Tom Taylor, the playwright, Zoe Thomson, the beautiful Anglo-Greek wife of William Thomson, the Provost of Queens College Oxford, whom Jane described as the 'insipidest little thing you ever saw under the name of beauty' (*Cornhill Magazine* 633-5), Edward Twisleton with his American wife and her young sister from Boston, and John Tyndall, professor of natural history at the Royal Institution. Tyndall sat next to Jane at dinner when they spent most of their time talking about Thomas. She charmed him and summarising the atmosphere at the Grange, he declared to a friend: 'If this be the so-called formality of aristocratic life, I must say that I have seen it a million times intensified in a party of trades people'. Tyndall left the gathering 'with a perfume of kindness hanging round my thoughts' (JT to Thomas Hirst, 12 Jan. 1856; Tyndall Papers).[2]

Against this background of elegance, opulence, eccentricity, and amusing talk small, dramas were played out and later discussed in letters and memoirs. A particularly controversial incident was Lady Ashburton's gift of a dress to Welsh Carlyle, on the advice of Jane Brookfield, which Jane deeply resented (*Brookfield* 2:426-7). The origins of the insult are mysterious, but Virginia Surtees speculates that a made-up dress would only have been given to someone socially inferior (226-7). Though it is doubtful that Lady Ashburton intended to insult her deliberately, Jane may have regarded the gesture as an effort to remind her of her inferior social position. This may have been the incident about which Henry Taylor was writing when he remarked that 'a little while ago there was a state of things in which she had had more difficulty in keeping things straight than she had ever had in her life before, and that the effort had been so dreadful that she could not have gone on with it for three days more' (*Correspondence* 214).

Perhaps the wittiest accounts of the people and events of the 1855 Christmas house party are those given by Ellen Twisleton and Elisabeth

Dwight in their letters to their sister, Mary Parkman. These sisters were in their mid-twenties, lively, good-looking, and clever, and Elisabeth Dwight was two months into her first visit to England. Their analysis of the surroundings and the relationships between the guests was acute, sardonic, and unaffected by clan loyalty. Their letters are a mixture of gossip, fashion news, satire, and clever observation. From the outset, they are aware of English reserve and propriety. As Elisabeth warns her sister on 26 December, 'I feel the wonderful difficulty of understanding these English people, without the observation of years, for the code of universal good-breeding which is so religiously observed, with all its charm and advantages has somewhat the effect of an universal mask, through which the different individualities are rarely seen on short acquaintance' (Houghton; *CL* 30:xix).

Elisabeth carefully recorded how hard both Ashburtons worked at keeping their guests entertained. Lady Ashburton's 'expression is almost wholly intellectual, her manner not haughty but exceedingly reserved and dignified'. At breakfast she 'talked to left and right, in the most agreeable manner. From the table the ladies went to the billiard room, & and the gentlemen followed very shortly. Books in every direction, & the newspapers for the gentlemen' (Houghton). To the delight of her young American guests, Lady Ashburton read some of James Lowell's *Biglow Papers* 'in a way which set everyone laughing'. All her 'talents were devoted to our entertainment' and 'she could not open her mouth without being agreeable'. She was like the princesses in fairy tales 'who spoke pearls and diamonds', and 'the indescribable charm of her voice, language and manner increases every day' (Houghton; *CL* 30:xix, xx). It was a joy for Elisabeth to listen to her host's management of the conversation: 'I am very much inclined to think, that Lady Ashburton deserves admiration & respect for more things than her wit, & that she is free from petty ways of thinking of, or dealing with other people. – To see her with Carlyle is better than any play I ever saw; for she turns his howls into the merriest of laughs, & evidently refreshes *him*, as much as she does the rest of the company. You will see that I am consistently in love with her' (Houghton; *CL* 30: xix, 144).

In the same letter Elisabeth writes of Lady Sandwich, Venables, and others making exploratory expeditions in her direction, 'to see what was to be picked up, so that I had no solitude to complain of' (Houghton). As Americans and to some extent outsiders, the sisters witnessed every detail of the ritual. They saw affectation, generosity, snobbery, and constant movement as each guest sought agreeable conversation. One evening Elisabeth watched while her sister and Mrs Carlyle 'coalesced' and Lady Ashburton tried to get away from a particularly tiresome group of women. Through another entrance came Jane Brookfield, 'Thackeray's ideal woman...an exceedingly pretty person, who does not speak above her breath, comes 'the startled fawn' perpetually, & dresses in true English style, with a net on her head and a mantle over her shoulders. The gentlemen admire her and the ladies want to set a dog on her' (Houghton; *CL* 30:xx).

In a postcript to the same letter, Ellen Twisleton called Jane Brookfield 'a regular "intrigante"' and described relations between her and Jane as 'preternaturally civil' (Houghton) because they disliked each other. Elisabeth found Thomas 'a younger and smoother looking person than I expected, & and was so well dressed and combed that when he came into dinner I could not believe it was he who looked so much like other people...He came out at dinner with one of his tremendous Jeremiads, against the age, sent us all to perdition without the slightest deference to our feelings, and talked so loud that the whole company inevitably stopped to listen several times. – I cannot say he attracted me in spite of his evident genius'. At the end of the stay in her letter of 26 December she wrote, 'We left Carlyle scolding, Lady Ashburton entertaining, Mrs Brookfield smiling and toadying, Mrs Carlyle neither smiling nor toadying...certainly no one could pass a more amusing week than we have done; & yet it was not the kind of life that made one's heart stay behind' (Houghton; *CL* 30:114, 44).

Jane Welsh Carlyle is not mentioned as frequently as Thomas in memoirs. To Goldwin Smith, she was 'a modest person always in the background with no reputation for cleverness amongst those at the Grange' (142-3). Zoe Thomson called her 'poor Mrs Carlyle' (Rickards 63). This was in striking contrast to the way she was seen outside the Ashburton circle. Her *Journal* for the period shortly before and after the Christmas visit to the Grange, although often introspective and gloomy, gives an impression of a busy, sociable life. In her own circle, which at the time included Ruskin, Geraldine Jewsbury, the painter Robert Tait, the actress Sarah Anderton, and the Irish poet William Allingham, she was in demand (see JWC's *Journal*, *CL* 30:197-262). She did take part in the social intercourse of the Ashburton circle and other members enjoyed her company. She could be exhilarating and charming, although she did not command as large an audience as Thomas. Certainly Ellen Twisleton, Elisabeth Dwight, and John Tyndall did not see Jane as Goldwin Smith's nonentity. The Grange was not a natural milieu for her. Like Thomas, she disapproved of idleness and extravagant opulence. Had she not been jealous of Lady Ashburton, the Grange might have provided her with an amusing and temporary diversion but like Elisabeth Dwight it was not the place where her heart would have stayed behind. She would certainly have appreciated the irony of her own jealousy being the chief source of present interest in Lady Ashburton, while her gifts as a writer are increasingly recognised (Pope Hennessy 158).

George Venables said that both the Carlyles' lives would have been impoverished without the Ashburtons' friendship (629), but it is equally true that without the Carlyles, the Ashburtons' lives would have been duller. In spite of the impact the friendship had on the Carlyles' private lives and their marriage, there were many other relationships which had far more intellectual significance for them. Thomas was more at ease at the Grange than Jane for many reasons; there was his admiration for Lady Ashburton, undoubtedly reciprocated, the opportunity for long wild rides through the countryside, the elegance of the surroundings, but there was also the fact that although the Ashburtons belonged to the 'idle rich', they avoided many of the excesses of their class. They were able to see beyond social hierarchy and appreciated the value of intellect. They also had a moral worthiness that Carlyle venerated and found reassuring.

Notes

1 The Ashburton Movement influenced Dickens and his friend Angela Burdett Coutts; see Fielding.

2 I am grateful to Kenneth J. Fielding for giving me a copy of this letter.

Works Cited

Annual Register (May, 1857).

Ashburton Correspondence. 100M70/F1-4. Hampstead Record Office (HRO).

Ashburton Papers. Acc. 11388. NLS.

Ashburton Prizes for the Teaching of 'Common Things'. An Account of the Proceedings of a meeting between Lord Ashburton and the Elementary Schoolmasters, assembled at Winchester, on... December 16, 1853. London, 1854.

Brookfield, Charles and Frances. *Mrs Brookfield and her Circle*. New York: Scribner, 1905.

Council of Education. *An Account of the King's Sombourne School*. In 'Minutes of the Committee of Council of Education, 1847-8'. London, 1849.

Fielding, K. J. 'Hard Times and Common Things'. *Imagined Worlds: Essays on some English novels and novelists in honour of John Butt*. Ed. M. Mack and I. Gregor. London: Methuen, 1968. 183-203.

Greville, Charles C. F. *A Journal... 1852-1860*. Third Part of *The Greville Memoirs*. 2 vols. London: Longmans Green, 1887.

Houghton Library, Harvard University. Letters of Ellen Twisleton and Elisabeth Dwight. *45M-98 (18)-(88) .

Huxley, Leonard. 'A Sheaf of Letters from Jane Welsh Carlyle'. *Cornhill Magazine* 124 (1926): 493-510, 622-38.

Kent, David. *Popular Radicalism and the Swing Riots in Central Hampshire*. Hampshire Papers, No. 11. Hampshire County Council, 1997.

Milnes, Richard Monckton (Lord Houghton). *Monographs Personal and Social*. London: Murray, 1873.

Moore, Richard. 'New Letters from Tennyson to the Ashburtons'. *Tennyson Research Bulletin* 7 (1998): 75-82.

Pope-Hennessy, James. *The Flight of Youth*. London: Constable, 1949.

Rickards, E. C. *Zoe Thomson of Bishopthorpe*. London: John Murray, 1916.

Smith, Goldwin. *Reminiscences*. Ed. A. Haultain. New York: Macmillan, 1910.

Surtees, Virginia. *Jane Welsh Carlyle*. Salisbury: Michael Russell, 1986.

Taylor, Henry. *Correspondence*. Ed. Edward Dowden, London: Longmans, Green, 1888.

———. *Autobiography*. London: Longmans Green, 1885.

Tennyson, Alfred Lord. *Letters*. Ed. Cecil Y. Lang and Edgar F. Shannon. Oxford: Clarendon, 1987.

Tyndall Papers, Royal Institution.

Venables, G. 'Carlyle in Society and at Home'. *Fortnightly Review* 33 (1883): 622-42.

Chapter 15

The Uses of German Literature in the Carlyles' Courtship

ROSEMARY ASHTON

On 2 April 1866 Carlyle was installed as Rector of Edinburgh University. Having processed into the hall with the Principal, Sir David Brewster, Carlyle 'threw off his robe, like an ancient David declining the unproved armour of Saul' (362), in John Tyndall's words, and delivered a memorable speech. He concluded with a passage from Goethe - not one of his teachers at this same University of Edinburgh, but the man from whom he had learnt the deepest and most enduring lessons. Quoting from a favourite Goethe poem, 'Symbolum', in his own translation, Carlyle called it 'a modern psalm', 'a kind of marching music of mankind'. The last two verses rang out:

But heard are the voices,
Heard are the Sages,
The worlds and the Ages:
'Choose well, your choice is
Brief, and yet endless.

Here eyes do regard you
In Eternity's stillness:
Here is all fullness,
Ye brave, to reward you!
Work, and despair not'.

(Tarr/McClelleand 95-6)

This Goethe poem was one that Carlyle had often cited in his writings, beginning with his essays on German subjects he wrote for Francis Jeffrey of the *Edinburgh Review* in 1827. Its theme had also been echoed in *Sartor Resartus*, the great utterance which came forth from Thomas's solitary life with Jane in the 'Dunscore Patmos' of Craigenputtoch in Dumfriesshire (TC to John Carlyle, 21 Aug. 1830; *CL* 5:141-2). When he began writing *Sartor* in the autumn of 1830, he was corresponding with

Goethe, writing dramatically about his solitary Scottish moorland home. He liked Goethe to think of his life as a heroic isolation, physical and cultural. In representing himself to his mentor as a solitary voice crying out in the wilderness to his uncomprehending fellow men, he turned Jeffrey's teasing caricature of him as a 'German mystic' into a positive portrait of the lone champion of German culture (TC to Eckermann, 25 Sept. 1828; *CL* 4:404).

Carlyle confessed to Goethe in November 1829 that he was 'still but an Essayist, and longing more than ever to be a Writer in a far better sense'(*CL* 5:29). He took up the theme again in August 1831, alluding to the poem 'Symbolum', which, being a celebration of the brotherhood of man and ideal freemasonry, became a favourite source of quotation for Carlyle, not least because of the link between freemasonry and the honest trade of stonemason which his own father had pursued. He was ambitious, he told Goethe, for 'higher honours' than mere literary journalism, for 'till one knows that he *cannot* be a Mason, why should he publickly hire himself as a Hodman!' Regarding Goethe as a genial repository of his slowly ripening creative idea, he continued:

> When I look at the wonderful Chaos within me, full of natural Supernaturalism, and all manner of Antediluvian fragments, and how the Universe is daily growing more mysterious as well as more august, and the influences from without more heterogeneous and perplexing, I see not well what is to come of it all; and only conjecture from the violence of the fermentation that something strange may come. (*CL* 5:153-4)

'Wonderful Chaos', 'natural Supernaturalism' (which became the title of an important chapter in *Sartor*), 'fragments' and influences 'heterogeneous and perplexing' – Carlyle could not have described better *Sartor Resartus*, the 'something strange' that was growing in his mind but had not yet (to use the masonic metaphor) been chiselled into an outward form.

In 1818 Carlyle had given up studying for the ministry at Edinburgh University and was teaching alongside his friend Edward Irving in a Kirkcaldy school. By November he had decided that Kirkcaldy and school-teaching were not for him, and he left for Edinburgh once more, not hopeful, but thinking he might manage there for two years, living on his savings, which he could supplement by taking private pupils. The next few winters were spent in Edinburgh, half-heartedly attending lectures in different subjects, teaching private pupils maths and astronomy, frequently moving lodgings in vain attempts to escape the noises and smells of the city and in general leading 'a miscellaneous, undescribeable life' (TC to Thomas Murray, 19 Feb. 1819; *CL* 1:163). Summers saw him moping on his parents' Dumfriesshire farm, trying to hide his religious doubts from his mother (*Reminiscences* 262). At all seasons Carlyle suffered agonies from dyspepsia and from the drastic remedies he applied, in the form of frequent large doses of mercury and sulphate of magnesia. In his unfinished autobiographical novel, 'Wotton Reinfred', begun and abandoned in 1827 and later cut up for passages to use in *Sartor Resartus*, Carlyle describes the equivalent period in the life of his alter ego Wotton as a time of inner anguish: 'He...hurried into the country, not to possess his soul in peace as he hoped, but in truth, like Homer's Bellerophon, to eat his own heart' (*Last Words* 31).

Some gleams of light relieved the gloom. In February 1819 Carlyle met the man who would preside over his installation in Edinburgh in 1866. Dr David Brewster, as he then was, had invented the kaleidoscope, and was editor of the *Edinburgh Encyclopædia*, for which he commissioned some twenty articles from Carlyle over the next few years on miscellaneous subjects mainly beginning with M and N (including Montaigne, Newfoundland, Norfolk and Northumberland). Carlyle also began taking German lessons from a Dumfriesshire acquaintance, Robert Jardine, in return for lessons in French, and was soon reading Lessing and Klopstock. On 25 September 1819 he makes the first mention of Goethe. At this very time, September 1819, Jane Welsh was almost overwhelmed with grief at the sudden loss of her father, Dr John Welsh, who died aged forty-four of typhus fever contracted from a patient. Jane struggled to fulfil his wishes by continuing her own education - learning French and Italian - while also making use of her accomplishments to teach a group of younger girls. Her life was settling into a routine of quiet days at home with her mother, varied by short visits to Edinburgh to stay with her friend Eliza Stodart at Eliza's uncle John Bradfute's house in George Square. Having lost the person she had loved and admired most in the world, she was vulnerable to the rediscovered attractions of her childhood tutor, Edward Irving, who was making a name for himself in Glasgow and preparing to be ordained by his native presbytery at Annan.

As for Carlyle, nothing seemed to go right for him. Finding he had a talent for writing, he decided in January 1820 to send a trial review article to Jeffrey. Choosing a French work on the theory of gravitation, he wrote his review, 'penned some brief polite Note to the great Editor', and took it to George Street. The result was 'absolute *zero*, no answer, no return of MS, absolutely no notice taken; which was a form of catastrophe more complete than even I had anticipated!' (*Reminiscences* 358). Dr Brewster was more encouraging, but a magazine he hoped to found, with Carlyle as chief contributor, never materialised. Another plan, that of using his newly acquired knowledge of German to translate Schiller's history of the Thirty Years' War (*Geschichte des Dreissigjährigen Krieges*, 1791-3), was turned down by the publisher Longman.

To set against these negatives, however, was the growing conviction that he would be a writer. 'Confound the knaves!' he wrote to his brother John in January 1821, 'I will write a *book* and shame them all' (*CL* 1:303). The growth of such defiant self-confidence was linked to the discovery of Goethe's works, which would be momentous both for him and Victorian culture generally. Carlyle confided the first of many expressions of excited admiration to Irving in June 1820. The subject was *Faust*:

> I wish Goethe were my countryman, I wish - O, how I wish - he were my friend. It is not for his masterly conception of human nature - from the heroes of classical story down to the blackguards of a Leipsic alehouse - that I admire him above all others; his profound sentiment of beauty, his most brilliant delineations of all its varieties - his of head and melancholy of heart, open all the floodgates of my sympathy. Faust is a wonderful tragedy. I doubt if even Shakespeare with all his powers had sadness enough in his nature to understand the arid and withered feelings of a passionate spirit, worn out by excessive studies and the want of all enjoyment; to delineate the chaos of his thoughts when the secrets of nature are bared before him; to depict his terrible volition and the bitter mockery of the demon [which] gives scope to that volition. (*CL* 1.255)

Carlyle was not the first discontented youth to respond so heartily to Goethe's drama. For him, however, Goethe would come to seem nothing less than an aesthetic and spiritual prophet, and he would in due course deliver that message to British readers. In the more immediate future, Goethe and German literature - with its revelation of a 'new Heaven and new Earth' (*CL* 1:268) - became a vital ally in the struggle to win, and keep, the affection of Jane Welsh.

They met at the beginning of June 1821, when Irving took his sullen, awkward, dyspeptic friend to visit his former pupil, now an attractive girl of nearly twenty and known as the belle of Haddington. Carlyle was thoroughly smitten and not so shy that he could not gratify his longings by writing to Jane immediately on his return to Edinburgh. Addressing her boldly as 'my dear Friend', he plunged into an impressive list of prescribed reading for her. It might seem 'presumptuous' of him to 'act as your tutor', but he was prepared to take the risk. He advised her to read Noehden's German grammar when he could procure it for her, and Madame de Staël's famous book on Germany, *De L'Allemagne* (1813). A novice in the genre of the love letter, he entered self-consciously into the realms of flirtation, asking her to 'tell me in three words what you think of the Lady de Staël' and say whether 'her cousin, the Lady Jane is well and happy; and whether the latter has ever deigned to cast one glance of recollection on those few Elysian hours we spent together lately?' He wound the letter up with a saving expression of self-irony – 'this wonderful compound of pedagogy and sentimentality and absurdity must conclude' (4 June 1821; *CL* 1:359, 60, 61). The only reply he received to this letter and the accompanying set of books, sent in late June, was the following line: 'To M*r* Carslile [sic], with Miss Welsh's compliments and very best thanks' (*CL* 1:366).

This was an inauspicious beginning. If Carlyle had not been singularly determined, Jane's unfriendly note might have strangled at birth one of the most extensive exchanges of letters surviving between two people. But he was determined and replied with spirit to Jane's discouraging note. He did not hide his disappointment or hurt pride, not least at her misspelling of his name, but he quickly moved on to the ground he instinctively knew to be the firmest on which to pursue the relationship – books. He was careful to address her now as 'My dear Madam', rather than presuming on a friendship she had not bestowed. He sensed that this young woman, already well educated at the behest of the father whose memory she held sacred, would respond positively to the pedagogy, while she scorned the sentimentality and absurdity, in his letters. Encouragingly, her second reply, on 6 July, was a little longer and a little less frosty: 'I return your books; and heartily thank you for the pleasure they have afforded me - I fear you think I have kept them long; nevertheless I have not been idle - I have dismissed my German Master (for the enormous offence of asserting all words beginning with capitals to be the names of towns) and I think I get on faster without him' (6 July 1821; *CL* 1:368).

Carlyle was not slow to step into the space so conveniently opened up by the departure of the unnamed fool of a teacher. 'My project', he replied emphatically, 'is no less than *to set out in person to inspect and accelerate your progress in the German tongue*!' For this he planned to visit her in August: 'Will you let me come?' Masterful and pleading by turns, he both lectures and flatters Jane, begging her to 'sit down *instantly*, and say *La Reine le veut*', assuring her that he thinks her more than merely 'a very accomplished young Lady', and asking her 'most humbly' not to address him as 'Car-*slile*' again (16 July 1821; 1:368-9). Jane graciously accepted the offer of his advice on German matters, but indicated that Mrs Welsh was uncertain about a visit from him. However, she was to be in Edinburgh at Mr Bradfute's house towards the end of July, and Carlyle would be welcome to call on her there.

So began the relationship. There is no record of what Jane thought of Carlyle on first view, though it is clear that she did not fall in love with him. He, on the contrary, laid his cards on the table straight away, yet his feelings were changing and complex. He pursued her single-mindedly, but was capable of procrastination and temporary withdrawal, so that the story of their long courtship is no simple one of the dogged, devoted suitor gradually wearing down the resistance of the fair object of his attentions. A pattern emerged of mutual struggle, of progress and reversal, of shifting mastery and submission, of genuine fondness and sharp criticism, in the letters which travelled between Haddington, Edinburgh, and Dumfriesshire. From the summer of 1821 until they finally married in October 1826, Thomas and Jane met in person only two or three times a year, sometimes less, and then either in snatched half hours at Mr Bradfute's house in Edinburgh or under the generally baleful eye of Mrs Welsh in Haddington. Their correspondence was the lifeline between them; though it sometimes threatened to snap, it never did. German literature is partly to be thanked for this. It not only formed the first and most common subject matter of the letters, but was also to be the means by which Carlyle began, somewhat belatedly, to make a living and – equally important in Jane's eyes – a reputation as a writer.

During the early summer of 1821 Carlyle was in Edinburgh, corresponding with Jane about German literature and working at articles on the Netherlands and Newfoundland for Brewster's *Encyclopædia*. He wrote to his mother and brothers, indicating that he was 'moderately comfortable or even happy at present', but making no direct mention of Jane (*CL* 1:371). By mid-August he was at home on his parents' farm at Mainhill, from where he wrote to Irving, revealing that during his last few weeks in Edinburgh 'sleeplessness and so forth had rendered me a fitter inmate for Bedlam than a study' (*CL* 1:379). It is difficult to imagine Carlyle's state of mind in June 1821, newly in love but aware that he is not yet loved in return, hopeful yet doubtful of his success as a suitor; at the same time he suffers the tortures of dyspepsia and its embarrassments – how could he contemplate intimacy with anyone in such a condition? Then there is his anxiety about religion. Recognizing in himself a religious cast of mind, he knew that his critical faculties were constantly undermining passive acceptance of the old faith. Finally, at twenty-five, he was still far from fixed in a career, though he strongly suspected that he has found his *métier* in writing. But what should he write? Who would publish him? How would he survive financially in the meantime?

In the midst of his difficulties, Carlyle did not know it then, but his eventual expression of the chaos of thought and emotions of that summer of 1821 became archetypal, speaking to many who were suffering their own doubts and difficulties. The 'Everlasting No' chapter of *Sartor Resartus* annotates the inner-experience of Diogenes Teufelsdröckh, 'shut-out from Hope' and wandering 'wearisomely through this world': 'Doubt had darkened into Unbelief…shade after shade goes grimly over your soul, till you have the fixed, starless, Tartarean black' (SR 121). Teufelsdröckh and his author alike envy those with uninquiring minds and strong stomachs:

'With Stupidity and sound Digestion man may front much. But what, in these dull unimaginative days, are the terrors of Conscience to the diseases of the Liver!' (SR 122). The world is an alien place, reflecting the younger Carlyle's own sense of dislocation.

There follows the most famous passage in *Sartor*, which mingles autobiographical fact with myth, as Teufelsdröckh recounts his moment of revelation on 'the dirty little *Rue Saint-Thomas de l'Enfer*' in Paris, when he threw off 'the EVERLASTING NO (*das ewige Nein*)...and then was it that my whole ME stood up, in native God-created majesty, and with emphasis recorded its Protest' (SR 125-6). Carlyle noted later that this incident, set in Paris and incorporating a joke on his name - St Thomas of Hell - was based on an actual experience that 'occurred quite literally to myself in Leith Walk, during those 3 weeks of total sleeplessness, in which almost my one solace was that of a daily bather on the sands between Leith and Portobello' (Clubbe, *Two Reminiscencess* 49). Inasmuch as Carlyle did reach some kind of peace and resolution, first in June 1821, and again over the next few years of vicissitudes - not least in his courtship of Jane - he owed it to Goethe.

The reading of Madame de Staël on Germany and of Goethe's *Faust* in 1819-20 began a process that continued with his translating *Wilhelm Meister's Apprenticeship* (1824) and *Wilhelm Meister's Travels* (1827), writing several articles on Goethe, quoting him widely as 'the Wisest of our time', and exchanging letters with him from 1824 until Goethe's death in 1832. In this period Carlyle acquired an intimate knowledge, as Tyndall later noted, of 'every nook and cranny' (356) of Goethe's huge literary output. To Goethe himself Carlyle wrote, 20 August 1827, in answer to an inquiry about 'my bygone life':

> Your works have been a mirror to me; unasked and unhoped for, your wisdom has counselled me; and so peace and health of soul have visited me from afar. For I was once an Unbeliever, not in Religion only, but in all the Mercy and Beauty of which it is the symbol; storm-tossed in my own imaginations; a man divided from men; exasperated, wretched, driven almost to despair; so that Faust's wild *curse* seemed the only fit greeting for human life, and his passionate *Fluch vor allen der Geduld*! [Cursed above all be patience!] was spoken from my very inmost heart. But now, thank Heaven, all this is altered: without change of external circumstances, solely by the new light which rose upon me, I attained to new thoughts, and a composure which I should once have considered as impossible. (*CL* 4:248)

Goethe seemed to have risen above the Faustian torment of soul to land on a high plateau of peace and resignation, and Carlyle felt he had been enabled to follow him there.

To others Carlyle confided at different times that he owed everything to Goethe – even life itself, as Henry Crabb Robinson noted after talking to him in February 1832 (Robinson, *Reminiscences* 3:2). In a letter to Thomas Spedding in November 1851 he answered the question so often asked about his religious beliefs. His 'creed', he writes, 'is all in the most compact quiescent condition', and gives me no trouble at all for the last thirty years or so, – fierce as the struggle was, almost to the edge of death or insanity, that I had with it before. But ever since, as Goethe says, 'With God, or with the Gods, my affairs have stood on a very tolerable footing!' (*CL* 26:239). This is deliberately evasive, for Carlyle's 'religion' was a strange and shifting entity, as he himself knew. Though he suffered from religious doubt in the 1820s, that doubt was intertwined with non-religious worries, with self-doubt, depression, illness and anxiety, probably including sexual anxiety. In his journal in December 1823 he even toyed briefly with the notion of suicide (31 Dec. 1823; 56-7). With his Olympian aloofness yet general tolerance of erring humanity, Goethe offered a saving influence across the whole range of Carlyle's troubles, not just in religious questions.

Curiously, at no time in Jane and Thomas's courtship correspondence did the topic of religion arise. One reason was Carlyle's sense of isolation: his spiritual struggles were worked out in the privacy of his journals, and released gradually and in transformed ways in his writings during the 1820s and 1830s. Another reason may have been that Jane, though not yet out of her teens when she met Thomas, had already given up her religious faith, perhaps chiefly as a result of her father's death. She had written to her paternal grandmother soon after the catastrophe, striving to express her belief in the wisdom of 'the Almighty' in cutting off 'one who was the Glory of his family, & a most useful member of society, one who was respected & beloved by all who knew him'. Though Jane is writing to a religious grandmother and trying to submit to God's will, bitterness is the keynote. One almost suspects satire at God's expense as she struggles with the idea that the 'ways of the Almighty are mysterious…& though he has afflicted those whom we thought deserved to be happy – *yet* his intention appears to me clear and intelligible – Could the annihilation of a Thousand useless and contemptible beings have sent such terror & submission to the hearts of the survivors as the sudden death of one whom their love would if possible have gifted with immortality – Oh no' (JWC to Elizabeth Welsh, 5 Oct. 1819; *CL* 1:201). In later years Jane was known for her scepticism; she shocked some acquaintances with her 'sweeping declamation against Christianity and the Church', and according to Charlotte Williams Wynn in January 1856, led her interlocutors to expect to be 'scalped' if they ventured to disagree (Hansons 443-4).

Religion, then, was not a topic for Jane and Thomas in 1821, though it formed such an important part of the latter's inner struggles. German literature was their common language, with Carlyle eagerly playing Abelard to Jane's Eloisa. Irving performed an important function in the early months of this new relationship between his two friends. A three-way correspondence evolved, with Irving voicing his suspicions of the 'entanglements' of German literature generally and of Goethe in particular. He urged Carlyle not to encourage 'our fair acquaintance' in what was already a visible tendency to religious scepticism (9 & 24 July 1821; *CL* 1:370, 380). Carlyle later recalled that his friend 'did not much know Goethe; had generally a dislike to him, as to a kind of Heathen *un*godly person and idle Singer, who had considerably seduced *me* from the right path' (*Reminiscences* 347).

Jane attempted a translation of Goethe's poem 'Der Fischer' ('The Fisherman'); Carlyle, styling himself 'Hypercriticus Minimus', corrected it (*CL* 1:375; 2:121). German proved useful as a language to convey personal comments that Mrs Welsh (who read his letters to Jane) could not understand, as in September 1821, when Carlyle asked plaintively in German why his 'dearest friend' had not written for three weeks (*CL* 1:383). Jane was hampered by her mother's caprices; one moment she was permitted to invite Carlyle to call, the next forbidden even to correspond with him. She herself added to Carlyle's torment by writing teasingly yet sharply, boasting of the young men who admired her and rebuking Carlyle for writing too romantically. However, she never told him to stop corresponding, but always kept the lines of communication open, usually by asking him for help with her translations from German.

Carlyle himself now had better prospects, for which he had Irving to thank. While preaching at the Caledonian Chapel in Hatton Garden in December 1821, Irving had met Isabella Buller, the wife of a retired Anglo-Indian judge. Mrs Buller was looking for a tutor for her sons Charles and Arthur when the family moved to Scotland, and Irving recommended Carlyle. Mrs Buller, Carlyle later recalled with a deft stroke of the pen, was 'a Calcutta fine lady, a bright princess of the kind worshipped there, a once very beautiful, still very witty graceful airy and ingenuously intelligent woman, of the *gossamer* kind' (*Reminiscences* 269). The offer, at £200 a year, came just in time, as Carlyle had had no regular income since giving up teaching three years before. The Bullers came to Edinburgh, and Carlyle began the tutoring experiment, staying for the moment in his old lodgings in Moray Street, which he now shared with his student brother John. He found he got on with the Bullers, Charles Buller senior being a good-natured, 'very deaf' type of English squire, and Mrs Buller gracious, if inclined to show 'a lively appetite' for 'the Ex-Indian accidental English-gentleman, and native or touring *Lion* genus' (*Reminiscences* 270, 272). Thomas was no doubt glad to be able to tell Jane, who in turn would tell her socially conscious mother about his new appointment with the glamorous Bullers.

Despite a brutally clear message from Jane in January 1822 that a visit to Haddington would be unwelcome to both her mother and herself, on account of the 'impertinent conjectures' it might arouse in 'this tattling, illnatured place', as well as his 'too ardent expressions of Friendship' (*CL* 2: 21, 20), Thomas persisted in threatening to come and see her. He finally did go, which was a mistake. Mrs Welsh was cold, and Jane made him feel like a country bumpkin. She told Eliza Stodart about his two-day visit in February, during which they had successfully read German together – 'it is a noble language!' she exclaims to Eliza – but he had annoyed her with his clumsiness: 'He scratched the fenders dreadfully – I must have a pair of carpet-shoes and hand-cuffs prepared for him the nextime – His tongue only should be left at liberty his other members are most fantastically awkward' (*CL* 2:38).

Carlyle might have felt soothed if he could have read the part about 'the nextime', but he only knew that the visit had been 'unfortunate' and that Jane and her mother felt socially superior to him. By a lucky chance Irving now enclosed a letter for Jane in one to Thomas, asking him to send it on to Haddington. This Carlyle did, taking the opportunity to assure her he fully understood 'what is your rank and what your prospects', but asking her to forget 'the roughness of my exterior, if you think me sound within' (13 Feb. 1822; *CL* 2:41). Once more the awkward young man had struck the right note, appealing to the one advantage he had over other young men in Jane's eyes – his intellect. Carlyle had the common sense not to propose any more visits. He simply resumed the role of epistolary Abelard/St Preux to Jane's Eloisa/Julie, advising her about her German reading and translating while also getting on with tutoring the Bullers and translating Legendre's *Eléments de Géométrie* for David Brewster.

Carlyle kept cool, replying after a decent interval of nearly two weeks, when he let her know how busy he had been, perhaps recalling Goethe's words in *Wilhelm Meister* that '[p]ractical activity and expertness are far more compatible with sufficient intellectual culture than is generally supposed' (*Works* 24:321). He reminded her that she might yet become a 'true-minded woman of genius' if she could put her undoubted literary talents to use, under his guidance, on worthwhile subjects, including the study of German (13 July 1822; *CL* 2:148). Jane continued to blow hot and cold when he returned in his letters to expressions of love and hope. But in November 1822 she told him that their first meeting had been memorable for her, though the reason was a troubling one. She had still been full of 'grief at the loss of the only being I ever loved with my whole soul'; the 'pole-star' of her life was lost and she had 'no counsellor that could direct' her. Casting Carlyle in a quasi-paternal role, she recalled: 'You spoke like him – your eloquence awoke in my soul the slumbering admirations and ambitions that *His* first kindled there'. The comparison may have frightened Carlyle, yet there was evidence in this letter that she was again asking him to 'direct' her: she complained about her failure to grasp 'the first part of Wallenstein', at the very moment when 'I was just beginning to congratulate myself upon my progress in the German Tongue' (11 Nov.; *CL* 2:196-7). Once again, her study of German had coincided with her expressions of affection for Thomas.

All the time they kept their difficult epistolary relationship going by constantly reverting to their German reading, which now had an added impetus, as Carlyle was translating *Wilhelm Meisters Lehrjahre* for the Edinburgh publishing house Oliver and Boyd. Goethe's novel, full of its own romantic entanglements and mistakes, was his steady point of reference while visions of Jane as his wife rose and fell. He was also writing a life of Schiller, which the *London Magazine* was to publish in monthly parts, thanks to Irving's influence with the editor. Goethe and Schiller fill the pages of their letters during the many months in which they were unable to meet. In May 1823 Carlyle went with the Bullers to the Highlands; they had rented Kinnaird House, near Dunkeld, for several months. Here he worked on Goethe and Schiller in a small house near the great one, suffering the tortures of dyspepsia all the while.

The *Life of Schiller* appeared in the *London Magazine* from October 1823 to September 1824, and was published as a book the following February. *The Times* carried an extract, which it praised as 'eloquent'. Carlyle was to remember this in 1866 as 'the *first* public nod of approval I had ever had' (*Reminiscences* 277). He was obliged to follow the existing German biographies, full of errors and omissions, but he managed to go beyond these and, by an effort of sympathetic imagination, to give a lively picture of the vicissitudes of his subject's life. Indirectly, he was also making claims about himself in his description of the young Schiller:

> The hard circumstances of his fortune had prevented the natural development of his mind; his faculties had been cramped and misdirected; but they had gathered strength by opposition and the habit of self-dependence which it encouraged. His thoughts, unguided by a teacher, had sounded into the depths of his own nature and the mysteries of his own fate; his feelings and passions…accumulated till their force grew irresistible. (*Works* 25:13)

Having found in Carlyle a replacement for her own 'pole-star', Jane would have recognised the affinities between him and the young German 'genius' in this passage.

Early in February 1824 Thomas was in Edinburgh, visiting Jane at Mr Bradfute's house in George Square and seeing the first of two volumes of his translation of *Wilhelm Meisters Lehrjahre* through the press while he continued translating the third. He negotiated £180 for a run of 1,000 copies, thereby impressing Jane, who was anxious that her 'beloved Genius', as she now encouragingly called him, should finally publish a book (29 Feb. 1824; 3:37). 'I would rather be able to make £180 by my wits than fall heir to a million', she wrote flatteringly in April, though she was far from sure of the merits of *Wilhelm Meister*, which she was then reading. 'The unaccountable propensity to kissing which runs through all your dramatis personae preplexes me sadly', she teased (4 April 1824; *CL* 3:55).

Jane was not really much shocked by *Wilhelm Meister*, but she guessed correctly that others might be, and she feared for Carlyle's reputation as its translator. In fact, he toned down some of the rather direct sexual references in the book. In his preface to the translation he showed some anxiety about these, explaining that he had 'dropped as evidently unfit for the English taste' some 'few phrases and sentences' (*Works* 23:10), while assuring his readers that such passages amounted to less than a page in all. The preface is cautiously apologetic about the two criticisms to which he felt Goethe's novel was vulnerable, that of indecency and that of tediousness. He confessed that the novel had its *longuours*, but claimed, rather diffidently, that if persevered with, it might be found to be 'a light airy sketch of the development of man in all his endowments and faculties, gradually proceeding from the first rude exhibitions of puppets and mountebanks, through the perfection of poetic and dramatic art, up to the unfolding of the principle of religion, and the greatest of all the arts, the art of life' (*Works* 23:6-7). For both Thomas and Jane, 'the art of life' had transcended religion in their lives, and become an essential bond between them. German literature had opened up a 'new Heaven and new Earth' (*CL* 3:87) to them, at once deepening their mutual feelings and teaching them 'to see the horizon of their certainties widened' ('Preface to WM', *Works* 33:8).

They both regarded Goethe now as a kind of 'saviour', who had rescued them from the spiritual quagmires that would soon engulf their friend Edward Irving. Recalling this period in *Reminiscences*, Carlyle spoke of his obligation to the Weimar sage: 'I then felt, and still feel, endlessly indebted to Goethe in the business; he, in his fashion, I perceived, had travelled the steep rocky road before me, – the first of the moderns' (321). In June 1824 he sent a copy of his *Meister* translation to Goethe, expressing the hope that he might 'one day see you, and pour out before you, as before a father, the woes and wanderings of a heart whose mysteries you seemed so thoroughly to comprehend' (24 June 1824; *CL*

3:87). Six months later, the seventy-five-year old Goethe replied graciously, in a letter which seemed to Carlyle 'almost like a message from Fairy Land' with its 'simple patriarchal style'. Fittingly, Carlyle associated his love for Goethe with his feelings for Jane, and instructed her to 'transcribe my copy, and your own translation of it, into the blank leaf of that German paper, before you lay it by; that the the same sheet may contain some traces of him whom I most venerate and her whom I most love in this strangest of all possible worlds' (20 Dec. 1824; *CL* 3:235-6).

In October 1825 Carlyle went to Annan to see Irving, who was visiting his parents there. Irving told him about the plans for the new University of London (now University College London), with which he had been involved until he found that 'religion was not cared for'. The non-allegiance of the new foundation to the Church of England did not upset Thomas, who told Jane he had 'some faint thoughts of looking after some appointment there' (19 Oct. 1825; *CL* 3:391). Jane rather hoped he would succeed. She wondered in December what he would do once *German Romance* was off his hands: 'Perhaps you will write a novel, or a tragedy, or become Editor of a literary newspaper at Edin*r*, or Professor of Lord knows what in the University at London' (*CL* 3:438). It was now settled that they would marry when he had finished his translation and realised some money for it, but Jane was naturally keen that something more noteworthy should follow. Nothing came of this, or any other attempt by Carlyle to get a university chair, though he tried for several over the next few years before finally resigning himself to the fact that he would be a professor 'nowhere' (TC to John Carlyle, 12 March 1828; *CL* 4:340). In *Sartor Resartus* he took private revenge on all the universities which failed to appoint him – University College London, Edinburgh, and St Andrews. Diogenes Teufelsdröckh is '*Professor der Allerley*-Wissenschaft, or as we say in English, "Professor of Things in General"', and 'he had never delivered any Course; perhaps never been incited thereto by any public furtherance or requisition' (SR 14). No doubt Jane enjoyed the shared joke which she had initiated with her prediction in 1825 that Thomas might become 'Professor of the Lord knows what' in London.

They married, at last, in October 1826. In notes written in 1866, Carlyle remembered how in August 'Hadd*n* became aware of what was toward; a great enough event there, the loss of its loved and admired "Jeannie Welsh", – "the Flower o' Haddington"' (*CL* 4:143). Jane herself wrote a fine letter to an aunt, defending him in the language of Wilhelm Meister, explaining that though others would say that Carlyle was poor and would 'indulge in some criticisms scarce flattering, on his birth', they 'would not tell you he is among the cleverest men of his day; and not the cleverest only but the most enlightened! that he possesses all the qualities

I deem essential in my husband, - a warm true heart to love me, a towering intellect to command me, and a spirit of fire to be the guiding star-light of *my* life'. She spoke of Thomas as she and Thomas had spoken of Goethe and Schiller. He was her 'genius':

> Such then is this future husband of mine; not a *great* man according to the most common sense of the word, but tru y great in its natural, proper sense - a scholar, a poet, a philosopher, a wise and noble man, one who holds his patent of nobility from Almighty God, and who's high stature of manhood is not to be measured by the inch-rule of Lilliputs! - Will you like him? no matter whether you do or not - since *I* like him in the deepest part of my soul'. (1 Oct. 1826; *CL* 4:141)

Many vicissitudes lay ahead, first at Comely Bank in Edinburgh, then at Craigenputtoch, and finally in London, where Carlyle became first the acknowledged German enthusiast of the age, then a sage and prophet in his own right, without need of a university chair from which to pontificate. The Carlyle marriage did not fulfil all Jane's hopes. Appropriately, though, even when complaining, as she often did, that her 'I-ity' was ignored or 'merged' in 'what the world doubtless considers my better half', she turned her discontent into wit by reaching for an analogy from Goethe. Writing to John Sterling in 1835, she explains: 'Little Felix, in the Wanderjahre [*Wilhelm Meister's Travels*], when, in the midst of an animated scene between Wilhelm and Theresa, he pulls Theresa's gown, and calls out, "Mama Theresa I too am here" only speaks out with the charming trustfulness of a child, what I am perpetually feeling, tho too sophisticated to pull peoples skirts, or exclaim in so many words; Mr Sterling "*I* too am here"' (4 June 1835; *CL* 8:138). Whatever the well-publicised problems in the marriage, Jane always retained her pride in her husband's 'genius', which she had first discovered during their courtship when together they explored the 'Fairy land' of Goethe and German literature.

Works Cited

Carlyle, Thomas. *Last Words*. Inro. Kenneth J. Fielding. 1892; rpt. Berlin: Gregg International, 1971.

Clubbe, John, ed. *Two Reminiscences of Thomas Carlyle*. Durham, NC: Duke UP, 1974.

Hanson, Lawrence and Elisabeth. *Necessary Evil: The Life of Jane Welsh Carlyle*. London: Constable, 1950.

Robinson, Henry Crabb. *Diary, Reminiscences, and Correspondence*. Ed. Thomas Sadler. 3 vols. London: Macmillan, 1869.

Tarr, Rodger L. and Fleming McClelland, eds. *The Collected Poems of Thomas and Jane Welsh Carlyle*. Greenwood, Fl: Penkevill, 1986.

Tyndall, John. *New Fragments*. London: Longmans, 1892.

Chapter 16

Geraldine Jewsbury: Jane Welsh Carlyle's 'best friend'?

IAN CAMPBELL

Prophecy is a dangerous art and, sometimes, events overtake even good guesses. When Norma Clarke wrote in *Ambitious Heights* that 'No long lost manuscript will be found under a Chelsea floorboard or in a Scottish peat bog' (2) to shed new light on the life of Jane Carlyle, she was happily only partly right. For important and long-lost manuscripts of Jane – her *Notebook,* (1845–52), missing parts of her *Journal* (1855–56), and Geraldine Jewsbury's letter to Froude of 22 November 1876 about the *Journal* – have now been published in volume 30 of the Duke-Edinburgh edition of the *Carlyle Letters*. Preserved in private hands and generously made available to the editors, this material gives an opportunity to reconsider the friendships of Jane Carlyle, and more specifically to focus on her often tempestuous relationship with Geraldine Jewsbury, who Froude claimed was Jane's 'most intimate and most confidential friend' (*My Relations* 20). But this claim is not easy to assess with two such complex women.

Geraldine's is a difficult personality, riddled with contradiction: admittedly, she was one who 'by sheer persistence in the face of Jane's discouragement at times, retained a close relationship from 1841 till Jane's death in 1866' (Christianson 288). At the same time, it is difficult not to believe such witnesses as Jessie Hiddleston, a servant at Cheyne Row in 1865, who recalled Geraldine's frequent afternoon visits to the house when Thomas was having his after-dinner sleep:

> This was the hour Miss Jewsbury used to come, almost every day while I was there. She sat on a footstool beside Mrs. Carlyle in the drawing-room and rubbed her ankles and gossiped, and she always went away about the time when master was wakened. At tea Mrs. Carlyle's talk was the same as at breakfast and dinner – the news, – and she would often quote 'Geraldine' and laugh contemptuously at her sayings. (Wilson 4:36)

Rosemary Ashton reasonably observes, 'Over the years Geraldine adored and quarrelled with and was patronised by Jane, while also throwing herself at a succession of alarmed or indifferent men. Jane came to rely on Geraldine's devotion, clinging and irritating though it was; already in her early letters Geraldine demonstrated an unfortunate tendency to magnify Jane's sufferings and feelings of neglect' (222-3). This is fair, both in its observation of Jane's first treatment of Geraldine and in its identification of the adverse effects of her tendency to over-dramatise. Jane certainly could play one acquaintance off against another. Aileen Christianson has commented persuasively on the ways in which Jane tailors her letters according to her correspondents, and constructs identities and characteristics that would be recognised or inferred by the recipients:

> There is a gap between Welsh Carlyle's self-critical statements and her assertiveness of her own individuality, her 'I-ity', which leads the reader to question not just the presentation of herself for the recipients of her letters, but also her presentation of herself for her own consumption. It has been assumed by most interpreters that the ironic self of her letters contains an unexpressed pain about her life. But it seems possible, given her skill at constructing herself, that it was rather another construction of a self which could contain her pain and which was then proffered for the admiration of the recipients. (288)

Jane's 'I-ity', to use her own term, was flexible enough to hold many friendships in suspension, and to move from one generation of friends – those soon after she arrived in Chelsea – to other sets in the 1850s and 1860s. She was resilient as well, and could hold in co-existence a detestation of Lady Harriet Ashburton and her baleful effect on her marriage with the honest comment that 'she proves by all her behavior that she is rather fond of me – the mere fact of her having *kissed* me at parting and meeting again proves more affection for me than twenty reams of protestations from a Geraldine would do' (*CL* 20:119). Yet Geraldine's affection included a good deal that was genuine, and Jane was certainly pleased to be comforted by that affection even to the rubbing of ankles. Sceptical though she might be of Geraldine's histrionics, she admired her ferocious energy and commitment and her resistance to 'fine-lady' conventions.

Two newly-found letters throw fresh light on Geraldine's relations with Jane. The first, published in full in Fielding and Sorensen's *Jane Carlyle: Newly Selected Letters* (2004), is a letter from Jane to the American actress Charlotte Cushman in 1862. It is a remarkably frank document:

> 5 Cheyne Row—Chelsea
> January [31 1862]
>
> My Dear! My Dear! I want to put my arms round your neck, and give you – oh! such a good kiss And then, if you can stand that sort of thing, once in a way, – I should like to lay my head on your shoulder and take a good cry! That is how nature prompts me to acknowledge your

dear letter, and dear newyear's tokens, - with a good kiss and a good cry; rather than with any written sentences *that* my poor nearly extinct Brain can cobble together in these Hard Times!. (I am so worn out and disheartened with long illness and confinement to two rooms!) But alas Dear! The 'gods', however entreated, will *not* 'annihilate Time and Space, to make two Lovers happy'! That has been clearly ascertained some time since! And so, *faute de mieux*, I must have recourse to *writing* 'under difficulties', and that without further delay, on penalty of passing for both fickle and ungrateful; when - God bless you! - I am far as possible from being either! and as unwilling as possible that such an idea should be entertained of me - by *you*!

Mrs Dilberoglue, being the precisest and faithfulest of dear little 'Goods', would do infallibly what she promised, nay volunteered to do, namely '*explain* to Miss Cushman all about *it*' - 'It' meaning my happiness at having a letter from you, - my true Scotch woman impatience to make '*a suitable return*', - and then my illness - the extreme weakness and nervousness which made any - the least - use of my *head* intolerably irksome besides being especially prohibited by my Doctor; - *all that* the little *Good* was to 'explain'! and trusting that she did so with her accustomed accuracy and lucidity, I will not go back upon the causes of my long silence. It is enough to have been *four months ill* and shut up in two rooms; without 'renewing grief' by details of one's fit-for-nothingness, so soon as ever one has recovered *a certain* use of one's tongue and pen!

But if I shut down the lid and turn the key on my sick room tribulations; what is there left out of these weary four months to tell you? This - first and foremost; that I am not a bit cooled on the sudden affection I took for you; and believe it to be one of those Elective Affinities on which one does not *cool - ever*! I have seen you twice - that's all! and already you are mixed up with my life like an old friend! Something new and good *in* my life - not outside it! I look forward with pleasure to seeing you again; but, without seeing you without interchanging words with you, it is a pleasure to know of you in the same world with me. The influence of a strong, brave, loving true woman may be felt at any distance, I firmly believe, without outward visible sign. And then, Dear, you are come to me just at the right time - to be a consolation as well as a possession! For, of late years, it had been all loss, loss with me! never gain! One Friend after another out of 'dear old Long ago', that had cared for me and that I had cared for all my Life, had gone to their rest, leaving me so lonely on the Earth! *Playing at Friendship* with the new people I was thrown amongst; and so discouraged in my secret heart that I despaired of both my chances and my ability to ever make myself a *new real* Friend! - My Heavens! when I went to Barnsbury Park that day to see *you*; how very very little I dreamt of jumping into your arms! and 'swearing eternal Friendship', like any Boarding-school Girl! But it was all right! After so many months and after a severe *fit of illness* (which I take to be the best possible test of realities and shams) I feel no misgivings about that somewhat German-looking transaction! rather compliment myself on having so much *Life* left in me after all! and on having turned it to such account! My *Life* has been making another *pronunciomento* with which I could throw you into fits of laughter if I had you beside me! My Dear! I have had a fearful row with Geraldine Jewsbury! which has made 'pigs and whistles' of *that* everlasting friendship! and 'Like cliffs that have been rent asunder

A dreary sea now flows between!'

I should be more overpowered with grief than I am (in fact I have shown an insensibility unexampled!) had the cliffs been rent by *one* explosion; but the rent has been the gradual work of many years. And the cliffs were only of *Land* or some very loose Material to begin with! I do think that sort of emotional woman, all 'finer sensibilities' and no feeling, all smoke and no flame is one of the most intolerable inventions of Civilization, should be put down by act of Parliament, and prayed against in all Churches!

You asked for Mrs Hawks's (Madame Venturi's) address after the 1st of January (she wrote to me) I was to address *Emelia Venturi nata Ashurst poste restante Milan* - She had been living up to that date in some rooms of an old château, near Bresica [Brescia], dismantled and unfurnished, in the midst of all sorts of inconveniences and discomforts; waited on by a girl of the Country whom she named *Bare* legs (as Mr Carlyle would say) 'significative of much!' But caring for none of these things! very fond of her new Husband (I think, and very happy with him) - happy as a young girl! - and with a touching air of consciousness that not *being* a young girl she has no claim to that sort of happiness and no sure hold of it! She writes to me 'I am so glad you like Charlotte Cushman. She is a dear good noble soul!'

Aren't you glad that we are not to be natural enemies? It would have been so absurd that war as well as so vexatious!! When will you come? And how long will you stay?

I cannot put into words how touched I was by your new years bouquet, and the little scarfs! I took them not only as tokens from *you* but as omens of a fortunate year; and - next day I had a relapse and was thrown into bed again for a fortnight!!

Does your friend remember me? I do her - and offer her my kind regards and just one word more and the paper is full. Please love me ever so much but *don't* flatter me for it makes me *'think shame'*! Yours faithfully and affectionately / Jane Carlyle

Charlotte Cushman is one of the figures now in the sequence of the Carlyle letters who, like many others of the 1850s, have been all but invisible. Yet clearly this letter (and others) suggests she must be taken seriously as someone to whom Jane felt she could write in an uncharacteristically spontaneous and confiding way. Her offer to lay her head on Charlotte's shoulders and 'take a good cry' suggests the kind of emotional release possible only among the closest of friends, though the enthusiasm was hardly to last. Geraldine's passionate advances irritated Jane and made her uneasy. But writing to Cushman, she openly employs terms of physical intimacy, while excusing them by appealing to her infirm condition. Though the two women barely know one another, already Jane strangely thinks of Charlotte as 'mixed up in my life like an old friend'. A 'strong, brave, loving true woman', Cushman exists in Jane's imagination even at a physical distance - she was in Rome - a consolation to someone whose friendships have been thinned by the passing years, 'leaving me so lonely on the Earth'.

Jane makes a dusty distinction between 'playing at Friendship with the new people' she meets, and '"swearing eternal Friendship", like any Boarding-school Girl. But it was all right!' It is worth noting that this is not Jane's usual epistolary style, particularly in correspondence outside the family. To cousins, uncles and in-laws, a kiss and a kind message tend to suffice. To swear eternal friendship like a 'Boarding-school Girl' is unusual. So too is her sharply disloyal ridicule of Jewsbury: 'I do think that sort of emotional woman, all "finer sensibilities" and no feeling, all smoke and no flame is one of the most intolerable inventions of Civilization, should be put down by act of Parliament, and prayed against in all Churches!' Jane distinguishes between 'finer sensibilities' and 'feeling', clearly to the advantage of the latter. While she is apparently glad to seem to take the tribute of the 'finer sensibilities' offered in the form of Geraldine's devoted service and embarrassingly obvious friendship, she suggests that she wants to establish a relation with someone as solid and consistent as Cushman.

The full story of the friendship with Charlotte Cushman remains to be teased out; but Jane's willingness to jettison Geraldine's affection is clear. The *Newly Selected Letters* show Jane exploding in exasperation to Ellen Twisleton about how she resented Geraldine's fussy jealousy, and how delighted she was when Geraldine flounced out when Ellen once called on her in 1856. 'Evidently', added Ellen, 'the next "best friend" has no sort of self-control, & knows nothing about illness, cries over Mrs Carlyle, spills her jellies, knocks over the coal-pail, kisses her, & writes her a letter of fourteen pages sent in before breakfast, to complain of "coldness"... & altogether there was a considerable glare of light thrown on the subject of their relations!' As early as 1855, Jane writes in her *Journal* that Geraldine has just sent her 'the kindest of letters', and shows how she enjoys her constant company, but also notes how it can put her 'in bad humour' or 'in a huff' when she is met by Geraldine's 'little *cankered* look' (CL 30:208, 233, 224).

Yet the second newly-found letter brings Geraldine's feeling and character into sharper focus. For though that letter to Froude of 1876 has partly been published before, the rediscovery of the original allows it to be read in full for the first time. It gives a final and clearer view of Geraldine, which has been obscured by editorial interference. It is now (as in *CL* 30) given from the manuscript found within the pages of Jane's *Journal*; and the passages previously unknown, since they were deleted by Froude, are here given in bold type:

> **Walnut Tree House/ 7 oaks Kent Nov 22—76**
> **dear M*r* Froude—Until *today* I have not been able to open the little book you lent me I now it return it as registered *letter.*—**
>
> **Many thanks for the same the reading of it has been like calling up Ghosts – There are many *lacunae* in the Journal – not only of blank days but of events & incidents. It was a very bad time with her just then – no one *but* herself or one constantly with her knows what she suffered *physically* as well as [mentally]. In many ways** I feel how poor & *misleading* is all I have said to you about her - I have told you *facts* but I have failed to give you any real clue to them - She was miserable - more abidingly and intensely miserable than words can utter - her *Misery* was a *reality* no matter whether her imagination made it or not. With her habit of pushing every thing to the extreme - and of *expecting* to find the most *logical* consecutiveness in what people said did or professed - I don't know w*h* fared the *worst* the people or herself. - M*r* C. once said to me of her that she had the *deepest* & tenderest feelings - but *narrow*. Any other wife *wd* have laughed at M*r* C's *bewitchment* with L*y* A **but to *her* there was a complicated *aggravation* w*h* made it *very* hard to endure.** L*y* A. was admired for sayings & doings for w*h she* was - *snubbed. She* saw this L*y* A's little ways & *grande dame* manners **& knew** *what they were worth*. she contrasted them with the daily hourly endeavours she was making that *his* life sh*d* be as free from hindrances as possible. He put *her* aside for his WORK, but lingered in the 'Primrose path of dalliance' for the sake of a great lady who liked to have a philosopher in chains [the transcript renders this as 'in the chair'] - **L*y* A was excessively capricious towards her, & made her feel she cared more about *him* than about *her* – w*h* was always *lèse majesté* with *her* – she was never allowed to visit anywhere but at the G[rang]*e* – & the mortifications & vexations she *felt* tho' they were often & often *self made* were none the less intolerable to her. At *first* she was charmed with L*y* A. – but soon found she had *no real hold on***

***her*, nor ever *cd* or *wd* have. The sufferings were *real* intense & at times *too grievous to be borne*. – C. did *not* understand all this & only felt her to be *unreasonable*.** Mrs. C. was *proud*, & proud of her Pride. It was indeed enormous but a quality she admired *in herself & in others*.The only person who every had any influence over her was her Father – he died when she was 14 & she was left to herself. Her *mother* & she never agreed well when *together*, tho' she adored her at a distance – and worshipped her after she was dead.

Now about another point on *wh* you have perhaps wrong ideas. Wrong because they are the natural conclusions you *wd* be quite led to make from certain facts, some of *wh* I told you myself, & you remarked. But was it not behaving very ill to C—-? no. her allegiance was *never* broken – that, *you must* please believe on my word – she liked to be worshipped & to have people give their life & soul & spirit to her – I mean those whom she '*allowed* to love her' as she *wd* have put it, but *all* even the only two she *really cared for*, & who had the *power to make her suffer* – broke themselves against a rock, her *will* was as strong as her *Pride* & she *never* did anything in her life *wh* she *wd* have considered ignominious. **The feelings of pity tenderness generosity (false if you will) *wh* softens & bewilders most women NEVER disturbed her**, the clear pitiless common sense *wh* she *always* kept to never failed her. She was not heartless, for her feelings were *real* and *strong*, but she had a genuine *preference* for *herself* From her earliest girlhood this was her characteristic in all matters where *men* were in question –

She *would* be the *first* person with every body man *or* woman whom she cared for enough to wish to subjugate – **& her *power* to inspire the most *intense desire* to lay life soul body to *consecrate* to *her* all one had of the best & strongest in one's nature was something like *enchantment* – she had the power of appealing to & of exciting all that was *really* the best & most heroic in one's nature, & of really keeping one up to being one's best – & she *could* & she *did* inspire those who loved her with the desire to give themselves & *all* that was in them just to supplement & to fill up all that was lacking to her happiness in life – It was like trying [to] fill the sea – *shortcoming* & *unprofitableness* were marked on all we did or ever *could* do – the *more* we cared for her, the more lame & poor seemed the best we *cd* offer**. – The lines on *wh* her character was laid down were very grand – but the result was blurred & distorted & confused – **If when she flung off the outside doctrine of the Scotch Kirk she *cd* have felt & believed that the spiritual religion contained in the hard rough shape she had broken continued as real & vital as if the Kirk had never been, she *wd* have had a source of help & strength *wh wd* not have failed her like human beings, but she never did or could realise**

that religion & the Scotch Kirk were *not* identical, there never was a creature who so intensely yearned after & felt the need of religion in her soul.

In marrying - she undertook what she felt to be a grand & noble life-task A task w*h* as set forth by himself touched all that was noble & heroic & inspired her imagination from its difficulty - she *believed* in him - **& her faith was unique – *no one else did* – Well but** she was to be the *companion friend* - help mate - *her own* gifts were to be cultivated & recognised by him - she was bright & beautiful with a certain *star like* radiance & grace - **she had devoted to him her life – w*h* so many other men had desired to share.** She had gone off into that Desert with him, w*h* you know. - she had taken up poverty obscurity *hardship* even, cheerfully willing & with an enthusiasm of self sacrifice only asking to be *allowed* to minister to him. The offering was accepted - but like the precious things flung by Benvenuto into the Furnace where his Statue was molten they were all consumed in the fierce flame - & *he* was so intent & occupied by what he was bringing forth that he c*d* take no heed of the individual treasures - they were all swallowed up in the great whole - in *her* case it was the *living creature* in the midst of the fire w*h* felt & suffered - he gave *her no human* help nor tenderness; - bear in mind that *her inmost life was solitary* - no tenderness no carresses [sic] no living words - nothing out of w*h* one's heart can make the wine of life. A *glacier* or a *mountain* w*d* have been as human a companionship. She once told me what the earliest period of her married life was **& of the way in w*h* her whole nature was crushed & ground down & wounded, *he* suffered too. but he put all into his work. *She* had only the desolation & barrenness of having all her love & her life laid waste.** Six years she lived there, & she held out - she *had* undertaken a task & she *knew* that whether recognised or not, that she *did* help him, her strong persistent Will kept her up to her task of pain - Then they came back to the World - & the *strain* told on her then. She did not falter from her purpose of helping & shielding him *but* she became *warped*. 'We have this treasure in earthly vessels' - **and the vessels get cracked & broken & disfigured & people do not see or understand the treasure w*h* is thus carried & they *misjudge* & measure & criticise but the Treasure *is* there, & the broken blackened misformed unshapely *outside appearance* is swallowed up by Death and '*I believe* in the forgiveness of Sins & the Life Everlasting Amen!' G. E. Jewsbury**

(*CL* 30:263-6)

She is careless in points of fact such as Jane's age when her father died, and questionable about her dismissal of 'the Scotch Kirk'. Visitors to Cheyne Row frequently remarked that Geraldine spent a great deal of time in Jane's company, and that they were both skilled at making fictions. Of course they shared confidences. Yet when controversy broke out in 1881 after the publication of the *Reminiscences* and Froude's biography, Geraldine's status as Jane's supposedly 'best friend' meant that her recollections and attitudes were drawn into the public arena of debate. David Alec Wilson even argued that Geraldine's personality was a central issue:

> Miss Jewsbury...was neurotic and unstable, 'never happy', in Mrs Carlyle's opinion, 'unless she has a *grande passion* on hand, and as unmarried men take fright at her impulsive and demonstrative ways, her *grandes passions* for these thirty years have all been expended on married men'; which has led not unnaturally to the assumption that what she said of Carlyle could be traced to pique at his persistence in treating her with punctilious kindness as a friend of his wife. (6:75)

Did Geraldine really nurture a passion for Thomas as implied, in line with her reputation for *grandes passions* for other men, available or otherwise? Wilson goes so far as to suggest that Carlyle's remarks and family jokes about Geraldine, which inevitably found their way back to her, 'embitter[ed] poor Geraldine, and explain why she always delighted to think the worst of him, and also what she may have meant when she said to Espinasse, – Mrs. Carlyle "pours oil into your wounds, but it is oil of vitriol"' (6:353). Geraldine retaliates. Speaking of Carlyle, she remarks, 'Of course, one would never have the wild expectation that Mr. Carlyle will ever approve or admire any human effort' (6:110). Yet Jane allowed herself to admit Geraldine's good points as well as her bad. She told Helen Welsh: 'People who are at ease in Zion – I myself when I have been so to a certain extent – may have found Geraldine very teazing and absurd – but let one be ill – suffering especially *morbidly* suffering – and then one knows what Geraldine is! – all the intelligent sympathy and real practical good that lies in her!' (19 Aug. 1846; *CL* 21:18). But was Geraldine a reliable witness? When the Froude controversy first raged, this was the question. Carlyle wrote about it in a private letter he sent her in 1866, published in the *Reminiscences*, after she had returned him her 'Book of Myths':

> Dear Geraldine, – Few or none of these Narratives are correct in all the details; some of them, in almost all the details, are *in*correct...Your *recognition* of the *character* is generally true and faithful; little of *portraiture* in it that satisfies me. On the whole, all tends to the mythical; it is very strange how much of *mythical* there already here is! –
>
> As Lady Lothian set you on writing, it seems hard that she should not see what you have written: but I wish you to take *her word of honour* that none else shall; and my earnest request to you is that,

> directly *from* her Ladyship, you will bring the Book to me, and consign it to my keeping... – Affectionately yours, T. Carlyle. (Chelsea, 22 May 1866)

The notes were once accompanied by a letter from Geraldine too close to his wounded feelings to be read: '*25 May 1866.* Geraldine returns me this little Book of Myths, *un*shown to anybody, and to be my own henceforth. I do not yet burn it; as I have done her kind and respectful Letter ("Narratives long ago, on our first acquaintance" etc. etc. and fermenting and agglomerating in my mind ever since!) – in fact, there is a certain mythical truth, in all or most parts of the poor scribble, and it may *wait* its doom, or execution' (*Reminiscences* 66).

Froude was convinced that Geraldine was right, not least because he knew that when she wrote to him in 1876, she had not long to live; she died 23 September 1880, several months before Carlyle. Of Jane's crucial allusion in her *Journal* to 'blue marks on my wrist' (26 June 1856; *Reminiscences* 446), Froude commented: 'In her last illness, when she knew that she was dying, and when it is entirely inconceivable that she would have uttered any light or ill-considered gossip, she related all this to me, with many curious details' (*My Relations* 22-3). He and Geraldine had shared the experience of seeing Jane's body after her sudden collapse and death. He recalled that 'I have seen many faces beautiful in death, but never any so grand as hers. I can write no more of it. I did not then know all her history. I knew only how she had suffered, and how heroically she had borne it. Geraldine knew everything. Mrs Carlyle, in her own journal, calls Geraldine her *Consuelo*, her chosen comforter. She could not speak. I took her home' (*Life* 4:221). It is difficult to take the statement seriously that Geraldine 'knew everything'. Jane would almost certainly have delighted to ridicule such an assumption to Thomas. The same passage also requires us to believe that, because of Lady Harriet, Jane definitely made up her mind to leave Carlyle, and 'even to marry someone else' (*My Relations* 23), which is inconceivable. She is not to be taken literally, but the complete text of Geraldine's letter to Froude of 22 November 1876 does provide *Geraldine's* perception of the relationship she had with Jane, and her idea of Jane's relations with Thomas. Thomas's grudging assent that 'Your recognition of the *character* is generally true and faithful' (*Reminiscences* 47) suggests in outline, if not in detail, that Jewsbury had a gift of portraiture which went some way to capturing the 'real' Jane.

The letter to Charlotte Cushman and the complete version of Geraldine's letter to Froude are vital reminders that we categorise and simplify 'Mrs Carlyle' at our peril. Writing to Cushman, Jane extends the range of her epistolary powers into the new territory of the female confessional: it is an adoring testimony of affection from a woman in her

60s to a stranger and foreigner whom she has met only twice before. It contradicts Geraldine's account of her as a woman without 'the feelings of pity tenderness generosity...which softens and bewilders most women'. In other ways the letters partly overlap. Geraldine's summary underlines the price Jane paid in physical suffering. The spiritual and emotional drain of these later years may explain why she wrote to Charlotte, apparently demanding attention and affection. Writing to Charlotte, Jane suppresses some of the reality of her suffering and presents a gentler face, though she cannot resist bitterly ridiculing Geraldine. In turn, Geraldine's letter to Froude is a record of Jane, ten years after her death, perhaps set down to counter what Geraldine took to be the world's misconception of the Jane she had known. Yet what did Jane say when Geraldine had left the room? And what unwritten confidences did she share with Thomas? No 'best friend' could ever penetrate her secret thoughts. As the *Collected Letters* continue to demonstrate, she was forever refining the art of expressing her 'I-ity'.

Works Cited

Ashton, Rosemary. *Thomas and Jane Carlyle: Portrait of a Marriage.* London: Chatto & Windus, 2002.

Christianson, Aileen. 'Jane Welsh Carlyle and her Friendships with Women in the 1840s'. *Prose Studies* 10 (1987): 283-95; 288.

Clarke, Norma. *Ambitious Heights: Writing, Friendship, Love: The Jewsbury Sisters, Felicia Hemans and Jane Carlyle.* London: Routledge, 1990.

Fielding, Kenneth J. and David R. Sorensen, eds. *Jane Carlyle: Newly Selected Letters.* Aldershot, UK: Ashgate Press, 2004.

Froude, James Anthony. *My Relations with Carlyle.* Ed. Ashley A. and Margaret Froude. London: Longmans, 1903.

Wilson, David Alec. Life of Carlyle. 6 vols. London: Kegan Paul, Trench, Trubner; New York: Dutton, 1923-34.

Chapter 17

'The Victorian Lady' - Jane Welsh Carlyle and the Psycho-Feminist Myth: A Retrospective

RODGER L. TARR

Parts of this essay were first delivered as the College of Arts & Sciences Lecture, Illinois State University, Spring 1986.

The alleged tragedy of Jane Welsh Carlyle's life is one built upon ignorance and founded upon falsehood. For over one hundred years, she has been damned and defamed. In spite of her nobility of character and wit, and her talents as a writer and thinker, Jane Carlyle has been consistently condemned because she dared to marry the irascible Thomas Carlyle. Many psychoanalytic critics and feminist scholars feel, in varying degrees, betrayed by her - she has become the symbol of the presumed oppression in Victorian marriage. She is at once the martyr and the scapegoat for unbridled indignation. How dare she marry someone not suitable for marriage; how dare she betray the growing conviction that women (and men) are destined for higher goals than slavish devotion to legalised cohabitation?

The Prufrockian challenge - 'How dare?' - is not exclusively a modern or post-modern perspective - in fact, the seeming pathological violations of Jane Carlyle's life have been going on - largely unchecked until the recent and welcome appearance of Rosemary Ashton's *Thomas & Jane Carlyle: Portrait of a Marriage* (2002), and Kenneth Fielding and David Sorensen's *Jane Carlyle: Newly Selected Letters* (2004) - since her death in 1866. The maltreatment of her character has even wider implications, for she has become a symbol of what happens when so-called scholars and intellectuals choose to live outside the realm of accepted taste, common decency and historical perspective. The question that emerges is crucial: do we as scholars have an obligation to the truth, or do we have free licence to any opinion regardless of the consequences? Over one hundred years ago John Stuart Mill set an ethical standard when he argued that we do not have a right to any opinion; rather we have only the right to responsible opinion. If Mill is correct, then what has happened to Jane Carlyle should serve as a demonstration of what can and still does happen when patent falsehood is presented as scholarly truth.

The known facts of Jane Carlyle's life can be repeated. She was christened Jane Baillie Welsh, the daughter of a distinguished medical doctor from Haddington, a tiny village of classical character to the east of Edinburgh. Documents indicate that Jane was a precocious child who spurned the habits of her domestic mother and instead persisted in being close to her professional father. As she told the Anglo-Indian journalist William Knighton in 1857, 'My father was very anxious for a boy. He was disappointed that I was born a girl. However, he brought me up as much as possible as a boy. I was taught as a boy. When my mother remonstrated he would say, at eighteen I will hand her over to you, and you can teach her all a girl ought to know' (915). Her father, who had already witnessed his daughter finishing a five-act tragedy at fourteen, never stood in her way. As the fates would have it, at the age of twenty Jane met Thomas Carlyle, a young man of Calvinist peasant stock from Ecclefechan, a village in the southwest of Scotland, a land immortalised in the poetry of Robert Burns. Under the tutelage of Carlyle, she read voraciously and eclectically, but the passion that drove her was her love of Byron

The unsettled state of the Regency period in Britain had spawned the Byronic misanthrope, and Jane identified immediately with this Byronic solitary. With some reluctance she also followed Carlyle's urging to learn German and to read particularly the pronouncements of Goethe, Schiller, and Kant. But in the end Byron's 'Manfred' spoke to her of other ideals - and at one point she proclaimed the intention of physical celibacy with the view of achieving intellectual chastity. On the other hand, the letters exchanged between Jane and Thomas during this period demonstrate that Carlyle's attraction to her was almost instantly transformed to love. He persisted, and she resisted, writing to him some of the most comic rejections ever penned. After all, what future would the Belle of Haddington have with a crude peasant from Ecclefechan? She was wealthy, he poor; she was sophisticated, he bumbling; she was the epitome of grace, he rude beyond words. Still, they did have Byron in common; and, yes, she was coming to appreciate the Germanic longing of Carlyle. Indeed, in the prophetic words of Byron from *Don Juan*,

> But who, alas! can love, and then be wise?
> Not that remorse did not oppose temptation;
> A little still she strove, and much repented,And whispering 'I will
> ne'er consent' - consented.

In 1826, two Romantics became Victorian, a marriage that was to become the most famous in nineteenth-century Britain.

During the early years of their marriage, the Carlyles were nourished by their idealism. Thomas made a sufficient but not extravagant living. He was already well-known in critical circles for his translation of *Wilhelm Meister* (1824), his biography of *The Life of Friedrich Schiller* (1825), and his four-volume translation of German fiction, *German Romance* (1827). The novelist Sir Walter Scott was an acquaintance, the classical critic Francis Jeffrey a mentor, and the immortal Goethe an epistolary friend. However, the Carlyles did suffer early failure. He was turned down for the chair of Moral Philosophy at Saint Andrews University, in spite of letters of recommendation from Professor John Wilson, Jeffrey and Goethe; he had failed at writing a novel; and the remoteness of their farm Craigenputtoch - one hour by horseback from the nearest village - put a strain upon his young wife, who was accustomed to refinement. Thomas composed *Sartor Resartus* and tended the livestock; Jane wrote poetry and worked in her beloved flower garden. Isolation had its impact, but as their letters of the period indicate, it seldom caused domestic acerbity.

In 1834, the Carlyles removed to London and for the next three decades their home in Chelsea became a centre of Victorian intellectual life; the liberals John Stuart Mill and Harriet Taylor were constant visitors during the 1830s; Dickens knew them; Thackeray came by for walks by the river; Emerson visited and revisited, taking home to America a renewed transcendental faith; the Brownings, Robert and Elizabeth, became friends and admirers; Tennyson was a constant companion, who on occasion came specifically to visit Jane; Leigh Hunt was so overcome by the aura that he penned the famous poem 'Jenny Kissed Me', after an impulsive greeting from Jane; and then there was the confused but brilliant John Ruskin, who was to address Carlyle as 'Papa'. Chopin was there, as well as the young German intellectuals of the day. The list of prominent visitors is endless. By 1854, George Eliot was to declare without equivocation that Carlyle was an 'oak' among 'acorns'.

The Carlyles shared an incredible life. If Jane suffered neglect when Thomas was at work, it was all but made up for by their associations. True, she complained when she felt ignored; she once wrote him a lengthy letter, entitled 'BUDGET *of a Femme* incomprise' (7 Feb. 1855), addressing him as a government minister after Carlyle complained of her extravagances. She was also upset, even bitter, over what she perceived as Carlyle's increasingly intimate relationship with Lady Harriet Ashburton. They endured periods of great emotional pain, but in the end the strength of their union was preserved, a strength confirmed in the passions of their letters. Carlyle called her 'Goody', 'My Necessary Evil', and in return, she called him bluntly 'Carlyle'.

Jane was Thomas's host, but never his ring bearer. She was a host in the medieval sense, one who was responsible for the moral as well as the physical well-being of the guests, most of them friends of hers. And, she knew cleverly how to irritate Carlyle: she pressed the French feminist George Sand upon him, and he responded by denouncing her novels as 'Phallus-Worship'; and she brought her feminist friends before him. The Americans, Margaret Fuller and Lydia Maria Child, and their English counterparts, Harriet Martineau and Geraldine Jewsbury, were welcomed, if somewhat reluctantly, by Thomas. George Eliot pestered Jane to get Thomas to read *Adam Bede*; Jane pestered Thomas to read the Brontës; each pestered the other with their literary tastes. In all this, Jane was always at the front, never did she trail, never did she cower. Certainly she suffered – so many visitors, so much bombast, became an intrusion. Thomas would retire cursing in broad Scots, while Jane was left to increasing migraines and the opiate laudanum. Colds, influenza, and unidentified ailments became her constant companions. Yet her wit never abandoned her; she persevered, defending Carlyle to the end. In 1866 she died, without a struggle or sound, during a ride in her brougham in Hyde Park; Carlyle, almost at the very moment, was at Edinburgh University accepting the Lord Rectorship. Jane Carlyle was born a Romantic and died a Romantic, even though she suffered the tragedies and triumphs of being what Virginia Woolf called 'The Victorian Lady' (150).

Without doubt, the Carlyles lived a tumultuous life. As intellectuals, both held fervently to the past; both lived uneasily in the present; and each had an apocalyptic vision of the future. Their marriage was not perfect. Carlyle was demanding, punctual and certainly stern. Jane was acerbic, witty and equally stern. They clashed frequently. There was thunder, but always it was followed by periods of redemptive rain. Yet they seemed to have a single flaw – a flaw whose magnitude has been exacerbated in the minds of those whose passion it was and is to examine the passions of the Carlyles. Quite simply, they were childless. Childless couples are childless because one or both suffer from sexual dysfunction. One is impotent, or the other is frigid. It cannot be any other way. Choice and/or ill-fortune were hardly possibilities. To the psychoanalytic mind that believes this, to the feminist who finds sustenance in it, there can be no other answer. The Carlyles were flawed – they must be exposed.

The primary architect of this exposure forces another irony upon the situation. One of Jane's best friends, the celebrated feminist and novelist Geraldine Jewsbury, in 1873, upon her deathbed and thus presumably in candour, imparted the news to Carlyle's official biographer James Anthony

Froude: 'Carlyle was one of those persons who ought never to have married' (*My Relations* 21). Froude translates this confession by Jewsbury into a portrait of pain. Throughout his biography he implies, suggests, cajoles; and, when the reader is finished, the portrait is sharp: Thomas was a cruel, insensitive and uncaring husband. Froude, however, avoids direct discussion of the Jewsbury allegation, that Carlyle suffered from either impotence or sexual dysfunction. Instead he paints a long-suffering Jane whose life was mercifully cut short in 1866. The Carlyle descendants were stunned by Froude's conclusions. Mary Aitken, Carlyle's niece and amanuensis, demanded an apology and return of the papers that Carlyle had entrusted to Froude. Froude declined, and the whole affair was taken to the pages of the London *Times*.

Charges and countercharges were filed. Friends and acquaintances were appalled. Froude subsequently appealed to Jane's first biographer, Mrs Alexander Ireland, to tell the truth, and to discuss openly Carlyle's impotence and its impact on Jane. Mrs Ireland declined, although her work is decidedly sympathetic to Jane. The furor continued. By the turn of the century, some corrections were attempted. Carlyle's nephew Alexander published *New Letters and Memorials of Jane Welsh Carlyle* (1903), and in his preface he challenged Froude's pronouncements. Froude, now dead, was defended by his family, and the rejoinder *My Relations with Carlyle* (1903), a short book of 80 pages founded upon a manuscript Froude left behind, was hurried to press. In it we are told explicitly that the only source for Froude's assertions was in fact Geraldine Jewsbury, who claimed a special intimacy with Jane. The 'mystery', as Froude calls it, was finally exposed: Carlyle had been impotent; the proof: 'The morning after his wedding-day he tore to pieces the flower-garden at Comeley Bank' (*My Relations* 23), the Carlyles' residence in Edinburgh. Just who saw Carlyle do this is unclear, and it did not seem to matter that there was no flower garden at Comely Bank.

The implication is clear: men who despoil flower-gardens after their wedding-night are confirming their sexual impotence. To this Froude adds, '[Jane] had longed for children, and children were denied her' (*My Relations* 21). In response to these new allegations, the prestigious *British Medical Journal* in 1903 offered a lead article by Sir James Crichton-Browne on the impossibilities of this all being medically provable, much less true. The noted writer Andrew Lang wrote a summary of the sordid situation, entitled 'The Carlyle Scandal' (1903). Crichton-Browne and Alexander Carlyle next devoted a book to the subject, *The Nemesis of Froude* (1903), in which they denounced such insufferable innuendo. Still, this now barebones psychoanalytic controversy would not go away. The crowning achievement to psychoanalysis was yet to come, however.

In 1911 the already infamous Bloomsbury addict Frank Harris reported with his usual sincerity that in 1878 Carlyle in a state of remorse had confided to him that he 'had never consummated the marriage or lived with his wife as a wife' ('Talks' 432). Carlyle was eighty-three when this alleged discussion took place; Harris was twenty-two. Harris insists that his knowledge was later corroborated at the Garrick Club in London by the distinguished physician Sir Richard Quain. Harris then reports at length Dr Quain's alleged club-room confessional. As the story goes, Quain was visiting the Carlyles when Jane suffered abdominal pains and retired to her room. Quain followed to offer assistance. The following excerpt from Harris's *My Life and Loves* (1925) suggests the extent of his retreat from the truth:

> Mrs. Carlyle was lying on the bed with a wooly-shawl round her head and face. I thought it an absurd affection in an old married woman, so I resolved on drastic measures: I turned the light full on, then I put my hand under her dress and with one toss threw it right over her head. I pulled her legs apart, dragged her to the edge of the bed and began inserting the speculum in her vulva: I met an obstacle – I looked – and immediately sprang up 'Why, you're a virgo intacta!' (209)

Harris's vulgar, demeaning, and insulting description marked the birth of the central myth of the Carlyles' supposedly disastrous marriage: Jane died a virgin.

It is discouraging to think that such psychoanalytic twaddle would be taken seriously by intellectuals, especially one as distinguished as Virginia Woolf. Yet in 1929 in her article 'Geraldine and Jane', she accepts and contributes to the myth. In general her account of the friendship of Geraldine Jewsbury and Jane Carlyle is remarkable for its depth of passionate understanding. She recounts deftly how Geraldine gave tea parties with Jane, where Geraldine 'discussed literature rather boldly, with a cigar in her mouth' (149). She points out how Geraldine 'dressed herself in a low-neck dress to receive visitors on Sunday' (149). And she observes how Geraldine revised the manuscripts of her first novel *Zoe* (1845) because Jane thought it too 'indecent' (150). To Woolf, both women are feminists. Jane was quiet, usually observing, whereas Geraldine was outspoken, always pugnacious: her 'blood boiled in her at the power men had over women'. Woolf's own blood boils at the thought of Jane's marriage to Carlyle, who 'hated…strong-minded women of the George Sand species' (150).

Woolf's anger leads her to extreme conclusions. She argues that Geraldine was unnaturally jealous of Jane, and quotes the latter's remark that Geraldine had 'some sort of strange, passionate…incomprehensible *attraction* towards me…such mad, lover-like jealousy' (150). Decorously but firmly Woolf raises the issue of lesbianism. She seems convinced, in the absence of any concrete evidence, that there was a passion between the two – a bodily attraction, at least on Geraldine's part. As if sorry for intruding upon the friendship, Woolf offers an apologia: 'It is difficult to persuade ourselves that we can judge Geraldine Jewsbury and the true nature of her feeling for Jane Carlyle' (150). Woolf almost seems to be appealing on her own behalf. In the end, however, she had left her impression for the future to consider: Geraldine Jewsbury and Jane Carlyle, Woolf concludes, 'discussed everything' (150). Unwittingly and without malice, she added a new chapter in the life of Jane Carlyle, who was linked on an intimate level with the 'Feminist from Manchester'. Woolf understood lesbian yearnings in the context of volatile marriage, and intuitively, she read her own life into Jane's. She could not possibly have anticipated how her impressions would become facts in the eyes of future (and lesser) psycho-feminist critics, and serve as a springboard for ludicrous charges and false innuendo.

To a certain extent, post World War II criticism attempted to salvage Jane Carlyle's reputation. In 1949, Trudy Bliss edited a selection of her letters in a noble and partially successful attempt to present the real Jane Carlyle. In 1952, Lawrence and Elisabeth Hanson wrote a sympathetic biography that relegates the whole controversy to an appendix. For a moment Jane Carlyle was restored, her dignity returned. However, it was only a brief respite. As psychoanalytic study and feminist perspective increased in the 60s and 70s, Jane Carlyle again became fair game. The myths created by the Victorians and Edwardians were once again translated into facts. The Victorians, seemingly notorious for chauvinistic behaviour, became the staples to feed the myth. In her book, with the leading (and misleading) title of *Seduction and Betrayal* (1975), Elizabeth Hardwick concedes from the outset that the Carlyles' marriage was '*the* Victorian marriage' (165), and then proceeds to dismantle it. Hardwick sees the marriage as a 'domestic comedy' because Jane had to subvert her 'genius' to Thomas's 'gigantism' (165). Hardwick insists that while Thomas chased the bitch-goddess success, Jane was 'cleaning, dusting, chasing bedbugs, sewing, [and] supervising redecorations' (168). In the midst of these unsupported observations, Hardwick repeats Frank Harris's mythical assertion that Jane was a lifelong virgin as a result of Carlyle's fumbling (174). With no more understanding than taste, Hardwick concludes that Jane Carlyle was no different from other Victorian women who had no 'bulwark against sufferings of neglect and the humiliations of lovelessness' (181). Perhaps such nonsense needs no refutation, but we can only regret that it comes from a woman who identifies herself as a feminist.

What Hardwick lacks in judgement is more than compensated for by the ebullient Phyllis Rose, who stretches decency to its nadir. In *Parallel Lives* (1984) - another best seller - Rose devotes upwards of four chapters to the Carlyles' marriage. She recounts as facts all previous myths, and concludes confidently that Carlyle 'is a great man, a great thinker, but a pathetic human being…a terrible, a cruel, husband. The idol has feet of clay' (257). To prove her point, Rose retreats to the well-known story of Carlyle and his neighbour's rooster, sometimes called cock, which much to Carlyle's consternation awoke him at all hours of the night and early morning. The story is true enough. Thomas was so put out with the noise that he implored Jane, among others, to do something about it. They planned all sorts of intrigues, including buying the cock and killing it. Victorian intellectuals sat around and ruminated on what the Carlyles should do. Thomas fumed, Jane sympathised, they all laughed, and in the end a sound-proof study was built at Cheyne Row.

Rose subjects this comic interlude to humourless psychoanalysis. Jane was always 'her husband's protector, slaying the serpents without so that he could concentrate on slaying the serpents within' (246). For Rose it follows that 'no one who has been awakened in darkness by cock crows will be tempted to put down [Carlyle's] resentment of cocks as wholly symbolic' (246). Thomas's resentment of the rooster has taken a Freudian turn. Of course, Jane herself is implicated. Referring to a letter in which Jane mentions a dream about a cock, Rose triumphantly declares, 'Even in her dreams, [Jane Carlyle] fended off cocks' (247). Rose's prurient implication is clear - Jane had phallic dreams because of her sexless marriage. Fred Kaplan embraced similar conclusions in his Freudian biography of Carlyle, written in the same period. Without a shred of evidence, he asserts that Carlyle suffered from an Oedipal complex so deep-seated that as a child he was afraid to masturbate (35). With equal certainty (and with no evidence) he states that Jane Welsh was 'frightened of sex' (72).

Perhaps inevitably, post-modern criticism has perpetuated the myth of Jane Carlyle, to the point where the windmill of illusion spins to a blur. Sandra Gilbert and Susan Gubar emerged as the chief spokespersons of psycho-feminist theory, and they comfortably and without hesitation asserted that the Victorian pen and the Victorian penis were indistinguishable, at least metaphorically. *Madwoman in the Attic* (1979) - an immediate best seller - was devoted to the proposition that the 'poet's pen is in some sense…a penis' (93-4). This link supposedly explained why women such as Jane Carlyle were intellectually unfulfilled. Males were the controlling force in literature and publishing, and of course, Carlyle was one of the central figures at the helm. In a rather dense syllogism Gilbert and Gubar hold him responsible for promoting the maleness of Victorian society. They argue that Carlyle was responsible for canonising Goethe, and that Goethe was the progenitor of 'the eternal feminine, the angel women' (23). In his climactic injunction in *Sartor Resartus* – 'Close thy *Byron*; open thy *Goethe*' – Carlyle encouraged the oppression of women. The suggestion that *Sartor Resartus*, with its emphatic transcendentalism, is a specific articulation of Victorian chauvinism is absurd. Typically, Gilbert and Gubar overlook the fact that Carlyle's bildungsroman was especially admired by feminists such as Lydia Maria Child, Margaret Fuller, Harriet Martineau, and Geraldine Jewsbury. It was also a favourite of Virginia Woolf's. Are we to believe that these distinguished women and others – Elizabeth Barrett Browning, Louisa May Alcott, Elizabeth Gaskell, and Emily Dickinson, among others, missed the anti-feminist thrust seen by Gilbert and Gubar? Their claim is embarrassing as well as inaccurate.

Feminists since Gubar and Gilbert have used increasingly sophisticated arguments to reinforce the myth of the Carlyle marriage. In *Ambitious Heights* (1990), Norma Clarke argues that Geraldine Jewsbury's testimony was discredited because she was a female novelist working in a patriarchal world: 'Geraldine had provided a convenient scapegoat. She had furnished Froude with some of the anecdotes which placed Thomas Carlyle in a particularly bad light...and her capacity to tell the simple truth was easily called into question by referring to her occupation: she was a novelist; her brain teemed with "romance"' (148). Clarke simply refuses to accept the possibility that Jewsbury may have exaggerated, and curiously defends her decision to destroy Jane Carlyle's letters to her as 'honourable' (149) without questioning her motives. Jane's own complaints about Geraldine's misdirected sentiment and excessive emotion are dismissed and turned against her. They are the consequence of her envy at Geraldine's 'capacity to go out and live her life in a way that suited her' (152). Of course Carlyle himself is finally to blame for this state of affairs, since he is the one who shapes Jane to be, in Jewsbury's language, 'the beautiful reflex of him' (190). The psycho-feminist argument here takes a new turn, transforming the victim into the aggressor.

Adopting a different tactic, Aileen Christianson in 1997 drew welcome attention to the literary qualities of Jane Carlyle's letters. But the attention, it should be noted, came at a heavy price where Thomas Carlyle himself is concerned. In her essay, Christianson subordinates the discussion of the letters to the question of 'Welsh Carlyle's' status as a writer. By referring to her as a 'life-writer', Christianson intends to raise Jane's literary reputation to that of a Victorian novelist, which according to Christianson, 'Welsh Carlyle' chose not to be: 'In the end her choice was not to seek fame, to publish, or to challenge social constraints. It was to accept the dictates of a conventional 'wifely' life of duty, of repression; and, in sarcastic and humorous counterpoint to that life, to weave her continuous web of commentary on her life and the lives surrounding her' (243). What begins as an appreciation of Jane's epistolary skills ends with a claim for her as a novelist manqué. In her conclusion, Christianson implies that Jane Carlyle fails to become a Dickens because of her 'repressed' existence as Thomas's wife – it follows that her achievement as a 'life-writer' is all the more significant, given her life of 'duty' and 'repression'. In a recent review of Rosemary Ashton's *Portrait of a Marriage*, Kathryn Hughes has trenchantly exposed the dubious psycho-feminist assumptions underlying these claims: 'While other commentators have rushed to see Jane as a thwarted artist, whose prolific and entertaining letters are a sad token of all the brilliant novels that marriage to Carlyle stopped her from writing, Ashton is far cooler in her analysis. Other women in difficult situations managed to write novels – the Brontës, George Eliot, and even Mrs Gaskell all succeeded in domestic circumstances that were far from ideal. If Jane Carlyle never managed to make it into print, then something more complicated than patriarchy must have been to blame'

In *Men of Letters, Writing Lives* (1999), Trev Lyn Broughton sought to explain the Froude controversy in the context of late nineteenth-century shifting attitudes towards the ideal of the 'man of letters'. Barely concealing her delight in the triumph of 'psycho-history' over history proper, Broughton blithely disregards the moral implications of the charges made against Carlyle: 'With the publication of the impotence allegation, the Froude-Carlyle embroilment ceased to be a recognisably political struggle for justice...and devolved into an unsavoury struggle for the right to guarantee the meaning of sex: struggle, finally, for the phallus' (171). Truth here becomes a casualty of a larger and more important movement against the hegemony of 'autocratic' husbands and literary men. In her typically inflated idiom, Broughton observes that Froude's *My Relations* 'precipitated a crisis of legitimation for Victorian biography, and marks a faultline in biographical epistemology...[which]...calls a habitually psychoanalytic reader into being' (171). The arrival of psychoanalysis coincides with the disposal of old and tired complaints about accuracy and fairness: 'The fuss [the allegation of impotence] caused, and went on causing, was as much about this fracturing and redrawing of disciplinary and professional boundaries as about the truth, or otherwise, of Froude's revelations on ticklish topics' (172). For Broughton, the 'fuss' is incidental to these larger psycho-feminist concerns.

The myth of the Carlyle marriage has been resurrected in less obscure ways by Julia Markus in *Across an Untried Sea* (2000). She straightfowardly repeats Frank Harris's tale and declares that 'All the evidence points to the fact that both Quain and Harris were telling the truth' (300). As Brent Kinser has discovered, Markus's belief in Harris and Quain is the result of somewhat baffling logic. While she admits that Harris's memoir was 'ignored through the twentieth century, the message bearer in this case being long considered a liar' (167), she nevertheless maintains his truthfulness. Unfortunately, Markus has only Harris's version of Quain's testimony to offer as a defence of Harris's honesty. She undermines her position further by committing basic errors of fact and chronology. According to the *Dictionary of National Biography*, the Dr Richard Quain (1800-87) to whom Harris, Hardwick, Rose, and Markus herself refer is not the Dr Richard Quain (1816-98) who attended the Carlyles. As Kinser has further discovered, there were two Sir Richard Quains in London at this time, cousins, both of whom were physicians, and both of whom attended Queen Victoria. Markus claims that her Dr Quain 'was a literary man and a raconteur' (167), which is true: he published *The Diseases of the Rectum* in 1854. The Richard Quain who treated Jane Carlyle had a fashionable London practice and was an expert in diseases of the chest. Markus's mistake is no doubt an honest one. John Gallagher, who edited the 1963 Grove Press edition of *My Life and Loves*, identifies the wrong Dr Quain in Harris's account as well. It may be, however, that Harris was responsible for the error. If so, then his tale can be confirmed as an outright lie.

Markus further weakens her argument in her summary of Harris's report. She concludes her account of the examination after Dr Quain's pronouncement of 'virgo intacta', when Jane asks, '"What did you expect?"' (168). Harris, however, continues with Quain's response to Jane: '"Anything but that"', I cried, '"in a woman married these five and twenty years"' (210). It is surprising that Markus would leave out Quain's response, for it seems to date his examination to 1851 (the Carlyles married in 1826). However, in a letter to Betty Braid, dated 25 December 1862, Jane writes of Quain: 'My first words to him (he had never been in the house before) were "Oh Dr. Quain what has brought you here"' (Froude, *LM* 3:144). Thus, according to Jane, Quain's first visit to Cheyne Row is 1862, not 1851. Perhaps an aging Harris has confused his dates – if so, it is a peculiar testimony to what Markus calls his 'unusually retentive memory' (300). If Markus is correct about Harris's memory, then it seems reasonable to conclude that in constructing his lie, he chose the wrong Quain and the wrong date.

It is remarkable, given the weight of misunderstanding that surrounds Jane Carlyle and her marriage to Thomas Carlyle, that so few psycho-feminists have bothered to ask the relevant questions: what was Geraldine Jewsbury's motive in giving Froude such malicious gossip about the Carlyles? And armed with the gossip of Carlyle's alleged impotence, why did not Froude bother to check with other intimates of the Carlyles? Why, indeed, was he content to rely on the testimony of a woman whose propensity for exaggeration was well documented, especially by Jane Carlyle herself? The example of Jane Carlyle - an extraordinary woman in every respect - suggests how fragile the reputations of literary figures can be. Yet surely John Stuart Mill's injunction on responsible opinion still deserves to be respected. The foundation of any empirical truth should be fact rather than fiction. Psycho-feminists and their followers have, either wittingly or unwittingly, participated in the creation and the perpetuation of the myth of Jane Carlyle that undercuts the integrity of both feminism and psychoanalysis. Perhaps it is time for them to heed Carlyle's words in his essay 'Biography' (1832): '[I]t is good that every reader and every writer understand, with all intensity of conviction, what quite infinite worth lies in *Truth*' (*Works* 28:53).

Works Cited

Ashton, Rosemary. *Thomas and Jane Carlyle. Portrait of a Marriage*. London: Chatto & Windus, 2002.

Broughton, Trev Lynn. *Men of Letters, Writing Lives. Masculinity and Literary Auto/Biography in the Late Victorian Period*. London and New York: Routledge, 1999.

Christianson, Aileen. 'Jane Welsh Carlyle's Private Writing Career'. In *A History of Scottish Women's Writing*. Ed. Douglas Gifford and Dorothy McMillan. Edinburgh: Edinburgh UP, 1997. 232-45.

Clarke, Norma. *Ambitious Heights. Writing, Friendship, Love - The Jewsbury Sisters, Felicia Hemans, and Jane Welsh Carlyle*. London and NY: Routledge, 1990.

Crichton-Browne, James. 'Froude and Carlyle: The Imputation Considered Medically'. *British Medical Journal* (27 June 1903): 1498-1502.

———, and Alexander Carlyle. *The Nemesis of Froude. A Rejoinder to J.A. Froude's 'My Relations with Carlyle'*. London and New York: Lane, 1903.

Fielding, Kenneth J. and David R. Sorensen, eds. *Jane Carlyle: Newly Selected Letters*. Aldershot, UK: Ashgate, 2004.

Gilbert, Sandra, and Susan Gubar. *The Madwoman in the Attic*. New York: Yale UP, 1984.

Hardwick, Elizabeth. *Seduction and Betrayal*. New York: Vintage, 1975.

Harris, Frank. 'Talks with Carlyle'. *English Review* 7 (1911): 419-34.

———. *My Life and Loves*. New York: Grove Press, 1963.

Hughes, Kathryn. 'Marriage of Opposites'. Rev. of *Thomas and Jane Caryle Carlyle: Portrait of a Marriage*. By Rosemary Ashton. *The Guardian* (9 Feb. 2002): B3.

Kaplan, Fred. *Thomas Carlyle: A Biography*. Ithaca, New York: Cornell UP, 1983.

Kinser, Brent. 'Jane and Shirley'. Unpublished research. Used with the permission of the author.

Knighton, William. 'Conversations With Carlyle'. *Contemporary Review* 30 (June 1881): 904-20.

Lang, Andrew. 'The Froude-Carlyle Dispute'. *Independent* (Bombay, 1903): 1565-7.

Markus, Julia. *Across an Untried Sea: Discovering Lives Hidden in the Shadow of Convention and Time*. New York: Knopf, 2000.

Rose, Phyllis. *Parallel Lives: Five Victorian Marriages*. New York: Knopf, 1984.

[Woolf, Viriginia]. 'Geraldine and Jane'. *Times Literary Supplement* (28 Feb. 1929): 149-50.

Chapter 18

Jane Welsh Carlyle's Travel Narratives: 'Portable Perspectives'

AILEEN CHRISTIANSON

That Jane Welsh Carlyle controls her material and the presentation of her life in her writing through her literary skills is now generally accepted. Townsend Scudder, editor of her letters to Joseph Neuberg, wrote in 1931 that 'her literary effects...will be found to have something of a method in it' (Scudder xiii). Yet her skill as a writer contains much more than 'something of a method'. Her travels narratives in particular reveal the full range of her talents, conveying a subtle grasp of the ironies implicit in tourist narratives. In July 1858, she satirically headed two letters written from Cheyne Row with 'Notes of a Sitter-still' and 'Notes of a Still-sitter' (Froude *LM* 2:355; MS NLS 606.486). But her 'annals of visiting' that could 'fill a volume' (*CL* 21: 22), as she referred to a trip to Manchester in 1846, give evidence of a woman who was less sedentary – neither a 'Sitter-still' nor a 'Still-sitter' – than is sometimes assumed.

They provide examples of a self-conscious narrator travelling beyond that 'home' and contain different kinds of travel narratives: explorations of the return to the familiar, voyages into the new (which are then contained by literary metaphors), and awareness and a critique of the picturesque. In *Penelope Voyages: Women and Travel in the British Literary Tradition* (1994), Karen Lawrence refers usefully to the 'various plots of wandering (in romance, adventure, exploration, and travel narratives)' (17). The material explored here covers Lawrence's 'various plots', and includes Jane's trip to the Highlands in 1822, Manchester in 1846, Matlock (with Thomas) in 1847, as well as her notebook sketch of 'Tiger Wull', journey to Scotland in 1849, 'Letter of Travel and Romance' in 1852, and visit to Moffat in 1853.

In her youth, Jane Welsh was part of the world of romantic sensibilities that idolised both Byron and Napoleon as romantic icons. It was the revolutionary and Napoleonic wars, following earlier eighteenth century wars, which had contributed to the development of 'internal tourism' (Colley 186) in Britain. With the European tour no longer seen as safe, the upper classes travelled to 'the more isolated regions' of North Wales, the Lake Districts, and the Highlands. They carried with them, in Linda Colley's words, their fashionable 'aesthetic education: a knowledge of Edmund Burke's theory of the sublime, a properly developed understanding of the picturesque and the ability to read key texts like William Gilpin's *Observations on the River Wye* (1782), which was littered with untranslated Latin quotations and allusions to Old Masters such as Claude Lorraine and Salvator Rosa' (Colley 186-7). By 1822, when Jane was to make her journey to Fort Augustus, new elements had been added to the potent mix of Burke and Gilpin: Wordsworth's poetry and his cult of the sublime in the Lake District, *Ossian,* and Goethe's travel narratives.

There was also the satire of William Combe and Thomas Rowlandson's *Tour of Dr Syntax in Search of the Picturesque* (1809), with their conflicting tourist and anti-tourist tendencies. As Ian Ousby has pertinently remarked, 'almost as soon as the vocabulary of tourism emerged it was invaded by self-doubt and self-criticism' (19). Ousby points out that whereas the cult of the sublime 'concentrated on the masses of rock, hill and lake to solicit from their wildness and immensity an answering violence...of feeling in the spectator', the cult of the picturesque focused on 'the variegation and harmony expressed by the maundering curve of the river or lake shore, the grouping of the rocks and trees which flank it...and the subtle gradations of colour which blend the scene together' (152). Nonetheless, disagreement persisted as to whether the categories of the sublime and the picturesque really were 'distinct from each other or from the traditional concept of Beauty', with writers in the late eighteenth century using the terms 'almost interchangeably' (Ousby 153–4).

Jane's letter to Thomas recounting her trip to Fort Augustus provides a fine example of the young tourist in action, who is full of romantic sensibility and adolescent aspirations and appreciates the wild landscape in the frame of the best romantic, historical, and literary reference points. In the central paragraph she demonstrates her range of descriptive powers:

> I am delighted with this country. My cousin's house stands near the top of Loch Ness, in the midst of a bright green lawn as smooth as velvet. The Tarffe flows down from Corryarrick through a deep wooded glen behind the house – and forms the boundary of this verdant spot. Steep wooded braes rise on the opposite side of the river. and behind these the vast range of heathy mountains that form the northern boundary of the Great Valley – a few yards from the house there is a bridge across Glen Tarffe the most romantic thing I ever saw. I sit there whole hours admiring Loch Ness with its gigantic ramparts of bold mountains – and the beautiful little Fort Augustus and the green braes where Cumberland encamped with his ten thousand men after the battle of Culloden...I

> have seen Ben Nevis, the king of Mountains, and various other Bens, and Craigs, and Corrys; that I am neither learned enough to spell - nor poet enough to paint…in short (to use my highland cousin's words) 'I have been at all the knows [knolls] and *dubs* [puddles] in the country' - Of all I have seen what I admire most is Foyers - It is worth travelling a thousand miles to see the magnificent scenery around the fall - no description can convey an idea of its rude bold grandeur - while I stood on a projecting pocket between the stupendous rocks that seemed to have been torn asunder by some horrible convulsion I shuddered as if I looked upon an earthquake - and had not one of our party drawn me from the brink of rock I verily believe I should have thrown myself into the gulph beneath from absolute terror.
> (24 Sept. 1822; CL 2:166-7)

Jane responds to landscape in terms of both the picturesque and the sublime, climaxing in her proper response of fear and terror at the 'stupendous rocks', yet she adroitly resists their formal requirements in her description. In her opening paragraph she satirises both the plight of the tourist in face of Highland weather and her own romantic tendencies, and invokes the names of Byron and de Staël to add weight to her predicament:

> I was looking to the south and wondering if any living creature thought on me when your letter was put into my hand. Never did letter meet a warmer welcome. It was so unexpected and so different from anything I have read or heard these many weeks! - not a word of hogs, cheviots, Falkirk-fair or the Caledonian-canal!…I anticipated much enjoyment from our journey hither but, Alas! the wind blew, and the rain fell, and I was cold wet and wofully sick - From Glasgow to Fort-William I lay on the deck of the Steamboat praying to be again on terra firma and heedless of the magnificent scenery through which we passed - Every thing is ordered for the best - had I been at all comfortable I should assuredly have fallen in love - deeply hopelessly in love with a handsome fascinating Colonel of the Guards who held an umbrella over me for four and twenty hours - You will wonder I escaped when I tell you this charming stranger is intimately acquainted with Lord Byron and enjoyed the friendship of our own de Stael - I never saw his like. He is all heart and soul - with the look of a Prince and the manners of a courtier - I could have wept at parting with him - but I could not get at my handkerchief without unbuttoning my boat-cloke and that was inconvenient - (*CL* 2:165-6)

The portrait of the 'fascinating' Alexander Mair, deputy governor of Fort Augustus, serves to remind Thomas that he can make no assumptions about his possible status as a suitor. In the final paragraph she completes the frame for her picturesque and sublime tendencies by specifying the further 'sights' she has seen, including George IV's infamous orchestrated 'Scottish' parading in Edinburgh (although she does not refer to his appearance in an invented 'Highland' dress), and her failure in Glasgow to meet the Baron de Staël, the son of her heroine Madame de Staël. She also tells Thomas '*by the bye* I have got a new friend. I intend filling a sheet with his merits so shall say nothing of him at present' (*CL* 2:167-8). A month later in her next letter to Haddington, she satirises her 'new friend' Benjamin Bell, who has pretensions to being an artist but has 'no *genius*' (*CL* 2:280). In the same letter she offers a returned traveller's effusion on the superiority of the Highlands:

> [W]ere it not for the magic in that word *home* which rivets the heart to the spot where it first beat, I verily believe I should emigrate to the North – Oh the 'Land of hills, glens and warriors!' It's wild romantic grandeur forms such a contrast with our flat, wearisome cornfield' and the people there so frank, natural, and true-hearted! so different from the cold selfish well-bred beings lives among! (24? Oct. 1822; *CL* 2:179)

Here Jane conforms to the necessity for the traveller to find authenticity amongst the more 'natural' surroundings of the picturesque landscape, whether of the Highlands, the Lakes, or Switzerland.

Elsewhere in her travel narratives, she participates in the tourist currencies of her time, and follows a pattern that Ousby discusses in relation to the Peak District, conveniently near Derby and Sheffield: '[I]ts growing industries appealed to the early generation of travellers whose eclectic interests always made them ready to break the journey with a visit to a porcelain factory, a lead mine, a cotton mill or a cutlery workshop' (Ousby 132). In 1846, she identifies herself with the practical traveller rather than the more frivolous tourist, by announcing that 'I am afraid I should not take half as much interest in the *Lakes* as in the Manchester Mills! My tastes being decidedly *Utilitarian* for the moment!' (*CL* 21:30). In a practical mood, she invests the 'mechanical' world with sublime features:

> [D]ay after day has passed for me in going up and down in '*hoists*' and thro forest of machinery for every conceivable purpose – I have seen more of the condition of my fellow-creatures in these two weeks than in any dozen years of my previous existence...there is no lack of interesting people here – and they have a great superiority over the London people...Whitworth the inventor...has a face not unlike a baboon...to my taste worth any number of the Wits 'that go about'. (27 Aug.; *CL* 21:22)

Disdainful of the picturesque, she captures the natural beauty of this 'forest of machinery'. But this passage is not just an example of Jane doing the utilitarian, as opposed to the picturesque. Earlier in the summer she had left Thomas and London in a state of depression and anger over his friendship with Lady Harriet Ashburton. As a result, the 'natives' in the North of England are shown as more useful and more truly interesting than the 'Wits' of London who, like Thomas, dance attendance on Lady Harriet.

Jane's practical outlook in this period is apparent too in her treatment of exotic subjects. In an April 1845 excerpt from her Notebook, she refers to her cousin William Dunlop, known as 'Tiger Wull', because of his zeal for stalking game in India:

> 'Tiger Wull' and some friends of his sailed once to Ailsey Craig in search of the picturesque and went on shore there. Was there ever such 'beautiful Nature'? So sublime a scene? Their Lyrical recognition of it had just reached the highest point of ecstacy when turning a corner they found themselves face to face with *a Paisley Weaver*, wearing his unmistakable green apron - They did not strangle him - tho his apparition there had been death to their picturesque enthusiasm they merely expressed a courteous surprise that he should be 'so far from home'. It *was* a wonder he owned; he had 'never been to that *spot* before'; but could they tell him how he might lay his hands on a young Solan goose? He had 'come for *two Goose* to eat the snails in Provost Dagleish's garden -' The Gentlemen made themselves very merry over his *wild goose Chase* - might he not have done the same over theirs. (13 April; *CL* 30;163)

Welsh Carlyle here responds satirically to the idea of the picturesque in 'beautiful Nature'. She also opposes the legendary hunter and author of *Sketches of Upper Canada by the Backwoodsman* (1832) to the simple 'native' of Paisley, who has made a journey 'so far from home' (about 50 miles) in search of the common gannet to eat the snails in the Provost's garden. Their obligatory lyrical expression of Ailsa Craig's picturesqueness is cut short and challenged by this intrusion into their 'beautiful Nature' of the Scottish industrial world in the person of the weaver. With her closing suggestion that the search for the picturesque itself might be the 'wild goose chase', Jane turns the table on her cousin's and his friends' witticism of the 'wild goose chase' and identifies herself firmly with the weaver.

In August 1847 she and Thomas, imitating the example of Ousby's early travellers, took a trip to Matlock in Derbyshire and the surrounding Peak District. She writes to Anna Jameson of their new situation:

> It is three weeks to-day since we started on *The Pursuit of the Picturesque under Difficulties*, - the first time in our married lives that we ever figured as declared Tourists. And I fancy we should have broken down in the first blush of the business, but for a special interposition of Providence in the shape of a spirited young Quaker who came to the

> rescue at Matlock, and guided us triumphantly thro' all the sights of Derbyshire, northwards to his own habitation, where we have remained stationary for ten days. (27 Aug.; CL 22:43-4)

Notable as the author of *Winter Studies and Summer Rambles in Canada* (1838) and recently returned from Italy where she had been preparing *Sacred and Legendary Art* (1848), Jameson was both travelled and 'cultured'. Jane's echo of Rolandson's satirical *Tour of Dr Syntax in Search of the Picturesque* and her characterisation of she and Thomas as 'declared Tourists' serves to establish them as anti-tourists. She is alert to the pretensions of nature-worship, and when she writes to Thomas during a visit to Barnsley in 1847, she juxtaposes 'nature' and 'industry', both of which provide tourists with entertainment. She reports that she and her hosts are 'going off now in a fourwheeled gig to see some *beautiful nature* somewhere and what is more to the purpose the largest shawl factory in Yorkshire' (7 Sept.; *CL* 22:55-6). The phrase '*beautiful nature*' seems to demand a source but remains untraced. It is apparently part of her coterie speech, used mainly as a satirical phrase to imply a composite critique of romantic attitudes to landscape.

In her 1849 piece 'Much ado about Nothing', Welsh Carlyle frames her memories of her childhood and education in Haddington within a rail journey from the North of England to Haddington, and then from Haddington to Edinburgh. Her journey takes her from her present into her past and then back again to the present. It ends with the foregrounding of her present self waving goodbye to her past self: 'And now having brought myself to Edin*r* and under the little protecting wing of Jeanie, I bid my self adieu and "wave my lilly hand" – I was back into the Present! and it is only in connection with the Past that I can get up a sentiment for myself – The Present M*rs* Carlyle is what shall I say? – *detestable*' (*CL* 24:171). The journey begins in Morpeth in July when William Forster sees her into the train: 'I was shot off towards Scotland' and in effect also 'shot off' into her past as 'The first locality I recognised was *the Peas Bridge*: I had been there *once* before, a little child, in a postchaise with my Father; he had held his arm around me while I looked down at the ravine; it was my first sight of the Picturesque, *that*, I recognised the place even passing it at railway speed, after all these long years' (*CL* 24:160). The Pease Bridge was built over a large ravine near Cockburnspath, Berwickshire; Welsh Carlyle's memory of her introduction to this example of the picturesque from the safety of her father's arms remains uninflected by irony *because* it took place in the arms of her father. She then returns to a more familiar ironic stance with the adoption of the personae in Haddington of the 'stranger-in-search-of-the Picturesque' and 'the character of the travelling Englishwoman' (*CL* 24:162,164). Stared at 'as a stranger, or even a *foreigner*' (*CL* 24:161) by a woman she recognises, Welsh Carlyle enacts the role of a travelling foreigner (that is an Englishwoman) in her progress round her childhood haunts in Haddington. These hints of the traveller-tourist become an element in the 'underlying narrative structure' and 'storyline' that constitute this most complicated of her 'travel performances' (Adler 1375; quoted Buzard 16). She plays in the piece as a whole with the ghosts of her former self and of her parents, and the idea of a lost and unattainable past and 'home'.

In other travel letters, Jane uses 'home' to establish a sense of her own 'discursive space' (Lawrence 18) with Thomas. In these instances she is always underpinned by a sense of dialogue with him, of communication (or refusal of communication), and of preserving a sense of her own authority. Burdened by renovations at Cheyne Row in 1852, she denies him his wish for a 'Letter of Travel and Romance' (6 Aug.; *CL* 27:211):

> Oh my Dear! If I had but a pen that would *mark* freely - never to say *spell* - and if I *might* be dispensed from news of *the house*; I could write you such a *Lettre d'Une Voyageuse* as you have not read 'these seven years'. For it was not a commonplace journey this at all! It was more like that journey of a *Belinda* or *Evelina* or *Cecelea*. Your friends 'The Destinies', 'Immortal Gods', or whatever one should call them, transported me into the Regions of mild romance for that one day. But with this cursed house to be told about, and so little leisure for telling anything, my Miss Burney faculty cannot spread its wings - so I will leave my journey to Sherbourne for a more favourable moment, telling you only that I am no worse for it - rather better - ...Except that I sleep less than ordinary mortals do, I have nothing earthly to complain of nor have had since you left me - Nor will I even tell you of the Macreadys in this letter - I cannot mix up the image of that dear dying woman with details of bricklayers and carpenters - . (3 Aug.; *CL* 27:200)

The postponed letter is one of Welsh Carlyle's consciously shaped pieces that refers to her journey to Sherborne in Dorset to visit the dying Catherine Macready. The pain of the visit itself is only briefly referred to, contained between the adventures of her journey there and back: 'I was wonderfully little tired and able to make them all (*her* too) laugh with my adventures...My two days at Sherborne House were as happy as could possibly be with that fearfully emaciated dying woman before my eyes...I am so glad I went it pleased her and all of them so much!' (5 Aug.; *CL* 27:209). The first and largest part of the letter exemplifies Lawrence's idea that 'much travel writing self-consciously places itself in a tradition with aesthetic forbears, a tradition of mixed parentage of travel narrative and fiction' (Lawrence 25). Jane herself presage this tradition in her reference to other female fictional journeys: George Sand's *Lettres d'un Voyageur* (1834-6), Maria Edgeworth's *Belinda* (1801), and Fanny Burney's *Evelina* (1788) and *Cecilia* (1782).

She describes the visit to Sherborne House as if it were a chapter in a novel. She travels to Frome on the railway and there finds that there are no coaches to Sherborne. She then leaves her parasol on the coach she takes to Sparkford Inn, eight miles from destination. An 'old gentleman' reminiscent of Richardson's Sir Charles Grandison offers to retrieve it the next day. Jane instructs the landlady, overheard by a gentleman in a barouchette with two horses, and her journey continues:

> I started myself, in a little gig, with a brisk little horse, and silent driver. Nothing could be more pleasant - than so *pirring* thro' quiet roads in the dusk - with the moon coming out - I felt as if I were *reading about myself in a Miss Austin novel*! But it got beyond *Miss Austin* when at the end of some three miles before a sort of Carrier's Inn, the gentleman of the barouchette stept into the middle of the road, making a sort of military signal to my driver ...I sat confounded - expecting what he would do next. We had halted; the gentleman came to my side, and said exactly as in a book 'Madam! I have the happiness of informing you that I have reclaimed your parasol...I judged that it *would* be more pleasing for you to take the parasol along with yourself, than to trust to its being brought by the other gentleman - So I just galloped my horses, overtook the coach as it was leaving this court, reclaimed the parasol, and have waited here - knowing you could take no other road to Sherborne - for the happiness of presenting it to you!'...and then I found myself making a speech in the same style, caught by the infection of the thing. I said; 'Sir! this day has been full of mischances for me, but I regard this recovery of my parasol so unexpectedly as a good omen...'! I never certainly made so long and formal a speech in my life! And how I came to make anything like it I cant imagine unless it were under mesmerism! We bowed to each other like first cousins of Sir Charles Grandison - and I *pirred* on. (*CL* 27:208-9)

In 1851, Geraldine Jewsbury, talking of a dinner party, remembered it as 'like being translated into a novel...we all seemed like people and things out of a novel, and one wondered where the real life and human nature of the people had been stowed away, and whether any of them knew anything of the practical and economical difficulties of life' (Ireland 408-9). Using Jewsbury's conceit, Welsh Carlyle's allusions to novels by Richardson, Austen, Edgeworth, and Burney, provide a fine illustration of the intersection between fiction and non-fiction in her writing, with fiction impinging on her actual travel in a literal sense. Lawrence writes in *Penelope Voyages* of the 'female traveller's particular baggage' including 'the historical link between female wandering and promiscuity', citing a review of Frances Trollope's travel books that 'link women's travel to promiscuity through a play on her name' (Lawrence 16). As if explicitly invoking this connection, Welsh Carlyle concludes the journey section of her August 1852 letter with 'My only *adventure* on the road back was falling in with a young *Unfortunate Female* on the Chelsea boat' (*CL* 27:209). The building works that had been used to postpone Thomas's pleasure in the earlier letter are confined in this letter to the postscript.

In Jane's later travel narratives, the sceptical anti-tourist who is resistant to the picturesque tends to dominate. For example, in her account of her visit to her brother-in-law and his new wife in Moffat in 1853, she provides an extended example of the interplay of the picturesque and the sublime, as well as a satire on the desirable pursuit of the exotic for the traveller:

> The most important thing I have to tell you is that you could not know me here as I sit from a red Indian! that I was kept awake the first night after my arrival by a — — *Hyaena*! (yes upon my honour! and *you* complain of a simple *cock*!) and that yesterday I was as near as possible for giving occasion for the most romantic paragraph of the 'melancholy accident' nature that has appeared in any newspaper for some years! But first of the Hyaena. on my arrival I found an immense caravan of Wild Beasts pitched exactly in front of this House and they went on their way during the night and the animal in question made a devil of a row – I thought it was the Lion roaring but John said 'no – it was ONLY the Hyeana'! I rather enjoyed the oddness of having fled into the country for 'quiet' and being kept awake by *Wild Beasts*! (8 July 1853; *CL* 28:188)

Taken together, these narratives illustrate the way in which Welsh Carlyle absorbs the genre of travel writing into other modes of life writing. She uses the 'dual 'theoretical position' of traveler and signatory of the discourse' (Lawrence 26), accommodating her journeys in her letters, and ensuring that the travel is satirised and controlled within the frame of her writer's eye. Her travel narratives belong to the same satirical tradition of Combe and Rowlandson, who 'mocked the sheep-like pilgrimages of tourists who, tinted Claude glasses in hand, trecked in their droves to the approved stations for a glimpse of the 'correct' view' (Manning xvi). Unlike these touring spectators or her friend Benjamin Bell who wore 'a steel chain with a very ingenious, portable perspective (to denote he is an artist)' (24? Oct. 1822; *CL* 2:180), Jane's 'portable perspective' is internalised, allowing her to record, organise, and satirise her material. She shapes her journey narratives so that they become both 'Travel as Performed Art' (Adler 1366) and her own 'portable perspectives' on travel.

Works Cited

Adler, Judith. 'Travel as Performed Art'. *American Journal of Sociology* 94 (1989):1366-91.

Buzard, James. *The Beaten Track: European Tourism, Literature, and the Ways to Culture, 1800-1918*. Oxford: Clarendon Press, 1993.

Colley, Linda. *Britons: Forging the Nation 1707-1837*. London: Vintage, 1992.

Froude, J.A., ed. *Letters and Memorials of Jane Welsh Carlyle*. 3 vols. London: Longmans, Green, 1883.

Ireland, Mrs. Alexander, ed. *Selections from the Letters of Geraldine Endsor Jewsbury to Jane Welsh Carlyle*. London: Longmans, Green, 1892.

Lawrence, Karen R. *Penelope Voyages: Women and Travel in the British Literary Tradition*. Ithaca and London: Cornell UP, 1994.

Manning, Susan, intro. *The Sketch-Book of Geoffrey Cannon, Gent*. By Washington Irving. Oxford: Oxford UP, 1996.

Ousby, Ian. *The Englishman's England: Taste, Travel, and the Rise of Tourism*. Cambridge: Cambridge UP, 1990.

Scudder, Townsend, ed. *Letters of Jane Welsh Carlyle to Joseph Neuberg 1848-1862*. London and New York: Oxford UP, 1931.

Chapter 19

'Wonderful Worlds Up Yonder': Rousseau and the Erotics of Teaching and Learning

NORMA CLARKE

In *Reminiscences*, Thomas Carlyle recalled his first sight of Edward Irving. It took place in 1808, at Annan Academy, where the older boy, Irving, had come on a visit to his former school. Carlyle, a pupil in the Latin class, was a mere looker-on as the English master, Adam Hope, and the mathematics master, Morley, displayed this 'flourishing slip of a youth' and for some ten or fifteen minutes discussed with him the new ideas then current in Edinburgh. 'We didn't hear everything; indeed we heard nothing that was of the least moment or worth remembering', Carlyle wrote. He took note of 'a certain *preciosity*' in some parts of Irving's behaviour but in the main he was as dazzled as the rest: 'the talk was all about Edinburgh, of this Professor and of that, and their merits and methods ('Wonderful world up yonder; and this fellow has been in it, and can talk of it in that easy cool way!') (*Reminiscences* 211-12).

The 'wonderful world up yonder' was a world of teaching and learning. The schoolboy Carlyle heard little of what was said between Irving and his masters, but as an adult looking back he remembered both the excitement in the air and his own yearning after it. Some of his feeling for Irving, so penetratingly explored in the essay in *Reminiscences* which is, amongst other things, a meditation on the vicissitudes of their relationship, was rooted in this shared passion for learning. Irving was a model to emulate and a rival to beat. Seven years passed before Carlyle encountered Irving again, by which time Carlyle was a dissatisfied young schoolmaster and Irving still the golden boy. Irving had gone on to a post as master of the school at Haddington, where his energy, confidence, ambition, and drive had turned around a failing school. Carlyle had heard much 'betrumpeting' of the young man, how 'splendidly successful' he was, how 'his new Academy and new methods were illuminating and astonishing everything there' (*Reminiscences* 213). Their second encounter in 1815, a chance meeting in Edinburgh, was not a comfortable one for Carlyle since he felt too acutely his own lack of success by comparison. Four unhappy years as a schoolmaster had led him to resolve against teaching as a career: 'my solitary desperate conclusion was fixed, that I, for my own part, would prefer to perish in the ditch, if necessary, rather than continue living by such a trade' (*Reminiscences* 213). Intense and bilious as he described himself, morose and lonely, Carlyle had 'peremptorily' given up teaching and he felt a failure. Neither his past nor his future looked to him prosperous - unlike that of Irving who had 'a kind of joyous swagger traceable in his manners, in this prosperous young time'. Irving was 'Trismegistus Irving, a victorious bashaw [pasha], while poor I was so much the reverse' (*Reminiscences* 213, 216, 215). The excitements of teaching and learning had been working for Irving and they were failing Carlyle.

At Haddington, Irving had been tutor to Jane Welsh, who 'loved to learn and...cultivated all her faculties to the utmost of her power' (*Reminiscences* 45). In 1821 Irving introduced Carlyle to his ex-pupil, thus bringing into being a tripartite relationship structured around teaching and learning, with a romantic component that was acknowledged between the young men in their private talk but rejected by Jane Welsh. Carlyle had by 1821 abandoned the notion that his future lay in teaching, preferring to think of himself as a writer, a struggling writer, unknown, of low social origins, but regarded by many, including Irving, as a genius whose soaring abilities would one day be recognised. Jane Welsh meanwhile was no longer a girl with a passion for knowledge - the sort of girl who left books of Latin and Greek lying about in her wake - but an heiress sought out by many suitors; her future seemed to be defined in terms of the choice of a husband. Carlyle could never have been considered an appropriate suitor but he was an appropriate tutor. In the difficult courtship that followed which eventually led to marriage in 1825, the role of unofficial tutor was a means for Carlyle to pursue closer intimacy with Jane Welsh. The romance of tuition provided the basis for romantic love, although it was a condition of the relationship that love, or erotic feeling, be denied. Jane Welsh flatly refused to allow Thomas Carlyle even to allude to it. In spite of his contempt for the probable results of the transaction between teacher and learner - 'three grains of knowledge mixed up in three bushels of error' (TC to JBW, 26 Feb. 1822; *CL* 2:57) - he bowed to her insistence that they operate within a pedagogic framework. He was to send booklists; he was not to write about his heart. She would be his friend and pupil, she would call him brother, she would be a fellow writer; but she would not be a lover; she would not be a wife. Insofar as Carlyle represented for her the 'wonderful world up yonder', it was to be a world of intellectual fulfilment not erotic gratification; the shared passion for knowledge serving at once as a conduit, a scaffolding, an excuse, a substitution, a sublimation, an intensification, and a defense. The intensity of Jane Welsh's refusal of the erotic - not only in relation to Carlyle but also in response to her other suitors - argues a powerful inner struggle. The force of denial required suggests not the absence of erotic awareness but such a heady eroticisation of teaching and learning that it had to be constantly restrained, for it was in the teaching and learning encounter that the erotic was most likely to erupt.

For Jane Welsh, accepting Carlyle as a teacher replicated the special relationship she had had with Irving as a child. Born in 1801, Jane Welsh was ten years old when Edward Irving became schoolmaster at Haddington. The little girl had already shown a desire for learning which her father encouraged and her mother, whatever reservations she had, did not obstruct. She excelled in the 'male' subjects: mathematics and classics. She would stay up late puzzling over Euclid and get up early to translate Virgil. This application to study was fully endorsed when her father invited Irving to become the private tutor in the household. In addition to his duties as master at the school - which Jane Welsh also attended - Irving came twice daily, between six and eight in the morning and again in the evening, and gave individual lessons to his star pupil, the child of '*electric* intellect' (*Reminiscences* 70). What kind of future was being imagined for Jane Welsh? What 'wonderful world up yonder' might *she* dream of entering as her intellectual powers were developed by the young man of whom everybody expected so much? It was certainly not the same world of which Irving and Carlyle dreamt. Her father wanted her to be 'wise, as well as good-looking and good'(*Reminiscences* 68). Improvement of the self, of property, and of the lower classes - was an unquestioned ideal of the times. As an only child, and a precocious one, she was left in no doubt about her own significance in the world. Fantasies of the future were implicit in the educational agenda of her upbringing. Yet the specific outcomes imagined as the end product of this commitment to education were never clearly defined.

By 1847, when Jane Welsh Carlyle looked back over her life (with considerable bitterness) she told Caroline Fox that she thought the intense early education of her childhood had been a 'mistake'. Caroline Fox recorded the gist of the conversation:

> She believes that her health has been injured for life by beginning Latin with a little tutor at five or six years old, then going to the Rector's school to continue it, then having a tutor at home, and being very ambitious she learned eagerly. Irving, being her tutor, and of equally excitable intellect, was delighted to push her through every study; then he introduced her to Carlyle, and for years they had a literary intimacy and she would be writing constantly and consulting him about everything. (Pym 219-20)

It is not immediately obvious that the experiences described would injure someone's health 'for life'. But the Victorians promoted the view that the health of girls was injured by over education, and since something had clearly been 'injured for life' in the middle-aged Jane Welsh Carlyle, the idea of excessive learning was a convenient rationale. But two years later, visiting Haddington in 1849, Mrs Carlyle expressed a different point of view, lamenting what she saw as a sharp decline in educational standards there. She was dismayed to find that her old schoolroom displayed religious texts where once the walls had been covered with maps and geometrical figures. On this occasion, the memory of her childhood hours of hard study with Irving served as a positive counter. Education in itself, then, was not necessarily the problem. Caroline Fox's choice of words in her account directs us to read something awry in her friend's early experiences with the exceptional men who fired her intellect and imagination. Irving's later fate – religious schisms and speaking in tongues – is registered in the description of his 'excitable intellect' and that in turn casts a lurid colouring over Jane's 'literary intimacy' with Carlyle that followed. Experiences that in a boy's life would have marked him out as uniquely fortunate – a literary intimacy with a major writer – here acquire shiftily negative connotations that cannot quite be spelled out. The two women, both writers, grapple with a problem that seems to lack a vocabulary. They try to explain Jane's misery and ill health but in fact use words that carry not only a positive but, more strikingly, a sexual or erotic charge: 'eagerly', 'excitable', and 'delighted'.

The question about the purpose of her education was inevitably linked with her choice of a husband. Her pained reflections on her education and her experience at the hands of her tutors were often accompanied by expressions of generalised grievance at having been let down, or having been led to nurse false expectations about the future. The men she loved – her father, Irving, and Carlyle – had all urged intensive education on her, teaching by prescript and example the value of intellectual cultivation. More important still, they engaged with her, intellect to intellect, producing some of the excitements Caroline Fox reported that were inextricably bound up with the daughter's erotic feelings for her father, the child's erotic feelings for her tutor and the sexually mature young woman's erotic responses to suitors and husband. Adoring her father, she had sought to be like him as well as to be what he would like, adopting the posture of the good pupil. As a pupil, first of Irving's and then of Carlyle's, she had sought to imitate *and* please her tutors. It meant choosing the kind of husband of which he would have approved. Thomas Carlyle was welcomed for his 'eloquence' because it reminded Jane of her father: 'I had never heard the language of talent and genius but from my father's lips...you spoke like him – your eloquence awoke in my soul the slumbering admirations and ambitions that *His* first kindled there' (11 Nov. 1822; *CL* 2:196). What were those admirations and ambitions? How could they be incorporated into becoming a wife? This was a riddle neither the young Jane Welsh nor the mature Jane Carlyle managed to solve. For an intellectually gifted female in the early nineteenth century, the options were limited, though this did not prevent any of the men who admired and loved her from using a language of aspiration on her behalf.

The intimacy between Jane Welsh and Thomas Carlyle developed around a shared set of imaginative identifications. In this process both were familiar with Rousseau's *Julie, ou La Nouvelle Héloïse* (1761), an important fictional guide in a realm where the boundaries between the spoken and unspoken, and the real and the fictional were fluid. Rousseau's novel built on the public's fascination with the legendary story of Abelard and Héloïse to offer a thoroughly contemporary tale which fused the erotic and the intellectual. Abelard, a twelfth century monk who was acknowledged as an outstanding intellectual, fell in love with his brilliant pupil, Héloïse. The affair that followed had tragic consequences for both of them. Abelard was castrated. He insisted on separation. They renounced worldly love, ceased to have any communication with each other, and went into religious orders, but their love did not die. Many years later Abelard wrote an account of their story that led to a correspondence in which Héloïse made clear that her longing for him had not subsided. Rousseau's novel, as its double title suggests, focuses on a modern Héloïse, whom he named 'Julie'. Like Samuel Richardson, whose *Pamela* (1740) had taken Europe by storm, Rousseau put the ardent young woman at the centre of his tale. Unlike Pamela, Rousseau's Julie was not a servant but a middle-class woman of enormous intellectual gifts and erotic passion. Rousseau describes her using her intellect to maintain and justify the heroic renunciation of her passion. The erotic element in her intellectuality is at once constantly present and denied. Finishing the novel in February 1822, Jane Welsh told her friend Eliza Stodart that it was 'the most moral book' she had ever read: 'Divine Julia! – What a finished picture of the most sublime virtue! ... Julia never *relapses*! – to the last hour – last minute of her life, she is pure and bright as the silver Moon...Oh she is a glorious creature!' (12 Feb.; *CL* 2:36).

No less glorious was Julie's tutor, St Preux. His love was 'so pure, so constant, so disinterested, so exalted – that no love the men of this world can offer me will ever fill up the picture my imagination has drawn with the help of Rousseau' (Jan. 1822; *CL* 2:17). Thomas Carlyle resembled St Preux, having '*his* talents – *his* vast and cultivated mind – *his* vivid imagination – *his* independence of soul and *his* high souled principles of honour' (*CL* 2:18), but he lacked elegance, and more significantly, his passionate eroticism. For his part, Carlyle could enact the poor and brilliant philosopher in gentry circles with a conviction that he too had learned from his enthusiastic reading of Rousseau. Adopting the approved role of tutor, he urged his 'Julie' to 'press forward towards the golden summit of mental eminence'. The love of knowledge was a 'noble' passion. He and she could 'assist each other in many a noble purpose'. Good readers of Rousseau, they agreed that a 'vulgar wedding' and the erotic implications of mere sexual union would be 'a pitiful conclusion' for one of her Julie-like talents and virtues (TC to JBW, 26 March 1823; *CL* 2:313).

Eighteenth-century literature is filled with images of teacher and taught, images in which the journey of life is dramatised in terms of the transmission of knowledge. The cultural myth declared that there was a body of knowledge that could be possessed by one and transmitted to another, and that virtue resided in this transaction. In an early *Rambler* essay, Samuel Johnson expressed the view that 'virtue is the highest proof of understanding'. This also worked with the terms reversed: understanding was the highest proof of virtue, vice was 'the natural consequence of narrow thoughts' (*Rambler*, No. 4, 31 March 1750, 'The New Realistic Novel'). The model of teacher and taught can be found in Rasselas (1759), in which the philosopher Imlac, who knows about the real world beyond the happy valley, teaches *Rasselas* and Nekayah who do not. What he teaches them has to do with desire, but it is not eroticised as it is in *La Nouvelle Héloïse*, the biggest best-seller of the eighteenth century. In France, demand for copies was so high that booksellers rented it out by the day and even by the hour. At least seventy editions were published before 1800.

Rousseau offered readers a form of reading that allowed for self-creation. Through imaginative identification with the characters, the reader's own life was transformed. The reader became something and someone else. This was accomplished through external signs of emotional affect: readers sobbed, sighed, and wept their way through the pages. In his essay, 'Readers Respond to Rousseau', Robert Darnton summarises examples from Rousseau's own postbag: '[O]rdinary readers from all ranks of society were swept off their feet. They wept, they suffocated, they raved, they looked deep into their lives and resolved to live better, then they poured their hearts out in more tears' (242). In *La Nouvelle Héloïse*, the tutor comes into the household in order to teach, which in essence means to read with the pupil and share the experience. St Preux tells Julie: 'To read little and to meditate a great deal upon our reading, or to talk it over extensively between ourselves, that is the way to thoroughly digest it' and adds that she is someone who puts into her reading more than she takes out of it, whose 'active mind makes another and sometimes better book of the book you read'. The reader becomes the writer and the imagined becomes part of the real. St Preux says to Julie: 'In this way we will exchange our ideas. I will tell you what others have thought about the subject; you will tell me what you yourself think about it; and I will often leave the lesson better instructed than you' (Rousseau 1997:46-7).

The passion for knowledge, which is shared, is a virtue. The tutor and pupil spend hours privately apart from others, engrossed in their studies, in the pursuit of virtuous improvement. These highly charged intimate encounters may or may not find libidinal expression, but they were nevertheless liable to it, and once libidinised or eroticised, might be acted upon and thereby become a non-legitimate passion. By 1821 when Jane Welsh joined the vast ranks of those who were driven to ecstasy by *La Nouvelle Héloïse*, its effects were well known. As she said to Bess Stodart, 'ask your heart, or rather your judgement, if Julia be vicious. *I do not wish to countenance such irregularities among my* female *acquaintances*' (Jan. 1822; *CL* 2:16-17). But the quality of St Preux made it understandable to this twenty-year-old female reader that 'irregularities' might follow. Of course she ridiculed the emotional excess. A sophisticated and satirical reader, Jane Welsh was unlikely to reproduce the reactions of Rousseau's correspondents who were so emotionally overwhelmed they had to take to their beds or run away with the adored tutor. Her response suggested her awareness of such reactions. But what was vice and what was virtue? What was regular and what irregular? Rousseau's writing turned the world upside down so that vice looked like virtue. Something of the licence granted by these reversals can be found in her account of the poor suitor Dugald Gilchrist, who cried his eyes out for three days because she would not marry him. In this scene, Jane Welsh the reader of Rousseau became Jane Welsh the writer who could command a critical distance from a Rousseauistic reading while 'one would need a heart of flint to bear a destiny like mine' (JBW to TC, 11 Aug. 1824; *CL* 3:128). Like Rousseau, she too had a strong sense that she was 'unlike anyone I have ever met; I will even venture to say that I am like no one in the whole world' (Rousseau 1953:17).

In his *Confessions* (1782) Rousseau announced that Nature had broken the mould in which he was formed. His book would display what he had made of himself. At twenty, Jane Welsh contemplated two possible futures: on the one hand, there was marriage and wifely subordination; on the other, there was the cultivation of her unique self through reading and writing. Clearly, the erotic, associated with marriage, was identified with loss of the unique self. But the erotic was also linked to her reading and writing, and to the charismatic men who bestowed loving attention on her and made her feel unique. The ten-year-old child privately tutored by Irving received from him not just knowledge, but also a message about the kind of person it was imagined she might become. Like Irving, she too had permission to imagine a future equal to her abilities. Just as he and Thomas believed in their uniqueness, so too did Jane.

For her, the tutorial relationship offered a form of protection so long as the erotic element in it could be denied. Carlyle attempted to make the claims of love an open part of the exchange with her, informing her that 'it is the heart that makes us great or little; and who would not rather be the meanest creature that can *love*, than the highest that could but *perceive*?' (22 Feb. 1822; *CL* 2:57). He was rebuffed and did not dare speak the language of love again for many months, confining himself to the language of tuition and praising her intellectual ambition. His observation, it should be noted, was a question. In posing the possibility of being 'great' or 'little', Carlyle asked a question about an imagined future self. The version Jane Welsh chose took the tutorial relationship as its model: as a tutor Carlyle offered guidance and gave encouragement, and bound himself to her through a shared vision of what she might become. Writing to her on 23 Sept. 1822, he declared, 'I consider my own credit as partly implicated in your progress; I have pledged myself as to the extent of your natural endowments, and if I do not live to see you by far the most distinguished female of all I ever knew, I shall die disappointed' (*CL* 2:162-3). At the same time, he understood that other feelings were working in him: 'You bid me write to you as a *friend*. Vain injunction! I must exhibit the true state of my feelings when I write, or else write like a shallow fool: and I never felt *friendship* of this sort towards any one' (13 Feb. 1822; *CL* 2:40). Jane Welsh's rejection of these avowals of the erotic meant that Carlyle left the lesson much less well instructed than he might have been. So also did she. Julie, it should be remembered, allowed herself to be seduced by St Preux.

Carlyle's essays on Jane Welsh Carlyle and Edward Irving in *Reminiscences* were written in 1866 after Jane's death and they were a means of coping with grief through an attempt at understanding what the past might be able to teach. To reflect on their lives and expectations was, inescapably, to reflect upon his own. Carlyle linked his own progress from unknown country youth to celebrity with Irving's career. There was much for his analytic imagination to investigate as he recalled a friendship rooted in a powerful sense of identification. He could hardly help writing about himself since urgent personal questions drove his narrative, questions directly related to matters of success and failure in loving, learning, and teaching, and the being great or small. In a more diffuse sense, as a recent widower, he was preoccupied by questions about love in its varied forms: love of and by others, and love of oneself which might or might not be a necessary component of getting on in the world. The memories he found himself 'languidly' following as he recalled wonderful long walks, snatched visits, stimulating talks, moments of 'fine manly sociality' (*Reminiscences* 216) and, above all, Irving's constant encouragement of him as a man of great promise, were full of a sense of an imagined future which, at the time of writing, was now past. Carlyle recalled that Irving's predictions 'about what I *was* to be flew into the completely incredible. 'You will see now', he would say, 'one day we two will shake hands across the brook, you as first in Literature, I as first in Divinity – and people will say, "Both these fellows are from Annandale: where is Annandale?"' (*Reminiscences* 266).

Carlyle appreciated Irving's mock-heroic deflation which functioned, perhaps, as a defence against the 'incredible' utterance 'about what I was to be'. Conscious of his own powers and optimistic for the future, Irving lightly and lovingly contradicted Carlyle's 'gloomy prognostications' about 'obstructions and "impossibilities"' (*Reminiscences* 265) and reinforced his passionate dream of being 'first in Literature'. In 1866, Carlyle looked back over a life in which he had become if not *the* first then one of them, with an international reputation and disciples every bit as devoted as those who had followed Irving in his prime. As a writer he had achieved 'incredible' honours and recognition. This bit of the imagined future had come to pass more or less according to the most extravagant expectations, and in so doing validated the self-belief (or self-love) which drove it.

But if Irving was right about Carlyle, he was wrong about himself. Irving had gone from high promise to catastrophe. Moving from teaching to preaching, the charisma so evident in his youth found a ready audience amongst religious enthusiasts and fashionable followers of 'genius'. He had gone from being a celebrity in the 1820s to a wreck in the 1830s, in Carlyle's view a victim of adulation and fanaticism working on culpable levels of self-love. People flocked to learn what Irving had to teach them; they were inspired by him as Carlyle had himself been inspired. Carlyle's low opinion of Irving's followers partly served to obscure some identification with them. At the very least, he was wary about the operations of loving, teaching, and learning. Irving's life offering a moral of some sort, but what that moral might be is not explained in *Reminiscences*. Shrewd and elastic as his observations are, and generous and deep as his feeling is, Carlyle's *thinking* about why Irving's life went to smash is inhibited. Similarly, to *think* about his own success produced discomfort.

This inhibition of thought also characterises Carlyle's reminiscences of Jane Welsh Carlyle. The imagined futures of the young men Carlyle evoked were part of the meaning of their present: each self in the present contained the imagined selves of the future, credible or incredible as these might be, 'right' or 'wrong' as they might prove. In the case of Jane Welsh, his puzzlement at what fate delivered is made more explicit, perhaps because of his intimate involvement in her imagined future. Carlyle was implicated in what became of Jane Welsh in a way that he never was with Edward Irving. By marrying her in 1825, Carlyle *became* Jane Welsh's future. Through the several years of courtship that preceded their marriage, the question of who Jane was and what she would become was addressed by Carlyle with the same apparent seriousness that he brought to the question in his own life. Just as the curve of Irving's prospects went from high to low, so too did that of Jane Welsh Carlyle. By taking them both as subjects for autobiographical musings, and by setting against *his* success *their* inexplicable failure to achieve the 'incredible' futures their gifts seemed to promise, Carlyle invites his readers to ponder - as he appears to do - how these outcomes transpired.

Yet the imagined future that was part of the unmarried Jane Welsh's present had none of the scope for action that Irving and Carlyle - young men of whom much was expected - could dream of. To a large extent, her imagination was the place where such dreams began and ended: her aspirations, those 'admirations and ambitions' kindled by her father - were never likely to be realised. In helping to form these dreams, both Carlyle and Irving enthusiastically entered into fictions that flew more obviously into the '"impossibilities"' than anything Irving predicted for Carlyle. The imagined future implied by her early education was a fiction and Carlyle's urging her to join the ranks of literary women was also essentially fictional: 'Literary women have many things to suffer, but they have likewise something to enjoy. I confess it appears to me more enviable to be a sister of Madame de Stael's for half a year, than to "suckle fools and chronicle small beer" for half a century' (26 March 1823; *CL* 2:314). As many commentators have observed, Carlyle's language changed after marriage; the radical equality of his early vision was supplanted by his desire to build her up as his wife. No longer a tutor and rejected lover, he discovered the new pleasure of being a man with a wife, and of having wifely attentions bestowed on him. The erotic was released - or at least, a new imaginary was opened to him as a married man that made erotic expression of a particular sort available. In this new world the really exciting thing was the *difference* in their roles: he thrilled to the idea of having his 'Dear little Wifie' (27 March 1828; *CL* 2:346) in his life, beside his fireplace, and behind the closed front door.

It could also be said (though Carlyle does not say it) that Jane Welsh Carlyle's life went, like Edward Irving's, from high promise to catastrophe. That was the construction she herself came to put on it. Irving's life stood as a warning: his 'excitable intellect' (Pym 219-20) had led him astray. Instead of the soberly successful future of a man of promise, what the Carlyles witnessed was a decline into histrionics and excess. By marrying Thomas

Carlyle, Jane Welsh made the move from pupil to wife, replacing the tutor with the husband in the hope, evidently, that loving, teaching, and learning could go on in much the same combination. The choice of marriage was a choice for the continuation of the tutorial relationship in a slightly altered form. Among the altering components was the erotic, that element which in the tutorial model had been so powerfully present and so fiercely denied. Sexual difficulties and inhibitions present in the early years deepened as the years went by. The marriage declined into histrionics and excess.

It is surely no accident that Carlyle wrote his *Reminiscences of Edward Irving* shortly after completing his *Reminiscences of Jane Welsh Carlyle*, and that his recollections began with Irving's death in 1834, the very year that he and Jane moved into the house at Chelsea that was to be their home for the rest of their married lives and the site of Carlyle's successful progress from promising young author to Victorian Sage-celebrity. What Carlyle produced in these accounts can be read as a covertly triumphalist narrative, history as written by the victorious. The mournful account of Jane's life serves as a prelude to the longer and more probing meditation on Irving, the two narratives suggesting each other in Carlyle's mind. Of the three young people brought together when Irving introduced Carlyle to Jane Welsh in 1821, the year she read Rousseau, it was Carlyle who lived to tell the tale. If he was like St Preux, his Julie certainly resembled the original in heroic renunciation. She not only renounced sexual fulfilment but also the possibility – so excitedly canvassed between them during the years of courtship when she was his 'dear Pupil' – of being 'a sister of Madame de Stael's'. Irving represented for both of them, at different times, the fantasised and feared 'wonderful world up yonder'. Ironically though, it was Jane who was fated to follow Irving's path to disappointed and disappointing ambitions, while Thomas Carlyle swerved off into 'completely incredible' honours and success.

Works Cited

Darton, Robert. 'Readers Respond to Rousseau: The Fabrication of Romantic Sensitivity'. *In The Great Cat Massacre and Other Episodes in French Cultural History*. London: Allen Lane, 1984. 215-256.

Pym, Horace N., ed. *Memories of Old Friends, being extracts from the Journals and Letters of Caroline Fox from 1835-71*. London: Smith & Elder, 1882. Rousseau, Jean-Jacques. *Confessions*. Trans. J. M. Cohen. Harmondsworth, UK: Penguin, 1953.

———. *Julie, or the New Heloise, Letters of Two Lovers who Live in a Small Town at the Foot of the Alps*. Trans. Philip Stewart and Jean Vaché. Lebanon, NH: U Press of New England, 1997.

Chapter 20

A 'Creative Adventure': Jane Welsh Carlyle's 'Simple Story'

KATHY CHAMBERLAIN

Jane Welsh Carlyle's principal contribution to English literature lies in her letters, but she occasionally experimented with becoming a public author. Three pieces in particular, not published in her lifetime, read as if they were intended for a larger audience: her 1849 autobiographical essay 'Much ado about Nothing', prompted by a visit to her Scottish birthplace, Haddington; her 1852 story of her first love; and her 1855 report on household expenses, 'BUDGET of a *Femme* incomprise' (in which the 'unappreciated woman' addresses a formal request for funds to her husband, 'the Noble Lord'). Of the three, it is the second – '*The simple Story* of my own first Love' – in which Jane Carlyle, however unconsciously, makes her most ambitious attempt to transform an incident from her life into a clearly shaped piece of fiction.

Throughout her life, Jane toyed with the notion of being an author. In his *Reminiscences* Thomas Carlyle alludes to her efforts to write autobiography. She 'had written at one time something of her own early life; but she gave up, and burnt it' (72). Some pages later, he is moved to refer to the incident again, saying she was engaged 'at one time, upon a kind of Autobiography (had not *Craik* [Professor George Lillie Craik]...stept into it with swine's foot, most intrusively, though without ill intention, – finding it *un*locked, one day; – and produced thereby an instantaneous *burning* of it, and of all like it which existed at that time)' (157).

As a letter writer Jane Carlyle had what amounted to 'a private writing career' (Hardwick 174; Christianson 232), but she often expressed a desire to find more ambitious and fulfilling creative work. This yearning seems to have been strongest in middle age, when her major transitional pieces were written. At the age of forty-four, she informed her cousin Jeannie Welsh that 'the natural sadness of the latter part of ones life may be cruelly *embittered* by the reflection, that ones best years, which might perhaps have produced something good have been suffered to run to waste, fertile only of tares and nettles!' And she added, 'I wish I *could* find some hard work I could do – and saw any sense in doing – If I do not soon it will be the worse for me – ' (*CL* 20:193,194). A remarkable number of the Carlyles' friends believed that she was capable of writing for the public, and her husband was no exception. During their courtship, they had contemplated the idea of writing a novel together, and as late as 1842 he told her that 'My prayer is and has always been that you would rouse up the fine faculties that *are* yours into some course of real true work' (*CL* 14:134). Yet Thomas delivered mixed messages on the subject, and at times tried to discourage her. 'Do you know', he wrote in January 1825, 'I heartily rejoice that you *cannot* write a book at present!...as a woman it would have proved your ruin' (*CL* 3:270).

When Jane was fifty, her novelist friend Geraldine Jewsbury wrote a letter pleading with her to consider writing 'as an occupation': '[I]t not only blunts one's *amour propre* – or, as we politely term it, our sensibilities – so that we not only feel less acutely things that would otherwise irritate beyond endurance, but these things are transformed for us into artistic studies, instructions, experiences, and this goes a long way towards softening their intensely personal application to ourselves. Besides which, one's work is an "ark of refuge", into which one flings oneself on all occasions of provocation'. Geraldine even volunteered to help: 'Now, do set to work resolutely. I am just now open to any sort of arrangement you like to make. I will give the staple of my time to this mutual tale if you will begin' (Jewsbury 425-6).

There had been other offers to collaborate. In the 1840s Jane contemplated writing a novel with Jewsbury and Elizabeth Paulet, and later told her cousin Jeannie: '[L]ong ago – Geraldine and Mrs. P. and I were to write *a book* among us in the form of letters. I told them to start it and I would take it up when I saw their scheme – they *did* send me a screed of MS. which I augured no good of, it was so *stormy* – and so I backed out of my engagement' (*CL* 25:37). Jane later believed that pages resulting from Elizabeth and Geraldine's early collaborative efforts had found their way into Jewsbury's *Marian Withers* (1851): 'I remember much of *this* tale that seems bare-faced painting of Seaforth [where the Paulets lived] was in these pages *they* wrote between them!!' (*CL* 25:37; 15:246). The epistolary form was right, but the '*stormy*' approach was incompatible with Jane's ironic and satirical novel-of-manners style.

In her correspondence, Jane frequently mentioned novels and novelists. In turn, literary London occasionally attributed anonymous works to Mrs Carlyle, such as Charlotte Brontë's *Shirley* (1848). Half-imagining herself as a collaborator, Jane asked her friend John Forster if he could tell her who had written the novel, stating that if the writer 'have not *kept company* with *me* in this life, we must have been much together in some previous state of existence – I perceive in her book so many things I have said myself printed without alteration of a word' (*CL* 24:280). Though initially offended by Jewsbury's *The Half Sisters* (1849), perhaps because she feared that it was based on the story of her own marriage, she later admitted to Mary Russell that it was 'the one of all her novels which I like the best. And it has *bonafide* arguments in it, betwixt her and me, written down almost word for word as we spoke them in our walks together' (28 November 1856; MS NLS 605.429).

In 1866, at a dinner given by John Forster, Jane discussed the plot of a novel with Charles Dickens. She began by describing a house down the street, which provided her with imaginative inspiration. As Forster recalled in his biography of Dickens, she constructed a narrative based on 'the condition of its blinds and curtains, the costumes visible at its windows, the cabs at its door, its visitors admitted or rejected'. He went on to describe how 'the subtle serious humour of it all, the truth in trifling bits of character, and the gradual progress into a half-romantic interest, had enchanted the skilled novelist' (2:252). Humour, character, and half-romance – these were elements that may have been missing from the 'stormy' plot of the Jewsbury-Paulet novel.

One other 'novel' by Jane Carlyle suggests the frustrations she experienced in trying to write fiction. In the Strouse collection at the University of California, Santa Cruz, there is a leather-bound volume entitled *The School for Husbands*, by Jane Carlyle, 1852. The title suggests a novel, or possibly a humourous advice book for men to balance comportment manuals for women, such as Sarah Stickney Ellis's *The Wives of England, Their Relative Duties, Domestic Influence, and Social Obligations* (1843), which she and Geraldine frequently ridiculed in their letters. But inside this beautifully made volume, all the pages are blank. Though she could not articulate her own public voice, Jane Carlyle formed friendships with women who did, including Harriet Martineau, Geraldine Jewsbury, Elizabeth Paulet, and Margaret Oliphant. Yet unlike them, she was unable to negotiate between her private world and the larger world around her. In the blank pages of her 'novel', she left a record of her inability to transcend the conventions that had frustrated her throughout her life.

From the early stages of her life, Jane Carlyle's inclination to take creative risks were checked by her deference to custom and authority. When she announced in childhood, 'I want to learn latin – please let me be a boy', her parents had what Geraldine Jewsbury later called, in a narrative included in Thomas's *Reminiscences*, 'a division of opinion on the subject' (42). According to her first biographer Annie E. Ireland, Jane's mother 'considered Latin and mathematics sadly out of place in the little girl's education. Herself an accomplished and somewhat intellectual woman, she had kept to the old traditions, and desired nothing further for Jeannie. But the father divined his child's unusual capacity, and determined that it should have scope' (12). Dr John Welsh thought so well of his daughter's abilities that he overrode his wife's objections. Jane pleased him by being a precocious pupil, but she was only 18 when he died. The next year she lamented in a letter, 'I have lost my dearest and my best friend, whose love was my most valuable blessing' (*CL* 1:280). During her courtship with Thomas, she frequently reminded him about the efforts her father had taken to cultivate her mind and encouraged her ambitions and talents (*CL* 2:196). Her new 'genius' was fated to live in the shadow of Dr John Welsh.

Jane valued her mostly idyllic Haddington childhood and the years she spent there as a playful, cosseted, and spoiled only child. These experiences contributed to the antic and cavorting style of her letters. But clinging to an identification as a child can keep a woman in the position of an eternal daughter, and in Jane's case this may have been made more difficult by the ambivalent, unresolved feelings she had about her mother. Even after Grace Welsh died in 1842, Jane tried to be dutiful, and took up her needle to mend old clothes when she might have turned her mind to more ambitious pursuits. Yet she always sensed that duty was a poor substitute for more serious occupations. Writing in her *Journal*, 31 October 1856, she remarks bitterly: 'The evening devoted to mending; *Mr* C's trousers among other things! "Being an only child", I never "*wished*" to sew men's trowsers - no, never!' (*CL* 30:209). Guilt mixed with grief in her character. These two emotions can be seen at their most dramatic and extreme in 1847, five years after her mother's death, in an opium-induced dream she described to her young friend Caroline Fox. Jane told Caroline she had had 'a miserable feeling of turning to marble herself and lying on marble, her hair, her arms, and her whole person petrifying and adhering to the marble slab on which she lay. One night it was a tombstone - one in Scotland which she well knew. She lay along it with a graver in her hand, carving her own epitaph under another, which she read and knew by heart. It was her mother's' (Froude, *Life* 2:80).

This strong identification as a daughter placed Jane beyond reach of one of the more socially acceptable roles for women writers at the time, that of motherly advisor. In the same letter in which Geraldine urged Jane to take the idea of being a writer seriously, she also implored her to speak as a mother: 'It is not, however, altogether for your own sake that I am anxious you should set to work upon a story or a book of any kind that you are moved to do. You have more sense and stronger judgment than any other woman I ever knew...also, you have had such singular life-experiences that it is in your power to say both strengthening and comforting things to other women...If you had had daughters, they would have been educated as few women have the luck to be, and I think you might have enough maternal feeling, sisterly affection…to wish to help other women in their very complicated duties and difficulties. Do not go to Mr. Carlyle for sympathy, do not let him dash you with cold water. You must respect your own work and your own motives…So begin, begin!…You ought to have had a dozen daughters…So let your work be dedicated to your "unknown daughters". I am one of your children, after a fashion' (426-7). But Jane Carlyle was inhibited by the nagging sense that she had been undutiful. She was also someone who loved laughter, satire, and wit, and found the role of delivering 'strengthening' messages to a female public peculiarly tiresome. She could not imitate a woman such as Harriet Martineau, who confidently served as a counselor to the great, and a promoter of patriarchal ideas. As Deirdre David has remarked, Martineau's 'relatively untroubled acceptance of popularizing work in the service of male political ideas liberated her for a confident presentation of herself to the world' (227). Jane made friends with younger women and offered sisterly advice, but when she was obliged to dispense maternal wisdom, she tended to undercut her efforts with self-mockery.

In the fall of 1852, however, when she was 51, events in her life coalesced in such a way as to make her more creatively adventurous. In September of that year while Thomas was travelling in Germany, Jane was home in Chelsea supervising renovations. Her health and spirits were better than usual, and she was involved in literary matters, having read and critiqued chapters of Geraldine's next book, *The History of An Adopted Child* (Jewsbury 440-1). On 10 September, she answered a letter from an old suitor, John Riddle Stodart, who had been infatuated with her when she was a young girl. She informs him that she has been trying to get a 'female M S' published – perhaps the religious novel written by the mother of her artist friend Penelope Sketchley – and wryly remarks 'if it were [*my own*] I would give more for its chances of getting published' (*CL* 27:280). Two days later she mentions to Thomas that on an errand to his publisher she had been offered '"very advantageous terms" for a novel of my own!' (*CL* 27:281).

The exchange of letters with a former lover seems to have inspired her. She lets Thomas know that Stodart 'thought himself sufficiently master of his emotions, to dare to tell me that for nearly *40* years (!) he had loved me with the same worship-ful love' (*CL* 27:272). Replying to Stodart, she mixes serious reflection with humour. His letter, she tells him, 'has produced considerable bewilderment of my matronly wits – so that I could almost fall to doubting for the moment, Whether I be the present flesh-and-blood M*rs* Carlyle or the Ghost of little Miss Welsh! a perpetually recurring form of doubt with me, to say the truth' (*CL* 27:278). He has awakened her sense of the past: 'Oh dear! a little old love, bringing with it airs from *long ago* (God bless it!) is worth a vast deal of new love - at least to my retrospective turn of thought' (*CL* 27:279).

In this letter, as well as in the '*simple Story*' she was about to compose, Jane hovered between the impulse to express herself in a risky context and the need to observe propriety. She informs Stodart that it is 'in the highest degree unconventional to tell another man other than one's lawful husband, that one cares about his love and is grateful to him for it', yet she insists that she 'may speak with freedom' because their love is so old and they are so widely separated (*CL* 27:279). It was later said of John Stodart that while courting Jane Baillie Welsh, he had 'reached the point of trying to slip a ring over one of [her] fingers, only to see his ring sail through the air while Jane stamped with annoyance' (Chalmers 739). However ambivalent her feelings, Jane Carlyle expresses excitement at being back in touch with a man with whom she had once danced quadrilles.

In November or December 1852 she was confident enough to take up her pen and write a story in a notebook. Her aim was to contradict a remark that Thomas had made in his judgement of Thackeray's recently published novel, *The History of Henry Esmond* (1852): 'What "the greatest Philosopher of our day" execrates loudest in Thacke[r]ay's new novel—finds, indeed, "altogether false and damnable" in it, is, that "Love is represented as spreading itself over one's whole existence, and constituting the one grand interest of existence"; whereas Love, - *the thing people call Love*, is confined to a very few years of man's Life, - to, in fact, a quite insignificant fraction of it; and even then is but one thing to be attended to, among many infinitely more important things'. Indeed, 'so far as he (M*r* C) has seen into it, the whole concern of Love is such a beggarly futility; that, in a Heroic Age of the World, nobody would be at the pains to think of it particularly; much less to open his jaw on it' (14).

In contrast to Mr C's 'infinitely more important things', Mrs C concentrates on a '*simple Story*'. Her straightforward, understated title is intended to distance herself ironically from her husband's 'genius' and to ease expectations of her own. Like 'Much ado about Nothing' and 'BUDGET of a *Femme* incomprise', the title also disguises the importance of this piece to Jane. As Kenneth J. Fielding rightly observes, Jane's story 'can be read as an attempt to define herself' (*simple Story* 3). Looked at from this perspective, it is anything but 'simple'. In a letter to her young friend Kate Sterling in December 1852, she refers to her new endeavour casually, though dignifying it with the word 'occupation': 'One of my occupations is teaching the little Countess [Reichenbach] English - with what *success* you may partly figure Another (not an *imperative* one you will say) has been writing the narrative of my *First Love*; good Heavens! you shall have it to read someday - it is short' (*CL* 27:383).

In the story she describes an engaging childhood incident that allows her to reflect on the vagaries of love and memory, and at the same time to challenge the statement Thomas had made. Is love merely an insignificant fraction of a life? Declares Jane, '[M]y whole inner woman revolts against such position, which I find to be neither true nor well imagined. and regard, moreover, as a personal affront' (14). She then tells how she fell in love for the first time at the age of nine: 'One night, at a Dancing-school-Ball, a Stranger-Boy put a slight on me which I resented to my very finger-ends, and out of that tumult of hurt vanity sprang my first love to life, like Venus out of the froth of the Sea!! - So my first love resembled my last in this at least, that it began in *quasi* hatred' (15). Jane overhears the Boy's mother telling him 'to ask little Miss W - h for a quadrille'. Like Darcy in *Pride and Prejudice*, he refuses. He leads up instead 'a fair, fat, sheep-looking Thing, with next to no sense' (16). The Boy, the son of an Artillery Officer at the Barracks, is named Scholey (Jane cannot recall his first name), and while a real Scholey may have been stationed at Haddington in her childhood - there were barracks in the Artillery Park, on the NE edge of the town - his name also suggests another early love: her scholarly ambitions at the important age of nine. According to Geraldine, this was the period in which Jane 'made great progress in Latin and was in Virgil' (*Reminiscences* 44).

Jane loves the Boy but he prefers the fat sheep girl. She then forms a friendship with his mother, believing Mrs Scholey would like to see them united. Later, when the Regiment is about to move on, Jane takes the mother a gold filigree needle case hoping to get a little portrait of the Boy in return. The mother, however, grabs the needle case, and gives nothing back. The next morning, the Regiment marches away 'with band playing gaily "*The Girl I've left behind me*"' (19). The Boy, Jane says as she winds up the tale, 'had slipt thro' my fingers like a knotless thread' and 'in no great length of time' he had 'passed for me into a sort of Myth; nor for a quarter of a century had I thought as much of him, put it altogether, as I have done in writing these few sheets' (20).

Her story lends itself to being interpreted mythically, as a kind of dream. Dreamlike elements dominate the story: a tale-telling cadence, simple figures with archetypal potency, and stock expressions and motifs. The mythical frame of mind matches her view of the world as a child. As she recalls in a footnote: 'Thus was my inner world at that period three fourths *Old Roman*, and one fourth Old Fairy' (24). The unnamed Boy may represent a masculine aspect of her creativity, an animus figure about whom she feels ambivalent. Like Jane, he is an only child. The picture she paints of him is vivid: he is twelve or thirteen, tall 'and very slight, - with sunshiny hair, and dark blue eyes, - a dark blue ribbon about his neck, and grey jacket with silver buttons', an 'Image', she says, 'stamped itself on my soul forever!' (16) The Boy's mother is also described in mythical terms as 'a sort of military *Holy Mother* for me', 'her Barrack...a sacred shrine!' (17)

But the Boy fails to unite with Jane, his true partner - the best dancer in her 'little white kid shoes' - choosing instead bland conventionality in the person of the fat sheep girl whose 'wax-doll face took the fancy of Boys at that period, as afterwards, it was *the rage* with men' (16). In an aside, Jane mentions that this archetype of conventionality came to a ghastly end in a Madhouse. The Boy has allowed himself to be captivated by a girl who, judging from her physical features, might have grown up to resemble Lady Harriet Baring, the woman Thomas Carlyle so admired. In the process Jane is abandoned, 'slighted, superfluous, *incomprise*' - that word again (17).

Jane Carlyle takes pains to portray her child self as not stepping *too* far beyond the bounds of the appropriate, as she explores the tension between prudent conventionality and potentially daring actions. At one point she even assures the reader that she would never have gone so far as to tell the Boy directly that she loved him. Ironically, she reinforces this impression of propriety by swearing: 'This project then; could it be the confession of my love to its object, you may be thinking? Christ Almighty! No! not *that*!' (18). In a further irony, Thomas's nephew Alexander Carlyle, the first editor of her story, changed this outburst to 'Almighty Gracious!' (*New Letters and Memorials* 2:54) in 1903.

Unable to have the Boy himself, the nine-year old Jane fixes her attention on the portrait of him, which belongs to his mother: '[A] dear little oval miniature of the Boy, in *petticoats*; done for him in his second or third year; and *so* like, I thought; making allowance for the greater chubbiness of Babyhood, and the little pink frock, of *no sex*. At each visit I drank in this "*Portrait charmant*" with my eyes, and wished myself artist enough to copy it. Indeed had one of the Fairies, I delighted to read of, stept *out of the Book*, in a moment of enthusiasm, to grant any one thing I asked; I would have said - I am sure I would - "the *Portrait charmant*, then, since you *are* so good, all to myself, for altogether!"' (18) She wants to possess an image of the little boy in pink petticoats of '*no sex*', a sign perhaps of her unconscious desire for what Virginia Woolf later called the 'androgynous mind', the union of opposite sets of qualities that are needed for creativity to flourish (98).

In the story Jane attempts to obtain the portrait by praying to the Roman goddess of art - 'Minerva was my chosen godess' (19). After Minerva fails her, she tries another tactic, presenting the Boy's mother with 'the only really valuable thing I possessed' (18), the gold filigree needle case from India. The object is possibly sexual, suggesting her ownership of instruments necessary for invention and synthesis. Jane even has a vague plan that when she is a wealthy adult, she will return a more dazzling version of the portrait: 'I would return it to her *set with diamonds*' (18). When Mrs Scholey snatches the needle case without any awareness of what Jane wants, the dream lesson seems to be that the greedy, self-absorbed mother is the wrong figure to appeal to for the gift of the boy baby in the pink frock.

The Boy and the image of the Boy are both lost. Traditional male qualities such as aggression, daring, and bravery of heart – the virtues of a soldier's son – will not characterise Jane's imaginative powers. The inner realignment she seems to be searching for has eluded her. She begins and ends the story with an image of her hand, suggestive of the writing process itself. In the beginning of the tale, she says she felt to her 'very finger-ends' the potent mix of resentment and love that burst out for the Boy. At the conclusion, the needle case is gone and the Boy has slipped through her fingers 'like a knotless thread' (a conventional phrase for her). The mystery of love, as she says, 'passeth all understanding' (20). It is as if an opportunity for Jane Carlyle to dream herself into being a more adventurous writer has briefly appeared, then vanished.

With the spell broken, the dream ends. She declares the loss of the needle case to be of no consequence. The thread did not get knotted so the story unravels. The ring sailing through the air did not land on her finger and her pen will not dance in this particular way again, largely because there was too great a risk involved. Had she been able to continue, she half-jokingly speculates, 'such reflections…might lead me too far, – to the length namely, of my whole pamphlet, *in petto* [in my breast] on *the Marriage-question*, which I fear is too much in advance of the Century for being committed to writing' (20). She concludes the story humorously with a quotation from a preacher who, not knowing how to wind up a worship service, addresses the Almighty with a stock phrase for ending a letter: 'So – So "I add no more, but remain, my dear Sir, your obedient servant",' and she signs herself: 'J — — ' (20).

In her '*simple Story*', she has extended the boundaries of convention – both personal and social – and found a small but fruitful space to engage her imaginative energies. Through the alchemy of fiction, she has transformed a childhood scene and returned it to her audience '*set with diamonds*'.

Works Cited

Carlyle, Alexander, ed. New *Letters and Memorials of Jane Welsh Carlyle*. 2 vols. London: Lane, 1903.

Carlyle, Jane Welsh. '*The simple Story* of my own first Love'. Ed. Kenneth J. Fielding and Ian Campbell, with Aileen Christianson. Introduction Kenneth J. Fielding. Edinburgh: University of Edinburgh, The Carlyle Letters, Department of English Literature, 2001.

Chalmers, E. B. 'Mrs Carlyle's Letters to John Stodart'. *Times Literary Supplement*. 25 June 1971: 739-41.

Christianson, Aileen. 'Jane Welsh Carlyle's Private Writing Career.' In *A History of Scottish Women's Writing*. Ed. Douglas Gifford and Dorothy MacMillan. Edinburgh: Edinburgh UP, 1997.

David, Deirdre. *Intellectual Women and Victorian Patriarchy: Harriet Martineau, Elizabeth Barrett Browning, George Eliot*. Ithaca, New York: Cornell UP, 1987.

Forster, John. *The Life of Charles Dickens*. 2 vols. New York: Dutton, 1966.

Fox, Caroline. *Memories of Old Friends, Being Extracts from the Journals and Letters of Caroline Fox of Penjerrick, Cornwall from 1835 to 1871*. Ed. Horace N. Pym. 2 vols. London: Smith, Elder, 1882.

Hardwick, Elizabeth. *Seduction and Betrayal: Women and Literature*. New York: Random House, 1973.

Ireland, Mrs Alexander [Annie E.]. *Life of Jane Welsh Carlyle*. London: Chatto & Windus, 1891.

Jewsbury, Geraldine. *Selections from the Letters of Geraldine Endsor Jewsbury to Jane Welsh Carlyle*. Ed. Mrs Alexander Ireland. London: Longmans, Green, 1892.

Woolf, Virginia. *A Room of One's Own*. New York: Harcourt Brace, 1989.

Chapter 21

Collating Carlyle: Patterns of Revision in *Heroes*, *Sartor Resartus*, and *The French Revolution*

MARK ENGEL

Historical editors are like those archaeologists who specialise in chipping away the accretions of time, so that other archaeologists can study the artifact underneath. Sometimes the accretions may yield as much knowledge as the artefact. Editors have to focus not on the relatively stable, authorial bulk of a work, but rather on the many textual variants that as a matter of historical fact did appear and accumulate in its various published versions. The challenge of editing Carlyle's works is a basic one: all of his works were published in multiple authorised editions during his lifetime, and no two editions of the same work are even close to identical. Typically there are two or three variants per page between any two sequential editions, and since each edition was based on the most recent previous edition, the variants tend to accumulate from edition to edition. The sources of these variants are three: Typesetters made changes either accidentally or deliberately, and Carlyle ordered revisions. Most of the variants from all three sources are admittedly minimal - colons change into semi-colons, or the reverse; commas appear, migrate, and disappear; a spelling is modernised here and there. Even many of the revisions that must have been made by Carlyle are quite minor, often involving the addition of a word or two. But however minor, the differences are there. Only one text can be published - the problem is therefore to choose, or rather to create, the best possible text.

The first step is collation, which is the creation of an accurate list of all the variants and the recording of the editions in which these variants appear. This is a tedious and painstaking job, computer technology notwithstanding. Each edition is put into a text file, and because of the unreliability of Optical Character Recognition, or scanning, for nineteenth-century hand-set type, typists must do the key-stroking. Once this process is complete, the computer can generate accurate collations of the text files virtually instantly, but typists do make mistakes, and these appear as variants in the raw collations. As a consequence, each variant has to be checked for accuracy against the edition in question. Proofreading of the collations has a valuable by-product. Every typist's error in the master text file, which contains the edition that will become the copy-text, is detected in this process that I call Computer-Assisted Proofreading. The individual responsible for the checking must look at every variant, in context, and usually in several different editions. By the time the collation has been corrected, the variants have become very familiar.

The main objective of the Strouse editorial policy is to create an 'authorial' edition. This means eliminating, as far as possible, the textual contributions of the typesetters while preserving Carlyle's intentions for the text. Each historical variant becomes what Carlyle might call a miraculous 'Fact'. A certain change appeared in the text at a certain date. Was Carlyle responsible for it, or at least, does it express his intentions? If so, the copy-text is emended accordingly. If not, the earlier version is followed. For *Heroes* and *Sartor*, the complete collation was published in the section entitled 'Textual Apparatus'. This enables scholars to reconstruct any of our source texts, and to reconsider specific editorial verdicts. The length of *The French Revolution* will make it impossible to create a similar kind of 'Apparatus', but the collation files will be preserved in the archives of the edition.

From the textual evidence of *Heroes*, *Sartor*, and *The French Revolution*, it is possible to offer some generalisations about what Carlyle did when he sat down to revise one of his texts for a new edition. His 'revision' when he was getting a book into print for the first time was very different from what he did for subsequent editions. The Victoria and Albert Museum has a set of page proofs for ninety pages of *The French Revolution* for Book I of Volume II, 'The Feast of Pikes'. This chapter, presumably like all others, was very heavily revised in proof. For example, it is instructive to compare a passage from 'The Feast of Pikes' as typeset in the surviving page proofs with the same passage as revised by Carlyle in proof and printed in the 1837 first edition. The first version reads: 'These same finances give trouble enough; no putting of that matter to rights. The very sale of the Clergy's Lands and superfluous edifices will not do it; for there is none to buy them, ready money having fled'. The second reads: 'These same Finances give trouble enough; no choking of the Deficit; which gapes ever, Give, give! To appease the Deficit we venture on a hazardous step, sale of the Clergy's Lands and superfluous Edifices; most hazardous. Nay, given the sale, who is to buy them, ready-money having fled?' (FR 1837, 2:12–13). It appears as if Carlyle is using the proofs here for what is in effect a second draft of the book.

There were further revisions between 'The Feast of Pikes' proofs and the first edition as printed – in effect, a third draft – though how these further changes were conveyed to the printer is something of a mystery, unless there was another iteration of pulling and correcting another set of proofs. For example, the first footnote in the chapter was revised in the proofs and then further revised for the final printing of the edition. The footnote as typeset and marked for revision in the surviving page proofs reads as follows:

range * Arthur Young's Travels.

In the first edition the same footnote is printed:

* Arthur Young's Travels, i. 264–280.

(FR 1837, 2:5)

On the proofs Carlyle deleted the reference to the *Histoire Parlementaire* and wrote 'range' in the margin next to the reference to Young's Travels. 'Range' evidently is a note to himself to look up and insert the range of relevant pages in Young's book, and this was subsequently done. But questions remain: what was the printer supposed to do with the 'range' notation? How did this note made on the proofs, which were subsequently sent to the printer, serve to remind Carlyle to attend to this footnote? How was the later revision conveyed to the printer? Such questions remain unanswered, and reinforce Carlyle's own argument that 'of our History the more important part is lost without recovery' ('On History', HE 6).

The same level of revision is not apparent in the other major set of surviving Carlylean proofs, the complete set for the 1841 third printing of *Sartor Resartus* in the Strouse Collection at Santa Cruz. The evidence here suggests that once a book was in print, Carlyle was on the whole satisfied with it. Though there are changes that are distinctly authorial in every lifetime edition of *Heroes* and *Sartor* (with the exception of the late People's Edition), these are few and usually quite minor. Contrary to the impression that he conveyed to others, Carlyle frequently re-read his early books in the course of his working life, reading closely with an eye to possible improvements. He proofread or revised *Sartor* in 1838, 1841, 1846, possibly in 1849, in 1858, and 1869, at least once a decade for four decades. But there is no sign in the few emendations that he did make of any temptation to revise extensively. In all the editions of *Sartor*, the most 'substantive' revisions do not amount to much, as the following four passages demonstrate:

If, indeed, the whole Parties of the State [all party- divisions in the State; 1846 –] could have been abolished, Whig, Tory, and Radical, embracing in discrepant union; and the whole Journals [and all the Journals; 1846 –] of the Nation cold have been jumbled into one Journal, and the

> Philosophy of Clothes poured forth in incessant torrents therefrom, the attempt had seemed possible. (SR 9)

> But what I do mourn over is, that the lamp of his soul should go out; that no ray of heavenly, or even of earthly knowledge, should visit him; but only, in the haggard darkness, like two spectres, Fear and Indignation. [Fear and Indignation bear him company; 1846 –] (SR 169)

> Were it not wonderful, for instance, had Orpheus [Orpheus, or Amphion; 1838 –] built the walls of Thebes by the mere sound of his Lyre? (SR 193)

> Well does he know, if human testimony be worth aught, that to innumerable British readers likewise, this is a satisfying consummation; that innumerable British readers consider him, during these current months, but as an uneasy interruption to their ways of thought and digestion, not without [digestion; and indicate so much, not without; 1846 –] a certain irritancy and even spoken invective. (SR 218)

These changes are relatively insignificant. In the proofs for the 1841 edition, in particular, the most 'substantive' authorial revisions are alterations from 'incredible' to 'incalculable', 'must' to 'had to', 'too' to 'also', 'opened' to 'founded', 'in this wise' to 'in this manner', and 'lived' to 'existed'. Changes of this kind appear in every edition Carlyle attended to, including the 1869 Library Edition, but they constitute tinkering, at most.

On the other hand, Carlyle was willing to make major revisions in the interest of truth, as is evident in both *On Heroes* and *The French Revolution*, which are non-fictional in contrast to *Sartor*. In the 1846 edition of *On Heroes*, for example, he added a passage of more than 300 words to Lecture VI, regarding Cromwell's assumption of the Protectorship:

> [1841] They failed, it seems, and broke down, endeavouring to reform the Court of Chancery! They appointed Cromwell Protector, and went their ways. The second Parliament, chosen by the rule these Notables had fixed upon, did assemble, and worked; – but got, before long, into bottomless questions as to the Protector's right, as to 'usurpation', and so forth; and had at the earliest legal day to be dismissed. Cromwell's concluding Speech to these men is a remarkable one. Most rude, chaotic, all these Speeches are; but the most earnest-looking.

> [1846 et seq.] They failed, it seems, and broke down, endeavouring to reform the Court of Chancery! They dissolved themselves, as incompetent; delivered up their power again into the hands of the Lord General Cromwell, to do with it what he liked and could. What will he do with it! The Lord General Cromwell, 'Commander-in-chief of all the

> Forces raised and to be raised;' he hereby sees himself, at this unexampled juncture, as it were the one available Authority left in England, nothing between England and utter Anarchy but him alone. Such is the undeniable Fact of his position and England's, there and then. What he will do with it! After deliberation, he decides that he will accept it; will formally, with public solemnity, say and vow before God and men, 'Yes, the Fact is so, and I will do the best I can with it!' Protectorship, Instrument of Government, – these are the external forms of the thing; worked out and sanctioned as they could in the circumstances be, by the Judges, by the leading Official people, 'Council of Officers and Persons of interest in the Nation:' and as for the thing itself, undeniably enough, at the pass matters had now come to, there was no alternative but Anarchy or that. Puritan England might accept it or not; but Puritan England was, in real truth, saved from suicide thereby! – I believe the Puritan People did, in an articulate, grumbling, yet on the whole grateful and real way, accept this anomalous act of Oliver's; at least, he and they together made it good, and always better to the last. But in their Parliamentary articulate way, they had their difficulties, and never knew fully what to say to it! –
>
> Oliver's second Parliament, properly his first regular Parliament, chosen by the rule laid down in the Instrument of Government, did assemble, and worked; – but got, before long, into bottomless questions as to the Protector's right, as to 'usurpation', and so forth; and had at the earliest legal day to be dismissed. Cromwell's concluding Speech to these men is a remarkable one. So likewise to his third Parliament, in similar rebuke for their pedantries and obstinacies. Most rude, chaotic, all these Speeches are; but most earnest-looking. (HHW 199–200)

Since the previous edition of *Heroes* in 1842, Carlyle had published *Oliver Cromwell's Letters and Speeches* (1845), and his letters in this period indicate that he had found more to say about the 'anomalous' acts of the Protector. Another interesting set of authorial revisions in *On Heroes* illustrates the way in which textual history can intersect with biographical issues. In preparing materials for the collation of *On Heroes*, Rodger Tarr drew the Strouse editors' attention to the existence of a previously unknown 1852 Fourth Edition – not listed in Dyer's bibliography, nor in the National Union nor British Library Catalogues. Collation of this edition disclosed a pattern of corrections, obviously authorial, of what G. T. Tanselle has called 'errors of external fact' (356–8). In the first three editions of *On Heroes*, Carlyle bid his readers to 'remember that fancy of Aristotle's, of a man who had grown to maturity in some dark distance, and was brought on a sudden into the upper air to see the sun rise' (HHW 8). The correction to 'that fancy of Plato's' was made in the Fourth and subsequent editions. It is ironic that Carlyle wrote of remembering, since the passage is a distant recollection of the allegory of the cave in Book 7 of Plato's *Republic*. The historical fact of the error will be of interest to students of Carlyle and of the reception of Plato in the nineteenth century, but to the historical editor it is even more interesting as part of a pattern of the correction of such errors in this particular edition. In the same lecture, Carlyle had referred twice to the '*Havamal*', one of the Norse Eddas, but in this edition changed both references to the '*Völuspa*', a different Edda (HHW 30, 34). Similarly, in previous editions Carlyle had made reference to '*Childe Etin* in the Scottish Ballads' in asserting that '*Etin* was a *Jötun*', an etymological link between Scottish and Norse mythology. In the Fourth Edition, however, '*Childe Etin*' is replaced by a reference to '*Hynde Etin*, and still more decisively *Red Etin of Ireland*' (HHW 32). Another element in this pattern of correcting 'errors of external fact' in the 1852 edition is found in Lecture III in the section on Dante's *Inferno*, where a previous reference to 'that poor Sordello, with the *cotto aspetto*, 'face *baked*', parched brown and lean' is corrected to 'that poor Brunetto Latini' (HHW 79). Sordello is a character in the *Purgatorio*; it is Latini whose *aspetto* was *cotto* in the *Inferno*.

Discovering this pattern of revision led to several assumptions. First, it proves that Carlyle certainly 'participated' in the 1852 Fourth Edition, thereby establishing it as an authoritative source text. An alert, unusually learned and officious typesetter might just have caught and corrected the Aristotle/Plato mistake independently, but when that is added to the other examples mentioned, it is clear that Carlyle himself was taking advantage of the new edition – the first in six years – to correct some errors to which his attention had somehow been drawn in the interim. Second, there must have been a correspondent or correspondents who had drawn his attention to these errors. Carlyle proofread the first edition and prepared revised printer's copies for the Second and Third Editions, but these errors escaped his notice on each of those three earlier occasions. Why were they all corrected at once in the Fourth Edition, unless someone else had only then pointed them out to him? An inquiry to the editors of the then not yet published volume 52 of the *Collected Letters* produced exactly the sort of correspondence that the collation evidence had predicted.

In 1852 Joseph Neuberg, one of Carlyle's assistants, was preparing an annotated translation of *On Heroes* in German. In a list of queries that he sent to Carlyle on 20 March, he mentioned the allusion to Aristotle. Responding on 31 May, Carlyle remarked, 'I have very little doubt *Plato* is the word, – tho' Plato's "fancy", too, in his *Republic* does not too well suit (if I remember now) what is there said of the Sun and the man. However, *say* "Plato", beyond doubt. I read the thing, forty years ago, in some poor Book or other, neither Aristotle nor Plato; and have ignorantly but now irremediably, twisted it to my own little uses a little' (*CL* 27:132–3).

Neuberg also referred to p. 55 (which indicates that he was working from a copy of the first edition), where 'the *Havamal* [is] described as *prophetic*: "rapt, earnest, sibylline". - I find this description to fit the *Völuspa* (the first *Lied* in *Simrock's Edda*) but *not* the *Havamal*; which latter (#13 in *Simrock*) consists of a series of wise saws after the manner of King Solomon, but not what you would call "sybilline". - The prophecy of the "Consummation", too, ascribed (page 60 of the Hero-Worship) to the *Havamal*, I find not in *it*, but in the said *Völuspa*'. Carlyle replied simply, 'p. 55 (Havamal, Völuspa) *do do*' (*CL* 27:132).

Typically thorough, Neuberg asked Carlyle, '"*Childe Etin*", where can I find some thing about him, with a view to an explanatory Note?' (*CL* 27:124). Carlyle was uncertain: 'There is a Ballad of *Childe-Etin*, wh*h* I have read in some Scotch collection (hardly *Scott*'s, I think), but cannot say where. I have written to R*t*. Chambers to tell me; and if his answer, which is already due, come before tomorrow's post go, you shall still have it' (CL 27:133). Chambers provided him with the correct information on 31 May: 'There is no ballad called Childe Etin, but there is one called Hynde Etin, which you will find in Chambers's Scottish Ballads [Edinburgh], 1829...In my Popular Rhymes of Scotland [Edinburgh, 1826] the tale of the Red Etin was first printed - a totally different thing from the ballad, as you will see by a copy which I enclose' (*CL* 27:124). Carlyle forwarded Chamber's letter to Neuberg on 1 June, with the comment, '*Childe* Etin, apparently, is a mistake, and should be Hynde Etin (*Hind* means, drudge, slave)... - it must have been in Chambers that I read of him. *Red Etin*, which I also send if you can read Scotch, is a much more conspicuously Norse business. He is also, you see, of venerable age as a myth. — —On the whole, you had better say, in translating the Text, "*Hynde Etin* in the Scottish Ballads, and still more conspicuously *Red Etin*, are Norse myths: *Etin*' &c. And add what brief Note, manufactured out of these materials, you find suitable" (*CL* 27:134).

Perhaps the most famous instance of Carlyle's willingness to revise in the service of truth occurs in 'The Sinking of the Vengeur' episode in *The French Revolution*. In a letter to 'Oliver Yorke' in *Fraser's Magazine* in 1839 (later included in the Centenary edition of his *Critical and Miscellaneous Essays*), he cites the views of Rear-Admiral Griffiths, a survivor of the naval battle of June 1, 1794. Griffiths had sent a letter to the *Sun* newspaper in 1839, in which he complained that the version of the battle described by Carlyle was 'a ridiculous piece of nonsense' (*Works* 29:213). The 'official' interpretation, promulgated by Bertrand Barère (1755-1841) in the National Convention's *Choix de Rapports* (1818-25), was that the episode produced 'a glorious victory *for France*'. Carlyle had repeated Barère's claim in the 1837 edition, but he now acknowledged that 'it becomes impossible to conceal that the glorious victory for France has yielded six captured ships of war to the English, and one to the briny maw of the Ocean; that, in short, the glorious victory has been what in unofficial language is called a sheer defeat' (*Works* 29:210). This 'victory' had become one of the founding myths of the French Republic, celebrated in verse and enshrined in the Pantheon.

Carlyle did further research, explored the complete historiography of the event, and emphatically retracted his earlier account. But with his usual insight, he recognised the usefulness of the myth: 'It was a successful lie too? It made the French fight better in that struggle of theirs? Yes, Mr. Yorke; – and yet withal there is no lie, in the long-run, successful' (*Works* 29:221). Ingeniously accommodating this paradox in the 1842 edition of *The French Revolution*, he did not change a word of his previous narrative. Instead, he cited his *Fraser's* article in a footnote, added a dash, and commented prophetically on the relevance of myth to historical memory:

> ——Reader! Mendez Pinto, Münchäusen, Cagliostro, Psalmanazar have been great; but they are not the greatest. O Barrère, Barrère, Anacreon of the Guillotine! must inquisitive pictorial History, in a new edition, ask again, 'How *is* it with the *Vengeur*', in this its glorious suicidal sinking; and, with resentful brush, dash a bend-sinister of contumelious lampblack through thee and it? Alas, alas! The *Vengeur*, after fighting bravely, did sink altogether as other ships do, her captain and above two-hundred of her crew escaping gladly in British boats; and this same enormous inspiring Feat, and rumour 'of sound most piercing', turns out to be an enormous inspiring Non-entity, extant nowhere save, as falsehood, in the brain of Barrère! Actually so. Founded, like the World itself, on *Nothing*; proved by Convention Report, by solemn Convention Decree and Decrees, and wooden '*Model of the Vengeur*;' believed, bewept, besung by the whole French People to this hour, it may be regarded as Barrère's masterpiece; the largest, most inspiring piece of blague manufactured, for some centuries, by any man or nation. As such, and not otherwise, be it henceforth memorable. (FR 1842, 3:300–1)

Works Cited

Carlyle, Thomas. *The French Revolution. A History*. 3 vols. London: Fraser, 1837.

———. *The French Revolution. A History*. 3 vols. London: Fraser, [1839].

Tanselle, G.T. 'External Fact as an Editorial Problem'. In *Selected Studies in Bibliography*. Charlottesville: U of Virginia Press, 1979. 355–401.

Index